*Princeton* 1746-1896

# Princeton
## 1746-1896

Thomas Jefferson Wertenbaker

BICENTENNIAL HISTORIAN
PRINCETON UNIVERSITY

PRINCETON UNIVERSITY PRESS, PRINCETON,

NEW JERSEY, 1946

# PREFACE

THAT the child is father to the man is as true of institutions as it is of human beings. It seems a far cry from the infant college which began its first academic year at Elizabeth two centuries ago, where a handful of students gathered at the feet of Jonathan Dickinson, to the Princeton University of today; yet a knowledge of the one is essential to an understanding of the other. It is proper, then, that Princeton, as a part of its Bicentennial celebration, should review its history, should evaluate anew the services of the men who contributed most to its development—Dickinson, Burr, Witherspoon, Maclean, and many others—should explain the educational policies which shaped its past, recount its services to the nation, bring back the student life of other days.

For this task the materials have been abundant. The Princeton archives are remarkably complete, the Trustees' Minutes, beginning on October 13, 1748, the Faculty Minutes, from November 10, 1787, and many of the account books having escaped both the fire of 1802 and the fire of 1855. Invaluable, also, is the voluminous correspondence of President John Maclean, which has recently been presented to the University. For a picture of college life we turn to the correspondence, journals and diaries of undergraduates—especially the diaries of J. R. Buhler and Edward Shippen—or to the reminiscences of T. W. Tallmadge and A. A. Woodhull. To those who, like Moses Taylor Pyne and Bayard Henry, have made gifts to the Library of many rare documents and letters which throw light on the origin and development of Princeton, gratitude is due.

To those friends who have been kind enough to read the manuscript or the proof of this book and make valuable suggestions the author returns his deep appreciation. He wishes to thank the staff of the Princeton University Library, also, for their unfailing courtesy and helpfulness.

T. J. W.

# CONTENTS

# CONTENTS

# CHAPTER I

# The Cornerstone Is Laid

**E**DUCATION in colonial America was the child of religion. It was the denominations who, through their own efforts or those of the provincial governments, founded schools and colleges, provided them with instructors and raised the funds for their support. In many cases the ministers themselves became teachers, and after expounding the Bible to their parishioners on Sunday, expounded Homer and Cicero to the children on week days. Education was important, they thought, not only to develop an enlightened citizenry and to insure an intelligent reading of the Scriptures, but especially to supply the churches with scholarly clergymen. So Harvard and Yale were established by the Congregationalists, William and Mary by the Anglicans, Rutgers by the Dutch Reformed, Hampden-Sydney by the Presbyterians, Brown by the Baptists. Since the founding of Princeton was the direct result of the great religious revival which swept through the colonies in the fourth and fifth decades of the eighteenth century, it becomes necessary for us to follow its course.

When the great evangelist, George Whitefield, made his remarkable tour through the American colonies in 1739 and 1740, he aroused many thousands to a high pitch of religious excitement. Wherever he went, New England, New York, New Jersey, Philadelphia, the south, such vast crowds flocked to hear him that he was forced to preach in the open. In Boston he spoke to 8,000 persons in the Common; at Newark, a window back of the pulpit in the old square stone meeting-house was removed so that he could preach to the people who crowded into the burying ground;[1] in Philadelphia, where he used the porch of the court house in Market Square as a pulpit, the throng extended in solid ranks for four hundred feet to

[1] Alexander MacWhorter, *A Century Sermon* (Newark, 1807), p. 14.

the river, while many attentive listeners found seats on the decks of shallops at the wharf.[2]

His arms extended toward Heaven, his round face flushed with ardent zeal, his sonorous voice raised in denunciation of human error and indifference, he wielded an extraordinary influence over his audience. When he spoke of the lost state of the human race, of the impossibility of salvation without a personal experience of grace, of the horrors of eternal damnation, many were overcome with terror and despair. Often he was interrupted by the sound of shrieks, of weeping and wailing, of shouts, "What shall I do to be saved?"[3]

Even more appalling was the preaching of Gilbert Tennent, who followed in Whitefield's steps. A man of large stature and grave bearing, simple, almost pastoral, in his loose greatcoat and leather girdle,[4] he stood like a prophet of old, denouncing the impenitent and the rebellious and warning them of "the awful danger they were every moment in of being struck down to hell."[5] His listeners paled as he laid open "their many vain and secret shifts and refuges, counterfeit resemblances of grace, delusive and damning hopes, their utter impotence and impending danger of destruction."[6]

As thousands were shaken out of their indifference to religion, or their habits of dissipation, to flock into the churches imploring guidance in the quest for salvation; as ministers began to search their own hearts in alarm lest the spark of divine grace had passed them by; as men gained a new insight into the meaning of religion; as the number of conversions continued to mount, it seemed that the old Puritan spirit had returned to reassert its influence over men's lives. The Great Awakening, the people called it.

The tours of Whitefield and Tennent marked not the beginning of this movement in America but its culmination. Two decades before the great English evangelist landed at

---

[2] Joseph Tracy, *The Great Awakening* (Boston, 1845), p. 52.
[3] *Ibid.*, p. 108.
[4] *Evangelical Intelligence*, 1807-1808, p. 244.
[5] Joseph Tracy, *The Great Awakening*, p. 116.
[6] *Ibid.*, p. 116.

Philadelphia,[7] the doctrines which he espoused had been heralded in New Jersey by the young Dutch minister, Theodorus J. Frelinghuysen. A graduate of Halle, the center of the Pietist movement which emphasized the religion of the heart rather than of empty forms, he aroused his congregations on the Raritan from their lethargy. He preached the doctrine of repentance, regeneration, and holiness, and excluded from the Lord's Supper any whom he judged had had no profound religious experience.[8] He created a tremendous stir among the "dry bones" of the Dutch Reformed Church in America, and aroused much bitter opposition and many acrimonious disputes, but in the end he brought about a sincere and lasting revival of religion.

Nor was Frelinghuysen a lone champion. In New Brunswick Gilbert Tennent preached the new gospel as early as 1728; two years later the people of Freehold were thoroughly aroused by the appeals of his youthful brother, John Tennent; at Northampton, Jonathan Edwards began a revival in 1734 so extensive "that there was scarcely an individual in town either old or young who was left unconcerned about the great things of the eternal world."[9]

The very heart of the Great Awakening was the insistence upon personal religious experience. Samuel Buell tells us that after the visits of Whitefield and Tennent to New Haven, certain pious students at Yale would go from room to room to search the hearts of their classmates. So when the saintly young David Brainerd paid him a visit, he was "wholly on the reserve," being conscious that he had had "no religious experience to tell of." But when Brainerd observed "that he believed it impossible for a person to be converted ... without feeling his heart, at some time at least, sensibly and greatly affected with the character of Christ," he was so convinced of his own peril that it changed the course of his life. It was this religion of experience, as contrasted with the religion

[7] His first American voyage was to Georgia.
[8] Abraham Messler, *Forty Years at Raritan*, pp. 165, 166, 170.
[9] *Works of Jonathan Edwards* (New York, 1830), p. 123.

of faith or formalism, which galvanized Whitefield, Edwards, the Tennents, Frelinghuysen, Samuel Davies and Aaron Burr, shook the churches to their foundations and brought to tens of thousands a new approach to religion.

Calvinism at the time held almost complete sway in New England, was strongly entrenched in New York, New Jersey and Pennsylvania, and was making headway in Maryland, Virginia and the Carolinas. In Massachusetts and Connecticut, despite an appreciable relaxation of Puritan austerity since the day of John Cotton and John Davenport, and despite the growth of rationalism and the widening of religious horizons, the figure of Calvin still loomed large. Although the congregations had emerged as separate bodies distinct from the towns, they still looked to the colonial governments for support and protection, still regarded the clergy as political as well as moral and spiritual guides. Congregationalism, though in Connecticut disguised as a mild form of Presbyterianism, was the established church, while other denominations were accorded a grudging, somewhat limited freedom of worship.

But New England Congregationalism, when it overflowed into New York and northeastern New Jersey, gradually took on a changed aspect. Finding themselves under the jurisdiction of governors who were seldom sympathetic with their views and often bitterly hostile, mingling with Quakers, Dutch Reformed and Anglicans, weak and isolated, the churches one after the other sought strength by embracing Presbyterianism. But the congregations of Newark, Elizabeth, Woodbridge and Orange, even though they joined the synod of Philadelphia and gave somewhat reluctant assent to the Westminster Confession, looked upon the Connecticut church as their mother and patroness, and drew their ministers from Yale, and occasionally from Harvard. At heart Jonathan Dickinson, Aaron Burr, Ebenezer Pemberton, and John Pierson were more Congregationalist than Presbyterian.[10]

[10] T. J. Wertenbaker, *The Founding of American Civilization—The Middle Colonies* (New York, 1938), pp. 174-175.

It was this which made them ill at ease with the Scotch-Irish who were pouring in through the port of Philadelphia and were rapidly becoming the predominating element in the synod. This sturdy people had been nurtured upon the Calvinism of John Knox and Andrew Melville, and they had little patience with congregational autonomy. They insisted that the individual be obedient to the congregation, the congregation to the presbytery, the presbytery to the synod, and the synod to the church general assembly. In Scotland and in Ireland authority had come from the top, not the bottom, and from the top it should come in America.

In the south here and there Calvinism was raising its head to combat the Church of England and to claim the right of dissenters to preach in licensed meeting-houses. On the frontiers especially, in Frederick County, Maryland, in the valley of Virginia and parts of the Carolinas, where the Scotch-Irish were making clearings in the forest, erecting log cabins and sowing their first crops, the foundations were being laid for Presbyterian congregations. But the people labored under great difficulties. The farms were few and far between, roads were almost nonexistent, there were very few meeting-houses and still fewer ministers. Fortunate indeed was the settlement which was favored by the visit of some itinerant preacher for a week or two each year, and none aspired to the services of a settled clergyman. But the region was potentially rich religious soil, which some day was to boast its congregations by the hundreds and its communicants by the tens of thousands.

To Calvinistic America the Great Awakening brought not only enthusiasm unequaled since the days of the Puritan exodus, but also a conflict within the churches so bitter as to threaten permanent disruption. The zealots who followed the teachings of Frelinghuysen, Whitefield and the Tennents were termed New Lights, but actually were firebrands who kindled a blaze that spread from Maine to Georgia. These good men had no wish to divide the church and so weaken the cause for which they had dedicated their lives, but division was the inevitable consequence of their methods, if not of their religious views.

They were unwilling to confine their ministrations to their own congregations, but went forth, armed with the mighty weapons of fervor and complete conviction, to snatch souls from the burning wherever there was an appeal for help. They would willingly ride scores of miles, perhaps through snow or rain or bitter cold, "to awaken the secure" or reprove the wicked or guide those in search of salvation. If the resident minister of the "invaded" congregation invited them to preach, so much the better, but if the request came against his wishes from some disgruntled communicants, the invaders did not hesitate to accept. If the minister barred the door of his church, they preached in some nearby barn or more frequently in a grove or orchard or field. This custom of "itinerating," as it was styled, or invading other ministers' congregations, was the occasion of many heart-burnings and lasting animosities. It was certainly no compliment, some of the clergymen said, to assume that they were so incapable of caring for their flocks, rebuking the sinful, and of leading the wavering to God, that strangers had to be invited in to do these things for them.[11]

If they were left in any doubt as to the contemptuous opinion the itinerants held of their abilities and their fitness they were not infrequently enlightened by open criticisms and even denunciations. You yourselves are blind, they were told, so how can you lead the blind? You are unconverted, so how can you point out the way to salvation? Gilbert Tennent, in his famous Nottingham sermon on the "Danger of an Unconverted Ministry," declared that their prayers were so cold that the poor Christians who were put to feed on such barren pastures and such "dry nurses" were stunted and starved. Such ministers were like "dead dogs, that can't bark." "Is a dead man fit to bring others to life?" he asked. "Is a madman fit to give counsel . . . an enemy to God, fit to be sent on an embassy of peace . . . a leper or one that has plague-sores

---

[11] Chas. Chauncy, *Seasonable Thoughts* (Boston, 1743), pp. 37, 40; Benjamin Trumbull, *History of Connecticut*, II, p. 164.

upon him fit to be a good physician?"[12] This stinging denunciation, published and spread far and wide, created intense bitterness and hastened the breach in the Presbyterian
church.

When once a minister had been singled out as unconverted,
he had no other alternative than either to defend himself
or resign. His defense led naturally to a counter-attack upon
the New Lights, their doctrines and methods, and so aligned
him with the conservatives. If he had the affection and respect
of his congregation he might hold them solidly behind him,
but if some were dissatisfied or had imbibed the new principles, a rupture was inevitable. Withdrawing from the old
meeting, the New Lights would erect a house of worship of
their own and, if they had the means to support a minister,
call one after their own heart. Thus devout Christians were
drawn into two hostile camps, disrupting communities and
often family ties, while preachers of the Gospel, who should
have been cooperating for the common good, exerted themselves to thwart each other's efforts.[13]

These disputes found their way into the synod of Philadelphia, where Old Side and New Lights glared at each other
and fought bitterly for the ascendancy. The contest was complicated by the efforts of the group from East Jersey, under
the leadership of Jonathan Dickinson, to maintain their traditional congregational autonomy in the face of the centralizing Scotch-Irish influences. When it was proposed that the
synod adopt publicly the Westminster Confession of Faith
and require every minister to subscribe to it, Dickinson re-
belled. None the less, at the meeting of 1736, when most of
the "Congregationalists" were absent, the measure was passed,
leaving them to choose between submission or withdrawal.[14]
In this dilemma they turned to the Scotch and Scotch-Irish
New Lights in the synod as their natural friends and allies.

[12] Gilbert Tennent, *Danger of an Unconverted Ministry* (Boston, 1742),
pp. 7, 8.
[13] Leonard Bacon, *Thirteen Historical Discourses* (New Haven, 1839),
pp. 219, 220; Archibald Alexander, *The Log College*, p. 51.
[14] Charles A. Briggs, *American Presbyterianism*, pp. 202-238.

Dickinson, John Pierson, Ebenezer Pemberton, and other New Englanders, although lacking the crusading spirit of Whitefield and Gilbert Tennent and condemning some of their methods, were heartily in sympathy with the concepts of the Great Awakening. At the same time the Tennents and their friends were forced to oppose the centralizing forces in the church because these forces threatened to leave them at the mercy of the Old Side.

It was the all-important matter of educating young men for the ministry which precipitated the breach between the New Lights and the Old Side. Dickinson and the Tennents, without minimizing the importance of a thorough education, insisted first upon piety and proof of religious experience. Is it right to reject zealous candidates because of deficiency in Hebrew, or theology, or metaphysics, they asked, while scores of congregations, not only on the frontiers but even in the older parts of the colonies, are imploring the synod to send pastors to guide them along the path to salvation? "Many calls are perpetually presented to our Synod and Presbyteries, which for want of ministers we are unable to comply with," wrote one New Light minister. "It grieves us . . . to hear the melancholy representations of their destitute circumstances and their affectionate longings after the Bread of Life, when we can in our present state do nothing further for them than to send now and then some occasional supplies. These demands for ministers are not confined to the Jerseys, but come from Maryland and even from the most distant parts of Virginia."[15]

To meet this demand the church could count upon a few young clergymen who had received their diplomas at the universities of Scotland—St. Andrews, Edinburgh, Aberdeen, Glasgow—together with a number of graduates of Yale and Harvard. But the Scotch and Scotch-Irish recruits were totally insufficient, while the graduates from the New England colleges had "a backwardness to leave their native home and settle at such a distance from all their friends."[16] In this im-

[15] *Princeton Library MSS*, AM 1424.      [16] *Ibid.*

passe it became customary for pious youths, after acquiring a smattering of classical learning in the schools, to study divinity under some learned preacher and then to present themselves as candidates for the pulpit.

At Nottingham, Maryland, the Reverend Samuel Finley gathered around him a group of young men, some of whom later became distinguished—the Reverend James Waddell, the famous blind parson of Virginia; the Reverend Alexander McWhorter, of Newark; Colonel John Bayard, and others.[17] The Reverend Samuel Blair conducted an equally well known school at Faggs Manor which, after his death, was continued by his brother John Blair and gave the ministry such able members as Samuel Davies, John Rodgers and James Finley.[18] In Elizabeth, Jonathan Dickinson, and at Newark, Aaron Burr, despite their arduous ministerial duties, found time to give instruction to a number of young men.[19] All of these so-called academies were partly grammar schools and partly colleges. Since they stressed preparation for the ministry and since they were conducted by distinguished divinity scholars, the students devoted their attention to a mixture of Greek, Latin, moral philosophy and theology.

By far the most important of these institutions was the so-called Log College, at Neshaminy, Bucks County, Pennsylvania. Whitefield was "much comforted by the coming of one William Tennent, an old gray-haired disciple of Jesus Christ. . . . He keeps an academy about twenty miles from Philadelphia and has been blessed with four gracious sons." Later Whitefield visited Neshaminy to preach, and noted further: "They intend bringing up gracious youths and sending them out from time to time into the Lord's vineyard. The place wherein the young men study now is in contempt called the College. It is a log house, about twenty feet long and near as many broad; and to me it seemed to resemble the school of the old prophets."[20]

[17] Archibald Alexander, *Log College*, p. 206.
[18] *Ibid.*, p. 172.
[19] Alexander McWhorter, *A Century Sermon* (Newark, 1807), p. 19.
[20] George Whitefield, *Journal*.

William Tennent, who came to America from Ireland in 1718, had been ordained as a priest in the Church of England, but was later converted to Presbyterianism. He was admitted to its ministry by the synod of Philadelphia,[21] and after several moves was settled as pastor of the church at Neshaminy. It was doubtless the necessity of educating his own sons, Gilbert, William, John and Charles, all of whom were destined for the ministry, which gave rise to the Log College. Mr. Tennent reared the crude structure across the road from his farm house, where probably most of the students resided, and there began his instruction in the classics and in divinity. His knowledge of Latin was remarkable even for those days when every educated man must know his Cicero and his Sallust, and it was said that "he could speak and converse in it with as much facility as in his vernacular tongue."[22]

More important than his skill with the ancient languages was the ability of this elderly man to impress his students with his own character and his views of religion. The handful of graduates whom he sent out into the ministry were impregnated with the Pietistic tenets of Frelinghuysen and Whitefield and fired with a crusader's zeal to spread them far and wide. In addition to his own sons, Tennent educated Samuel Blair, John Blair, Samuel Finley, William Robinson, John Rowland, Charles Beatty,[23] Charles McKnight, John Roland, and others.[24] We find these men preaching from Massachusetts to the Carolinas, now warning the "secure" of a sophisticated congregation of Boston or New York, now bringing their message to a handful of settlers on the upper Susquehanna or under the shadow of the Alleghenies in far-off Rockbridge County in the valley of Virginia. They wasted no time in discussing the finer points of theology or in denouncing the "errors" of Romanism, but explained and insisted upon

[21] *Records of the Presbyterian Church* (Philadelphia, 1841), p. 49.
[22] Archibald Alexander, *The Log College*, p. 20.
[23] *Ibid.*, p. 23.
[24] George H. Ingram, "Biographies of the Alumni of the Log College," *Journal of the Presbyterian Historical Society*, XIII, pp. 175ff.

the doctrine of religious experience as the only path to salvation.

The Old Side regarded William Tennent and his rustic college with mingled contempt and fear. How could this aged man, who himself lacked adequate training in certain branches of knowledge, without tutors to assist him, without an adequate library, without scientific apparatus, prepare young men for the ministry? They asked scornfully, will it not bring religion into discredit to ordain half-educated enthusiasts, who lack the scholarly background to controvert the champions of other religious faiths or to recognize error when it lifts its head? None the less, they were painfully aware that it was these very young men who were filling the vacancies in the church, building up congregations in the new settlements and gaining the hearts of deeply religious men and women everywhere. Whereas the conservative group were receiving only occasional recruits from the universities of Great Britain, one Log College man after another was coming up for ordination to strengthen the New Light faction.

So in 1738 the Old Side majority in the synod launched a frontal attack on the Log College by putting through a regulation that candidates for the ministry who had not studied at one of the New England colleges or European universities should be examined by a committee of the synod, skilled in philosophy, divinity, and the languages.[25] Realizing that their graduates were apt to receive short shrift from a committee controlled by Robert Cross, Francis Alison, John Craig and other irreconcilable Old Sides, the Tennents and their friends deliberately defied the synod. The newly formed presbytery of New Brunswick was entirely in their own hands and they decided to make use of it to admit Log College men or any other applicants whom they thought properly qualified. So, in direct disobedience to the synod, they ordained John Rowland, stating that they were satisfied with "his experience of a work of converting grace." They also resolved "that in point of conscience they were not restrained from using the liberty

[25] *Records of the Presbyterian Church* (Philadelphia, 1841), p. 139.

[ 13 ]

and power which Presbyteries all along have hitherto enjoyed."[26]

The synod answered this defiance by expelling the entire presbytery of New Brunswick, with the statement that no group would be permitted to "obtrude members" on their body contrary to the wishes of the whole.[27] As a parting shot the synod denounced the New Lights for invading other congregations, their "rash judging and condemning all who do not fall in with their measures," their insistence upon the need of "some invisible motions and workings of the spirit" as essential for conversion, the fact that they so frightened the people with the terrors of hell that many cried out and fell down in "convulsion-like fits."[28] The expulsion of their fellow New Lights with this "reflection upon the work of divine power and grace," so aroused their friends of the presbytery of New York that the latter entered a vigorous protest and, when this proved unavailing, withdrew to join with the presbytery of New Brunswick in creating the synod of New York.

As Jonathan Dickinson, Ebenezer Pemberton, John Pierson and Aaron Burr rode home from the fateful meeting in Philadelphia which marked this split in the Presbyterian church, the problem of educating young men for the ministry must have been a grave subject of discussion. With Old Side and New Lights now definitely aligned against each other, the future would belong to the faction which secured the larger number of recruits. William Tennent had become too feeble to continue actively his work at the Log College, and the occasional graduates sent out by Samuel Finley or Samuel Blair, or by Dickinson or Burr themselves, were entirely inadequate to meet the situation. Little could be expected from the European universities, while Yale and Harvard, these men sadly reflected, had both fallen into the hands of the enemy. So to these good men, as they urged their horses over the atrocious roads of Pennsylvania and New Jersey, or

---

[26] Archibald Alexander, *The Log College*, p. 234.
[27] *Records of the Presbyterian Church* (Philadelphia, 1841), p. 158.
[28] *Ibid.*, pp. 155-158n., "A Protestation presented to the Synod, June 1, 1741."

crossed the Delaware or the Raritan upon the dangerous ferries of the day, or sat around the table in the guest room of some wayside inn, probably came the idea of a new college where young men possessing the spark of divine grace could be prepared for the ministry. They were far-sighted, these four, but they could not have envisioned, as their horses jogged through the hamlet of "Prince Town," the great university that was to be built on the foundation they helped to lay. They little thought that the college of their dreams would train tens of thousands of young men, who would not only carry out their design of preaching the Gospel in every part of the country, but would play a major role in the creation and development of an independent America.

Jonathan Dickinson tells us that it was he, with Burr, Pemberton, Pierson, and three laymen—William Smith, Peter Van Brugh Livingston and William Peartree Smith, all of New York City—who "first concocted the plan and foundation of the college."[29] Some of our great educational institutions owe their origin to the initiative and devotion of one man—Thomas Jefferson was the father of the University of Virginia, Benjamin Franklin of the University of Pennsylvania—but Princeton had its origin in the deliberations of this little group of devout, able, zealous men. Jonathan Dickinson, the beloved pastor of the church at Elizabeth, was one of the most distinguished preachers and theologians in the colonies and the accepted leader of the "congregational" wing of the Presbyterian church. Aaron Burr, who at twenty-two had been called to the important congregation at Newark, had already gained a reputation as a pulpit orator, scholar, pastor, and educator. John Pierson, born in the New England tradition of the East Jersey church, was minister at Woodbridge, New Jersey; while Ebenezer Pemberton, "an eloquent preacher" and a "man of polite breeding, pure morals and warm devotion" was for twenty-six years pastor of the First Presbyterian Church of New York.

It was good policy for the four ministers to associate with

29 *Princeton Library MSS*, Letter of March 3, 1747.

themselves in their project the noted jurist, William Smith of New York. An accomplished scholar in the fields of theology, Hebrew, and the classics, he was to be found always on the side of piety, education and religious freedom. Of like spirit was the prosperous merchant, Peter Van Brugh Livingston, who was for many years a member of the New York Council of State, served as president of the first New York provincial congress and all his life was a stanch Presbyterian. William Peartree Smith was a "worthy religious young man" of a wealthy and cultured family, an ardent patriot, and interested in good works of all kinds; he not only cooperated in the founding of the new college but remained a trustee for forty-five years.

At first sight it would seem strange that this group, consisting of six Yale graduates and one son of Harvard, should have omitted the New England colleges from consideration in the problem which confronted them. Certainly it would have been less costly to establish a few scholarships at Yale for youthful aspirants to the ministry in the Middle Colonies than to create a new institution, erect buildings, secure an endowment, and employ a competent faculty. Dickinson and Burr, in explaining this point, dwelt much upon the distance to New Haven, the expense and difficulty of travel, and the inadequateness of the facilities at Yale to handle the increasing number of students. "We have received many excellent men from the colleges of New England," they declared, "but candidates among them are become so scarce and our vacancies are so numerous, that we find by experience that it is in vain for us to expect an adequate supply from them."[30]

But behind this rather labored explanation was the painfully evident fact that Yale was no place for young men with New Light leanings. When Whitefield and Gilbert Tennent visited New Haven[31] on their great evangelical tours, they left in their wake not only a genuine religious revival but a train of fanaticism and emotional excesses. Among others, the

[30] *Princeton Library MSS*, AM 1424.
[31] *Two Centuries of Christian Activity at Yale*, p. 19.

Reverend James Davenport of Southold, Long Island, completely lost his head. In 1740 he set out on a pilgrimage in which he played the role of a colonial Billy Sunday, stripping off his upper garments, climbing on seats, leaping up and down and crying: "The war goes on, the fight goes on, the Devil goes down!"[32] In New Haven, speaking from the pulpit of the Reverend Joseph Noyes, minister of the congregation attended by the Yale faculty and students, he denounced Noyes himself as an unconverted hypocrite, a wolf in sheep's clothing whom thousands in hell were cursing as the cause of their damnation.[33] This aroused the ire of President Clap, of the college, and of many others who respected Mr. Noyes and had faith in his godliness and ability, but it so impressed certain others that they withdrew from the congregation and formed a separatist meeting.

This incident and others like it turned Clap and all his tutors into open enemies of the Great Awakening. They published a letter to Whitefield, blaming him for all the recent troubles—the excesses of itinerants and lay exhorters, the denouncing of ministers as unconverted, the splitting of congregations.[34] And even when Jonathan Edwards, Joseph Bellamy, and other prominent ministers entreated them not to condemn the "entire work of grace" because of the excesses of a few ill-balanced persons, they remained adamant and went to work to eradicate all traces of New Light doctrines from the college.

Edwards, Dickinson, and Burr resented especially Clap's harshness to an undergraduate named David Brainerd. This pious youth was one day conversing with several fellow students in the hall just after Mr. Chauncey Whittelsey, one of the tutors, had concluded prayers. When Brainerd was asked what he thought of Mr. Whittelsey, he replied: "I believe he has no more grace than the chair I am leaning upon." Unfortunately, a freshman outside the door overheard this re-

---

[32] Leonard Bacon, *Thirteen Historical Discourses*, pp. 212, 213.
[33] *Ibid.*, p. 214.
[34] "Letter from Rector and Tutors of Yale College to George Whitefield," in *Church Controversy*, vol. 104.

mark, and reported it to a "towns-woman," who in turn told President Clap. Brainerd was already in disgrace for attending a meeting of the New Haven separatists and he was now promptly expelled.[35] So outraged were some of the moderate New Lights at Brainerd's expulsion that they sent Aaron Burr all the way from Newark to New Haven to plead for him, but in vain.[36] Later Burr is reported to have said that "if it had not been for the treatment received by Mr. Brainerd at Yale College, New Jersey College never would have been erected."[37]

It was not the Brainerd incident alone, however, but the accumulated evidence of Clap's hostility to the Great Awakening which made Edwards, Burr, Dickinson, and others turn their backs upon their alma mater. They looked on with resentment while several students were fined for following Gilbert Tennent to Milford during his evangelical tour;[38] while two young men, Ebenezer and John Cleaveland, were expelled for attending with their parents a meeting of the separatists at Canterbury during Christmas vacation;[39] while certain students who had subscribed for the printing of a new edition of Locke's *Essay on Toleration* were reprimanded and ordered to make a public confession. And no doubt they applauded when one of them, a young man possessed of a fair estate, not only refused to submit but forced the president and the corporation to give him his degree by engaging an attorney and threatening to take the matter to the King in Council.[40]

Many and earnest must have been the consultations before the seven founders of the new college could decide upon the draft of a charter. We may imagine Dickinson and Burr, for the moment deserting their clerical duties, making the danger-

[35] Jonathan Edwards, *Life of David Brainerd*, H. W. Hodge, ed. (New York, 1925), p. 28.
[36] *Works of President Edwards* (New York, 1830), I, p. 203.
[37] J. F. Stearns, *Historical Discourses* (Newark, 1853), p. 176.
[38] Jonathan Edwards, *Life of David Brainerd*, H. W. Hodge, ed. (New York, 1925), p. 28.
[39] Benjamin Trumbull, *History of Connecticut* (New Haven, 1818), II, p. 179.
[40] *Ibid.*, p. 183.

ous voyage through Kill Van Kull and across the Upper Bay to talk matters over with the four New York partners; while it is certain that the college was an important topic of conversation when Pierson, Burr, Dickinson, and Pemberton met in Elizabeth in September 1745 for the first meeting of the synod of New York.

All were agreed that the control of the institution must remain in the hands of ministers and pious laymen who accepted the tenets of Calvin and were convinced of the necessity of religious experience for salvation. It was to be a college for the New Lights, controlled by New Lights. Yet they realized that if they made their purposes too narrow, if they excluded all save Presbyterians from the board of trustees, faculty, and student body, they not only might have serious trouble in gaining legal sanction for their project but also might lose public approval. It was quite doubtful under any circumstances whether they could secure a charter, either from the King in Council by running the gantlet of bishops and lords at court, or from Governor Lewis Morris, of New Jersey, who was an Anglican and none too friendly to dissenters. So they decided to cite in their charter the Fundamental Concessions of the proprietors of New Jersey in 1664, granting religious freedom to the people, and promised that in conformity with this principle young men of every religious denomination should have equal liberty of education in their college. But they were resolved, none the less, that all or most of the trustees should be of like faith with themselves, so that they could control the policies of the institution.

They were wise, however, in so broadening their plans as to include the education of laymen as well as of candidates for the ministry. "Though our great intention was to erect a seminary for educating ministers of the Gospel," they declared, "yet we hope it will be a means of raising up men that will be useful in other learned professions—ornaments of the State as well as the Church. Therefore we propose to make the plan of education as extensive as our circumstances will admit."[41] Since at the time there was no college in existence in the great expanse of territory between New Haven, in Connecticut, and Williamsburg, in Virginia, the need for an institution of higher education in the Middle Colonies was urgent. Was there any wonder that "rudeness, incivility and ignorance" were so widespread, they asked, when "the necessary means of improvement" were lacking?[42] So the founders decided that at their college "persons who would otherwise be useless members of society would be trained to sustain with honour the offices they may be invested with for the public service."

Moreover, they made their plans for a course of instruction so wide and comprehensive as to disarm in advance the criticisms of their enemies. There must be no excuse for Old Sides to say of this new institution as they had said of the Log College, that its graduates were deficient in certain important branches of learning. There were to be courses in the classics, in divinity, in philosophy and in science comparable to those at Harvard and Yale, or the Scottish universities or the English dissenting academies. This was not to be another advanced grammar school of the stamp of Faggs Manor or Nottingham, or even the Log College, but an institution of full collegiate grade.

The wisdom of this was soon apparent. It appeased to some extent the hostility of the Anglicans, it enlisted the support of many members of the Dutch Reformed Church, it produced financial contributions from scores of persons who were in no way concerned in the training of Presbyterian ministers and in spreading New Light doctrines. It offered, also, grounds for a legitimate appeal to the people of Great Britain and Scotland, and this was to prove indispensable in placing the institution upon a firm basis; and it provided the governor of New Jersey with an excuse for granting a charter to a group of dissenters.

Their first step was to solicit financial aid, and for this pur-

[41] *Princeton Library MSS*, AM 1424.
[42] *Rise and State of the College* (Edinburgh, 1754), p. 4.

pose they appointed Robert Hunter Morris and Andrew Johnston, of New Jersey, and James Alexander and William Smith, of New York, as their representatives. In March 1745, subscriptions amounting to £185 New Jersey currency were made to one paper alone, James Alexander promising £50, William Smith £20, Abraham Lodge £20, John Coxe £20, and Robert H. Morris £20.[43] Armed with this financial and moral support, they now applied to Governor Lewis Morris for a charter, but to their great disappointment met with a positive refusal. The governor realized that the influential Quaker party in New Jersey had no interest in the proposal, that the Anglicans regarded it with suspicion and that by yielding he might incur the anger of the diocesan of the colonial church, the influential Bishop of London.[44] So he took refuge behind his Instructions. Spreading the document before the petitioners, he put his finger on the clauses which, he insisted, "inhibited" the granting of a charter for a dissenting college.[45] That this was an excuse rather than the real reason becomes obvious upon a perusal of the Instructions, for they expressly directed him to "permit a liberty of conscience" and also to encourage "the erecting and maintaining of schools, in order to foster the training up of youths to reading and to a necessary knowledge of the principles of religion."[46]

But at the very moment when all their hopes seemed to have been blasted, fortune smiled upon Dickinson and his associates. On May 21, 1746, Lewis Morris died, and the duties and powers of the governorship devolved upon John Hamilton, president of the Council. Hamilton, like Morris, was a member of the Church of England, but he was "infirm, deaf, suffering from palsy"[47] and very old, so that he had to depend upon a group of advisers for his more important decisions. Chief among these were James Alexander, Robert Hunter Morris, John Coxe and his secretary, Charles Reade,

[43] *Princeton Library MSS.*, AM 13140.
[44] *Princeton Library MSS*, AM 1424.
[45] *S.P.G. Papers*, Rev. William Skinner to Secretary of the Society, Jan. 9, 1749.
[46] *New Jersey Archives*, First Series, VI, pp. 15-51.
[47] W. A. Whitehead, *Lewis Morris Papers* (1852), p. 219.

all of them friends of the proposed college and liberal sub-scribers to the endowment. There can be little doubt that it was these men who persuaded the aged governor that he had the power to grant a charter and that it was his duty to do so. The Anglican clergy of the Middle Colonies were as bitterly opposed as ever, but they reported that the charter was granted "so suddenly and privately that" they "had no oppor-tunity to enter a caveat against it."[48]

A momentous occasion it was when, on October 22, 1746, the old governor affixed his signature to a charter empowering in the king's name the seven founders as trustees to establish their college, and granting all the privileges and powers "ac-customary in our universities or any of our colleges in our realm of Great Britain." It is assumed that the charter itself was drawn up by William Smith who was the only one of the founders whom experience had fitted to foresee and eliminate from the documents points which might afford opportunities for quibbling or attack. For a century and a half Princeton historians had to speculate as to the wording of the "birth certificate" of their college, for it was not recorded in Prince-ton's archives, and the original instrument was lost. President Ashbel Green in 1822, President MacLean in 1877, and later writers were more or less in the dark concerning it, and one historian went so far as to state that no "complete version of the text has survived." Fortunately, a transcript has recently been unearthed from the library of the Society for the Propa-gation of the Gospel, in London, where apparently it has reposed for nearly two centuries.

Great was the rejoicing among the New Lights when the news of Hamilton's action spread throughout the colonies. Ed-wards, Bellamy, and Prince in New England, and the entire synod of New York regarded it as a stroke of Providence; in Scotland John Erskine and other evangelical ministers wrote their congratulations, while many a remote congregation on the frontiers of Pennsylvania, Maryland, or Virginia looked forward eagerly to the day when the new college would send

[48] *S.P.G. Papers*, Joseph Wetmore to Bishop of London, March 26, 1747.

them pious, learned ministers. But their hopes were dashed again when it was reported that the Anglicans were attacking the charter, declaring that Hamilton was in his dotage when he made the grant, that since he was merely acting as governor *ad interim* he had exceeded his authority, and that they were "resolved to try the validity of it in chancery."[49] Many think this design "will be of ill consequence to the Church," wrote the Reverend William Skinner of Perth Amboy, for the dissenters "will be trusted with the education of our youth, will endeavor to warp them from all other principles and form them according to their own."[50]

Whatever their apprehensions from this source, Dickinson and his associates went ahead vigorously. So far the whole affair had been conducted by New York and East Jersey Presbyterians of New England Congregationalist traditions and New Light affiliations. Certain historians have contended that the College of New Jersey grew directly out of the Log College, perhaps even might be regarded as a continuation of it, so that Princeton should date its origin back to the founding of the institution on the Neshaminy. In fact, as early as 1761 one writer spoke of "the original of the new-light Log-College that is now become a great building at Princeton, in New Jersey."[51] Yet there were no Log College men among the original founders who applied for and received the charter of 1746 and were constituted a board of trustees under it.

But there was every reason for the founders to secure the cooperation and support of their fellow New Lights of the presbytery of New Brunswick. The Tennents and their friends had a powerful and growing influence among the Scotch-Irish who were rapidly moving into some of the very regions which the college was largely designed to serve, and Burr and his associates had from the first envisaged an inter-colonial rather than a provincial college. Accordingly we find Dickinson writing, on March 3, 1747, that the seven trustees, under the

[49] *Princeton Library MSS*, AM 1424.
[50] *S.P.G. Papers*, Letter of January 9, 1749.
[51] *A Second Letter to the Congregations*, etc. (Philadelphia, 1761).

authority granted in their charter to elect five more, had "thought of choosing Messers. Gilbert Tennent, William Tennent,[52] Samuel Blair, Richard Treat and Samuel Finley. Mr. Pemberton and I propose a journey the week after next to Philadelphia, in order to meet with those gentlemen and prevail with them to accept the character of trustees."[53]

This probably proved an easy matter. The Tennents, now that their father was dead, could have no especial interest in continuing the Log College. They too were desirous of finding some practicable means of educating pious young men for the ministry, were disgusted with conditions at Yale, were just as alive to the inadequacy of the classical schools. So announcement was made in the *Pennsylvania Gazette*[54] that the original trustees "have chosen the Rev. Messrs. Gilbert Tennent, William Tennent, Samuel Blair, Richard Treat and Samuel Finley" to their body. Although it had already been advertised that the college would open its doors in the spring of 1747, it is probable that the election of the president was deferred until after the new trustees had been chosen.

There could be little doubt as to their choice. It was to Jonathan Dickinson, "the eminently learned, faithful and pious" minister of the Elizabeth church, and "the glory and joy of it,"[55] the champion of congregational autonomy, the acknowledged leader of the synod of New York, the distinguished writer and theologian, that all eyes were turned. Dickinson had for some time either conducted a classical school in connection with his ministerial duties or admitted a few students to his residence,[56] and his scholars probably formed the nucleus of the new student body.[57] So, during the last week in May 1747 the first eight or ten undergraduates of what was to become Princeton University assembled at Elizabeth

---

[52] William Tennent, Jr., son of the founder of the Log College.
[53] *Princeton Library MSS*, Letter dated Elisa. Town, March 3, 1747.
[54] Aug. 13, 1747.
[55] *New York Gazette and Weekly Post Boy*, Oct. 12, 1747.
[56] Ashbel Green, *Discourses* (Trenton, 1822), p. 299.
[57] Otherwise it is difficult to explain the graduation within eighteen months after the opening of the college, of a group of six students.

charter. Now followed prolonged conferences with the original founders, letters to Jonathan Edwards and other distant
friends of the project, consultations on this legal point or
that. Nor was there perfect agreement. Belcher insisted that
the college should have a closer affiliation with the province
of New Jersey so as to fortify it from attack in that direction.
There should be four members of the Council always on the
board of trustees,[62] he said, and the governor should always
be its chairman.

This caused much shaking of heads among the trustees and
not a few mutterings of disapproval. No one objects to having
Mr. Belcher on the board, they said, but how do we know
that future governors will not be men of no religion or
Deists? Gilbert Tennent, especially, was so uneasy that it was
with some difficulty that he was dissuaded from washing his
hands of the whole affair.[63] There was discontent, also, at
Belcher's plan to drop some of the present trustees to make
room for new nominations. In the end the only one left out
was Samuel Finley, the additional appointments being provided for by enlarging the board from twelve to twenty-three.
Belcher strengthened the Pennsylvania interest by adding
three prominent laymen—Edward Shippen, John Kinsey and
Samuel Hazard—but the influential James Logan refused
to become a member. John Reading, James Hude, Andrew
Johnson, and Thomas Leonard, all members of the Council,
together with the governor, represented the provincial government while the clerical majority was preserved by the
appointment of Joseph Lamb, David Cowell, Timothy Jones,
Thomas Arthur and Jacob Green. The total included nine
Yale graduates, four sons of Harvard, and three Log College
men.

There was intense interest in the little town of Newark
when, on November 9, 1748, the trustees assembled to elect
a president. With the aged governor presiding over the group
of politicians, businessmen, and clergymen, the ballot was

[62] *Works of President Edwards* (New York, 1830), I, pp. 266, 273. Belcher
eventually had to give way on this point.
[63] *Ibid.*, p. 273.

taken and Aaron Burr was the unanimous choice.[64] A wise selection it was. Young, of pleasing personality, popular with his congregation and his students, an inspiring teacher and eloquent preacher, a distinguished scholar, a man of untiring energy, devoted to the interests of the college, Burr more than fulfilled the hopes reposed in him.

After the election the trustees and students repaired to the famous old square stone meeting-house, with its roof receding on four sides to the belfry in true New England style, where the elite of the surrounding country had crowded every bench to witness the first commencement exercises. After President Burr, ascending the steps to the "wine-cup" pulpit, had "delivered a handsome and elegant Latin oration," the students displayed their accomplishments by "the customary scholastic disputations." The degree of bachelor of arts was then conferred on Enos Ayres, Israel Reading, Benjamin Chesnut, Richard Stockton, Hugh Henry, and Daniel Thane.[65] This done, the president rose and, addressing the governor, declared that under the authority granted by the charter and after the manner of the academies of England, he admitted him to the degree of master of arts. A salutatory oration was then delivered by young Thane, the president pronounced the benediction and the commencement came to an end.[66]

To the Princeton undergraduate of today the life of the students in the little college at Newark would have seemed dull indeed. Every morning and every evening they assembled to hear the president or tutor read from the Scriptures and hold prayers, while on Sundays if they absented themselves from divine services at the Presbyterian meeting-house or some other place of worship, they had to pay a fine of four pence. The student who so far forgot himself as to "frequent taverns" or to "keep company with persons of known scandalous lives" likely to vitiate his morals, or indulged in "cards or dice or any other unlawful game," was liable to expulsion. And even had the expense and danger of

[64] *Trustees Minutes*, I, p. 13.      [65] *Ibid.*
[66] *Boston Weekly News-Letter*, Dec. 1, 1748.

the boat trip not prevented, there would have been no week-end trips to New York, as the undergraduate bold enough to leave town without permission might have to pay a fine of five shillings.[67]

Some of the students resided with President Burr, others boarded out in town with Mrs. Camp or Mrs. Sayers.[68] Their belongings were very simple—a chest to hold a few coats, jackets, shirts, stockings, caps, shoes, breeches, and handker-chiefs; a small shelf for Latin and Greek lexicons, the Bible, copies of Virgil, Xenophon, Cicero, and other texts; a plain table for the candle, ink, quill, and paper; a pile of logs in the corner for the fire; a single bed and a chair or two.[69] That President Burr was wise enough to encourage innocent di-versions we gather from Ezra Stiles' statement that when he visited Newark in 1754, "two young gentlemen of the college acted Tamerlane and Bajazet, &c."[70] None the less, it was a joyous occasion for the student when with the advent of Christ-mas vacation he hired a horse from one of the townspeople, packed his saddlebags, bade goodbye to the president, his tutor and his classmates and set off for home.

Great was the excitement when announcement was made of Mr. Burr's engagement to be married. "He made a visit of but three days to the Rev. Mr. Edwards' daughter at Stockbridge," wrote young Joseph Shippen, "in which short time, though he had not . . . seen the lady these six years, I suppose he accomplished his whole design." The fair Esther Edwards, he thought "a person of great beauty" but "rather too young for the president."[71] Nor did it escape the sharp tongues of gossips that the bride-to-be came with her mother to Newark for the wedding, instead of having the ceremony performed in her father's meeting-house at Stockbridge. But these criticisms soon subsided before the general admiration for the new first lady of the infant college. "I think her a

[67] *Trustees Minutes*, I, p. 15.
[68] *Aaron Burr Account Book*, MSS, Princeton Library.
[69] *Ibid.*; *Account Book of Samuel Livermore, Jr.*; *Princeton Library MSS*.
[70] *Princeton College Bulletin*, IV, no. 3.
[71] *Princeton Library MSS*, AM 9261.

woman of very good sense," wrote Shippen, "of a genteel and virtuous education, amiable in her person, of great affability and agreeableness in conversation and a very excellent economist."[72]

President Burr during these early years of the college was a busy man. Devoting to his new charge every moment which could be spared from his clerical duties, he was now holding a class in divinity, now counseling some backward student, now endeavoring to raise funds in New England or Pennsylvania or Scotland, now meeting with the trustees, now procuring financial aid for a divinity student. "By his pupils he was beloved as a friend and, like a father, revered and honored."[73] He was president, professor, secretary, librarian, purchasing agent all in one, and the musty old account book in which he made all his financial entries gives eloquent testimony of his devotion, his energy, and his multiform duties. On one page we find him charging Joseph Reed with £3.9.7 advanced for board at Mr. Baldwin's, with nine pence for Watts' *Logic*, or 4s. 9d. for a pair of shoes; on another, David Hull with £3.4.0 for tuition, £3.18.0 for board at Mrs. Camp's, £1.16.0 for a Hebrew lexicon, 18s. for "Elijah Crane's horse," 16s. for firewood; on another, paying out £14.3.3 to one of the tutors, or crediting the Honorable W. Pepperell with a gift of £72, or entering 1s. 10d. freight on "books from Boston."[74]

Meanwhile the problem of finance became acute, for the number of students had so multiplied that they had difficulty in finding rooms and board in Newark, while the lack of adequate lecture halls, a library, and scientific equipment began seriously to handicap the work. Moreover, the strain of serving both the college and his congregation was beginning to tell on the president.[75] Despite the friendship of the governor, nothing could be expected from the assembly, where the Quakers and other hostile groups united to vote down every

[72] *Ibid.*            [73] *New York Mercury*, Oct. 10, 1757.
[74] *Aaron Burr Account Book*, MSS, Princeton Library.
[75] *Rise and State of the College* (Edinburgh, 1754), p. 7.

proposal for financial aid.[76] "The principal thing we now want is a proper fund to enable us to go on with this expensive undertaking," said one of the founders. "Though there are many Presbyterian congregations in these parts, yet the most of them are but lately formed, are struggling with the difficulties" of the frontier and so "are able to afford us but little assistance."[77] In 1750, Burr wrote that the college so far had been carried on "almost without anything to support it,"[78] and we know that he served as president for three years without salary.

Yet he was cheered from time to time by the announcement of a fair sized gift or legacy. Colonel John Alford of Boston gave £100, James Alexander £50, Sir William Pepperell £40, General William Shirley £50; over £100 was collected at Newark; William Kings of Delaware left a legacy estimated at £700. By 1754 it was stated officially that "the trustees have received about £1,200 sterling," or the equivalent of £1,800 New Jersey currency. This sum had been invested and the yield was "applied to the support of the president and tutors," although it had proved "hardly sufficient for that purpose."[79]

The president and the trustees, although they punished severely the student who indulged in "cards or dice or any other unlawful games,"[80] saw no harm in holding a lottery for the benefit of the college, for it was not until later times that this method of raising money was condemned as immoral. So they got Benjamin Franklin to print 8,000 tickets, distributed them in Philadelphia, New York, Boston, Virginia and elsewhere, and appointed committees to sell them and to distribute the prizes. A large sum might have been cleared had not the Philadelphians been trying at the moment to carry out Franklin's suggestion that they establish a college of their own.[81] The Old Side, also, not only opposed the lottery but questioned its legality and demanded that the governor of Pennsylvania bring suit against the managers. Although

[76] *New Jersey Archives*, First Series, VII, pp. 146, 579-580.
[77] *Princeton Library MSS*, AM 1424.   [78] *Ibid.*, AM 9971.
[79] *Rise and State of the College*, p. 7n.   [80] *Trustees Minutes*, I, p. 15.
[81] Later the University of Pennsylvania; *Princeton Library MSS*, AM 9260.

the latter escaped with a fine of £100, no less than 876 tickets were left on their hands.[82] Even this was not enough to prevent a fair profit, which gave Burr "such pleasure that his spirits were quite revived by it, which before were very low."[83] Having exhausted this resource, having tried another lottery in Connecticut with only fair success, and having been denied the right to hold one in New Jersey, the trustees now turned their attention to Great Britain and Ulster as their last hope for funds for buildings and endowment.

Accordingly, in September 1751 they requested Ebenezer Pemberton to make the voyage, and when his congregation refused to part with him, turned to President Burr.[84] But Burr was eliminated by the urgent need of the college for his services, by the fact that he had never had smallpox, and by his recent marriage. Thereupon they asked the Reverend Samuel Davies of Hanover, Virginia, together with Gilbert Tennent, to undertake the important mission. Davies was long torn with uncertainty, "all the tender passions of the husband, the minister, the father and the son" causing an insurrection in his heart.[85] In the end, however, he consented, and after making a farewell address to some thousands "of his friends and religious charges" and leaving his family in tears, set out on horseback for the north, there to join Tennent. On November 17, 1753, the two ministers climbed aboard the *London* at Reedy Island, and the next day were out in the Atlantic.[86]

These good men realized keenly that the future of the college might depend upon their mission, and despite seasickness, the smell of the ship, and Davies' toothache, prayed alternately in their cabin for its success.[87] A month later they were sailing up the Thames and wondering at the panorama of villages, old Gothic churches "with square steeples without spires," the numerous windmills, green cornfields, forests, a

[82] S. *Hazard Letters*, MSS, June 7, 1750, Princeton Library.
[83] *Princeton Library MSS*, AM 9261.
[84] *Trustees Minutes*, I, pp. 22, 31.
[85] *Samuel Davies Diary*, MSS, vol. II, p. 4, Princeton Library.
[86] *Ibid.*, p. 55.    [87] *Ibid.*, p. 57.

gibbet with the remains of a criminal hanging on it. At last the dome of St. Paul's came into view, then the Tower, then the masts of the ships in the river looking "like a vast forest." It was Christmas day and the bells were ringing merrily in all the churches.[88]

Now followed many strenuous weeks in the city, marked by calls upon scores of dissenting clergymen and upon Dr. Avery, Lord Lothian, the Duke of Argyle, and others influential at Court, by sermons in the Little Wild Street church or the Miles Lane Meeting House or the Berry Street church; by visits to Westminster Hall, "a spacious old building where courts are held"; by walking the "tedious, crowded streets of London from morning to evening till quite exhausted."[89] The two Americans, discovering that the Presbyterian ministers had a habit of congregating at Hamlin's coffee house and the Independents at the Amsterdam coffee house, began to visit these places at frequent intervals to meet influential men and present the claims and needs of the college. Here they had many long and interesting conversations which enlightened them upon conditions in the various dissenting sects, and which pointed out the men upon whom they could rely. Despite their reverence for Whitefield, they declined an invitation to make his residence their home, lest they "blast the success of their mission among the Dissenters" with whom he was far from popular.[90] In the end they learned that they could rely especially upon four prominent ministers—Thomas Gibbons, Samuel Stennett, David Jennings and John Guyse—and so consulted them in every step they took.

With Samuel Chandler, of the Old Jewry Meeting House, famous as the defender of toleration and Christian rationalism, they had a mortifying experience. One of them remarked that the college would be a means of uniting the various Calvinistic sects in America. "Upon which Mr. Chandler says, 'I have seen a very extraordinary sermon against union,' and immediately reached to Mr. Tennent his Nottingham Ser-

[88] *Ibid.,* pp. 82-92.
[89] *Samuel Davies Diary,* MSS, vol. II, p. 1, Princeton Library.
[90] *Ibid.,* I, pp. 126, 127.

mon," with its violent abuse of "unconverted ministers." This threw them into confusion, and drew forth a long and not too convincing explanation. Although they succeeded eventually in regaining Mr. Chandler's confidence, they now realized that wherever they went they would have to combat the accusations of their enemies in America. Within a short while the Nottingham sermon was "dispersed through the town from hand to hand," so that for a time Tennent's "spirits were quite sunk and he gave up hope of success."[91]

On the advice of their friends, Davies and Tennent drew up a petition or appeal for aid to the college, secured the endorsement of sixty-eight prominent persons, most of them ministers, had it printed and distributed hundreds of copies among the dissenting congregations. They also published a new edition of a pamphlet put out in 1752 entitled *A General Account of the Rise and State of the College*, adding several paragraphs and footnotes to bring the narrative up to date. So effective did these measures prove that by May 1754 they had collected £1,700, a sum far beyond their most sanguine hopes. "To be instrumental of laying a foundation of extensive benefit to mankind, not only in the present but in future generations, is a most animating prospect," Davies wrote down in his *Diary* in a mood of pleasing prophecy.[92]

But the work was not yet completed, for there were rosy prospects of aid from Scotland and Ulster. So the two Americans set their faces toward Edinburgh, to attend the general assembly of the Church of Scotland on May 27. The way had been prepared by the correspondence of Edwards, Burr, Pemberton, Davies himself and others in America, with John Erskine, and other prominent Scottish ministers, and by two petitions, one from the synod of New York and the other from the trustees of the college. On the other hand, they constantly ran across the trail of the Old Sides of the Philadelphia synod, who did their best here as in London to balk their efforts.

The night before the meeting, when the general assembly

[91] *Ibid.*, I, pp. 161, 162.　　　　[92] *Ibid.*, II, p. 3.

was to vote on the advisability of endorsing the two petitions, Davies could not sleep and the next morning, worn out and anxious, he sat in the church as the Duke of Argyle, the Earl of Breadalbine, Lord Dunmore, the Marquis of Lothian, many members of the gentry, and one distinguished minister after another came in and took their seats. When the credentials of the two Americans had been read, Mr. Lumisden, professor of divinity at Aberdeen, arose to speak. "As I knew not whether he was a friend or foe, my heart palpitated," says Davies, "but I soon found he was a hearty friend." After the Reverend Mr. McLagan had added his voice in approval, the vote was taken to endorse the petitions without "one objection through the whole house."[93] Davies was right in predicting that this approbation would be "attended by many happy consequences," for the general assembly next directed that collections be made for the college at the "church-doors of all the parishes through Scotland upon any Lord's day" until the New Year.[94]

The two friends now parted, Tennent going to Ulster, and Davies heading south through Durham, Nottingham, Bury St. Edmunds, Braintree, to London. On October 5 they met again in London, where Tennent brought the joyful news that he had raised about £500 more.[95] A few weeks later they bade each other an affectionate goodbye and embarked, Tennent for Philadelphia and Davies for Virginia. For Davies it proved a most uncomfortable voyage, for storms threatened to engulf the little vessel, while the curses of the sailors brought sad thoughts of the wickedness of human nature. They are "so habituated to blasphemy that oaths and imprecations flow spontaneously from them and I am in pain and perplexity what measures I shall take for their reformation," Davies wrote in his *Diary*.[96]

In the meanwhile, as news drifted in of the success of the mission, the trustees busied themselves with plans for the col-

[93] *Ibid.*, II, p. 13.
[94] *Rise and State of the College* (Edinburgh, 1754), p. 15.
[95] *Samuel Davies Diary*, MSS, vol. II, p. 83, Princeton Library.
[96] *Ibid.*, vol. II, p. 87.

lege building and president's house, having already, after long and occasionally rather heated discussions, decided on the permanent site of the institution. The good people of the Newark congregation signed a petition asking that the college remain there, so that they would not lose the services of Burr as their pastor,[97] while Elizabeth, too, had its advocates, a Mr. Woodhouse proposing "to give the trustees good security to build a fine college" in that town, "to be worth £3,000 at least, light money."[98] Either of these places would have been acceptable to the trustees and ministers from East Jersey and New York, but not to Governor Belcher or the Philadelphia and Scotch-Irish group. New Brunswick or Princeton would be better, they argued, for both were more centrally located, both were more remote from the proposed college at New York,[99] both were more healthful. "We had great struggles and long debates," wrote Edward Shippen. "Newark and Elizabeth Town were first brought up but soon voted out."[100]

Even when the issue had narrowed down to Princeton and New Brunswick, the contest between the eastern and western interests continued unabated. Young Joseph Shippen wrote to his father, on September 17, 1750, to stop at Princeton to gather some "good arguments to use with the trustees, as there is a great part of the trustees already of opinion that that place" is the proper site. But the trustees astutely bided their time and played off one town against the other. As the college would bring trade and enhance real estate values, they thought it only fair that the people of the favored place should contribute £1,000 New Jersey money, ten acres of land for the campus, and 200 acres of woodland to provide fuel. For a while it seemed definitely settled that the New Brunswickers would secure the prize, but at the last moment they fell short of the requirements.

Meanwhile the people of Princeton were busily at work

[97] Joseph Shippen, Letter of May 13, 1751.
[98] Edward Shippen to Joseph Shippen, May 16, 1757.
[99] *Princeton Library MSS*, AM 9260.
[100] Edward Shippen to Joseph Shippen, May 16, 1751. *Shippen Papers*, Pennsylvania Historical Society.

securing subscriptions, and at the meeting of the trustees on January 24, 1753, triumphantly announced that they had complied with all the conditions.[101] So the die was cast and the college fixed permanently at the little village hitherto known chiefly as a stopping place for travelers between New York and Philadelphia. A wise choice it was. Reposing amid fields and groves on a high ridge half encircled by Stony Brook and the little Millstone River, it was well protected from the once famous New Jersey mosquito. It was quite in the center of New Light America, near enough to New England to serve that region and yet within easy reach of Pennsylvania, Delaware, and Maryland. Had the college been founded a few decades later a site further south would probably have been chosen, but the trustees in 1753 had no way of foreseeing that the waves of Scotch-Irish immigration to Pennsylvania, western Maryland, Virginia, and North Carolina would shift the center of Presbyterian influence so far to the southwest.

The site once fixed, the trustees hastened the preparations for the erection of the college building. When Edward Shippen arrived in Newark for the trustees' meeting of January 24, 1753, he brought with him a plan for a structure 190 feet long and 50 feet deep.[102] This probably was the basis of the design made by Shippen's brother, Dr. William Shippen, in collaboration with the distinguished Philadelphia architect and builder, Robert Smith, which in July 1754 was accepted by the trustees.[103] Smith was a member of the Carpenters' Company and designer of Carpenters' Hall (famous as the meeting place of the First Continental Congress), lovely St. Peter's, the Pine Street Church, and other notable edifices. To him, rather than to the amateur, Dr. Shippen, credit is probably due for the charming proportions and quiet dignity of the college building which is now known as Nassau Hall.

We may imagine Smith and Shippen poring over the architectural volumes in their libraries—Batty Langley's *Builder's*

---

[101] *Trustees Minutes*, I, p. 29. It was Nathaniel FitzRandolph who gave the land.

[102] Edward Shippen to his son, Jan. 27, 1753.

[103] *Trustees Minutes*, I, p. 40. Nassau Hall, without the end towers, was 176 feet, 8 inches long.

*Treasury of Designs*, or Gibbs's *A Book of Architecture*, or an English edition of Palladio—for inspiration and details. "We do everything in the plainest . . . manner . . . having no superfluous ornaments," said President Burr. If we remove the "superfluous ornaments" from Gibbs's design for King's College, Cambridge, we have a close approach to Nassau Hall —the proportions, the hipped roof, the central façade topped by a pediment, the ornamental urns. The central doorway, with a head of Homer dominating the flat arch, clearly was borrowed from Langley's *Treasury of Designs*, while the cupola is a replica of the upper part of the cupola of St. Mary-le-Strand, London, shown in Gibbs's book.

On September 17, 1754, while Nathaniel FitzRandolph, John Stockton, John Horner, Thomas Leonard, and others looked on, the cornerstone was laid in "the north westerly corner of the cellar."[104] Thereafter the work went ahead slowly but uninterruptedly under the supervision of Robert Smith—the rearing of the massive walls of uncut native stone, the fitting in of the three front doorways with their flat arches and stone quoins each approached by a flight of stairs, the raising of the roof, set off by decorative urns and the little cupola, the plastering of the rooms. In July 1756 Edward Shippen wrote that "our college is almost finished and looks exceedingly well."[105] To President Burr, the trustees, and the friends of the college, as they viewed the broad expanse of the front façade and wandered through the prayer hall, the dining room, the students' chambers, the library, and the lecture rooms, it seemed a beautiful building "well calculated to answer the design and the most spacious on the continent."[106]

On entering the central door one found oneself in a hallway which led directly to the prayer hall and was bounded on either side by classrooms. In this room, which was about 32 feet by 40, occupying the north end of what is now the Faculty Room, the students were called to morning worship, often before dawn, at the sound of the bell in the cupola. Here was

[104] *Princeton Library MSS*, AM 8035.
[105] *Ibid.*, AM 9260.          [106] *Ibid.*, AM 1983.

the first organ used in Presbyterian services in America, a bit of liberalism which brought a frown from the strait-laced Ezra Stiles of Yale. In the basement were the kitchen, dining room, and steward's quarters; the library occupied a room on the second floor in the upper part of what is now the War Memorial Room, while the two rooms over the library were probably used for recitations. The wings were subdivided into small suites, most of which consisted of a bedroom and two studies. The basement chambers were left unfinished until 1762[107] when the increase in student enrollment made it necessary to house a number of unfortunate youths there, to hover over their wood fires and write home complaining of the dampness and darkness.

As one stone was laid upon another and the building began to take shape, the trustees decided to express their gratitude to Governor Belcher by naming it for him. "As the College of New Jersey views you in the light of its founder, patron and benefactor," they asked permission "to dignify the edifice now erecting at Princeton" with his name. "And when your Excellency is translated to a house not made with hands, eternal in the Heavens, let Belcher Hall proclaim your beneficent acts."[108] The governor not only declined this honor but, in his turn, made a suggestion. May I ask "the favor of your naming the present building Nassau Hall," he said. "This I hope you will take as a further instance of my real regard to the future welfare and interest of the college, as it will express the honor we retain . . . to the immortal memory of the glorious King William III, who was a branch of the illustrious house of Nassau."[109] Thus did the building which became so sacred to generation after generation of Princeton students receive its name.

In the early days within its stone walls the entire college had its life, for here slept students and tutors, here they held their recitations, attended religious exercises, ate their meals, and held their debates. But the president was privileged to

[107] *Trustees Minutes*, I, p. 99.　　[108] *Ibid.*, p. 43.
[109] *Ibid.*, p. 44.

have a residence of his own. As one views the simple dignity of the old President's House with its regularly spaced windows capped by flat arches, the pedimented doorway, the beaded cornice, one recognizes the Philadelphia Georgian and is not surprised to learn that its architect and builder was Robert Smith. Here it was that Burr brought his youthful bride for a few short months of happiness before his untimely death. Fortunately the old house has survived to the present day with only a few alterations, after looking out serenely for nearly two centuries upon the passing traffic of Nassau Street, as the pack horse gave way to the stage wagon, the stage wagon to the coach, the coach to the automobile and the motorbus.[110]

It was in November 1756, during the fall vacation, that the move to Princeton was made. Those students who had remained at Newark paid their bills to their boarding-house keepers, gathered their clothing, books, and other belongings and, mounting their horses, set out along the Elizabeth-New Brunswick road. We find Burr advancing one of the young men 5s. 6d., "for bringing his chest and expences in going to Princeton," while the cost of moving the chest of another was 3s. 4d., and of sending his horse back to Newark, 3s. 6d.[111] As for the college equipment, it seems to have consisted of "two large boxes of books," and sundry other things which the president shipped by water to New Brunswick, whence they were carted to Princeton.[112] Although carpenters and plasterers were still working in Nassau Hall when the session began on November 28,[113] the students and tutors moved in. The college had furnished each chamber with bed, mattress, table, and chairs[114] so that when the students had purchased rugs, blankets, and sheets from Mr. Yard or Mr. Patterson and

[110] At present it is the official residence of the Dean of the Faculty. The cost exceeded the original estimate of £600 and Burr himself advanced part of the money for its completion. *Trustees Minutes*, I, p. 74; *Princeton Library MSS*, AM 1972.

[111] *Aaron Burr Account Book*, MSS, pp. 122, 176, Princeton Library.

[112] *Ibid.*, p. 145.

[113] *Princeton Library MSS*, AM 1983.

[114] *Trustees Minutes*, I, p. 131.

firewood from Mr. Norris, their new quarters were home-
like and comfortable.[115]

It was well for the college that its foundations were laid so
securely by Dickinson, Burr, Belcher, and the other devoted
men who gave liberally of their time and thought, for it was
now destined to face a series of shocks which otherwise would
have brought disaster. Today the president of an American
college, as its educational leader and chief administrative
officer, is vital to its prosperity and progress, but two centuries ago he was still more important, for the entire life of
the institution centered upon him. It was an extraordinary
trial for the College of New Jersey, then, that it lost by death
no fewer than four able and devoted presidents during the
second decade of its existence. Again and again the trustees,
having by long deliberation selected the ideal man to direct
the institution, in sorrow followed his body to the old cemetery
on Wiggins Street almost under the shadow of Nassau Hall.

"The fatigue I have had in the care of the college this
winter has been greater than ever," Burr wrote in February
1757, "being obliged to do the duty of tutor as well as my
own, one of them being taken off from duty by illness."[116] The
next summer found him worn out and ill, and in no condition
to undertake a series of unexpected journeys and other calls
upon his vitality. In August he made a hasty visit to his
father-in-law, a hundred and fifty miles away at Stockbridge,
and returned only to remount his horse to ride to Elizabeth
on college business. Here he received news of the death of the
tutor, the Reverend Caleb Smith, whose funeral sermon he
preached extemporaneously. He next made a tiring trip to
Philadelphia, returning a very sick man racked with intermit-
tent fever. Instead of remaining in bed, he again rode his
horse to Elizabeth to preach the funeral sermon for Governor Belcher.[117] When finally he relaxed it was too late, and
his strength slowly ebbed. He died on September 24, 1757,

[115] *Aaron Burr Account Book*, MSS, pp. 124, 176, Princeton Library.
[116] *Princeton Library MSS*, AM 8569.
[117] Jonathan F. Stearns, *Historical Discourses* (Newark, 1853), pp. 207, 208.

just four days before commencement, to the grief of his students, the trustees, his colleagues of the ministry, and his former congregation.[118]

To Aaron Burr, more than to any other man, Princeton is indebted for its foundation. One of the original seven who "concocted" the plan, to his lot fell chiefly the task of putting it into successful operation. When he took over the college after Jonathan Dickinson's brief presidency, it consisted of one tutor and a handful of students, without dormitories, lecture rooms, library or equipment, with no more than the beginning of an endowment, without a single graduate. When he died there were about seventy students[119] and three tutors,[120] housed in the largest and one of the handsomest buildings in the country, working under a system of instruction justly acclaimed for its proficiency, while the institution was buttressed by a small endowment and had won the admiration even of its enemies. The trustees stated that under God the college owed "its existence and present flourishing state" to Governor Belcher's "patronage and influence," but his services, great as they were, did not equal those of the enthusiastic, able, indefatigable, beloved young president.

Five days after Burr's death the trustees, who had assembled for the commencement exercises, "after earnest prayers" elected as his successor his father-in-law, Jonathan Edwards.[121] This eminent theologian, whose writings profoundly influenced the trend of religious thought in America and Great Britain, had from the first been one of the leaders in the Great Awakening and an ardent friend of the college. No choice could have been more acceptable for, as Gilbert Tennent declared, he was universally acclaimed "in all the churches," for his "acumen, orthodoxy, learning, piety and courage."[122] Edwards had formerly been pastor of the meeting at Northampton, Massachusetts, but after a disagreement with part of

[118] *New York Mercury*, Sept. 19, 1757.
[119] John Maclean, *History of the College of New Jersey*, I, p. 155.
[120] Isaac Smith, Jeremiah Halsey, and John Ewing.
[121] *Trustees Minutes*, I, p. 59.
[122] *Princeton Library MSS*, AM 1983.

his congregation had taken over the church and Indian mission at Stockbridge. Since the presidency of the college offered a field of usefulness wider than the work of this outpost of civilization, the trustees were hopeful that he would accept.

But Edwards hesitated. He had found time at Stockbridge for his scholarly pursuits and he shrank from the exacting duties of the administrator and teacher; his rather poor health he feared would handicap him; the expense of moving his "numerous family" to Princeton seemed beyond his means; he thought himself deficient in some parts of learning, "particularly in algebra, the higher parts of mathematics and in the Greek classics."[123] None the less, when a group of trusted friends advised him that it was his duty to accept, and when the Indian Commissioners released him from his duties, he reluctantly yielded.

So in January 1758 he set out for Princeton, where he was received with joy by the students and tutors. Once more the President's House was occupied by an able scholar and teacher and the college looked forward to a long period of prosperity and progress. But they did not count upon the malignant fate which in these early days hovered over Nassau Hall. Smallpox was prevalent in Princeton at the time and Edwards had never had the disease, so it was decided after long consultation that it would be wise for him to submit to inoculation. This was before the days of vaccination, so that the patient subjected himself to a supposedly mild case of the disease in the hope of rendering himself immune to a more virulent infection. Dr. William Shippen came from Philadelphia, and on February 23, inoculated the president. Although "he had the small pox favourably," Shippen reported, "yet having a number of them in the roof of his mouth and throat, he could not swallow a sufficient quantity of drink to keep off a secondary fever which proved too strong for his feeble frame."[124] So, for the second time within six months the college was subjected to another interim without a leader.

[123] *Works of Jonathan Edwards* (New York, 1830), I, p. 569.
[124] *Ibid.*, p. 579.

When the news of this new disaster reached the trustees, they mounted their horses and set out for Princeton to decide upon a successor to Edwards. Their eyes turned again to the section which had already given them three presidents, their choice falling this time upon the Reverend James Lockwood of Wethersfield.[125] Four months later they were back again, for Mr. Lockwood had declined the invitation.[126] After long and heated debates, in which some expressed a strong preference for Samuel Finley, the board elected Samuel Davies. But the messenger who went all the way to Virginia to notify him was tactless enough to convey the impression that as president he would not have the united support of the trustees, and the peace-loving young Davies sent in his refusal.[127] This was unfortunate, for when the trustees met again the roads were so bad that they mustered barely a quorum and, not desiring to make a final decision with so many absent, they requested the Reverend Jacob Green to act as president *pro tempore*,[128] and it was not until May 1759 that they reassembled and elected Davies again.[129] This time he was persuaded to accept, although he entered upon his work with grave misgivings as to his fitness for the place. "A tremor still seizes me at the thought of my situation," he said, "and sometimes I can hardly believe it is a reality."[130]

But his own doubts and those of the trustees soon vanished. "I believe there never was a college happier in a president," wrote David Bostwick. "He far exceeded the expectations of his best friends. . . . You can hardly conceive what prodigious, uncommon gifts the God of Heaven had bestowed on that man."[131] Modest, lovable, scholarly, eloquent, acquainted with recent trends in education, he was ideally equipped to lead the college. Unfortunately, the trustees had overlooked

---

[125] *Trustees Minutes*, I, p. 71.       [126] *Ibid.*, p. 73.
[127] *Bellamy Papers*, Presbyterian Historical Society, Letter of David Bostwick, Jan. 1, 1759.
[128] David Cowell to Davies, Dec. 25, 1758, Presbyterian Historical Society.
[129] *Trustees Minutes*, I, p. 78.
[130] New Jersey Historical Society *Proceedings*, I, pp. 77, 78.
[131] *Bellamy Papers*, Presbyterian Historical Society, Bostwick to Bellamy, March 17, 1761.

the important matter of health, for Davies for years had been a sufferer from tuberculosis.[132] In Virginia the incessant riding through forests and fields in his five hundred mile circuit to serve his scattered congregations, had no doubt aggravated his illness. And the confining work at Princeton, where he drove himself mercilessly to remedy fancied defects in scholarship, rising at dawn and seldom retiring before midnight, proved too severe for his weakened constitution.[133] His death in February 1761 struck the college with dismay "and spread a gloom all over the country."[134]

All eyes now turned to Samuel Finley and he was unanimously elected president on May 21, 1761.[135] Finley, whose squat figure and round, ruddy face, presented a strange contrast to the slender, well-formed, esthetic Davies, arrived at Princeton in July. He had no reason to complain of his welcome, for the college officers met him a few miles out of town and escorted him to the President's House. After donning his academic costume, he proceeded to Nassau Hall where, after the students had received him with the greatest respect, he ascended to the desk in the Prayer Hall to make an introductory address.[136] We know that Finley was no orator, for Dr. Shippen tells us that he was awkward and stammered. But, he adds, he is honest and he has "all the essential qualifications of a president," which is more important than being the "finest orator in England."[137] Shippen was right, for Finley was a popular, energetic, able president, and a teacher to whom every branch of study seemed familiar.

Fate was somewhat kinder this time, for it was five years before death struck again. Finley died in Philadelphia, where he went for medical treatment, on July 17, 1766, and was interred in the churchyard of the Second Presbyterian Church beside his friend Gilbert Tennent. Many of the students

[132] W. H. Foote, *Sketches of Virginia* (Philadelphia, 1850), pp. 157, 162.
[133] Ashbel Green, *Discourses* (New York, 1822), p. 351.
[134] *Bellamy Papers*, Presbyterian Historical Society, Bostwick to Bellamy, March 17, 1761.
[135] *Trustees Minutes*, I, p. 91.
[136] *Pennsylvania Gazette*, July 30, 1761.
[137] *Princeton Library MSS*, AM 9260.

journeyed all the way from Princeton to pay a last visit to their beloved preceptor, and eight members of the senior class were his pallbearers. Although his grave is not in President's Row in the Princeton Cemetery beside Burr, Edwards, and Davies, a cenotaph there stands as a tribute of the college to his services and character.[138]

With the death of Finley the formative period of the college may be said to have ended. His successor, the Reverend John Witherspoon of Paisley, Scotland, found, in place of the little group of eight or ten students who had congregated around the scholarly Dickinson in May 1747, a full-fledged college of 120 undergraduates, housed in the spacious and beautiful Nassau Hall. Many graduates had gone out to fill important positions in civil life or to occupy the pulpits of New Light congregations from New England to North Carolina. Already the college had established the reputation which Princeton was to maintain for more than a century as the religious and educational capital of Presbyterian America.

To the little group who accomplished this great work— Dickinson, Burr, Edwards, the Tennents, Davies, Finley, and others—latter-day Princetonians must accord gratitude and respect. It is not easy for the present age to understand the psychology of these men, to brush aside the changes of two centuries and think with their minds, feel with their hearts, tremble with their fears. To many today the spectacle of a Gilbert Tennent in the pulpit threatening his auditors with eternal damnation and driving scores to despair, is an unlovely one. But if we understand that Tennent had devoted his life to rescuing souls—that as the physician must warn his patient of the progress of disease so he considered it his duty to warn of the fatal progress of sin, that he would willingly have undergone privation, hardship, death itself to save the humblest from the burning—we glimpse the real man.

When we peer behind the cold metaphysics of Jonathan Edwards, we see the affectionate husband and father, the quiet, modest scholar, the wise counselor, the forgiving op-

[138] Ashbel Green, *Discourses* (New York, 1822), p. 383.

ponent. We follow Davies, Finley, and the others on their long and tedious journeys, now ferrying over broad rivers, now riding through the forests, now exposed to rain or snow, now splashing along the muddy roads to preach to some remote congregation, or to console the sick, or to attend a meeting of the synod, or to solicit funds for the college. We find them surrounded by their students, giving unsparingly of their time and energy, acting the father and friend as well as the teacher, winning their deep affection, stimulating their minds, molding their characters. Nassau Hall with its fine proportions, its sturdiness and beauty, is a reflection of their vision, resolution, and devotion.

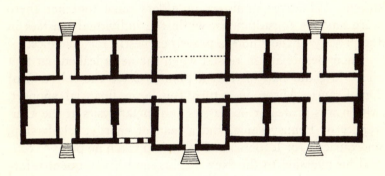

# CHAPTER II

# The Cradle of Liberty

HE news that Samuel Finley was dead brought sorrow and deep concern to Presbyterians from the Hudson to Georgia. Who now would unite the church, who defend it from the attacks of its enemies, who prepare young men for the work of the ministry? At a time when the air was full of rumors of the creation of an American bishopric and of an attempt by Governor Franklin to turn Nassau Hall over to the Anglicans, the selection of a president eminent enough to gain the support of both New Lights and Old Side was urgent. Wherever ministers or elders came together there were anxious consultations, while the individual trustees in the privacy of their homes prayed earnestly for guidance.

Their perplexity increased when the news leaked out that the Old Sides had on foot a plan to force the selection of Dr. Francis Alison in return for large financial support. Alison was professor of classics and metaphysics at the University of Pennsylvania, and a man of energy, scholarship, and capacity for leadership. But he had taken no pains to conceal his aversion to the New Lights, and his frequent references to "narrowness" and "bigotry," had done much to keep alive the embers of hostility and bitterness. To place such a man at the head of a college founded and built up by the devotion and labors of New Light ministers for the purpose of fostering New Light doctrines would be a base betrayal, the trustees thought. At the same time the urgent demands for unity might force them to yield unless they could produce a suitable candidate of their own.

From this dilemma they were delivered by the suggestion that if the proper man could not be found in America, why not turn to Great Britain? Why not elect Dr. John Witherspoon, a Scotsman distinguished as scholar, author, preacher, and church leader? Since he had had no part in the contest between Old Sides and New Lights and would bring with him the prestige of success in the Old World, he would be acceptable to both parties. He would be the rallying point for the church, be the unmitered bishop, and the most prominent divine in America.

When the trustees assembled on November 19, 1766, they found a committee of five gentlemen from Philadelphia who had arrived at Nassau Hall to present the Old Side plan. These visitors were ready to propose Alison or John Ewing, professor of natural philosophy at the University of Pennsylvania, for the presidency and the Reverend Matthew Wilson for the chair of mathematics, and to agree to the Reverend George Duffield or Jeremiah Halsey for other professorships. Since they were fortified with a "very strenuous letter" signed by twenty-six influential men they were confident of success.

But the trustees, though greeting them with grave courtesy, retired behind the closed doors of the library and kept them waiting impatiently outside. When at last they were admitted they listened with undisguised astonishment as the chairman smilingly informed them that the board had just elected Witherspoon president. This put an entirely different face on things, the committee said. They had come to Princeton with the hope that they could unite both factions behind the college, but this precipitate election, made before they could present their proposals, had changed the entire situation. They could do nothing until they had consulted their friends and received new instructions.[1]

The trustees wrote Witherspoon to offer him the position at a salary equivalent to £206 sterling, with the use of the President's House, a good garden and land for pasturage and firewood. They had been moved by his eminence in the Church of Scotland and in the learned world, and pointed out that they were calling him to a position of first importance, where he could be of untold service to religion and learning

---

[1] Ashbel Green, *Life of Wtiherspoon*, MSS, p. 95, New Jersey Historical Society.

"throughout all the colonies." To make certain that he should not miss the full meaning of the invitation they commissioned Richard Stockton, who happened to be visiting in London, to go to Scotland and explain it to him. This was fortunate, for certain irreconcilable Old Sides, in revenge for the maneuver which had defeated their well-laid plans, had written Witherspoon an "artful, plausible, yet wickedly contrived letter" designed to prevent his acceptance of the presidency.[2] In the quiet parsonage at Paisley there were long and earnest conversations between the polished, handsome, quick-witted American and the eminent Scottish divine. They were offering him no financial advantage, Stockton pointed out, but they did offer a prospect of rescuing religion and education in America from grave dangers. But though Stockton brought Witherspoon to the verge of acceptance, he could not persuade the quiet, home-loving wife, who "continued in such distress" at the thought of going to America that for weeks "she was scarcely ever half a day out of bed." In the end her husband yielded and promised that he would remain in Scotland.[3]

When word of this decision reached America it brought deep discouragement to the trustees and renewed hope to the Old Sides. When the board met on September 30, 1767, the same committee of five appeared again with new proposals and new promises. But they did not insist upon the acceptance of their plan if any other reasonable alternative were presented. They promised their support to any properly qualified person "chosen without regard to party distinctions." Thereupon the trustees, taking them at their word, selected as president young Samuel Blair, Jr., the recently installed pastor of the Old South Church, Boston. They then appointed his uncle, the Reverend John Blair of Faggs Manor professor of divinity and moral philosophy; Dr. Hugh Williamson of Philadelphia professor of mathematics and moral philosophy; and Jonathan Edwards, Jr., professor of languages and logic. Since of this group Dr. Williamson alone was of the Old Side party, the trustees made an additional gesture of friend-

[2] Varnum Lansing Collins, *President Witherspoon*, I, p. 79.    [3] *Ibid.*

ship by appointing George Bryan, one of the committee of five, as a member of the board.

This program was unsatisfactory to the Old Sides. It was partisan folly, they asserted, to bring to the presidency of the college a young man of twenty-six, who had graduated only seven years ago, when there were available such able scholars and divines as Alison and Ewing. Clearly the New Lights were merely angling for financial support while keeping the control of the institution in their own hands. Thereupon they washed their hands of the whole matter, so that the new plan was only partly put into effect.

At this moment, when the future of the college seemed dark, events in Scotland were taking a favorable turn. Young Benjamin Rush of the Class of 1760, who was studying medicine at the University of Edinburgh, visited Paisley in an attempt to dispel Mrs. Witherspoon's fears that if her husband went to America he "might soon die and she be left in a strange land." And though she remained outwardly adamant, declaring that to leave home "would be as a sentence of death to her," grave doubts as to the wisdom of her course began to assail her. In the end she yielded and declared her willingness to move if her husband should be reelected.[4] This news the doctor discreetly passed on to Stockton, who in turn informed young Blair. Blair, who had been facing the responsibilities of the presidency with justifiable misgivings, wrote at once to the trustees declining the office. Then, at a special meeting of the board in December 1767, Stockton produced his letter and "the said Dr. Witherspoon was again unanimously chosen."[5]

On August 7, 1768, the *Peggy*, from Glasgow, sailed up the Delaware to one of the Philadelphia wharves.[6] There stepped ashore a heavy-set man of forty-six, with brown hair, large nose and ears, a strong face, and blue eyes which looked out from beneath bushy brows. With him were his wife and

---

[4] John Witherspoon to Benjamin Rush, Aug. 14, 1767. *Princeton Library MSS*, AM 12648.
[5] *Trustees Minutes*, I, p. 141.
[6] *New Jersey Archives*, First Series, XXVI, p. 240.

five children. The Witherspoons received a hearty welcome in the Quaker city, many leading Presbyterians vying for the honor of entertaining them. After five days under the hospitable roof of Andrew Hodge, they set out for Princeton. At the old province line, about a mile from the village, they found Vice-President William Tennent and the three tutors, with the entire student body waiting to greet them and escort them to their temporary quarters at Morven, the residence of Richard Stockton. That night Nassau Hall celebrated their arrival with a tallow dip in every window.

Dr. Witherspoon was deeply moved by these manifestations of joy and impressed with the responsibility which he had assumed. This satisfaction "plainly implies an expectation of duty and service which I fear I shall be ill able to perform," he said. Yet not only the trustees, faculty, and students, but even his rival for the presidency, Francis Alison, rejoiced that at last the proper man had been found to unite the warring factions within the church and repel attacks from without. "I'm every day determined to combat with and stifle our own trifling prejudices and endeavor after consolidating the Presbyterian interests," said another Old Side. When Witherspoon attended the meeting of the synod in May 1769, he was welcomed as the new leader of the church, appointed to no less than eight committees, and made head of an important delegation to the convention of the associations of Connecticut.

Dr. Witherspoon discovered that he was expected to be a financier as well as scholar, teacher, and church leader. Alison stated that the trustees "are bad oeconomists and have squandered away much money," and a survey of the musty old college ledger dating to 1769, together with the minutes of the board, fully bear him out.[7] Part of the college funds had been lent to private individuals upon personal security, or in some cases with land as collateral; large sums had remained for years in the treasurer's hands yielding no return; part of the college assets consisted of scattered bits of real estate; the college accounts were in hopeless confusion; losses from

[7] Varnum Lansing Collins, *President Witherspoon*, I, p. 90.

bad debts ran into hundreds of pounds; arrears of tuition and room rent piled up at the end of each session;[8] the steward was permitted to fall behind in his accounts by no less than £810,[9] the trustees had drifted into the habit of meeting current expenses by dipping into the endowment. In April 1769 total assets amounted to only £2,535, of which a mere £1,310 was out at interest, and it was obvious that additional sums must be raised to avert bankruptcy. One wonders why the trustees, comprising as they did several well-known businessmen, should have permitted the college finances to become so muddled.

Witherspoon himself, with little experience in such matters, was slow in putting things in order. But in raising money he was more successful. Although the synod refused his request for aid from the church funds, it appointed twenty-five members to "use their utmost endeavors to obtain subscriptions" in Pennsylvania, Maryland, New Jersey, Virginia, and South Carolina. Some of the trustees and other friends of the college had already set a good example, William Peartree Smith giving £100, Robert Ogden, 128 acres of land, Elias Boudinot, £15, Elias Dayton, £15, Cornelius Hetfield, 100 acres of land. In far-off Georgia contributions exceeded £1,000, but "largely in produce," so that the trustees were forced to charter a vessel to go south to get it.[10] In Charleston, South Carolina, the Reverend James Caldwell raised £700,[11] Philadelphia contributed £316, little Cohansey £17.2, New York £123, Boston £360, Judge John Berrien gave £25, John Hancock £166.13.4.[12]

Dr. Witherspoon himself proved the greatest drawing card. Journeying far and wide through the colonies during the vacation periods, he preached in many of the foremost churches and met many prominent men, always stressing the needs of the college and its influence for good. In November 1769 a

[8] *Princeton Library MSS*, AM 10716.
[9] *Trustees Minutes*, I, p. 303.
[10] *Ibid.*, I, p. 172.
[11] *New Jersey Archives*, First Series, XXVII, p. 112.
[12] *College Ledger*, 1769, pp. 11, 22.

great multitude assembled in the yard of the capitol at Williamsburg, Virginia, were so deeply impressed that they at once contributed £66, to which Governor Botetourt added £50 from his own pocket.[13] The next year the president turned eastward, visiting New Haven, Providence, and Boston and returning with gifts amounting to £1,000,[14] of which £535 was subscribed by William Phillips, of Boston, and his two brothers.[15] In the one year ending October 1, 1770 Witherspoon turned over £1,541 to the treasurer.[16] No community was too poor, no congregation too small to escape his attention. One finds in the college ledger, sandwiched in between the larger donations, entries of £18 from Peter Grove and Cape May, £11.15 from Marsh Creek, £34.10 from Conogocheaqua, £20 from Rocky Spring—which must have meant real sacrifice to many of the donors.

In striking contrast was the ill-starred attempt to secure donations in the West Indies. As it was known that many in Jamaica revered Witherspoon as a great scholar and divine,[17] the trustees decided to send him to the island to present the needs of the college. At the same time his son James, accompanied by the Reverend Charles Beatty, was to visit Barbados, Antigua, etc.[18] This plan was never carried out. Witherspoon, instead of making the long, dangerous voyage, decided to publish a brief account of the history, educational methods, purposes and needs of the college for distribution in the islands.[19] But the brave Beatty, who had repeatedly risked his life in the wilderness to bring the Gospel to the Indians, insisted upon sailing. "It is all the same to me whether I die at home, on the seas or in the West India Islands; so that I am about my Master's business," he said on the eve of de-

[13] *Virginia Gazette*, Nov. 2, 1769.
[14] *Trustees Minutes*, I, p. 159.
[15] Ashbel Green, *Life of Witherspoon*, MSS, p. 116, New Jersey Historical Society.
[16] *College Ledger*, I, p. 46.
[17] Ashbel Green, *Life of Witherspoon*, MSS, p. 118, New Jersey Historical Society.
[18] *Trustees Minutes*, I, p. 186.
[19] *New Jersey Archives*, First Series, XXVIII, pp. 289-308.

parture.[20] He reached Barbados, but became ill there and died before securing any gifts for the college.[21]

The increase in the endowment was seconded by a more businesslike administration, by closer attention to the collection of debts and by economy in college affairs. The trustees appointed Dr. Witherspoon and Richard Stockton a committee "to examine into all writings, instruments of conveyance, records and papers . . . to see that all deeds be properly acknowledged and recorded . . . and provide a . . . strong box or chest" in which to keep them.[22] Chamber rent for students was raised to 40 shillings a year to be paid semi-yearly in advance.[23] A lottery was planned for Delaware. A committee was appointed to confer with the treasurer as to the best ways of investing college funds. A considerable sum was saved by the acceptance of John Blair's resignation as professor of divinity and moral philosophy.[24] So far was retrenchment carried that the trustees, apparently taking the stand that a college was not the proper place for the study of art, refused to reimburse Witherspoon for Boyden's *Collection of Prints* which he had paid for from his own pocket.[25] As a result of these multiform efforts the college finances were gradually placed upon a firmer footing and, despite the purchase of costly scientific equipment and the paying off of old debts, the invested funds began to mount. On September 24, 1770, the college owned bonds and securities totalling £5,114.8.3,[26] yielding an income which, with the returns from tuition and room rent, was sufficient to meet current expenses.

If, during the first two decades of the college, religion held the dominant place in the minds and hearts of faculty and students, in the next ten years patriotism became a strong rival. The injustice of the Stamp Act, the stimulating of American manufactures, the right of the subject to resist royal aggression, the Boston Massacre, were discussed in the refectory, on the campus, and in the chambers of Nassau Hall by excited

[20] *Extract from Sermon of Jas. Sproat,* Presbyterian Historical Society.
[21] He died Aug. 13, 1772. *Ibid.*      [22] *Trustees Minutes,* I, p. 174.
[23] *Ibid.,* pp. 181, 183.      [24] *Ibid.,* pp. 162, 163.
[25] *Ibid.,* p. 304.      [26] *College Ledger,* I, p. 33.

groups of undergraduates. Each commencement became the occasion for harangues on patriotism,[27] or debates on the thesis that "all men are free by the law of nature." In September 1765, seven months after the passage of the Stamp Act, the graduating class when assembled to receive their degrees were attired in cloth of American manufacture, an act of patriotism which brought forth warm praise from the public and the press. "If young gentlemen of fortune and education, many of whom will probably shine in the various spheres of public life, would thus voluntarily throw aside those articles of superfluity and luxury which have almost beggared us," said one writer, their example will have a profound influence on "the lower ranks of mankind."[28]

A year later, although presumably again clothed in "articles of superfluity and luxury" because of the repeal of the Stamp Act, the graduates treated the audience to a debate on the thesis that "Civil liberty is necessary to give birth to the arts and sciences," while one young man delivered "a very spirited nervous harangue on Liberty."[29] Nor were they content to vent their patriotism in oratory and debates alone. On July 13, 1770, they intercepted a letter written by a group of merchants in New York, and addressed to the merchants of Philadelphia, in which they stated their intention of ignoring the Non-Importation Agreement. As the undergraduate body gathered on the campus in their flowing black gowns, the tolling of the bell in Nassau Hall adding a note of somberness, a public hangman hired for the purpose burned the letter, as a warning to all "betrayers of their country."[30] Whatever the Tory merchants thought of this act of violence, it was warmly applauded by all true lovers of American rights. In September, at commencement, the graduating class were back in American made clothes, which Franklin's *Pennsylvania Ga-*

---

[27] *New Jersey Archives*, First Series, XXIV, pp. 631-639.
[28] *Ibid.*
[29] *Ibid.*, XXV, pp. 218, 219.
[30] G. Hunt, *Writings of James Madison*, I, p. 7; *New York Gazette or Weekly Post Boy*, July 16, 1770.

*zette* thought more brilliant than the "borrowed plumage" of the "gayest butterfly in all the assembly."[31]

In time, as the controversy with the mother country became heated, the spirit of patriotism on the campus grew more and more intolerant, so that the unfortunate youth whose father was aligned with the Tory party might become the butt of his classmates or even pay for his loyalty to the King with a ducking under the college pump. One excited young patriot wrote that he hoped two or three "possessed swine" of Tories would be "turned off" as soon as Dr. Witherspoon could attend to their cases.[32] In January 1774 the students held a "tea party" on the campus, in which the "steward's winter store of tea" together with a few extra pounds from the chambers in Nassau Hall, were burned to the ringing of the bell and the passing of "many spirited resolves." When an effigy of Governor Hutchinson, with a tea canister suspended from his neck, also went up in flames,[33] one of the trustees made a futile effort to end the "riotous proceedings" but received an "insulting" rebuff for his pains.[34]

In April 1776 the grim news of Lexington and Concord reached Princeton and spread like wildfire through the college. The time for orations or for demonstrations had now passed and the business of preparing for war began. The students organized a company of fifty men, so that the usually peaceful campus now resounded to the sound of sharp commands and the tramping of feet. "Every man handles his musket and hastens in his preparations for war," wrote one young patriot.[35] After so much excitement it was perhaps to be expected that the students would receive the news of what seems to us the culminating act in the great drama in which they were playing their part—the Declaration of Independence—in comparative calm. True, Nassau Hall was "grandly illuminated," and the proclamation read under a triple volley

---

[31] *Pennsylvania Gazette*, Oct. 18, 1770.
[32] *The Journal of Philip Vickers Fithian*, Hunter D. Farish, Ed., pp. 14, 15.
[33] *Princeton Library MSS*, AM 1591.
[34] *Trustees Minutes*, I, p. 203.
[35] *Princeton Library MSS*, AM 9641.

of musketry and with cheers for the prosperity of the United States, but the ceremony was conducted with the "decorum" proper to men who were exchanging the life of the undergraduate for that of the soldier.[36]

Those who thought that President Witherspoon, as a native Scot and a recent arrival in the colonies, would frown upon or repress the patriotic enthusiasm of his young charges were greatly mistaken. From the day of his arrival at Philadelphia he had been an admirer of things American—the high standard of living, the freedom from beggars and highwaymen, the astonishingly large and self-respecting middle class, even the invigorating climate. He was surrounded with ardent supporters of the colonial cause—his friends and neighbors, the trustees, the fathers of his students, his colleagues in the Presbyterian synod—and had he attempted to stem the tide of revolution, it would have swept him away from his safe moorings in the church and the college. But Witherspoon had no desire to stem the tide; he rode triumphantly on its crest. When the students "rioted" on the campus, he was probably peeping from behind the curtains of his study window, smiling as the letter of the New York merchants or the steward's tea, or Governor Hutchinson's effigy went up in flames. We find him a member of the Somerset County Committee of Correspondence, sitting in the provincial convention where he played a leading role in the overthrow of the loyal government and the imprisonment of Governor William Franklin; again a few weeks later we find him in the Continental Congress pleading for the immediate passage of a Declaration of Independence.

A cloud of apprehension hung over the college in the closing weeks of the session which ended in September 1776, and the students must have found it difficult to keep their minds on metaphysics, the classics, or natural philosophy, with Howe's invading army a mere fifty miles away and driving the Americans from post to post. Scarcely had one messenger brought the news of the defeat on Long Island than another

[36] *New Jersey Archives*, Second Series, I, p. 142.

told of the evacuation of New York and a third the defeat at Kips Bay. Commencement was a dismal affair, even though the senior class went through the usual round of debates and orations, for the lack of a quorum at the trustees' meeting made it impossible to confer the degrees.[37]

Six weeks later, when the students reassembled after the autumn vacation, they began recitations with the consciousness that any day they might have to take to flight. They were not surprised, then, when on November 29 Witherspoon summoned them to the Prayer Hall, to announce the rapid approach of the Red Coats. The president was deeply affected as he looked down into the serious faces of the young men and, after giving them "much good advice," bade them an affectionate farewell.[38] Immediately all was excitement as the students packed their belongings and scoured the village for vehicles to carry them to places of safety, or went from room to room in Nassau Hall to bid their classmates goodbye. Some, whose homes were in far-off Virginia or South Carolina, had to leave their effects behind and so "lost their all." Witherspoon himself loaded a few valuables in a wagon, placed his wife in the "old chair," mounted his sorrel mare and set out for Pequea, in Pennsylvania.[39]

Three days later Washington passed through Princeton with the remnant of his shattered forces, followed on December 7 by the British. Then began what an eye-witness called the "twenty days tyranny." The rough soldiery went from house to house pillaging and plundering and dragging off to imprisonment in Nassau Hall all who were suspected "of being rebels or aiding and assisting them."[40] The house of Jonathan Sergeant was burned to the ground, Richard Stockton's "furniture, apparel and even valuable writings" were destroyed and his cattle, horses, hogs, sheep and grain carried off.[41] A regiment of regulars crowded into Nassau

[37] *Trustees Minutes*, I, p. 214.     [38] *Princeton Standard*, May 1, 1863.
[39] *Christian Advocate*, II, pp. 443, 444.
[40] "A Brief Narrative," p. 34, *Princeton Library MSS*, Pyne Henry, AM 1123.
[41] R. H. Lee, *Memoir of the Life of Richard Henry Lee*, II, p. 164.

Hall, sleeping in the recitation rooms and Prayer Hall as well as the students' chambers, and using the basement as a stable for horses. Although a sentry posted at the door of the room containing the scientific apparatus preserved the Rittenhouse orrery from damage, the library was plundered and great damage was inflicted upon the building.[42]

On the morning of January 3, 1777, before the break of day, the British soldiers were awakened by the buglers and, after eating a hasty breakfast, marched off toward Trenton, leaving one regiment as a garrison for Princeton. A few hours later those who were not dead or wounded or scattered came streaming back, a disorganized mass of fugitives. They had been disastrously defeated outside the village by Washington's army, which had eluded Lord Cornwallis at Trenton, and had reached Princeton by an all night march over back roads. Some of the British fled down Witherspoon Street, past Rocky Hill and on toward New Brunswick. Others took refuge in Nassau Hall and, knocking out the panes of glass, stationed themselves at the windows prepared to resist every assault. But the Americans, bringing up their artillery, opened fire with such deadly effect that the building soon became untenable. A cannonball passed through a window of the Prayer Hall, and blasted the portrait of George II.[43] Apparently regarding the downfall of his "late majesty" as a signal of defeat, the regulars waved a white flag from a window and, marching out a humiliated, "haughty, crabbed set of men," laid their arms down on the front campus. Later on in the day Cornwallis' army retreated through Princeton "puffing" and "swearing," but they were too intent on heading Washington off from their base at New Brunswick, to give more than a passing glance at the college.[44]

It was a sad sight which greeted the frightened inhabitants of Princeton when they returned to their homes. "Princeton is indeed a deserted village," wrote Benjamin Rush. "You

[42] Ashbel Green, *Life of Witherspoon*, MSS, p. 110, New Jersey Historical Society.
[43] *Trustees Minutes*, I, p. 236.
[44] *Account of Sergeant R.*, Princeton Library, p. 8.

would think it had been desolated with the plague and an earthquake, . . . the college and church are heaps of ruins, all the inhabitants have been plundered."[45] Even though the college was now in the hands of friends, worse was to come. A body of Continental troops who moved into Nassau Hall and remained through more than five months[46] conducted themselves more like a swarm of vandals than the defenders of liberty. They amused themselves by playing with the orrery until the delicate machinery was so badly deranged that it could never be entirely repaired.[47] They used benches and doors for firewood, ripped up floors, punched holes in the partitions, ruined the organ. When they were gone the doctors who arrived to convert the building into a military hospital found the rooms stripped of plaster, "which, with an accumulation of other filth," covered the floor.[48] Yet in the months from October 1777 to November 1778 scores of the ill or wounded were brought to this cheerless place for treatment.[49]

Meanwhile the student body had dispersed, some having returned to their homes, while others were fighting as members of the militia or the Continentals. One was seized by a press gang and forced to serve on the American brigantine, *Andrew Doria*.[50] James Ashton Bayard, a boy of sixteen, was taken by the British on his way home from college and escaped hanging only by the intervention of General Washington. In April 1778 the trustees petitioned the New Jersey government to exempt both faculty and undergraduates from military duty,[51] a plea which was seconded by a letter in the *Gazette*, signed "Cato," probably written by Witherspoon himself.[52] Parents will not enter their sons in college if they may at any moment be called forth to serve in the militia, he

[45] R. H. Lee, *Memoir*, II, p. 164.
[46] *Princeton Library MSS*, AM 1973.
[47] Ashbel Green, *Life of Witherspoon*, MSS, p. 110, New Jersey Historical Society.
[48] *Ibid.*, p. 157.
[49] *Princeton Library MSS*, AM 1973.
[50] Varnum Lansing Collins, *President Witherspoon*, II, p. 92.
[51] *Trustees Minutes*, I, p. 218.
[52] *New Jersey Archives*, Second Series, II, pp. 14-16.

pointed out, so that the minor service they can render the nation as soldiers is putting an embargo on the seat of the muses and preventing the development of future leaders.

In the summer of 1777, a handful of undergraduates put in their appearance in answer to an announcement in the *Gazette* that classes would be resumed.[53] The students engaged board and lodging in the village and assembled daily in the President's House, where Witherspoon, if he happened to be in town, devoted himself to their instruction. At other times they were under the care of William C. Houston, professor of mathematics, and of one tutor. A pathetic little group they were, cheated out of their normal college life, missing old friends and classmates, deprived of their library and scientific apparatus, fearing that the enemy might appear again to interrupt their studies. In August the senior class, reduced to seven, were examined and awarded their degrees, but the usual commencement was omitted.[54]

The government added to the troubles of the college by drafting its president for service in Congress. In the years from 1776 and 1782 Witherspoon's squat figure was familiar to the farmers as he jogged along the road to Philadelphia to attend important committee meetings or back to Princeton to resume his lectures. Despite the prejudice against the "clergyman in government," he played a major role in the counsels of the nation, for he served on no less than one hundred committees. As one of the Board of War he was partly responsible for military affairs; as a member of the Committee of Secret Correspondence he had a voice in concluding the treaties with France and in instructing the peace commissioners; he entered actively into the debates over the Articles of Confederation, and assisted in organizing the executive departments. And throughout the trying months and years, when lesser men were driven into despair and recklessness, his patience, calmness, and courage proved a rock of strength to the national cause.[55]

[53] *Ibid.*, I, pp. 322-323.     [54] *Ibid.*, II, pp. 435-437.
[55] Varnum Lansing Collins, *President Witherspoon*; Ashbel Green, *Life of Witherspoon*, MSS, pp. 128-141, New Jersey Historical Society.

The misfortunes of the college and the problem of restoring it to its former vigor, weighed heavily on the president's mind. His first step was to render a bill to Congress for the damage done to the property of the college, which he pressed to such good purpose that by November 6, 1779, he had received payments totaling £7,250,[56] or $19,357, in Continental currency. Had this money been available a year earlier, before depreciation was fully under way, it would have been sufficient to make the needed repairs, but by the time the first payment reached his hands, the paper dollar had sunk to about 5 cents in hard cash. Elias Woodruff, the steward, who superintended the work of restoration, had to pay $4,178 for window glass, $1,077 for lime, $1,076 for nails, $3,571 for carpenter's work, $2,200 for ordinary labor, $330 for glazing.[57] Yet the money held out long enough to mend the leaky roof, put in the broken windows, restore the classrooms, and plaster some of the chambers.[58] When Ashbel Green entered college in May 1782, the whole building inside and out still showed the effects of war, for the outer walls were scarred by the cannonade, two of the four floors were "a heap of ruins" and the other two but imperfectly restored.[59]

In the meanwhile the life of the institution continued, though at a low ebb. Several students had moved into Nassau Hall in the autumn of 1778, and spent an uncomfortable winter there with the cold winds howling through the broken windows. Although at the summer session of 1779 there were only ten undergraduates conning over their studies to the sound of hammering and sawing,[60] a "numerous and respectable" company assembled for the commencement in September. Six seniors received their degrees and went through the usual rounds of Latin and English orations, in which a dis-

---

[56] £1,250 on May 29, 1779, £3,000 on September 3, and £3,000 on November 6. *Maclean MSS*, 1779. Princeton Library.

[57] *Ibid.*

[58] *New Jersey Archives*, Second Series, III, pp. 324, 325.

[59] Ashbel Green, *Life of Witherspoon*, MSS, pp. 150, 151, New Jersey Historical Society.

[60] *New Jersey Archives*, Second Series, III, pp. 671, 672.

course on the "horrors of war" was sandwiched in between one on "true nobility" and one on "affability."[61]

It now became necessary to find someone who could give his undivided time to the instruction of students and the restoration of the institution, for not only was Witherspoon still in Congress but in June 1779 Professor Houston joined him there. The choice of the trustees fell upon Samuel Stanhope Smith, the husband of Witherspoon's daughter Ann and the founder of Hampden-Sydney College. Witherspoon resigned to him one-half of the presidential salary of £400, together with the President's House on the campus, and took up permanent residence at Tusculum, his farm about a mile north of the village.[62] Tall, handsome, eloquent, courtly, Smith was an ideal selection, and it was due in no small part to his ability and energy that the college emerged successfully from the trying days of the war.

But it proved to be slow, uphill work. In 1780 there were seventeen or eighteen students in college, of whom six received their degrees; in 1782 there were forty undergraduates, working under Professor Smith and Mr. Riddle, the tutor; two years later the number had mounted to sixty-eight, and in 1786 to ninety. In 1782 Witherspoon resigned his seat in Congress and thereafter rode over from Tusculum regularly to take charge of the senior class.[63] Life in Nassau Hall at this time must have been dull in contrast to the exciting days of 1775 and 1776, for the war weariness of the nation was reflected on the campus. The boys complained of the difficulty of their work and of the "rye bread half-dough," the "old oniony butter," and the "lean, tough, boiled fresh beef with dry potatoes."[64] Early in 1783 the deserters who passed through Princeton almost every day brought rumors of peace, but the students "heard that story so often" that this created little interest.[65]

But things took a different turn when Congress, fleeing

---

[61] *Ibid.*, pp. 669-671.     [62] *Trustees Minutes*, I, p. 222.

[63] Ashbel Green, *Life of Witherspoon*, MSS, p. 151, New Jersey Historical Society.

[64] *Princeton Library MSS*, AM 8797.     [65] *Ibid.*, AM 9511.

from a body of mutinous soldiers, came to Princeton and resumed their sessions in the library room in Nassau Hall. "The
face of things inconceivably altered," wrote young Ashbel
Green. "From a little obscure village we have become the
capital of America," where "the passing and rattling of
wagons, coaches and chairs, the crying about of pine apples,
oranges, lemons and every luxurious article"[66] creates an air
of bustle and excitement. The students must have found it
difficult to keep their minds on their books as one distinguished
man after another drove up to Prospect on the edge of the
campus and the footman handed out the luggage. The excitement culminated on August 26 when Congress received
George Washington in Nassau Hall. Passing through cheering crowds of students and townspeople, the general entered
the building and mounted the stairs to the library, where
Elias Boudinot read a congratulatory address.

For the students the great moment came on September 24,
at the commencement exercises in the Presbyterian church. It
is probable that no other graduating class in any American
college have received their degrees before so distinguished a
gathering. As the youthful speakers debated the question,
"Was Brutus justified in killing Caesar?", or "Can any measure that is morally evil be politically good?" they looked into
the faces of the Father of his Country, the French Minister
(the Marquis de la Luzerne), seven signers of the Declaration of Independence, nine signers of the Articles of Confederation, eleven future signers of the Constitution of the
United States, and many members of Congress. Washington
was visibly embarrassed when Ashbel Green, the valedictorian
of the class, turned to him to predict that "some future bard
. . . shall tell in all the majesty of epic song the man whose
gallant sword taught the tyrants of the earth to fear oppression
and opened an asylum for the virtuous and free." The next
day the general, chancing to meet Green in Nassau Hall,
shook his hand, praised his oration, and requested him to
present his best respects to his classmates. For the college

[66] H. C. Alexander, *Life of J. A. Alexander*, I, p. 16.

itself Washington expressed his esteem in a more substantial manner with the gift of fifty guineas. Not to be outdone, the trustees requested the general "to sit for his picture to be taken by Mr. Charles Wilson Peale," so that it might hang in the hall in place of the picture of "his late majesty."[67] This portrait, traditionally occupying the frame from which a cannonball ejected the portrait of George II, has escaped the destruction of two fires, and today hangs on one side of the president's chair in the Faculty Room, while another portrait of George II, recently presented by several alumni, hangs on the other.

The history of college endowments in America is discouraging. We find the friends and alumni of this institution or that going out to solicit funds or digging down into their own pockets until they have buttressed it with a fund sufficient for its needs. Then they have the mortification of seeing this dwindle or perhaps melt away because of mismanagement, or destruction of property, or inflation brought on by war, and the uphill struggle has to begin all over again. The College of New Jersey was no exception. The money raised during Burr's administration by the visit of Davies and Tennent to Great Britain, by contributions from congregations in America, by lotteries and legacies and private gifts, was in part wasted by bad financial management. Hardly had a new fund been built up by another "drive" than the Revolution swept it away.

Early in 1777 the trustees of the college saw the danger of currency inflation and looked around anxiously for some safe channel into which to divert their funds. New Jersey at the request of Congress had made Continental currency legal tender, and it was feared that the bondholders might soon be paying interest and principal at a half or a fourth of the original value. Before the paper currencies had made their headlong dive, the trustees took the seemingly wise step of investing every available penny in United States loan office certificates, protected as these were by a promise to pay inter-

[67] *Trustees Minutes,* I, p. 236.

est in hard cash borrowed from France.[68] And for several years this promise was kept. In 1779, 1780, and 1781, when other investments were melting away and, as Witherspoon said, creditors were running away from their debtors and the debtors were pursuing them in triumph and paying them without mercy, the college was receiving a tidy income on its certificates through drafts on France.[69] When Witherspoon, in April 1780, exchanged $240 received in this way for $10,320 in depreciated currency, he must have congratulated himself and the trustees on their foresight.

His happiness turned to alarm and resentment when, in 1782, Congress found it no longer possible to pay the interest of the certificates in cash, and instead issued indents, or acknowledgments of indebtedness.[70] Rising on the floor of Congress he protested against what he termed this last stab to the public credit, which would prove ruinous to widows and orphans and to endowed institutions. Of the last he could speak from personal experience, he said, since the College of New Jersey was a heavy investor in these securities. Had he dreamed that this revenue was to be cut off the trustees might have "disposed of their holdings for something," but now the country's best friends were reduced to beggary.[71] Witherspoon pleaded with Congress at least to appropriate additional funds for the restoration of Nassau Hall, but the finances of the nation were in such chaos that he could accomplish nothing.[72]

So once more the college was forced to appeal to the generosity of its friends. But the war had to a large extent dried up this source of assistance also, for many merchants had been impoverished, the rich had lost heavily by the inflation, landholders had been plundered by the armies, while some of the congregations who had formerly contributed liberally now were forced to spend every penny they could raise in rebuilding their ruined churches.[73] Yet vigorous efforts in every part

[68] *Princeton Library MSS*, AM 7490.    [69] *Ibid.*, AM 7491.
[70] C. J. Bullock, *Finances of the United States*, p. 145.
[71] Varnum Lansing Collins, *President Witherspoon*, II, p. 29.
[72] *Trustees Minutes*, I, pp. 220, 224.
[73] Ashbel Green, *Life of Witherspoon*, MSS, pp. 151, 152, New Jersey Historical Society.

of the country yielded enough to keep the faculty together and
to pay for further repairs to Nassau Hall. In 1779 the collection of £415 was reported from western Pennsylvania;
£663 came in from Philadelphia; Pequea, Faggs Manor, and
Chaceford contributed £380; the Reverend George Duffield
secured £391.[74] Unfortunately, before the money reached
Witherspoon it, too, had so depreciated that it is probable that
its purchasing power was less than $200. The old expedient of
a lottery was tried with indifferent success; one or two bits of
real estate were sold; but despite everything, the revenues
sank lower and lower.[75]

In this extremity it was decided to send Dr. Witherspoon
and Joseph Reed, president of the Supreme Executive Council of Pennsylvania, to solicit funds in Great Britain. This
action, taken against the advice of Witherspoon himself, was
extremely ill-advised. It is true that sentiment in the mother
country had at first favored the cause of the colonies during
the long-drawn-out quarrel with King and Parliament, as was
evidenced by letters to the gazettes, political cartoons, and
addresses in the House of Commons. But hostilities had
brought about a change, and the French alliance and independence had left resentment and bitterness. Witherspoon and
Reed were received with courtesy, but their friends made it
plain that the British people were in no humor to contribute
to any cause in America, no matter how worthy. The war had
left them with a huge national debt, they pointed out, taxes
were heavy and they did not consider it their duty to aid in
educating American youths now that the old tie had been
broken.

Witherspoon wrote to Franklin and Jay, to ask whether
there was any hope of securing contributions from France and
other countries of the continent, but the answer was equally
unfavorable. Franklin thought that "the very request would
be disgraceful to us by representing the United States as too
poor to provide for the education of their own children." Ut-

[74] *College Ledger*, I, p. 153.
[75] Ashbel Green, *Life of Witherspoon*, MSS, p. 152, New Jersey Historical
Society.

terly discouraged, the president took vessel for New York, where he arrived in September. After examining Witherspoon's accounts, the trustees found a balance in favor of the college of £5.14,[76] and even this was wiped out seven years later when they paid him £19, the "balance of his expenses to Europe."[77] The most important results of the mission were the loss of eight months of Witherspoon's time and of one of his eyes from an accident on board ship.[78]

So once more the trustees petitioned Congress for relief. Witherspoon could not bring himself to believe that the government, now that victory had been won, would desert the college which had suffered so severely for its patriotism.[79] Since the government itself was on the verge of bankruptcy and had no money to appropriate, he asked for a tract of land from the national domain. But once more he came home empty handed and discouraged. An appeal to the New Jersey legislature also failed, while the earnest efforts of the synod brought forth only a few scattered contributions, entirely inadequate to meet the pressing needs.[80]

Yet the restoration of Nassau Hall went forward from time to time, as the increase in students or an unexpected gift yielded a little ready cash. In 1783 the bricklayers, carpenters, masons, and plasterers were at work on the building repairing walls and partitions and stairs, while joiners fitted up the bare chambers with bedsteads and tables.[81] It was not until the next year, however, that the third floor was made habitable and new flooring and tables put in the dining room.[82] Finally, in 1791, fourteen years after the Battle of Princeton, a new roof was installed, the floors and windows were repaired and the building once more seemed in good order.[83] Even then an air of poverty still hung over the place. "The deplorable state of the enclosure wall, several urns from which have fallen to the ground," and of the "dirty and unkempt" court-

---

[76] *Trustees Minutes*, I, p. 246.  [77] *College Ledger*, I, p. 179a.
[78] Varnum Lansing Collins, *President Witherspoon*, II, p. 143.
[79] *Trustees Minutes*, I, p. 315.  [80] *Ibid.*, p. 221.
[81] *Princeton Library MSS*, AM 1596.  [82] *Ibid.*, AM 1584.
[83] *Ibid.*, AM 1592.

yard gave such an air of negligence that one was "angered that the pupils have such an unfortunate example under their eyes," noted a foreign visitor, in 1794.[84]

Had this visitor focused his attention on what was occurring inside Nassau Hall, he would have found the professors lecturing or holding recitations as usual, the boys studying or perhaps romping or crowding into the dining hall—for despite physical dilapidation the college was still doing good work in preparing young men for leadership in the nation. After 1779 the chief burden of teaching as well as much of the responsibility of administration fell to the lot of Samuel Stanhope Smith, and in 1786 the trustees paid recognition to his services by making him vice-president.[85] By the students Smith was universally respected as teacher and scholar, and not a little feared for his strictness as a disciplinarian. Yet he knew when to be lenient, as when he found the boys after a celebration at the local tavern disturbing the peace of Nassau Hall long after 11:00 p.m. and "just hinted at its being bed time."[86]

For Ashbel Green, the youthful professor of mathematics and natural philosophy, the students had a real affection. "Oh! he is a fine scholar, and a clever fellow," said one of them, "there is something so amiable and engaging in him that I like him more and more every time I meet him if it is a dozen times a day."[87] Nor was it a real reflection upon his ability as a teacher when another lad cut his lecture in navigation because he was "capable of giving us very little more than our books."[88] In a college where there were but three professors and two or three tutors, none could be a master of every subject he was called upon to teach. In 1787 Green resigned to become associate minister of the Second Presby-

[84] Moreau de Saint-Méry, *Voyage aux États-Unis*, pp. 114-117.

[85] *Trustees Minutes*, I, p. 260.

[86] *Ibid.*, "Journal at Nassau Hall," April 6, 1786.

[87] *Princeton Library MSS*, AM 11288.

[88] "Journal at Nassau Hall," June 8, 1786, *Princeton Library MSS*, AM, 10841.

terian Church of Philadelphia.[89] Twenty-five years later he
was to return to the college as its president.

It was in recognition of the increasing importance of science
in education that the trustees selected Walter Minto, one of
the most distinguished astronomers in America, to succeed
Green in the chair of mathematics and natural philosophy.[90]
A native of Scotland and a graduate of the University of Edinburgh, Minto had studied under Professor Giuseppe Slop of
the University of Pisa, and had published a work on the
*Theory of the Planets.*[91] In his inaugural oration at Princeton,
delivered the evening before the 1788 commencement, he
spoke on "The Progress and Importance of the Mathematical
Sciences." He addressed himself to the graduating class and
urged them to continue their studies in after life, "for a college education is intended rather to sketch out the plan and to
lay the foundation than to complete the fabric of the liberal
arts and sciences."[92] Since the new professor's meager salary
of £200, always far in arrears, was supplemented by free board
and lodging in Nassau Hall, one wonders how he could have
afforded to desert bachelorhood to marry Mary Skelton of
Princeton.

To the members of the three lower classes, Dr. Witherspoon was an unfamiliar figure. Even in 1786, when he was
but sixty-three years of age, they usually spoke of him as the
Old Doctor.[93] On Sundays when they took their seats in the
Presbyterian church to hear him preach, they always found
him wearing his gown but not the old clerical wig, which he
laid aside after the Revolution. Beginning in a low voice, his
words gradually rang out louder and louder as he warmed to
his subject, while he leaned forward in the pulpit and gesticu-

---

[89] *Trustees Minutes*, I, p. 263.     [90] *Ibid.*, I, p. 271.
[91] The copy in the Princeton University Library was presented to Benjamin
Franklin by Minto "in testimony of esteem and veneration."
[92] *Princeton Library MSS*, AM 1831. There are two copies of his manuscript
translation of Bossuet's "A Course in Mathematics" in the Princeton Library,
one in the handwriting of Minto himself, and one for class use by R. L. Beatty,
1797.
[93] "Journal at Nassau Hall," Sept. 21, 1786, *Princeton Library MSS*, AM
10841.

lated with graceful movements of his right hand.[94] They saw him, also, at commencement exercises and at various celebrations when he presided with dignity on the platform of the Prayer Hall, smiling quietly if all went well or pulling nervously on his heavy eyebrows or shifting his hands and feet, if something disturbed him. During one Fourth of July celebration, when someone fired a cannon near the building in the midst of an oration, "he sprang forward as if in a convulsion" and had great difficulty in regaining his composure.[95]

To the seniors the Old Doctor was familiar enough, for they had to sit under him in several of their courses, finding him an excellent and clear teacher, despite his strong Scots accent. Ashbel Green says that many of the ideas which Witherspoon implanted in his mind when he was an undergraduate remained with him fifty years afterward.[96] If a group of boys walked to Tusculum to pay him a visit they were apt to find him directing the affairs of his farm, for he prided himself upon being a scientific agriculturalist. Even though his theories often failed to work out in practice, his vegetable garden won the admiration of his neighbors. Once when a visitor remarked, "Why, Doctor, I see no flowers in your garden," he replied, "No, nor in my discourses either."[97]

There was sincere sympathy among the students when Witherspoon's faithful wife died, leaving him the prospect of a lonely old age. But he himself decided that his old age should not be lonely. One morning after prayers about two years later it was rumored that something was afoot, for he had been seen to set out from Princeton in the old family chaise drawn by an ill-assorted tandem of plow and riding horses. A few days later when he returned with a bride of twenty-four, the widow of Dr. Armstrong Dill, of York County, Pennsylvania, the boys sent a delegation to Tusculum to offer their congratulations and beg for a day's holiday in

[94] Ashbel Green, *Life of Witherspoon*, MSS, p. 177, New Jersey Historical Society.
[95] Ashbel Green, *Life of Witherspoon*, MSS, p. 120, New Jersey Historical Society.
[96] *Ibid.*, pp. 107, 108.          [97] *Ibid.*, p. 178.

celebration. When the Old Doctor gave them three, there was universal jubilation which culminated with the firing of the cannon, the illumination of Nassau Hall with six hundred candles, and music by the student orchestra seated in the belfry.[98]

This marriage proved doubly fortunate for Witherspoon, for he became totally blind soon afterward and needed the loving care of a wife. The accident to one eye on shipboard in 1784 had been followed by a fall from his horse which so injured the other that a cataract developed. The celebrated surgeon, James Tilton of Delaware, gave him some hope of relief from an operation, but when this proved unsuccessful he resigned himself to his fate. Despite this affliction, his interest in the college and affairs of the nation remained as keen as ever, and he employed an amanuensis to take his correspondence and read to him from the newspapers and his own manuscript sermons. He could still place his hand on every volume in his library, and if he found one missing, would tug at his eyebrows, exclaiming, "They use me vorry ill, vorry ill."[99]

Young Titus Hutchinson gives us an intimate glimpse of the life at Tusculum. Coming to Princeton to seek admission to the junior class when the session was half over, he called on the president one morning before breakfast. "The venerable old Doctor in his blindness felt his way along and opened the door into the room. . . . After compliments, he said, 'Be seated. You will take breakfast with us.' . . . Soon the family were called together and they sung a psalm or hymn, which they seemed to know by heart. . . . They all kneeled in prayer. We then took breakfast." This done, young Hutchinson went up to the study where the president gave him a grilling in Latin and Greek to determine his fitness for advanced standing. Later in the day they called on "Doctor Smith." The two older men retired to the back part of the hall where they held a consultation in "stage whispers." "This Mr. Hutchinson has

[98] *United States Gazette*, June, 1791.
[99] Ashbel Green, *Life of Witherspoon*, MSS, p. 179, New Jersey Historical Society.

[ 73 ]

come to enter college with a view to join the junior class," said Witherspoon. "I have questioned him as my manner is. He is behind . . . in the studies of the present term. . . . I believe we may as well admit him, and he can occupy the coming vacation in the studies in which he is behind." To this Smith replied, "Well, just as you think best."[100]

This deference to the decisions of the older man makes us think that Smith must have discussed at length with him the proposal for the union of the college with Queen's College, the present-day Rutgers. From the first there had been cordial relations between Presbyterians and Dutch Reformed, for their doctrines were almost identical. Had it not been that the Dutch regarded their church as a national institution, which must remain under the jurisdiction of the Classis of Amsterdam as a buttress to the Dutch language and Dutch customs in America, the two denominations might well have united. Among the trustees of the College of New Jersey in its early history were three Dutch ministers, John Frelinghuysen, John Leydt, and Lambertus De Ronde. When it was proposed to found Queen's College to educate young men for the Dutch pulpit, the Classis of Amsterdam, thinking the expense too great, suggested making use of Princeton, which they understood had been founded by "the purest Scotch Presbyterians," and already had buildings, library, and "celebrated professors."[101] Accordingly De Ronde, in June 1766, proposed to the Princeton trustees the founding of a chair of divinity, to be filled by a Dutchman, "for the service of the Dutch as well as the English Presbyterian churches."[102] But while Princeton hesitated a charter was granted to Queen's College and the matter, for the moment, was dropped.

In 1793, when Queen's was without a president and facing financial ruin, the proposal for a union was revived. On September 19, a joint committee from the two boards of trustees met at New Brunswick and drew up a plan under which there

---

[100] *Memoirs of Titus Hutchinson*, MSS, pp. 12-15, Princeton Library.
[101] William H. S. Demarest, *History of Rutgers College*, p. 64.
[102] *Trustees Minutes*, I, p. 113.

was to be a new charter for the united colleges, with twenty-eight trustees, the work of college grade to be done at Princeton under the existing faculty, and the preparatory work at New Brunswick.[103] Before the trustees of the College of New Jersey could act on this report it came before the Queen's board, where it was debated long and earnestly. But in the end Dutch traditions and Dutch blood triumphed over the necessities of the moment, though by the narrowest of margins, and the trustees voted nine to eight not to surrender their charter and permit their college to lose its identity.[104]

On November 15, 1794, Dr. Witherspoon was sitting in his accustomed chair at Tusculum, listening as his attendant read the newspaper, when he suddenly asked to be put to bed. Mrs. Witherspoon came in to assist, but the two had succeeded in getting the aged president only to another armchair when he breathed his last.[105] Three days later the body was brought from Tusculum to Nassau Hall where it lay in state as sorrowing friends, colleagues, and undergraduates filed by. From the Prayer Hall the casket was borne to the Presbyterian church for the sermon by the Reverend David Austin. Then the solemn procession started for the cemetery down the present Witherspoon Street—eight clergymen serving as pallbearers, followed by the faculty, trustees, the treasurer, the steward, the undergraduates and townspeople. And so John Witherspoon—educator, churchman, patriot, statesman—was laid to rest beside his predecessors in the president's lot.[106]

Witherspoon is one of the outstanding figures of America's early history. He was perhaps the greatest educator of the eighteenth century as well as the greatest ecclesiastical leader. It is remarkable that this Scotch clergyman should have taken his place in Congress beside Jefferson, Franklin, and John Adams to play an important role in directing the affairs of the

---

[103] *Ibid*, p. 318.

[104] William H. S. Demarest, *History of Rutgers College*, p. 176.

[105] *Princeton Library MSS*, AM 10228. Letter of David English to C. D. Green, Nov. 17, 1794. The account given by William Eltinge, '96, differs slightly in the matter of details from that of English. (*Ibid.*, AM 978.)

[106] *American Daily Advertiser*, Nov. 24, 1794.

nation throughout the critical years of the Revolution. For the college his services were invaluable, for he restored its finances, raised its prestige, increased the attendance, set a new direction to its educational policies. And though he had the misfortune to see much of his work temporarily undone by the ravages of war and inflation, his influence upon the college and upon American education was profound and lasting.

The most important development in the life of the college during the quarter of a century in which it was under Witherspoon's guidance could not have been entirely to his fancy, although his policies were in part responsible for it. Witherspoon found the college, if not a theological seminary, at least a place where religion struck the dominant note and where a very large percentage of the graduates went into the ministry; he left it a place devoted chiefly to training men for public life. The college had been founded with both ends in view, but in the days of Burr, Davies, and Finley, the emphasis was placed upon filling the vacant pulpits of the Calvinist denominations. Under Witherspoon the number of ecclesiastical students gradually became less, while those destined to become governors of states, congressmen, senators, judges, lawyers, and doctors steadily increased.

One must not imagine that Nassau Hall in the first decade of its history was given over entirely to devout lads who went about their daily tasks with long faces and spent all their spare moments reading the Bible. There were outbursts of exuberance even then, pranks, evasions of the regulations. But on the whole the students were a sober lot, many of whom were assisted through college by the fund for pious youths, or by private individuals interested in supplying the vacant churches. From time to time there would be religious revivals at college when few even among the frivolous escaped the general awakening. Then there would be frequent sermons in the Prayer Hall by the president or some visiting clergyman, prayer meetings by small groups in the college chambers, and earnest religious discussions in the dining hall or on the campus.

In Witherspoon's day, especially after the Revolution, all this was changed. We may take with a grain of salt the statement of Samuel Beach that the college "instead of being a nursery of piety" had become "a source and scene of almost every vice,"[107] or of Ashbel Green that the "moral conduct of the students" gave him pain every time he thought of it.[108] Yet Jonathan Dickinson, or Aaron Burr, or Samuel Davies would have been shocked could they have seen the undergraduates acting in a "tragedy and farce,"[109] or taking fencing lessons from a French master,[110] or dancing up and down the entry as a Negro played upon a violin with "twenty students hallooing and tearing about."[111] They would have been horrified when one of the students reeled into Nassau Hall after a Fourth of July dinner, cursing and swearing and threatening to kill Ashbel Green, and actually aiming a blow at him with an andiron.[112]

Occasionally one or two young men went forth from Nassau Hall to carry on the work of the Gospel, but they were few in comparison with former days. In the class of 1786 Thomas Grant and Henry Smalley alone assumed the cloth; in 1787 four entered the ministry; in 1788, two; in 1789, two; in 1790, one; in 1791, two. Of their classmates in the years from 1786 to 1791, thirty-four took up law or entered public life, many of whom became distinguished jurists or statesmen— J. H. Imlay, John Alexander, William Kirkpatrick, Nicholas Vandyke, E. K. Wilson, and Silas Wood entering Congress; David Stone being in turn congressman, senator, member of the United States Supreme Court; Mahlon Dickinson becoming governor of New Jersey, United States senator and Secretary of the Navy; William Johnson, associate justice of

---

[107] *Beach Family Letters*, MSS, July 10, 1782, Princeton Library.
[108] *Princeton Library MSS*, AM 11285.
[109] *Ibid.*, AM 8795.    [110] *Ibid.*, AM 11288.
[111] "Journal at Nassau Hall," March 18, 1786, *Princeton Library MSS*, AM 10841.
[112] *Beach Family Letters*, MSS, July 10, 1782, Princeton Library.

the Supreme Court; John Taylor and Jacob Burnet, members of the Senate. A fairly large group became doctors of medicine, others went into business or banking, a few became planters. The trend away from the ministry is illustrated by the experience of Charles Snowden who studied theology, and was licensed to preach, but who, after delivering one eloquent sermon, went into the newspaper business.[118] It must have grieved some of the stanch old Calvinist families when two of Jonathan Edwards's grandsons, as also the son of Alexander McWhorter, the son of Aaron Burr, and one of the New Jersey Piersons, turned their backs on the ministry to take up law.

For this great change the college itself was largely responsible. Not only had it loudly proclaimed from the first that it would educate for public life as well as for the ministry but it shaped its courses and its methods of instruction to this end. As the emphasis gradually shifted from the classics, metaphysics and divinity to mathematics, chemistry, astronomy, and physics, the college became more and more popular with those seeking a cultural background for law or business. It was symptomatic of the trend of the day that the efforts to establish a professorship of divinity were abandoned in favor of a chair of mathematics and natural philosophy.

The career and character of Witherspoon were also influential in bringing about the change. Whenever he spoke in Congress, or preached in some prominent church, or visited distinguished families in different parts of the country, he won friends for himself and the college. It was this admiration for Witherspoon which influenced James Madison, Sr., Henry Lee, John Van Cortlandt, and others of like stamp to send their sons to Princeton. And after they came it was Witherspoon who stimulated their interest in public affairs by encouraging them to debate on the great issues facing the nation.

It was a remarkable epoch in the history of the college, these twenty-six years of change and intellectual stirrings

[118] S. D. Alexander, *Princeton College during the Eighteenth Century*, p. 247.

under Witherspoon, an epoch marked successively by growth, disaster, and recovery. One wonders whether the institution would have played so important a role in the winning of independence and the creation of the nation, whether it could have maintained its position among the colleges of the nation, whether it could have risen from its ruins after the Revolution without the vision, the energy, the scholarship, the magnetic personality, the capacity for leadership of the great Scottish divine.

# CHAPTER III

## The School of Statesmen

MERICAN civilization had its inception in Europe, chiefly in England. It harks back to Westminster Hall, to Westminster Abbey, to the ports of London and Bristol, to the quiet country village, to the fishing towns of Suffolk and Devon. We inherited the English language, political institutions, common law, literature, and architecture. Since American education, too, had its origin in Great Britain, it becomes necessary for us in following its development and describing its character at Princeton, to turn back in our narrative to the mother country. There we discover that attention must be focused, not upon the great English universities, but upon those rather obscure, but not less important, institutions known as dissenting academies.

The average English dissenter in the eighteenth century regarded Oxford and Cambridge with mingled suspicion and resentment. He no more thought of sending his sons to these universities where they might be weaned from "true religion and piety," than to the College of the French Jesuits at Rheims or the College of Louis le Grand at Paris. It had not been long after the restoration of Charles II that Parliament, urged on by the Anglican hierarchy and tired of having Oxford and Cambridge "nurseries of heresy," purged their faculties of all save those who subscribed to the Anglican creed. So scores of the ablest and most pious Fellows took their departure, the Puritan *pileus* or skullcap gave way to the square cap, and orthodoxy reigned supreme. Moreover, for the youth of a dissenting family the peril to his morals was considered as great as to his religious faith, for he would have to associate with young noblemen and fellow-commoners, with their long hair and gayly colored clothing, who often scorned the classics and metaphysics, and wasted their time at drinking, gaming, hunting, and bear-baiting.

Some of the ejected university tutors, gathering around them groups of youthful students, founded what later became known as dissenting academies. They were chiefly concerned in educating pious youths for the ministry, so that the succession of able preachers would not be cut off from the Congregational and Presbyterian churches. The tutor usually began with two or three students, who perhaps boarded in his residence, giving what assistance he could in Greek, Latin, moral philosophy and divinity in the hours snatched from his ministerial duties. If his teaching proved successful so many might flock in that he would have to move to larger quarters, perhaps an old manor house, perhaps the former residence of an earl or a wealthy merchant. Here the academy would take on the character of an isolated college, with master, tutors, commons, chambers, and a full curriculum covering four or in some cases five years.[1]

The academies opened their doors to lay as well as clerical students. When one successful master wrote his former teacher of his intention to devote his entire time to preparing youths for the ministry, the latter convinced him that this would be unwise. "The support of our interest comes from the laity," he pointed out, "and they will not be constrained to bring up all their sons either as ministers or as dunces." Was it wise, then, he asked, to force them to send those, "who are designed for physicians, lawyers or gentlemen, to Oxford and Cambridge, or to make them rakes in the foreign universities?"[2] In fact, the academies not infrequently admitted the sons of Anglicans, some of whom attained eminence in the church— Thomas Secher, Archbishop of Canterbury; Joseph Butler, Bishop of Durham, and others. It was the dissenting academies which gave Britain Peter King, Lord Chancellor of England; Daniel Defoe and William Hazlitt; Thomas Malthus and Joseph Priestley; William Wickinson, inventor of the blast furnace.

[1] H. McLachlan, *English Education under the Test Acts* (Manchester, 1931), pp. 16-44.
[2] *Ibid.*, p. 145.

It was well that the dissenting academies upheld scholarship and high standards of education at a time when the universities were well-nigh palsy-stricken. At Oxford, Aristotle still reigned supreme in philosophy, science was looked upon with disfavor, the examinations for the sons of the wealthy had become a farce. Nor were conditions better at Cambridge. It is stated that the final examination there often consisted only of the question: "*Quid est nomen?*" to which the candidate was supposed to answer, "*Nescio.*" One student could not translate *Anno Domini*, another, when asked how long it was since the birth of Christ, replied, "About one hundred years."[3] On the other hand, at Northampton, or Daventry, or Warrington, the young man who secured his bachelor of arts degree had to earn it by hard work and real accomplishment. In the academies the terms were long, the vacations short, work began at six or seven in the morning and continued till late in the evening.

In the mid-eighteenth century, when scholars were shaking off the cobwebs of scholasticism, it was the academies which took the lead in emphasizing mathematics and natural philosophy. Formerly "if a man was well versed in the learned and dead languages and in Aristotle's logic and metaphysics and was master of the distinctions of the divinity school, he passed for a considerable scholar and divine," one tutor pointed out, "whereas now 'tis mathematical learning carries the bell."[4] So at Northampton, under the celebrated Philip Doddridge, or at Daventry, under Caleb Ashworth, the student got his full share of geometry, algebra, trigonometry, astronomy, conic sections, natural and experimental philosophy.

Though at first glance it would seem strange that men whose chief interest was religion and who were absorbed to the end of their lives in theological controversy should have taken the lead in achieving intellectual freedom, the key is furnished by dissent itself. It was the absence of ecclesiastical control which produced the wave of free thought in the

---

[3] *Ibid.*, p. 41.  [4] *Ibid.*, p. 27.

eighteenth century expressed in the congregations by Arianism and Unitarianism and in the academies by a zeal for astronomy or chemistry or physics. Had the tutors who were winning distinction by their discoveries in natural philosophy realized that they were paving the way for skepticism and spiritual disintegration, they would have been horrified. But they could see no incongruity in alternating mathematics with Greek and Hebrew, no danger in mixing experiments in electricity or chemistry with the study of divinity. So they became the champions of intellectual freedom and as such exercised a vast influence upon the future of scholarship and education.[5]

The academies led the way, also, in the study of the English language and literature. Since sermons had to be delivered in English, the masters broke away from the old tradition of lecturing in Latin, introduced new texts in English, and drilled the students in elocution. If suitable texts were lacking, they not infrequently passed on their manuscript lectures from academy to academy or, in many cases, had them printed for even wider distribution. The next step was the introduction of belles-lettres, with the study of literary works in which imagination and taste were of chief importance. Even John Colet, the great educational innovator of the sixteenth century, would have been shocked could he have visited Cowards Academy in 1770 to hear Andrew Kippis lecture on the variety and harmony of the English heroic verse.

Instruction in the academies was personal and intimate. Dr. John Aikin, master of Warrington, when conducting the work of divinity students on the Greek Testament, required them to construe portions of the text after which he would make "a minute, critical, doctrinal and practical explanation of each passage." Trial sermons or essays, after they were read before the group, were subjected to careful criticism. Then he "would generally turn to some of the finest passages of the English poets, Milton, Pope, Thomson," and after first reading a considerable portion himself, would ask the students to take

[5] W. A. Shaw in *Dictionary of Education*, I, pp. 468-469.

their turn, pointing out their defects and suggesting the proper remedy. It was the small number of students which made possible such individual attention. When a group of fifteen or twenty-five youths put themselves under the care of the master, slept under his roof, ate at his table, assembled around him for morning and evening prayers, sat at his feet every day for instruction, the progress each was making, his weaknesses, his difficulties, his aims, and ambitions became a matter of the teacher's keen interest and concern.

In comparison with the two great universities, the dissenting academies seemed weak and even temporary. Lacking adequate endowments, libraries, scientific equipment, and buildings; often following the master from town to town as he responded to different ministerial calls; subject to revolutionary changes in the course of study as one master succeeded another, they might be in their heyday one decade and close their doors the next. But their lack of stability was compensated for by their freedom from restraint. They were not hemmed in by ancient traditions or obsolete ordinances, there were no trustees to call the master to task for educational innovations, no patrons to meddle with the curriculum or to demand special favors for this lad or that. So when an academy grew up under the supervision of some remarkable scholar and teacher—a Philip Doddridge, a Joseph Priestley, or a John Eames—it profited to the full from his genius and his personality.

With the dissenting academies and with many of the masters the founders of the College of New Jersey were intimately acquainted. Dickinson, Burr, Edwards, and Davies corresponded regularly with Doddridge and other masters, kept them informed of religious conditions in America and questioned them upon courses, textbooks, and methods of instruction. When Davies and Gilbert Tennent went to England they took pains to visit as many of the academies as possible. In February Davies was at Hoxton, where Reverend David Jennings showed him the "philosophical curiosities, two orreries, an experiment to show all the colors of the rainbow blended from a white, a mushroom etc. petrified, two or three testaments in manuscript before the art of printing which were very elegantly written, sundry stones in the shape of a coiled snake, shells, minerals."[6] There can be no doubt that the information he gained at this time deeply influenced his own educational policies when a few years later he took up his duties as president of the college at Princeton.

But long before Davies and Tennent sailed for Great Britain, the college had turned to the English masters, especially to Philip Doddridge, for guidance and advice and to their academies as models by which to determine its own policies, curriculum, textbooks, methods of instruction. I hope you will not "defer the letter of advice to the students under my care, which is so much needed and so earnestly desired especially in the infant state of the college," Burr wrote Doddridge in May 1750. "I should be glad of your opinion of Grove's *Moral Philosophy* or what other system of that kind you think more suitable for the students. . . . The *Disquisitions* etc. were a very [welcome] present to our library. . . . I recommend myself, my people and my students to your prayers."[7]

The College of New Jersey, like the dissenting academies, had as its foremost purpose, the training of young men for the ministry, but like them threw its doors open to laymen and to youths of all Protestant denominations. Like them it consisted of a single college, not a group of colleges organized into a university after the manner of Oxford and Cambridge. Like them its reputation and progress depended largely upon the head of the institution, whether he was called president or master or tutor. Like them there was personal and careful supervision of studies and intimate relationship between teacher and pupil. Like them discipline was strictly enforced and students forbidden to waste their time in "worldly amusements." Like them there was a spirit of progressiveness in the choice of subjects to be taught and of liberality in the discus-

[6] *Samuel Davies Diary*, I, p. 153.
[7] *Princeton Library MSS*, AM 9971.

sion of controversial subjects.[8] True, in the College of New Jersey, unlike most of the dissenting academies, ultimate authority rested with a board of trustees, but during the first decades of its existence their chief function was to elect a president whose authority and policies they were forced to uphold.

It is a matter of profound moment in the history of American education, this influence of the dissenting academies in shaping the character of the colonial colleges, not only the College of New Jersey, but Yale, Dartmouth, Brown, Hampden-Sydney, and others. The colonies were settled in large part by dissenters—Congregationalists, Presbyterians, Huguenots, Dutch Reformed, etc.—who never lost touch with their co-religionists on the other side of the Atlantic. They looked to the British government, of course, for direction in governmental and economic matters, but in religion and education they were guided by the great dissenting divines and teachers. And as we must know Wesley, Whitefield, and Erskine to understand developments in the colonial churches, so we must know Philip Doddridge, David Jennings, and Joseph Priestley to grasp some of the forces which shaped early education.

Back in 1748, when Belcher clashed with Gilbert Tennent over the inclusion of the governor of New Jersey and four or five members of the Council in the board of trustees, perhaps neither realized that one was contending for the New England system of control, the other for an approach to the independent system of the dissenting academies. Belcher stated that he had been for thirty years a trustee of Harvard and had never observed any "inconveniency" from the close connection of the college with the government.[9] However, Professor S. E. Morison tells us that the overseers asserted their "right to examine into the principles of all those that are employed in the instruction of the students of the college, upon any just suspicion of their holding dangerous tenets," and insisted

[8] On this subject see Nelson R. Burr, *Education in New Jersey.*
[9] *New Jersey Archives*, First Series, VII, pp. 118-119.

upon quizzing every new tutor before confirming his appointment. In 1739, when three candidates for a degree were about to take the negative in a disputation on the proposition: "whether three persons in the Godhead are revealed by the Old Testament," they altered the printed questions with pen and ink to the affirmative. Such acts "were generally done by the Overseers who represented Church and State," says Professor Morison, "rather than by the President and Fellows of the college."[10]

Although Belcher succeeded in having the governor made *ex officio* president of the trustees, and included four of his Council in the new board of 1748, the College of New Jersey never fell under the control of the provincial government. It is stated that when William Franklin was governor he actually made an attempt to wheedle the trustees into consenting to a change in the charter surrendering important powers to the government in return for some slight financial advantage. Some of the trustees were praising "his Excellency's generous proposal" when William Tennent, looking around with his sharp and piercing eyes, rose and said: "Brethren! are you mad? I say, brethren are you mad? Rather than accept the offer of the President, I would set fire to the college edifice at its four corners and run away in the light of the flames."[11]

But the College of New Jersey, like both Harvard and Yale, was closely affiliated with the church, for on the board of trustees the ministers always outnumbered the laymen and they were always more punctilious in attendance. Their method of control was to elect as president the ablest Presbyterian scholar and preacher in the colonies, perhaps the recognized leader of the church, and if no man of sufficient eminence could be found in America they sought him in Great Britain. As a result it may justly be said that the college in the eighteenth century controlled the church even more than it was controlled by it. One day at a meeting of the Presbyterian

[10] Samuel E. Morison, *Three Centuries of Harvard*, p. 84.
[11] Archibald Alexander, *Log College*, pp. 154, 155.

general assembly, President Witherspoon, then an old man, remarked to Ashbel Green: "You can scarcely imagine the pleasure it has given me in taking a survey of this Assembly to observe that a decided majority of all the ministerial members have not only been sons of our college, but my own pupils."[12] To this day every president of Princeton has been either a Presbyterian minister, or the son of a Presbyterian minister.

And no matter how close their affiliation with the dissenting academies, no matter how eager they were to borrow from them the most progressive ideas, the founders of the college could not escape the fact that they themselves had been educated in New England. Jonathan Edwards had served as tutor for two years at Yale, in which time he was rector in all but name, and had exerted a powerful influence upon the policies of the institution. Nor can there be any doubt that Aaron Burr, when planning the course of study for the College of New Jersey, or selecting textbooks, or drafting rules for student conduct, not only drew upon his own experience at Yale but consulted his future father-in-law upon every point. Would it be wise to follow the example of Rector Cutler in using Wollebins' *Theology* and Ames's *Medulla*? Should he permit the students to read Locke and Newton, how much attention should be paid to Hebrew, should all conversation between students and tutors be conducted in Latin?[13]

But however great the influence of Yale upon the infant college in New Jersey it does not alter the fact that its character was shaped chiefly by the English dissenting academies, for Yale itself was no more than a dissenting academy somewhat altered to conform to local conditions in the province of Connecticut. Had an Englishman paid a visit to the little college in the Saybrook days, to see the twenty or more students pouring over their Tully and Virgil, or translating the Psalms into Hebrew, or coming to Rector Andrews for the

[12] Ashbel Green, *Life of Witherspoon*, MSS, p. 110, New Jersey Historical Society.
[13] Edwin Oviatt, *The Beginnings of Yale*, p. 418.

explanation of some knotty point in metaphysics, or seated at the long table in the hall asking for the butter or the milk in bad Latin, he could have imagined himself at Hoxton or Tewkesbury. The significance of the close contact of the founders of the College of New Jersey with Doddridge and other great educators in England was not so much that it gave them the tradition of the dissenting academies as that it brought that tradition up to date.

In the early years of the college a perplexing problem presented itself in the uneven preparation of the candidates for admission. Some who had studied at the better grammar schools or under private tutors were able to translate Cicero and Xenophon and perhaps speak Latin with some degree of facility, while others from the more remote districts were still struggling with Greek and Latin syntax. Dickinson and Burr found it expedient from the first to examine each youth upon entering to determine the class for which he was properly qualified. "Mr. Whittlesey is this morning leaving my house in order to go to college," wrote Samuel Finley from his Notingham school in August 1747. "I expect he will be admitted into the fourth class."[14] Apparently, however, he was a bit too sanguine, for Dickinson put him in the junior class and it was in September 1749 that he graduated. Finley himself may have been inclined to leniency in such matters. In 1761, when he was president he wrote Eleazar Wheelock: "I examined your son and though he was less prepared than the rest of his class, yet considering his age and good sense I concluded he would make a pretty good figure in it."[15]

In time it was found expedient before admitting a student not only to examine him for the upper classes but to require him to recite for a fortnight on trial. And it was announced that only in "very singular and extraordinary cases" would any be permitted to enter the senior class.[16] Even this seems to have proved unsatisfactory, for in December 1767 the

[14] *Bellamy Papers*, Presbyterian Historical Society, Finley to Bellamy, Aug. 3, 1747.
[15] *Princeton Library MSS*, AM 69.
[16] *An Account of the College* (Woodbridge, N.J., 1764), p. 33.

trustees decided that after September 1769 admission to the college should be only through the freshman class and that four full years of residence should be a prerequisite for the bachelor's degree.[17] But from this rather rigid requirement they were forced to retreat. In May 1769 they inserted a notice in a newspaper stating that so many urgent protests had been made against the rule that they had decided to rescind it. But "every scholar who pretends to enter any of the superior classes, must come fully prepared and expect a strict and impartial examination."[18]

Even more perplexing was the problem of the student who was not prepared even for the freshman class. As lad after lad stumbled over Virgil or Tully, could not tell the gerundive from the future passive participle, and had never opened a Greek book, President Burr began to realize that collegiate standards could not be maintained unless he opened and directed a preparatory school. This he did on his own responsibility, but after his death the trustees took it under their wing and appointed a Mr. Montgomery master at £45 a year and Mr. McWhorter usher at £15.[19] The boys toiled chiefly over their Latin and Greek, but they were supposed also to acquire "the graces of a good delivery," and spend a small portion of every day in improving their handwriting.

President Witherspoon was deeply interested in the school, and before leaving London for Princeton made himself conversant with the latest methods of instruction, "by conversing with some of the most eminent teachers in Great Britain."[20] In March 1769 he announced in the press that the master used a "book of directions" for teaching Latin, "drawn up by one who was long rector of the public grammar school in Glasgow." The school was provided with maps, he added, and with a "terrestrial globe" by which the pupils "may be taught geography by occasional exercises for amusement rather than a task." One hour a day was devoted to writing

[17] *Trustees Minutes*, I, p. 142.
[18] *New Jersey Archives*, First Series, XXVI, pp. 426-428.
[19] *Trustees Minutes*, I, p. 60.
[20] *New Jersey Archives*, First Series, XXVI, pp. 209, 270.

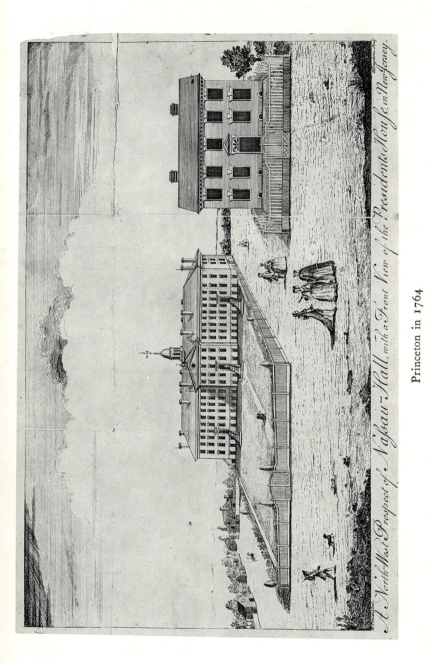

*A North-West Prospect of Nassau-Hall, with a Front View of the President's House, in New Jersey.*

Princeton in 1764

College of Princeton, New Jersey

View of Nassau Hall

Philosophical Hall

Stanhope Hall

East College

Library in Nassau Hall, 1868

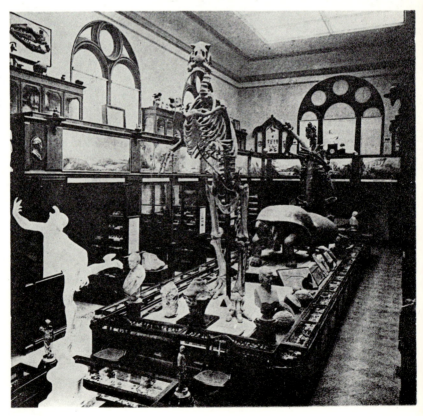

The Museum, 1879

Class of 1860

Faculty 1871

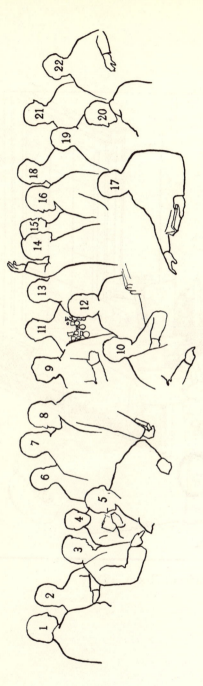

1. John Thomas Duffield
2. John Stillwell Schanck
3. Arnold Guyot
4. Henry van Dyke
5. James McCosh
6. Frederick Vinton
7. Henry Clay Cameron
8. William A. Packard
9. John Cross
10. Stephen Alexander
11. George Goldie
12. Henry T. Eddy
13. Stephen George Peabody
14. Cyrus Fogg Brackett
15. William McDowell Halsey
16. Joseph Kargé
17. Lyman Atwater
18. Theodore W. Hunt
19. Henry B. Cornwall
20. James C. Moffat
21. Charles. Woodruff Shields
22. John Seely Hart

A Student's Room, 1845

and arithmetic, while weekly exercises in reading English authors, with remarks on grammar and spelling, gave them greater proficiency in their own language.[21] In 1774 there were thirty boys in the grammar school, some apparently housed in Nassau Hall, others with "reputable householders in Princeton."

Witherspoon made clear just what he expected of his own and other grammar schools in a letter published in 1780. Masters were entreated to be thorough in their work, he said, for if boys who are "ill-founded in  classic learning" enter college, it is impossible fully to remedy the defect. It was more important to drill them in grammar and structure, he said, than to make them translate passages in poetry or prose, and it was wise to use at first easy books such as *Aesop's Fables* or *Carderias* instead of pushing them forward to the higher classics. "Nothing is more common than to meet boys who say they have read Virgil or Horace who yet cannot speak three sentences in Latin." Masters should make them read and pronounce properly, sending them to the bottom of the class as quickly for a false sound as for a wrong word.[22] Witherspoon added a few sentences about training in speaking, reading, and spelling English but it is clear that he regarded a knowledge of Latin and Greek syntax as the essential preparation for success in college.

In fact the trustees in 1748 based admission to the freshman class entirely upon a knowledge of these two languages. The president and tutors were to examine all candidates and reject those who could not "render Virgil and Tully's Orations into English" and "turn English into true and grammatical Latin" and translate "any part of the four Evangelists" from Greek into Latin or English.[23] Nothing whatever was said about mathematics, English, or the sciences. In 1760, however, the scope was widened slightly and entering freshmen not only had to "compose grammatical Latin, translating Virgil,

[21] *Ibid.*, pp. 383, 384.
[22] *New Jersey Archives*, First Series, IV, pp. 223-227.
[23] *Trustees Minutes*, I, p. 14.

Cicero's *Orations*, and the four Evangelists in Greek," but must also understand the principal rules "of vulgar arithmetic."[24] Nine years later the trustees explained that they took for granted that the candidates were well acquainted with such parts of education as preceded the study of the classics, "viz. reading English with propriety, spelling the English language and writing it without grammatical errors."[25]

When a youth entered college he could look forward to an introduction into the mysteries of science in his second year, for Burr and his successors followed in the footsteps of the dissenting academies in shifting the emphasis from the classics, logic, and metaphysics to mathematics and natural philosophy.[26] Yet they made the privilege of proceeding to the sciences the reward of an early mastery of Latin and Greek so that the freshmen and sophomores continued to pore over Homer, Tully, Erasmus, the Greek Testament, and Virgil[27] until they could read Greek fluently and had acquired some facility in speaking Latin.[28] In the commencement exercises the syllogistic debates were always in Latin and although one suspects they were worked out word for word in advance, they must have required considerable facility in pronunciation.[29] We have no evidence that Latin was bandied back and forth across the table in the tomblike dining room in the basement of Nassau Hall, or used by the tutors as a medium of instruction.

The students submitted to the curriculum as a matter of course, but as it was an age of intellectual stirrings when the imaginations of young men were caught by the new logic of Locke, the discoveries of Sir Isaac Newton, and the recent experiments in electricity, they longed for wider incursions into the fields of philosophy and science. Locke's *Essay Con-*

---

[24] *Account of the College* (Woodbridge, N.J., 1764), p. 33.
[25] *New Jersey Archives*, First Series, XXVI, pp. 426-428.
[26] *Princeton Library MSS*, AM 1424.
[27] *Aaron Burr Account Book*, MSS, Princeton Library.
[28] *Princeton Library MSS*, AM 1424.
[29] *New Jersey Archives*, First Series, XX, pp. 485-490, 616-618.

*cerning Human Understanding*[30] President Burr could himself expound, but though he attempted to aid several students "in the calculation of eclipses," he was not really prepared to teach astronomy, physics, or electricity. So the undergraduates even before the college moved to Princeton subscribed 25 shillings each to bring in Lewis Evans for lectures and experiments in natural philosophy. He had "already exhibited eight of his lectures . . . to the general satisfaction of us all," wrote young Joseph Shippen in September 1751. The youths sat open-eyed as he performed his experiments in that mysterious element—electricity—and Shippen was so enthusiastic that he procured a small electrical machine of his own for private experiments "in this useful branch of philosophy."[31]

Thirteen years later, when the college was housed in spacious Nassau Hall and there were three tutors to aid President Finley in teaching, the students enjoyed a more varied academic diet. The freshmen, however, still kept doggedly at Horace, Cicero's *Orations*, the Greek *Testament*, Lucian's *Dialogues*, and Xenophon's *Cyropaedia* and although the student in his sophomore year was introduced to "the sciences, geography, rhetoric, logic and mathematics," he continued with Latin and Greek. As a junior he took mathematics, moral philosophy, metaphysics, chronology, and physics and, if he were preparing himself for the ministry, entered upon the study of Hebrew. The senior year was devoted to reviews and composition, the student covering "the most improving parts of the Latin and Greek classics, part of the Hebrew Bible and all the arts and sciences."[32]

That the course of study was not much altered under Witherspoon we gather from a letter of an undergraduate to his brother who hoped to enter the junior class. "The studies you will be examined on . . . are Virgil, Horace, Cicero's *Orations*, Lucian, Xenophon, Homer, geography, and logic. Four books of Virgil's *Aeneid* together with the *Bucolics* and *Georgics*

---

[30] *Aaron Burr Account Book*, MSS, pp. 12, 16, Princeton Library.
[31] *Princeton Library MSS*, AM 9261.
[32] *An Account of the College* (Woodbridge, N.J., 1764), pp. 24, 25.

and four books of Xenophon are only looked for; but I would advise you if you come to college to study the whole of Xenophon. . . . Try to accustom yourself to read Greek and Latin well as it is much looked to here and be accurate in geography; study if you can the five common rules of arithmetic, interest, rebate, equation of payments, barter, loss and gain, fellowship, compound-fellowship, the double rule of three, comparative arithmetic, geometrical progression, vulgar and decimal fractions and the square root."[33]

Dr. Witherspoon when he arrived to take charge of his infant college in the "wilds of America," was no doubt surprised to find that the course of study was not less advanced and up-to-date than in some of his Scottish universities. Thus whereas the students of St. Andrews in their junior and senior years were still poring over Latin and Greek, the upper classes in Nassau Hall had spread out into the "arts and sciences."[34] On the other hand in a comparison with the dissenting academy at Daventry which gave courses in Hebrew, mathematics, geography, and logic in the freshman year and civil government in the sophomore year, the College of New Jersey did not fare so well.[35] But for an institution which was rounding out its second decade, with but one professor assisted by two or three tutors, with few efficient preparatory schools as feeders, with inadequate library and scientific equipment, its high standards, the scope of its curriculum, and the emphasis placed upon the sciences were matters of justifiable pride.

The devout men who controlled the policies of the college in encouraging the study of mathematics and natural philosophy were like the masters of the English academies in having no fear that they would undermine religion or weaken faith in the Bible. If new discoveries were made concerning the origin of man they would, of course, merely confirm the story of Adam and Eve; astronomy might throw new light on the

---

[33] Edward Crawford to James Crawford, Aug. 29, 1774, Presbyterian Historical Society.
[34] John Kerr, *Scottish Education* (Cambridge, England, 1910), p. 219.
[35] H. McLachlan, *English Education under the Test Acts*, p. 157.

origin of the world, it would not alter the version given in the Old Testament. So they directed the attention of the students more and more to physics, chemistry, mathematics, and astronomy, brought in able scientists as professors and tutors until under Minto, Maclean, Henry, and others the college became known as a center of scientific thought.

But that there were stirrings of uneasiness as to the ultimate results of this development is shown by the inaugural address of Minto in 1788. "It is said by some that science tendeth to make men skeptics in every thing which is not susceptible of mathematical demonstration and therefore that instead of being useful it is in the highest degree dangerous to the interests of morality and religion," he said. But then he immediately proceeded to answer these charges with the usual arguments. "It is the property of errors to clash with one another; but truth . . . can never be opposed to itself. Mathematical truth, therefore, is perfectly consistent with every other species of truth. . . . Instead of these sciences being hurtful to religion and morality, they will be found to be of the greatest advantage to them. Natural philosophy in particular, by leading us in a satisfactory manner to the knowledge of one almighty all-wise and all-good Being, who created, preserves and governs the universe, is the very handmaid of religion. Indeed I consider a student of that branch of science as engaged in a continued act of devotion. . . . This immense, beautiful and varied universe is a book written by the finger of Omnipotence and raises the admiration of every attentive beholder."[36]

Despite this note of optimism the battle to defend revealed religion from the attacks of scientists had already begun on the campus at Princeton. In 1776 the British jurist and scientist Henry Home, Lord Kames, had published a discourse on the "Original Diversity of Mankind," in which he sought to prove that the human species had diverse origins and so could not be descended from one couple. "Man must have been originally of different stocks adapted to their re-

[36] Walter Minto, *An Inaugural Oration* (Trenton, 1788), pp. 34-37.

spective climes," he argued, "there were therefore created different kinds of men at first according to the nature of the climate in which they were to live." It was absurd to assume that climate itself could create the marked differences among the races of men. Could the heat of Africa make a man black, was it possible "to account for the low stature and little feet and large head of the Esquimaux" by the action of the cold, was it the sharp air of America that kept hair from growing on the Indian's chin and body?

Against this thesis Samuel Stanhope Smith took up the lance. In February 1787, he delivered an address before the American Philosophical Society, at Philadelphia, on the "Causes of the Variety of Complexion and Figure in the Human Species," which he published with an appendix in which he handled his lordship without gloves. The Englishman had made the mistake of basing some of his reasoning on conditions in America of which he knew very little, and of this Professor Smith took full advantage. It was not true, he pointed out, that Charleston in Carolina was insufferably hot because it had no sea-breeze, or that its inhabitants died so fast that without constant recruits from Europe it would be depopulated, or that the North American Indians were cowards because they would not fight in the open, or that they had no hair on their chins and bodies. It was true, as Lord Kames said, that for protection from cold the northern nations have more fat than the southern, but he was wrong in deducing from this that they have no common origin. It merely showed that the Creator had not confined man to a bounded range beyond which he cannot pass, but had made it possible for him to adapt himself to different conditions of heat and cold, of humidity and dryness.[37]

Dr. Smith was not so withering in his answer to the argument that there never could have existed a diversity of languages had there been but one original race. "Every new region and every new climate will present different ideas and

[37] S. S. Smith, *Strictures on Lord Kaim's Discourse*, published with *An Essay*, etc. (Philadelphia, 1787).

create different wants that will naturally be expressed by various terms," he argued. "Hence will originate great diversity in the first elements of speech. . . . Tongues would become as various as the tribes of men." He then concluded: "In all the writings of this author there is not another example of so much weak and inconclusive reasoning. This ought in justice to be imputed to the cause, and not the author." He had failed, Smith concluded, because his thesis was incapable of defense.[38]

It is interesting to discover that instruction when the college was in its infancy had the basic elements of the preceptorial system. "They proceed not so much . . . by prolix discourses . . . by burdening the memory and imposing heavy and disagreeable tasks," it was stated, "as in the Socratic way of free dialogue between teacher and pupil or between the students themselves under the inspection of the tutors. In this manner the attention is engaged, the mind entertained and the scholar animated in the pursuit of knowledge. In fine the arts and sciences are conveyed into the minds of youth in a method the most easy, natural and familiar."[39]

It was President Davies, himself an orator and poet, who emphasized English composition and eloquence and instituted monthly orations by members of the senior class, a practice which survived for decades.[40] The seniors also discussed "two or three theses in a week, some in the syllogistic and others in the forensic manner," the latter always in English. At stated intervals members of the freshman, sophomore, and junior classes delivered original declamations "from the stage," as well as such selections "from Cicero, Demosthenes, Livy and other ancient authors and from Shakespeare, Milton, Addison and such illustrious moderns as are best adapted to display the various passions and exemplify the graces of utterance and gesture." Each class recited twice daily at this time and had always "free access to their teachers to solve any difficulties

---

[38] *Ibid.*
[39] *Rise and State of the College* (New York, 1752), p. 6.
[40] Ashbel Green, *College Discourses* (1822), p. 339.

that may occur." In the preparation of essays and debates seniors and juniors, and even some sophomores, were given free access to the room over the central entrance where the college library was housed, that they might "make excursions beyond the limits of their stated studies into the unbounded and variegated fields of knowledge."[41] In science when the students were sorely handicapped by the lack of apparatus for demonstration and experiment, it was usual for the instructor to quiz them on an assigned portion of the text and after explaining the subject more fully to encourage them to "propose any difficulties." This was far preferable it was thought to "the usual method of teaching by lecture."

Now as at other periods the college prided itself on its freedom from dogmatism on controversial points. We take care "to cherish a spirit of liberty and free enquiry," said the faculty, and not only to permit but even to encourage the right of the students "of private judgement," without dictating to them with "an air of infallibility."[42] And even though the youngster who dared to differ from Jonathan Edwards on some point of theology no doubt would have brought a frown to the face even of the gentle Davies, the college encouraged its students to do their own thinking.

Witherspoon made an innovation by lecturing as a substitute for the former method of quizzing the students on assigned texts. At first his lectures on eloquence, moral philosophy, chronology, history, and divinity were all delivered orally but in time, when every student had copies of the manuscripts and had memorized them, he contented himself with quizzing them and illustrating the important points. He always conducted the competition in speaking and writing Latin. On these occasions he would give out English sentences for translation, and if the first competitor began to stumble or hesitate, he would pass it on to the next. Nor was he satisfied until the students had brought out all the different ways in which an English phrase or sentence could be turned into correct and

[41] *An Account of the College* (Woodbridge, N.J., 1764), pp. 25-29.
[42] *Ibid.*, p. 28.

graceful Latin. He then reached for a book from the shelves or perhaps drew a newspaper from his pocket and marked a passage which all were to translate into Latin in their chambers.[43] When Witherspoon came to Princeton the tutors tried to convert him to the Berkeleian system of metaphysics, in which they were ardent believers, but they were no match for him. He confounded them on every argument and then so ridiculed the system that he soon had driven it out of the college.[44]

Instruction was badly handicapped in these early years by the constant changing of tutors. These young men were usually recent graduates who were preparing themselves for the ministry and so had no thought of retaining their positions permanently. Even had they been attracted by the life of the instructor, the £65 or £75 a year paid them by the trustees was so insufficient for their needs that unless they took a vow of celibacy they could not remain. There was some compensation, however, in the respect and friendship which they received from the serious and studious young men who made up the student body prior to the Revolution, and with whom they roomed in Nassau Hall and ate in the dining room and for whose instruction and discipline they were largely responsible. Yet on one occasion the whole freshman class was so dissatisfied with their tutor, "as not qualified for instruction" that they presented a written protest to the trustees. It was the custom for a tutor to devote himself entirely to one or more classes, and in 1759 we find John Ewing taking over the sophomores and juniors and Jeremiah Halsey the freshmen and seniors.[45] The trustees were aware that it would be "of eminent service" could they "support professors in some of the distinct branches of literature who might each make a figure in his own province," but the revenues at that time were insufficient.[46] So for the present the tutors and even the president

[43] Ashbel Green, *Life of Witherspoon*, MSS, p. 111, New Jersey Historical Society.
[44] *Ibid.*
[45] *Trustees Minutes*, I, p. 69.
[46] *An Account of the College* (Woodbridge, N.J., 1764), p. 40.

had to be jacks-of-all-trades and masters of none, to the obvious detriment of efficient instruction.

In instituting what amounted to extracurricular studies in the social sciences, for speaking and debating on the great issue of American freedom, Witherspoon was many decades ahead of his time. And like other innovators he received his full share of criticism. Was it wise to encourage immature students to take sides in political questions? it was asked. Could they, with their insufficient knowledge and immature minds, understand international affairs or economic laws or the development of state constitutions? One critic, of obvious Tory tendencies, wrote to the *Pennsylvania Chronicle*, expressing his astonishment that at the commencement of 1772, he found the graduating class discussing "the most perplexing political topics," which they solved "with a jerk." "I could almost have persuaded myself that I was within a circle of vociferous politicians at Will's coffee-house, instead of being surrounded with the meek disciples of wisdom, in the calm shades of academic retirement."

"Institutions of this sort," he went on, "I always understood were intended to enable our youth . . . to attain a competent acquaintance with classic lore, with the constitution and revolutions of ancient states, with the manners and customs and the philosophical tenets of antiquity, with the mathematics and natural history, to gain a knowledge of the operations of their own minds, the leading principles of ethics and an acuteness in distinguishing truth from falsehood and to accustom them to compose with accuracy and elegancy and to speak properly and persuasively. . . . An examination of questions which relate to the British constitution, or the present circumstances of the nation, must be highly unseasonable . . . as it leads them to speak of what they know not."[47]

One wonders what young Aaron Burr, the future Vice-President, who was one of the "meek disciples of wisdom" and who spoke during the commencement exercises of this year, or Henry Lee, who was a junior, or James Madison and Gun-

[47] *New Jersey Archives*, First Series, XXVIII, pp. 277-280.

ning Bedford who had graduated the previous year, or Luther Martin and Oliver Ellsworth of the class of 1766, thought of this sage letter. We may well wonder whether they would have played their great roles in the creation and development of the nation had they as students resisted the temptation to study the great questions of the day, to form their own judgments, and defend them in open debate. Witherspoon acted upon the assumption that college was not only a place to prepare for correct thinking, but to practice oneself in thinking; a place for "unfledged wings" to make trial excursions so that flights of later years might attain important goals.

The students must have dreaded the public examination for the bachelor's degree which was held on the third Wednesday in August. The candidate was then quizzed on all the work covered in college, not only by the president and tutors, but by the trustees and other "gentlemen of liberal education" who happened to be present. That they were not always so overawed that they could not do credit to themselves and the college is shown in a letter from President Burr to Philip Doddridge. "On the day of public examination . . . there accidentally came in a gentleman of considerable figure as to station and fortune, who had by some means or other got strangely prejudiced against our design and had done all that laid in his power to bring an odium upon it. He heard considerable part of the examination and at the conclusion one of the young candidates delivered an oration in Latin. He has since expressed himself very much pleased and turns his reproaches to praises."[48] The only compensation for the hard work and anxiety entailed by these examinations was the fact that the visiting trustees dined with the students so that punch, or ham and green peas or other delicacies might be added to the menu.[49]

In addition to the final comprehensive examination, public examinations were held at the end of the session for freshmen,

[48] *Princeton Library MSS*, AM 9971.
[49] "Journal at Nassau Hall," July 4, Aug. 8, 1786, *Princeton Library MSS*, AM 10841.

sophomores, and juniors to determine their fitness for admission to the class above.[50] These tests had nothing in common with some of the farcical examinations in the English universities, and many a lad who was unprepared to pass, "if his relatives were near," pretended illness so that he could drop back without dishonor.[51] To hold the students to their work and to permit the tutors to judge of their progress there were half-yearly tests on the material covered during the preceding period. These proved so helpful that President Finley instituted quarterly examinations, "whereby the instructors" could "observe the general progress each one makes and thence were enabled either to encourage or warn them."[52]

All of these examinations were dreaded by the students, even the mid-term tests, and they occasioned much hasty cramming, many conjectures as to what the professor or tutor would ask. Then, at the sound of the bell they would file into the library room "like so many criminals" and take seats in a circle around the faculty, awaiting the barrage of questions. When the ordeal was over they all withdrew while the professors and tutors consulted over their answers to decide whether this youth or that had earned promotion to the class above, or if he were a senior, his bachelor's degree. Then they were summoned back to receive their "sentence from the Old Doctor," to be complimented or admonished, or warned of their duties as graduates or as upperclassmen; after which they dispersed amid mutual congratulations, "saluting each other by the appellation of freemen."

The trustees and the presidents in the first decades never forgot that the education of young men for the ministry was the prime purpose of the founding of the college, and shaped the work from the very first with this in view. The courses in Latin, Greek, and Hebrew opened the door to inexhaustible fields of religious reading; every student had to know his Bible from cover to cover; the emphasis on elocution helped

[50] *An Account of the College* (Woodbridge, N.J., 1764), p. 34.
[51] *New Jersey Archives*, First Series, XXVIII, pp. 289-308.
[52] *An Account of the College* (Woodbridge, N.J., 1764), p. 34.

to equip the future minister for the all-important task of preaching; the presidents themselves conducted courses in theology.[53] As we have seen, the plan of reconciliation of Old Sides and New Lights in 1767 called for the establishing of a chair of divinity and moral philosophy with the Reverend John Blair as its incumbent, but the failure to secure an endowment forced him to retire.[54] Many of the clerical students after graduating with the bachelor of arts degree went to some distinguished minister for further instruction, perhaps living in his home and making use of his library. Jonathan Edwards, Jr., worked under Joseph Bellamy; Alexander McWhorter under William Tennent; Hugh McAden under John Blair; David Rice under John Todd.

The college prided itself upon its discipline. "The utmost care is taken to discountenance vice and to encourage . . . a manly rational and Christian behaviour in the students," said the trustees. Perhaps they ought not to take too much credit for their success in this respect, they admitted, since life in the little village of Princeton subjected the undergraduates to none of the intoxicating diversions of large cities, such as balls, concerts, plays, and races.[55] Yet the regulations which they drew up for student conduct show that they believed that "vice" might raise its head even in rural surroundings. In fact Nassau Hall, to some of its young denizens, must have seemed like a prison. No student was to be absent from his room without leave from the president or a tutor save at stated hours, or make any "treat or entertainment," or invite any young woman to his chamber, "nor jump and hollo nor make any boisterous noise in the hallways." When the president or a tutor presented himself at the door of a student's room he identified himself by stamping on the floor, a signal which any undergraduate imitated only at his peril. If the student

[53] *Rise and State of the College* (New York, 1752), p. 6.
[54] Ashbel Green, *Life of Witherspoon*, MSS, p. 108, New Jersey Historical Society.
[55] *New Jersey Archives*, First Series, XXVIII, pp. 289-308.

refused to open the door, the tutors were authorized to "break it down."[56]

These regulations in the first two or three decades seem to have caused little trouble, when so many students were pious youths studying for the ministry, and eager to improve their time and to keep in the good graces of the president. Moreover, Burr, Davies, and Finley knew how to win the affection and respect of their young charges by giving unsparingly of their time and energy to aid them in their work, by their personal charm and tact and their lack of pomposity. Yet even they admitted that to teach a classic author or a system of philosophy is a much easier task than to govern a group of young men "in the gay and volatile period of life," a group "collected from almost all the several colonies," with different manners, tempers, and upbringing. "To govern so as to have their veneration and conciliate their love, to grant every innocent liberty and restrain from ensnaring indulgence, . . . to cherish a sense of honor, . . . this is the task, the arduous task of a governor of the college."[57]

No one understood better than President Witherspoon the effectiveness of mingling kindness and strictness in matters of discipline. "Govern always, but beware of governing too much," he used to say. "Convince your pupils . . . that you wish to see them happy" and desire to impose no unnecessary restraints. Put a wide difference between "youthful follies and foibles and . . . a malignant spirit." But Witherspoon in the latter years of his administration was handicapped not only by the spirit of freedom and impatience of restraint inspired by the Revolution, but by the radical change in the character of the student body. Regulations which had been considered necessary and right by the earlier undergraduates now were resented as "slavish impositions." Moreover, the doctor's Scottish accent and his dignified and venerable carriage discouraged the affectionate relationship of preceptor and pupil, so noticeable under Burr and Davies.

[56] *Trustees Minutes*, I, pp. 62, 63.
[57] *An Account of the College* (Woodbridge, N.J., 1764), p. 22.

Whig and Clio Halls

The Gymnasium and Halsted Observatory

Princeton College, 1875

John Witherspoon

Jonathan Dickinson

Aaron Burr

Joseph Henry

Stephen Alexander

James McCosh

John Maclean

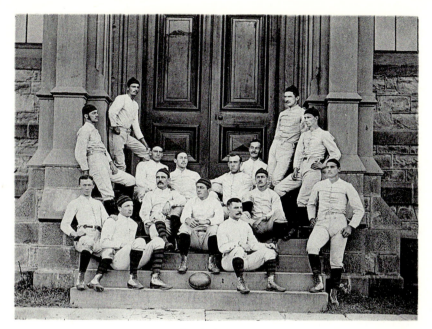

Football Team

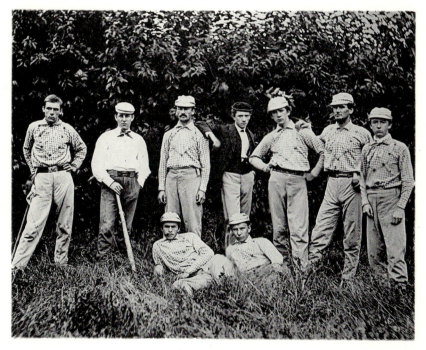

Baseball Team, 1870

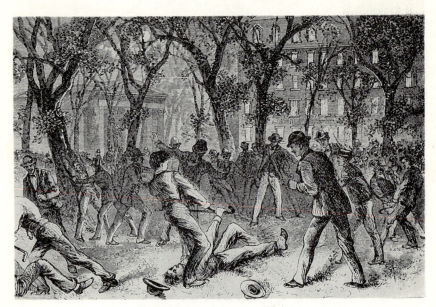

The Annual Cane Fight

Football at Princeton

On the other hand, it was a bold youth who dared defy him openly. On one occasion, hearing that a group of students had conspired to break one of the regulations, he summoned the undergraduates into the Prayer Hall to address them. He first dwelt upon the kindness and leniency with which he had always treated them and then sternly denounced by name the ringleader of the conspiracy. "Now, sir, what have you to say for yourself," he demanded. "I have to say that I am no more guilty then twenty others and we are all resolved to share the same fate." "Then you shall know and share it without delay, if your number should include the whole college. You, sir, are expelled and go you immediately out of the Hall." Then turning to the rest he said: "Now follow him just as many as please." But the conspirators left their leader to his fate and not one stirred from his seat.[58] Another group who tethered a calf in the pulpit of the Prayer Hall fared somewhat better, probably because the offense was not plotted but resulted from drinking too deeply in a village tavern. The leaders were expelled, it is true, but were later readmitted, while the others got off with a severe warning.[59]

Witherspoon's understanding of human nature is shown by his self-restraint on one occasion when his dignity and authority were threatened. Upon leaving a recitation room and walking down one of the corridors, he became aware of light footsteps behind him. Turning his head suddenly, he saw one of the students following him and shaking his fist back of his neck. The youngster immediately beat a retreat and waited fearfully for the summons to the president's office. But the summons never came, for the doctor preferred to keep him in suspense. Not knowing whether he had been detected and realizing that if he ever got into trouble this incident might be produced against him, he was on his good behavior to the day of his graduation.[60]

[58] Ashbel Green, *Life of Witherspoon*, MSS, p. 112, New Jersey Historical Society.
[59] *Faculty Minutes*, July 2, 1790.
[60] Ashbel Green, *Life of Witherspoon*, MSS, p. 113, New Jersey Historical Society.

In the infancy of the college at Elizabeth and Newark, the students, when they wished to consult books other than the assigned texts, had to resort to the libraries of Dickinson and Burr. But almost immediately gifts of needed volumes began to come in. The Society in Scotland for Propagating Christian Knowledge, as soon as they heard that a charter had been granted, set aside £30 for the purchase of good books[61] which probably arrived in 1750 when the trustees authorized the president "to buy a bookcase."[62] Davies and Tennent enlarged the little collection while in Great Britain through the generosity of various donors, while a few volumes came in from friends in Boston and elsewhere in America.[63]

But the real foundation of the college library was the donation by Governor Belcher of his entire collection consisting of several hundred volumes. This library was but a reflection of the governor himself, strict Puritan that he was, for it was full of orthodox reading of the old New England kind— *The Whole Duty of Man, Bunyan's Works,* Cotton Mather's *History of England, Milton's Works,* Burnet's *State of the Dead;* the sermons and other writings of New Light divines, Whitefield, Pemberton, Edwards, Tennent, Doddridge; the usual galaxy of classical writers, Sallust, Horace, Plutarch, Caesar, Cicero, Cato, Tacitus; an unusually large collection of English masters including Dryden, Defoe, Pope, Locke, and Bacon; and a number of volumes in history, biography, law, geography, navigation, and physics.[64]

Although the college library continued to grow until in 1760 it contained 1,281 volumes, the trustees appealed for further contributions. And as it consisted entirely of the donations of the charitable, which now and then were still coming in, they published a catalogue of their books so that all could see what was on hand and what was needed.[65] They were espe-

---

[61] *Minutes of the Society in Scotland for Propagating Christian Knowledge,* Nov. 2, 1749.
[62] *Trustees Minutes,* I, p. 19.
[63] *Aaron Burr Account Book,* MSS, p. 132, Princeton Library.
[64] *Trustees Minutes,* I, pp. 39-44.
[65] *An Account of the College* (Woodbridge, N.J., 1764), p. 29.

cially concerned over the "comparatively small assortment of modern authors," they said, and of "works on mathematics and the Newtonian philosophy, in which the students have but very imperfect helps, either from books or instruments." "A large and well-sorted collection of books on the various branches of literature is the most ornamental and useful furniture of a college, and the most proper and valuable fund with which it can be endowed. It is one of the best helps to enrich the minds both of the officers and students with knowledge; to give them an extensive acquaintance with authors; and to lead them beyond the narrow limits of the books to which they are confined in their stated studies and recitations, that they may expatiate at large through the boundless and variegated fields of science. If they have books at hand to consult upon every subject that may occur to them, as demanding a more thorough discussion in their public disputes, in the course of their studies, in conversation, or their own fortuitous thoughts, it will enable them to investigate truth through its intricate recesses and to guard against the stratagems and assaults of error."[66] The new catalogue seems to have been put in Witherspoon's hands before he left Scotland to become president, for he purchased and brought over with him "a very valuable addition to the public library" and left orders for so many additional volumes that the trustees at last regarded the collection as satisfactory.[67]

To the student of science today the lack of equipment of the College of New Jersey seems pathetic. Repeatedly the trustees appealed for gifts of "philosophical instruments" to aid in the study of astronomy, physics, and geography, and they were deeply grateful to Governor Belcher when he gave the college his "terrestrial globes." In 1760 the college possessed a "few instruments and some natural curiosities,"[68] though nothing to compare with the tanned Negro's hide, the skull of an

[66] *A Catalogue of Books in the Library of the College of New Jersey* (Woodbridge, N.J., 1760).
[67] *New Jersey Archives*, First Series, XXVI, pp. 304, 307.
[68] R. R. Wilson, *Barnaby's Travels* (New York, 1904), p. 104.

Indian warrior, the stuffed animals and birds at Harvard,[69] while in 1764 the trustees again complained that "with mathematical instruments and an apparatus for experiments in natural philosophy it is but very indifferently furnished."

But the situation suddenly changed when the college secured the celebrated orrery made by David Rittenhouse, said to be the "most excellent of its kind ever produced." When Witherspoon heard that this delicate bit of machinery was nearing completion he rode over to the home of the great scientist at Norriton, and after inspecting the apparatus purchased it for £416.13.4,[70] and in April 1771 had it installed in Nassau Hall. Great was the excitement of the students as they gathered around the orrery to turn the winch and see the little brass and ivory balls which represented the planets move in elliptical orbits around the gilded brass sun. The tutor must have explained to them that by setting the machine for a given year, day, and hour within 5,000 years in the past or 5,000 years in the future and then with a miniature telescope pointing from the ball representing the earth past Mars or Jupiter or Venus to a brass circle beyond, they could read there the longitude and latitude of the planet for that date and hour. Hardly less fascinating was the part of the machine which showed Jupiter and its satellites with their "eclipses, transits and inclinations" and Saturn with its "ring and satellites." Still another part gave the moon, with "her eclipses and those of the sun occasioned by her interposition."[71] The Academy at Philadelphia had made a strenuous effort to purchase the orrery, and the friends of the college at Princeton were triumphant when they carried off the prize.[72] When additional scientific instruments recently ordered arrived, the college apparatus for mathematics and natural philos-

[69] S. M. Morison, *Three Centuries of Harvard*, p. 95.
[70] *College Ledger*, 1769, p. 22.
[71] *Transactions of the American Philosophical Society*, I (Philadelphia, 1771), pp. 1-3; *Memoirs of David Rittenhouse* (Philadelphia, 1813), pp. 198-202.
[72] Rittenhouse later made another orrery for the Academy.

ophy would be equal, if not superior, to any on the continent, the trustees boasted.[73]

It was with grief, therefore, that they viewed the wreckage made by the British and American troops during their occupancy of Nassau Hall. Nothing remained "but the orrery, a small telescope and an electrical machine with a can of coated jars."[74] The orrery itself which was badly damaged was sent back to Rittenhouse, but the distinguished scientist died before he had made a real beginning at the repairs.[75] This was a real misfortune. Jefferson said that "the world has but one Rittenhouse and it never had one before," and the trustees feared it would be impossible to find anyone who could put back in their proper places the parts of the machine which he had constructed. It was not until 1804, more than a quarter of a century after the orrery had been damaged, that a contract was made with Henry Voit, to undertake the work.[76] Voit succeeded in restoring the delicate mechanism of the planetary system and of Jupiter and its satellites, but he seems to have failed with the part showing the phases of the moon.[77]

The purchase of new scientific equipment after the war was also long delayed, as whatever funds came in had to be used for current expenses and for restoring Nassau Hall. It was in 1790 that Professor Minto appealed in vain for a fund to procure a philosophical apparatus,[78] while six years later Elias Boudinot, Aaron Burr, James Madison, and other alumni subscribed $122 for "instruments and materials most necessary to exhibit the leading experiments in chemistry."[79]

The public commencement, which for a hundred years was held late in September, was an occasion of great interest, not only to the families and friends of the students but to the general public. On the preceding day the roads leading

---

[73] *New Jersey Archives*, First Series, XXVIII, pp. 289-308.
[74] J. H. Jones, *The Life of Ashbel Green* (New York, 1849), p. 136.
[75] *Trustees Minutes*, II, p. 3.      [76] *Ibid.*, p. 121.
[77] Ashbel Green, *Life of Witherspoon*, MSS, p. 110, New Jersey Historical Society.
[78] *Princeton Library MSS*, AM 499.      [79] *Ibid.*, AM 10667.

to Princeton were crowded with coaches and horsemen from every part of New Jersey and from New York and Philadelphia, while seats in the stage wagons went at a premium. Every house in the village was filled to overflowing with handsomely gowned women and men looking quite stiff and formal in white wigs, velvet coats, colored stockings, and shoes set off with silver buckles. For the graduating class it was a time of glory and anxiety, in which pride in receiving their diplomas before the distinguished audience mingled with nervousness over their orations and disputations. Joseph Shippen wrote in 1753 that the "wretched oration" he was to deliver robbed him of much of the pleasure of having his father at commencement.[80]

At Newark the exercises were held in the stone meeting-house, those at Princeton from 1757 to 1763 in the Prayer Hall of Nassau Hall, and after that in the newly erected Presbyterian church.[81] The academic procession began at the President's House with the graduating class in the van, followed by the candidates for the master's degree, the tutors and visiting ministers, the trustees and the president, and the governor of New Jersey in that order, all attired in the academic gown and cap. When the president called out *"Progredimini juvenes!"* they started off across the campus, accompanied by the ringing of the bell, to the central door of Nassau Hall, where they halted, lined up on either side of the gravel walk, and entered in reverse order. When all were seated, and the president had made the opening prayer, he announced: "Doctors and gentlemen, these young men wish to greet you with an oration." Thereupon the salutatory orator mounted the platform and addressed the gathering in Latin. After the applause had died down the president arose and said: "Whereas, learned doctors, it is a very worth while thing to carry on a rational argument leading to truth away from falsehood, these young men, about to be initiated,

---

[80] Joseph Shippen to his father, Newark, Aug. 20, 1753.
[81] *Princeton Library MSS*, AM 8486; *New Jersey Archives*, First Series, XXIV, p. 431.

will give you a sample of what they can do." So the gathering, many of whom could not understand a word of what was being said, listened to a debate in Latin on "Moral evil does not take away the perfection of the world," or some similarly abstruse premise.[82]

After this there would be an oration on the "Advantages of Health," or the "Blessings of Peace," or on "Patriotism." This was in English, so that it might entertain the "English part of the audience," as the president explained apologetically, and tend to the "cultivation of one's native language." At intervals musicians performed on the bassoon, clarinet, and other instruments, while the candidates gathered strength for further debates on "Whether moral as well as mathematical truths are capable of demonstration," or "Whether Noah's Flood was universal," or "Civil Liberty is necessary to give birth to the arts and sciences." Finally, late in the afternoon, the graduating class received their bachelor of arts degrees and advanced students and honored guests their master of arts degrees, the valedictorian delivered his address, the president prayed, and the commencement and the academic year came to an end.[83]

Of the seven founders of the College of New Jersey, two, Peter Van Brugh Livingston and William Peartree Smith, lived to see the institution fulfill all their hopes. Before it had rounded its fifth decade, despite the untimely deaths of so many of its leaders, despite financial losses and the ravages of war, it had become a powerful influence for good in the country. Its purpose was to train men for the pulpit, the bench, the bar, the seats of legislation, the schools, the founders had said from the beginning, and now the careers of their graduates as preachers and teachers, as leaders in the Revolution, as members of Congress, as framers of the Constitution of the United States, as eminent jurists, physicians, merchants, scientists, soldiers showed how successfully these purposes had been attained.

[82] *New Jersey Archives*, First Series, XX, pp. 616-618.
[83] *Princeton Library MSS*, AM 8486; *Diary of Ezra Stiles*, I, p. 139; *New Jersey Archives*, First Series, XX, pp. 616-618.

More than half of the graduates under Dickinson and Burr
entered the ministry. Imbued with the spirit of Whitefield
and Tennent, they went forth to keep burning the fires of the
Great Awakening and preach the gospel of the religion of
experience. We find them making the frontier circuit, or
preaching to a congregation in New Hampshire, or in far-off
Kentucky or South Carolina, as well as in the older churches
of New Jersey, Pennsylvania, or Maryland. John Todd, the
former weaver, followed in Davies' footsteps in ministering
to the Virginia dissenters; Eleazer Whittlesey made his way
over the mountains to Kentucky; John Harris moved to South
Carolina, where he endeared himself to his people not only
as minister but as the patriot who more than once preached
with his gun beside him in the pulpit; Hugh McAden became
one of the founders of the Presbyterian church in the south;
Nathaniel Sherman, brother of Roger Sherman, preached
first at New Bedford, Massachusetts, and later at Mt. Carmel,
Connecticut. John Ewing became pastor of the First Presbyterian Church of Philadelphia and won added distinction as
provost of the University of Pennsylvania and lecturer on
natural philosophy.

As the influence of New Englanders was paramount in the
founding of the college, so the college, in these early days,
exerted a powerful influence on the eastern colonies. Not only
Edwards, Bellamy, Prince, and other New Light divines,
but many prominent laymen looked to the college to supply
New England with pious ministers now that Harvard and
Yale had gone over to the enemy. Nor were they disap-
pointed. Of the first sixty-nine graduates certainly seventeen,
and probably more, entered the ministry in New England.
Among them were Daniel Farrand of Connecticut; Samuel
McClintock of New Hampshire, D.D. Yale 1791; Nathaniel
Potter of Brookline, Massachusetts, A.M. Harvard 1758;
Benjamin Chapman, Southington, Connecticut, A.M. Yale
1761; Ezra Horton, Union, Massachusetts, A.M. Yale 1772;
Sylvanus Osborne, East Greenwich, A.M. Yale 1757; Joseph
Sherman, Woburn, Massachusetts, A.M. Harvard 1758,

A.M. Yale 1765, A.M. Dartmouth 1765. In the civil life of
New England, Princeton graduates were equally prominent.
James Manning was the first president of Brown; Tapping
Reeve, founder of the Litchfield Law School, became Chief
Justice of Connecticut; the Reverend John Bacon represented
Massachusetts in the United States Senate; Oliver Ellsworth
was Chief Justice of the United States and a member of the
Constitutional Convention; Nathaniel Niles represented Ver-
mont in Congress; Micah Townsend was Secretary of the
State of Vermont.[84] In time, however, the bitterness between
Old Sides and New Lights dimmed and many of their dif-
ferences were ironed out. And with the founding of new col-
leges, the young men of New England turned once more to
Harvard and Yale, or matriculated at Brown or Dartmouth.

But the ground lost east of the Hudson was more than compensated for by the growing prestige of the college in the
southwest. As the Scotch-Irish immigrants spread out into
western Pennsylvania, or pushed up the valley of Virginia
between the Blue Ridge and the Alleghenies, or took up their
little farms in the North Carolina uplands or crossed the
mountains into Tennessee or Kentucky, they turned to Princeton for their ministers and their teachers. Nassau Hall became
the religious and educational capital of all Scotch-Irish America. Princeton graduates went forth, Bible in hand, to bring
the Gospel to the fringes of civilization, now preaching in a
barn or in the open, now baptizing, now conducting a wedding
ceremony, now catechizing a group of children. Philip Fithian
of the class of 1772 has left us in his journal a vivid picture
of the hardships these men endured, the eagerness with which
they were listened to, and the influence they exerted.[85]

When the circuit rider accepted one of the many invitations
to a pastorate which inevitably fell to his lot, his life might be
cast permanently with the people of the frontier. He would
probably serve two or more widely separated congregations,

[84] Samuel Alexander, *Princeton College in the Eighteenth Century.*
[85] *Philip Vickers Fithian: Journal.* Robert G. Albion and Leonidas Dodson,
eds.

must content himself with a log cabin for a residence, with the plainest fare, with homespun clothes. But having established himself in his crude home his first care was to erect places of worship for each of his congregations and the next to establish a classical school. The story of William Tennent and his Log College was repeated over and over under the shadows of the Alleghenies or in the forests of Tennessee and Kentucky. It was a strange sight, an inspiring sight, these frontier academies, where some recent Princeton graduate assembled a group of youths around him to drill them in Latin or Greek, to expound moral philosophy from his treasured copy of Witherspoon's lectures and, if he could contrive the necessary apparatus, to try a few crude experiments in physics or electricity.[86] When Samuel Doak founded the academy which later became Washington College, Tennessee, he brought the books for the library in sacks on horseback five hundred miles from Philadelphia through forests and over mountains.[87]

It was Samuel Stanhope Smith, Princeton 1769, who founded the Prince George Academy, which later became Hampden-Sydney College, and he served as its first president with three other Princeton graduates as assistants, one of them a son of Dr. Witherspoon. No fewer than 110 students gathered around these men the first session the academy opened, reciting in the unfinished buildings, and erecting their own log cabins in lieu of dormitories. Across the mountains in the valley of Virginia, John Brown of the class of 1749 conducted a grammar school in conjunction with his ministerial duties, which later was merged into Liberty Hall, the Washington and Lee University of today. As Brown grew older the work was taken up by William Graham of the class of 1773, who ran the academy so far as possible as a replica of Princeton, in the "hewed log-house, twenty-eight feet by twenty-four, one story and a half high." Here he housed his little library and his air pump, electric machine, sextant, microscope, telescope,

[86] William H. Foote, *Sketches of Virginia*, p. 444.
[87] Samuel Alexander, *Princeton College in the Eighteenth Century*, p. 185.

maps and two twelve-inch globes, and taught his classes in Greek, Latin, moral philosophy, and natural philosophy.[88]

Throughout the south the College of New Jersey was revered and loved. To mention Nassau Hall brought to mind sound scholarship, true piety, and men of high character. Congregations vied with each other in obtaining Princeton men as their ministers, and the father who could enter his son under Witherspoon considered himself fortunate indeed. Nor was the prestige of the college confined to Presbyterian families, for in an age when skepticism and free thinking were creeping into some of the institutions of learning, men of various denominations turned hopefully to Princeton as a bulwark of religion. Many a southern youth, whose life upon the tobacco or rice plantation and training in the Anglican church contrasted strangely with the stern Calvinistic spirit of Nassau Hall, rubbed elbows with the earnest and pious candidates for the ministry, and the soft accent of Virginia or South Carolina was as familiar in the classroom or the dining hall as the harsher tones of New Jersey or Pennsylvania.

Perhaps the college would not have attained such great prestige in the south had not her graduates acquitted themselves as well in civil life as in the ministry. Princeton was the alma mater of James Madison, of Henry Lee, of Charles Lee, of Luther Martin, of William Branch Giles. Of the southerners who studied under Witherspoon, one became President of the United States, four were members of the Continental Congress, ten entered the United States Senate, seven represented their states in Congress, nine became governors, one became a justice of the Supreme Court, one was Attorney General of the United States.[89]

In the middle colonies, even after the founding in 1750 of the Philadelphia Academy (later the University of Pennsylvania), King's College (later Columbia University), and Queen's College (later Rutgers), the College of New Jersey played a vitally important role. Men trained under Burr,

[88] W. H. Foote, *Sketches of Virginia*, pp. 438-470.
[89] John Maclean, *History of the College of New Jersey* (Philadelphia, 1877), pp. 359-362.

Finley, or Witherspoon went forth to fill important posts in the pulpit, bench, and legislative halls. From Witherspoon's regime alone there emerged, in New Jersey, five United States senators, six members of Congress, two governors, one chief justice, one attorney general; in New York two United States senators, seven members of Congress, one governor, two justices of the United States Supreme Court, one attorney general; in Pennsylvania four congressmen, two justices of the supreme court of the state, one United States attorney general, three presidents of colleges.

When Witherspoon signed the Declaration of Independence, he found affixed to that famous document the names of two Princeton graduates—Richard Stockton and Benjamin Rush. Had he visited the Constitutional Convention at Philadelphia in the summer of 1787 he would have been almost as much at home as in the Presbyterian general assembly. Leading in the debates he would have found his friend and pupil, James Madison, while W. C. Houston, Gunning Bedford, Jonathan Dayton, and W. R. Davie, all of whom had sat at his feet, together with William Paterson, Oliver Ellsworth, Alexander Martin, and Luther Martin, who had graduated from Princeton before his arrival, doing their part in shaping the great document which became the basis of American unity and liberty. More than 16 per cent of the members of the Convention were Princeton graduates.

The remarkable record made by this little body of fewer than eight hundred Princeton graduates may be accounted for in part by the fact that they were picked men. This was before the days of mass education, and the aim of the colleges at that time was to develop leaders. A large proportion of the youths who entered the College of New Jersey came from well-to-do and cultured families, had been prepared for college by tutors or in the best classical schools, and had every opportunity to assume after graduation important posts in their communities. Others, often from poor and obscure families, were selected for their native ability. The boy who stood at the head of his class in grammar school was encouraged to continue his work in some classical school. If he stood out above his fellows here, he probably could secure assistance from some wealthy neighbor or from the fund for pious youths to complete his work at Princeton, especially if he were destined for the ministry.

Nor must one overlook the fact that these young men received a training remarkable for its efficiency under that succession of able teachers—Burr, Davies, Finley, and Witherspoon. The Princeton undergraduate of the eighteenth century had his regular allotment of the classics, philosophy, and science and had to do his share of memorizing, but more important for his future were the discussions with fellow students and instructors over this phase of his work or that, his debates or his orations. It was this which gave him practice in exercising his creative ability. In after years when the graduate, now in his state legislature, or a justice of the supreme court, or a member of his state constitutional convention, was called upon to solve some important problem, he not only could draw upon the experience of other ages but could think the matter out for himself.

# CHAPTER IV

# The Stepchild of the Church

**F**ORTUNATELY for the college the death of Witherspoon caused no serious interruption in its life, gave rise to no anxiety for its future prosperity. For years all matters of instruction, administration, and educational policy had been largely in the hands of his able son-in-law, and it was taken for granted that Samuel Stanhope Smith would now have the title as well as the duties of president. At their meeting in May 1795, the trustees elected him by a unanimous vote, and five months later, at the commencement exercises, he celebrated the event with a distinguished inaugural address in Latin.[1]

A progressive educator, an advanced scholar, an able teacher, a renowned pulpit orator, a man of commanding personality, he seemed ideally fitted for the task which fell to his lot. He was a man of erect figure, penetrating blue eyes and a quiet dignity which was softened by a winning smile. "I have never seen his equal in elegance of person and manners," said Archibald Alexander. "Dignity and winning grace were remarkably united in his expressive countenance."[2] By the students of a period marked by undergraduate restlessness and insubordination, he was respected and even loved. Though few came to him for advice and guidance, they seem to have regarded him instinctively as their friend, always placing the blame for a severe penalty, a warning in Prayer Hall, or a suspension, upon some "obnoxious" tutor or the hard-hearted trustees, not on "Doctor Smith."[3]

As with Samuel Davies, Smith was greatly handicapped by ill health. It was while president of Hampden-Sydney that hemorrhages and fever gave warning of tuberculosis, so that

---

[1] *Trustees Minutes*, I, p. 345; John Maclean, *History of the College of New Jersey*, II, p. 5.
[2] James W. Alexander, *Life of Archibald Alexander*, p. 265.
[3] *Sermons of Samuel Stanhope Smith* (Philadelphia, 1821), p. 52.

he was forced to spend some time at the Sweet Springs. Here the water and the rest were thought for a time to have effected a permanent cure, but in 1782 the ominous bleeding began again, so that his life was despaired of. Against the advice of his physician Smith began the practice of bleeding himself and to this he attributed his recovery. Even though the disease was arrested, he was never afterwards a strong man, so that it is remarkable that he should have sustained for thirty years more the burden of teaching and directing the affairs of the college.

This able man, standing on the threshold of a new century, faced not only many and perplexing difficulties but also great opportunities. That Nassau Hall was still in need of repair, that the faculty consisted of a mere handful of underpaid men, that funds were low, that the number of volumes in the library was small and the scientific apparatus inadequate, were matters of minor importance which time would remedy. Far more significant was the fact that the college had the opportunity of becoming the leading institution of higher education in the country—the Oxford of the United States. With its alumni occupying positions of leadership in all parts of the country, with an enviable record for excellent teaching and for the emphasis which it placed upon the sciences, drawing upon the vast region west and south of the Hudson for its student body, its future seemed bright indeed.

That this vision was not realized was no fault of President Smith's, for his educational policies were in the main far ahead of his time. From the first he bent his energies toward widening the scope of instruction in the sciences, securing adequate equipment in astronomy, physics and chemistry, increasing the numbers of the faculty, strengthening the ties with the alumni, maintaining discipline without oppression, increasing the facilities for the study of religion, and perhaps, most important of all, using the weapon of research and modern scholarship to defend the tenets of revealed religion. But when he tried to put these policies into operation he found that the deciding voice was not his but the trustees', and that the latter insisted that the college be first of all a place for instilling religious principles and for turning out pious men who would carry on the tradition of Dickinson, Davies, the Tennents, and Witherspoon. If this conflicted with the ideal of a national institution, that ideal would have to yield.

That it did conflict became painfully obvious at the very outset of Smith's administration when the college made an appeal to the state of New Jersey for financial assistance, based upon the catholicity of the institution and its great services to the nation. Founded by the contributions of public-spirited men in various colonies, it had shown such liberality in education that students had flocked in from every section and every denomination, returning to become distinguished ministers and civil officers, the trustees pointed out. If it could secure adequate support so as to have more professors in the liberal arts, it would continue to be "the principal resort of American youth from the Hudson to Georgia," especially the youth of the southern states. How glorious it would be for New Jersey to become another Athens which governed Rome through her science, taste, and art, after she had succumbed to Roman military might.[4]

This appeal, seconded as it was by many prominent men in the state, ran afoul of the objection that the college could not expect aid from funds raised by general taxation so long as it "was under the sole control of one denomination."[5] Only when some of the trustees promised a more liberal policy did the legislature vote $4,800 for completing the repairs to Nassau Hall, and the purchase of books and scientific apparatus.[6] As a token of good faith the next two vacancies in the board were filled by influential Episcopalians—Joshua M. Wallace and the Reverend Charles H. Wharton, both of Burlington—and larger appropriations in the future were confidently expected. But when the people expressed their disapproval of the original grant by turning out of the legislature many who had voted for it, the matter was quietly dropped.

[4] John Maclean, *History of the College of New Jersey*, II, pp. 14-17.
[5] *Ibid.*, p. 13.          [6] *Princeton Library MSS*, AM 1325.

Perhaps this was fortunate, for it preserved for the college its status as a private rather than a state institution. It might have proved invaluable, had it impressed upon the trustees the fact that if they wished the college to be national in character it must be national in control. However conscientious might be the Presbyterian ministers who made up the majority of the board, they represented but one group in the population and but one point of view. Unfortunately, the mere suggestion that "outsiders" ought to have a voice in running the college brought a frown of disapproval to their faces. With President John Maclean they thought that so long as they remained "true and faithful" the college could not "be other than a Presbyterian college, and under the sole and exclusive control of a body of orthodox Presbyterian ministers and laymen."[7]

Although the president of the college was always a clergyman and the faculty usually members of the Presbyterian church, the trustees gave them no more authority than was absolutely necessary, and that grudgingly. Their writings were scanned anxiously for any signs of unorthodox opinion; their unpublished lecture notes were examined; their power of discipline was limited to admonitions and suspension, the right of expulsion being reserved for the board; their minutes were subjected to close scrutiny; one committee of the trustees pried into instruction in the college, another into discipline. If President Smith suggested mildness and tact in dealing with unruly students, he found the board unsympathetic; if he outlined new educational policies to keep the college abreast of the times, he was thwarted; if he attempted to interpret revealed religion in the light of modern science, he subjected himself to suspicion.

In 1804 Ashbel Green received a letter from one William Hill stating that he had heard with horror that "the President of Princeton College" in his lectures to his students tried to prove that "polygamy and concubinage" are not moral evils.

[7] John Maclean, *History of the College of New Jersey*, II, pp. 20, 21.

"If these things are so, and are not checked, I will venture to predict that very few students will attend Princeton hereafter from these parts."[8] Not a little alarmed, Green wrote to John M. Bradford, one of the college tutors, to examine a copy of Smith's lectures, and report to him just what had been said. So this young man, apparently seeing no impropriety in acting as informant against the head of the college, sent back the following extract, culled probably from the notes of one of the students: "Some writers have supposed that there is a natural immorality in polygamy independently of the laws of religion or of society. . . . I believe the wisest institutions and the greatest happiness and perfection of society are most commonly connected with the law of one wife, but I cannot suppose that there is a natural immorality attached to the law of polygamy. This opinion is justified by our religion which teaches us that the greatest and most pious men and those who have enjoyed the most familiar intercourse with Heaven have submitted to this law."[9] Charges could not well be preferred against the president for giving it as his opinion that Abraham and Moses were not immoral, but there was obvious disapproval of this introduction of so embarrassing a topic, and the suspicion of the trustees lingered.

Nor was this suspicion allayed by the reports of some of the divinity students at the college. Locke's works were not in repute at Princeton, wrote one, Jonathan Edwards had no standing, while Hopkins had scarce a place in the library. Another reported that their president strongly recommended Reid's *Essays*, although they were grossly Arminian and advocated self-determination, which, if it meant anything, meant that the creature is independent of the Creator. "Doctor Smith has some curious sentiments about the nature and efficacy of baptism—but he finds some, even in this quarter, that dare contradict him." It was to be regretted, he went on, that the philosophic, "velvet-mouthed" preaching which was most in vogue in Princeton, was imitated by the students of the-

8 *Princeton Library MSS,* AB 2778.
9 *Princeton Library MSS,* AM 2434.

ology, but what was most alarming was the open denial by many of the doctrine of total depravity.[10]

Smith was well aware of the distrust of his views and the dissatisfaction with his educational policies, but he went on his way unperturbed, without striking back at his detractors. At the outset of his administration he was planning changes in the course of study which would have put the college many decades in advance of the age. "The time is, I believe, now come or nearly so, that I can propose to the trustees ... that the study of languages, except modern ones shall cease after the Freshman class, unless as mere exercises in taste in translation ... and that three entire years be employed in the different branches of art and science," he wrote to Benjamin Rush in 1796. "I wish to digest a plan that shall be at once as useful and extensive as ... is consistent with ... the small number of our teachers."[11] Unfortunately, poverty and perhaps the opposition of the board forced him to drop this far-sighted plan and continue with the old curriculum. But he gained permission to admit special scientific students, who devoted their time to geography, logic, mathematics, natural philosophy, moral philosophy, astronomy, and belles-lettres. These students did not receive the bachelor of arts degree, but merely a "certificate of their proficiency in the said sciences." A fair proportion of the undergraduates tried this plan, but their numbers gradually diminished until after a ten-year trial the experiment was dropped.[12] Had the board, instead of mere certificates, granted the degree of bachelor of science and made it equal in dignity with the bachelor of arts degree, it would have given a tremendous stimulus to the study of science at Princeton and throughout the country. But they frowned on such an innovation, and the college had to wait three-quarters of a century longer before its first bachelor of science degree was awarded.

The president was encouraged, however, by his success in

[10] *Princeton Library MSS*, AM 11456b.
[11] Library Company of Philadelphia, Ridgeway Branch, Yi 2/7403 F 5.
[12] John Maclean, *History of the College of New Jersey*, II, p. 29.

filling the chair of mathematics and natural philosophy—left vacant by the death of Professor Minto—with another able scientist, John Maclean.[13] This young Scotch chemist, after studying at Glasgow, Edinburgh, London, and Paris, came to the United States and began the practice of medicine in Princeton. Attracting attention by his knowledge of science, he was asked to give a course of lectures in the college in chemistry which President Smith himself attended, and which proved a stepping stone to his appointment to the faculty. Maclean was universally popular with his students. He is "a Scotchman, of fine intelligent countenance, a great man, amiable and kind, profound in the exact sciences," wrote a former undergraduate. "He had vanquished Dr. Priestley in public controversy on a difficult principle in chemistry and had acquired an enduring fame as a professor."[14] Maclean's courses in mathematics, physics, and astronomy excited the keen interest of the students but his experiments in chemistry, said to be the first made in any American college, were the wonder of Nassau Hall.[15] The lack of adequate equipment often forced him to construct his own instruments, and some of his equipment for teaching physics—a galvanic battery and a voltaic pile—was treasured by the college long after he had gone.[16]

Better things were in store, however, when with the payment of the first installment of the money voted by the legislature, Smith wrote to an agent in London to purchase and send over "an apparatus of instruments for exhibiting experiments on natural philosophy." The agent must have found it necessary to have some of the instruments manufactured specially for the college, for five years elapsed before they arrived in Princeton. For the president and Professor Maclean it was a thrilling moment when they opened the crates and took out one interesting object after another—barometers, thermome-

[13] Father of President John Maclean.
[14] *Princeton Library MSS*, AM 2074.
[15] John Maclean, *History of the College of New Jersey*, II, p. 130.
[16] John Maclean, *A Memoir of John Maclean, M.D.* (Princeton, 1885), p. 29.

ters, two pairs of nine-inch globes, an astronomical quadrant, a "magnetical apparatus," a magic lantern, an air pump, a "fountain in vacua," a "lungs glass," an artificial eye, a "hydrostatical apparatus," an opaque and transparent microscope, a three-and-a-half-foot telescope, a four-foot reflecting telescope.[17]

Nor was this all. In April 1805 the president announced to the trustees that he had purchased a cabinet of natural history from M. De la Coste of New York, who had prepared it with great skill and elegance.[18] "If it is not equal to Mr. Peale's in Philadelphia," he declared, "it is probably the next to his of any upon the continent." As funds to repay Smith could not be taken from the college capital stock, Elias Boudinot made a gift of land to cover the cost of $3,000. We have provided for the cabinet "an elegant chamber in one of the new buildings which we have added to the college, and it is now an excellent place of deposit for all the specimens in the history of nature which we may at any time receive from the friends of science," the president wrote a friend in South Carolina. "I observe that a rattle snake of great size and age has lately died or been killed in the neighborhood of George Town. Would it be possible for us to obtain the skeleton and rattles?"[19] He had also "made some preparations for a botanical garden," and appealed to his southern friend to send him "the seeds and roots of any plants which are indigenous, or have been assimilated to the soil and climate of Carolina."[20]

With the acquisition of the new scientific equipment, the president could announce to the friends of the college that at last it had fully recovered from the effects of the Revolution. In 1800 the number of students passed the hundred mark and every sign pointed to a continued rapid growth.[21] The trustees found it necessary to restore the bedrooms in the basement of the west wing of Nassau Hall so as to make them

[17] *Trustees Minutes*, II, p. 49.
[18] John Maclean, *History of the College of New Jersey*, II, pp. 68, 69.
[19] *Princeton Library MSS*, AM 239.
[20] *Ibid.*
[21] *Faculty Minutes*, I, Feb. 25, 1801.

"dry, airy and wholesome" for the "expected additions of students."[22] There were thoughts of erecting additional buildings and establishing new professorships. Then, like a flash of lightning from a clear sky, came a disaster which seemed to bring all hopes and plans in ruin to the ground.

It was one o'clock on March 6, 1802; the bell was ringing for dinner, the servant had just opened the door of the dining room and a few students had entered and were standing at their places, when the cry of fire resounded through the room. One of this group, George Strawbridge, a senior, rushing out on the campus saw a crowd assembled there looking up at a blaze in the belfry. It was a matter of but a minute for him to mount the stairs to his room on the top floor, seize his water pitcher and empty it on the flames in the room under the cupola above his head, beside the trap door leading to the belfry. But this proved utterly futile, and at that moment President Smith appearing beside him and raising his hands, exclaimed: "This is the progress of vice and irreligion."[23] He then turned and left the room.

All attempts to extinguish the flames were useless. Once they had broken through the wooden ceiling into the belfry, they leaped instantaneously up to the bell-shaped cap and converted the whole into a giant torch.[24] A violent southwest wind was blowing; there was no adequate fire engine, no firemen; the shingles of the roof and the seasoned timbers of floors and window frames and doors were highly combustible.[25] Realizing that there was no hope of saving the building, the students busied themselves with rescuing the precious scientific apparatus and what books, furniture, and clothing could be brought down the crowded stairs and out on the campus, as the fire roared overhead, the cupola toppled, and the roof crashed in. All save one hundred of the three thousand volumes in the college library, the entire libraries of the

---

[22] *Trustees Minutes*, II, p. 46.
[23] *Memoirs of George Strawbridge*, transcript, Princeton Library.
[24] *Trustees Minutes*, II, pp. 59-64.
[25] *Trenton True American*, March 1802; Poulson's *American Daily Advertiser*, March 9, 1802.

two literary societies,[26] and most of the furniture and personal effects of the students were consumed. As evening came on the president gazed in despair at the blackened walls and empty window spaces of the noble building in which for half a century the life of the college had centered.[27]

Even after mature reflection, he still believed that the fire had been the work of a small group of students who had been infected with those Jacobinic principles which were tearing the bonds of society asunder and threatening to overturn the country. He had been told that hostility to religion and moral order was one of their chief characteristics.[28] An excited committee of the trustees reported after an investigation that the conflagration could not have been accidental. That the flames appeared first under the cupola, some distance from any of the chimneys; that they spread with great rapidity; that many persons detected a strong smell of turpentine; that the smoke was "dark and heavy," that "the fire was accompanied with an unusual crackling"; that a second flame burst from the west end of the roof at some distance from the cupola, all pointed to the work of an incendiary.[29]

This report is not convincing. Young Strawbridge, who took it upon himself to make an investigation of his own, declared that there was no reason to suspect the students "as a body or individually." The fire occurred in broad daylight, the room under the cupola was kept locked, the hallway upon which it opened was "as public as a street," there were then no "Locofoco" matches and no one would have dared bring fire in a shovel, there was absolutely no motive for such a dastardly deed. "I really regard it as the weakest charge of incendiarism I have ever heard," he concluded.[30] The finger of suspicion should have pointed not to the students, but to that humble individual—the chimney sweep—for neglecting his duty.

[26] The American Whig Society lost about 800 volumes. *Princeton Library MSS*, AM 496.
[27] *Sermons of Samuel Stanhope Smith*, p. 38.
[28] *Princeton Library MSS*, AM 2164.
[29] *Trustees Minutes*, II, pp. 62-64.
[30] *Memoirs of George Strawbridge*, transcript, Princeton Library.

Rumor had it that one of the chimneys had been on fire that morning, and the flames might easily have worked through an opening in the old brick work to a rafter or girder. It is probable that the fire had been spreading in the attic for an hour or more before it found on outlet in the cupola and a few minutes later at the west eaves of the building.

To place the suspicion of incendiarism upon the student body was not only unjust but very harmful to the college. It was worse to select this occasion to purge the institution of what the trustees called undesirable characters.[31] Certainly the five or six young men who were suspended had a right to complain that they were being punished for a crime with which they were not even openly charged, and that the college had put on them without the least proof the stigma of arson.

On the other hand, there can be nothing but praise for the determination and zeal with which the trustees set about raising a fund for the restoration of Nassau Hall. The president was asked to tour the south to secure contributions from the alumni and the friends of education and religion; the Reverend Alexander G. McWhorter was assigned to New England; the Reverend Joseph Clark and Judge John Bryan to Maryland and Virginia. The people of Princeton itself, alarmed at certain efforts to have the college moved to some other locality, set the example by contributing nearly $3,000 within a week after the fire, and $2,000 more later.[32]

President Smith, turning his classes over to the other members of the faculty and the general supervision of the college to Ashbel Green, set out on a tour which lasted more than a year. In April we find him in Baltimore where a number of gentlemen relieved him of the "pain of asking," by bringing up the matter themselves and joining the solicitors.[33] In Washington he found people less considerate, and he rather shrank from sitting on the doorstep of Congress to beg donations from senators and congressmen. Yet there were com-

[31] *Trustees Minutes*, II, p. 66.
[32] *Maclean MSS*, Princeton Library, March 11, 1802.
[33] S. S. Smith to Elias Boudinot, April 15, 1802, Presbyterian Historical Society.

pensations for his embarrassment, as wherever he went the alumni, many of them men of prominence in their communities, greeted him with reverence and affection, and did all in their power to aid his mission.[34] In the summer of 1803 we find him back in Princeton fully satisfied with the results of his mission.[35]

Massachusetts did not wait for the arrival of McWhorter but, unsolicited, immediately made a substantial contribution. President Joseph Willard of Harvard gave $30 in books, Benjamin Waterhouse, professor of physics, donated "the profits of a course of lectures to be given the present season in Boston," Oliver Wendell gave $50, Professor David Tappan $20, Stephen Higginson $200, David Hyslop $200, William Phillips $1,000. In all, sixty-five persons subscribed $4,274. Not less encouraging than the donations was the message which accompanied them. The college was requested to accept the gift, it said, "as a token of our sympathy on this melancholy occasion and of our cordial good wishes for the permanent welfare of an institution which through half a century has been so eminent a blessing to this country."[36]

In the south, where the well-to-do could be reached only by going from town to town and from plantation to plantation, Bryan and Clark found their task an arduous one. Now we find Clark in Richmond to present his subscription paper to the members of the legislature, now he is riding in a violent rain in King and Queen county, now he is visiting Ralph Wormeley, now detained by illness at Landon Carter's plantation, now lodging at Mt. Vernon. It was in April 1803, five months after setting out from New Brunswick, that he reached Philadelphia and turned over $3,300 to Elias Boudinot.[37]

For Judge Bryan the trip proved fatal. Early in December he left Clark and started up the James River Valley expecting to cross the Blue Ridge to Staunton and the upper Shenandoah

---

[34] *Sermons of Samuel Stanhope Smith*, p. 52.
[35] *Faculty Minutes*, I, Aug. 20, 1803.
[36] *Maclean MSS*, March 31, 1802, Princeton Library.
[37] "Joseph Clark Diary," *Princeton Library MSS*, AM 8094.

Valley.[38] He had reached Farmington, the charming residence of George Divers,[39] near Charlottesville, when he became ill "with a violent bilious collic," and despite the efforts of the local physician, died four days later. He was interred in the family cemetery, and his horse, watch, and about $60 in cash held for his family.[40] Some time afterwards a nephew[41] appeared at Farmington and inquired particularly concerning the disposition of the clothes. Mr. Divers told him that he had given them to the slaves, all save the vests, which negroes were never permitted to wear. When the vests were brought down from the attic, the nephew ripped open the linings and drew out several thousands of dollars, which he turned over to the college.

So generous and so immediate were the responses to the first appeals for aid that the work of restoration was begun within a few weeks after the fire. In August it was stated that "Nassau Hall is rebuilding with great speed. The parts of the walls which were broken are repaired, the window and door frames and all the large timbers are replaced. The roof is now putting on, which is to consist of planks closely jointed and covered with sheet iron. The planks are jointed for the floors ready to be laid down as soon as the building is covered. Doors and almost all the interior-work are also prepared. It is therefore probable that a great part of it will be fit to be occupied next session."[42]

It is fortunate that the original massive walls were left standing, otherwise the architect of the restoration, Benjamin H. Latrobe, might have converted the building into a Greek temple under the influence of the classical revival. As it was he made few changes. The "old graduate" of 1760 or 1765 probably complained that the new cupola was too large, or

---

[38] *Ibid.*

[39] Now the Farmington Country Club.

[40] New Jersey Historical Society *Proceedings*, VI, pp. 178, 179.

[41] The Clark Diary shows that Clark himself did not hasten to Farmington on hearing of Bryan's death, as is stated in the New Jersey Historical Society *Proceedings.* The account given here is based in part on the statement of members of the Wood family who for many years owned Farmington.

[42] *Princeton Library MSS*, AM 8408.

that the new pediments over the three front doors were unfamiliar, or that the floors of the hallways were now paved
with brick, or that he could not find the old Whig or Clio
rooms, or that he missed the urns on the roof, but in the
main the building would have seemed the same as in his day.

When the work was nearing completion the students, who
had been boarding with the good people of the village, moved
in and the life of the college resumed its not too even way.
Unfortunately Latrobe's iron roof proved a failure, leaking
so badly that the ceilings in every bedroom of the fourth floor
were damaged and threatened to collapse on the boys' heads.[43]
In the end the entire roof had to be done over. It was several
years later that the so-called moat was dug around the building. This was an area sloping up from the base of the foundation, paved with brick, and draining into the street, designed
to make the basement rooms dry and to admit more light
and air.[44]

The fire, in the end, proved a blessing in disguise, for it
placed the college and its claims prominently before the
public, brought a rapid increase in attendance and produced
a restoration fund large enough not only to rebuild Nassau
Hall but to erect two new buildings. In 1803 the masons laid
the foundations of the Philosophical Building[45] which was to
contain the kitchen, dining hall, a room for the "philosophical" apparatus, recitation rooms for the classes in mathematics
and natural philosophy, and an observatory. On the other side
of the campus, facing this building, was erected the present
Stanhope Hall, named for Samuel Stanhope Smith, with
study halls for the freshman and sophomore classes, the
library, a recitation room for the president, and rooms for the
two literary societies.[46] These two new buildings, harmoniz-
ing as they did with Nassau Hall and dominated by the en-

[43] S. S. Smith to Boudinot, June 27, 1803, *Princeton Library MSS*, AM
10699.
[44] *Trustees Minutes*, II, p. 169.
[45] On the site of the Trustees Room in the Chancellor Green Library.
[46] John Maclean, *History of the College of New Jersey*, II, p. 47; *Trustees
Minutes*, II, p. 98.

larged cupola, made a well balanced and dignified front campus.[47]

Even more important was the rapid extension of the faculty, which the enhanced returns from student fees made possible. In 1802 the trustees appointed William Thompson professor of languages, in 1803 young Henry Kollock took up his duties as professor of theology, and in 1804 Andrew Hunter was made professor of mathematics and astronomy. Of these new additions to the teaching staff President Smith was very proud. "Professors Maclean, Kollock, Hunter and Thompson concur with me in every exertion of which our finances will admit for the advancement of every branch of science and of natural science particularly," he wrote in September 1805.[48] Certainly the faculty meetings, with the dignified president in the chair and the four professors and two tutors distributed around the table, presented a striking contrast with the days when Smith, Maclean, and a tutor or two comprised the entire staff.

Some of the new professors seem to have been poor disciplinarians and uninspiring teachers. "Among other eccentricities" Professor Thompson had "translated our catechisms into Latin and required us to recite verbatim," complained one student. "It was hard labor and no profit."[49] One suspects that this had something to do with the "gross and repeated insolence" which one youth showed to Mr. Thompson during the class exercises, marked by "antic gestures" and the use of a "disrespectful nickname," for which he was ejected from the room and later suspended.[50] Andrew Hunter, who is described as a chaplain in the Revolution and a man of the old school, never permitted the students "to put any other letters on the black board than those which were in the book itself,"[51] certainly not a very good way to encourage initiative

[47] The Philosophical Building was taken down in 1873 to make room for Chancellor Green Library.
[48] Princeton Library MSS, AM 239.
[49] Princeton Library MSS, AM 2074.
[50] Faculty Minutes, I, Jan. 6, 1806.
[51] Princeton Library MSS, AM 2074.

and originality of thought. Kollock, though a burning and eloquent preacher, seems to have been a failure in the classroom, one student, at least, pronouncing his lectures in theology "unsatisfactory and lifeless . . . containing no profound argument, no ingenuity or originality."[52]

We may be more ready to excuse these shortcomings, however, when we follow the professors in their daily duties and realize how much was expected of them. From President Smith down to the latest tutor the faculty was overworked. The president taught the juniors and seniors in belles-lettres, criticism, composition, moral philosophy, natural theology, the philosophy of civil government, the law of nations, logic, geography, and revealed religion; attended evening prayers in the hall; met with the Theological Society for two hours on Mondays; took his turn in presiding in the dining hall; and advised and reproved delinquent or disorderly students. Professor Maclean had two sections of juniors six days a week and one section of seniors three days a week. Each lecture, with experiments and recitation, took from one to two hours, while preparing the apparatus took from two to three hours.

Professor Kollock, in addition to his duties as pastor of the Presbyterian Church, met his class in Hebrew three times a week, in theology three times a week, in Biblical criticism once a week. Professor Thompson's hours of work were as heavy as his teaching was dull, for he had to remain in the classroom six hours every day in the week. From nine to ten-thirty he taught the freshmen, from ten-thirty to twelve he presided over sophomore study hall, from two to three-thirty he quizzed the sophomores alternately in Latin and Greek, from three-thirty to five he took over freshman study hall. As for the tutors, their life was one round of teaching, holding prayers, inspecting the students' rooms, warning the unruly, and reporting the incorrigible.[53]

With such a schedule there was no hope that the faculty could accomplish very much for the advancement of human knowledge, and little that they could arouse the intellectual

[52] *Ibid.*                    [53] *Trustees Minutes*, II, pp. 126-130.

curiosity of the students. The life of the undergraduates themselves was equally dull and arduous. "At six o'clock the bell rouses us to morning prayers," wrote young James Iredell in 1804. "From this till breakfast, which is always at half past seven, I study the recitation. The time between breakfast and nine I spend either in conversation or reading. At nine the bell rings for the students to retire to their rooms, except the two lower classes which must attend in the recitation room where they are confined till twelve. From this till dinner, at one o'clock, I generally read. At two we again go to the recitation room and stay till five, when the bell rings for evening prayers. From this till supper, at six o'clock, I study or read, and also from supper till seven. Between seven and eight I usually take a walk and from eight till ten read. At nine the tutor visits the rooms to see that the students are all in."[54]

No further evidence is needed to show that there had been a discouraging decline in teaching efficiency since the days of Burr, Davies, and Finley. Instead of a small group of eager young men gathering around their teacher to catch his enthusiasm and stimulate their own interest by informal discussion, we find an overworked faculty, under the eye of an exacting board of trustees, driving a hundred and fifty half-rebellious youths through a dull, exhausting routine. We know that the students enjoyed Smith's demonstrations in chemistry and his lectures on physics, but in their other work for the most part their minds "bogged down" under the succession of written lectures, memory exercises, and quizzes.

The situation was aggravated by a complete lack of understanding of the students by the faculty and trustees. Since the Revolution a new spirit of liberty which emphasized the personal dignity and individual rights of man had spread through the country, especially among the younger generation. The boys at college, some of them only fourteen or fifteen years old, addressed each other as "gentlemen," resented the strict regulation of their personal conduct and stood up manfully for their "rights." To the trustees, not only of Princeton but

[54] *Letters of James Iredell*, transcript, Princeton Library.

of other American colleges, this seemed nothing less than rebellion against proper authority. It was necessary for young men to submit to discipline, not only for the sake of preserving order but for the development of character. "Melancholy must be the prospect of the future state of our country when those of the rising generation, who . . . are designated to become the chief pillars of church and state, undertake to insult humanity and justice, to prostrate the laws and overturn the social order," said President John Wheelock of Dartmouth,[55] and the heads of other colleges gave hearty approval to his words.

The situation at Princeton was intensified by the fact that a large part of the student body was recruited from the plantation aristocracy of the south, whose code of personal honor was especially obnoxious to the trustees. Great was their horror when it was reported to them that several students had been engaged in dueling. Discovering "that those false and wicked principles in regard to personal honor" were accepted by many in the college, they decreed that any student who gave or accepted or carried a challenge or acted as second in a duel should be expelled. We will "never fail to mark every instance of this crime with the highest expression of detestation and abhorrence."[56]

It would have been well if the trustees, instead of trying to suppress the spirit of liberty, self-reliance, and personal honor in the student body, had sought to turn it to their own purposes in preserving order and stimulating study. Had they permitted the boys some participation in the management of undergraduate affairs, consulting their representatives in certain cases of discipline, substituting student monitors for prying tutors, relaxing the severity of the regulations and trusting to their honor not to break them, the college would have been a pleasanter place to live in. But if such a course ever occurred to them, they at once repudiated it as unworthy of religious men whose duty it was to yield nothing to the degenerate tendencies of the time. So they went on repeating the old

[55] *Princeton Library MSS*, AM 4268.   [56] *Trustees Minutes*, II, pp. 25, 26.

mistakes, reproving the students when they refused to inform on each other, urging the tutors to greater vigilance, increasing the severity of the discipline, and reprimanding the faculty if they seemed too lenient in its enforcement.

Perhaps they would not have been so unyielding had not the spirit of liberty been associated in their minds with irreligion and infidelity. President Smith lamented the presence in Nassau Hall of a small group with "jacobinic and anti-religious principles," who made hostility to religion and moral order one of their chief tenets, and "recently celebrated a triumph over the Faculty by breaking into the Presbyterian church, removing the Bible and burning it."[57] We might suspect that the good doctor's fears had led him to exaggerate this matter, did not an alumnus, who had been in college at the time of the fire, confirm his statement. This man said that the leader in his class was an "infidel and avowed his creed on all occasions. Godwin's *Political Justice* was his Bible." In those days "infidelity was very popular through the United States."[58]

On the other hand, there is abundant evidence that most of the students were normal boys of accepted principles, representing leading families in the middle states and the south. With tactful and wise guidance they would have been studious and even orderly. But rebellious at the rigid regime to which they were subjected, resentful of the supervision of the tutors, bored at the round of lectures, classes, and study periods, they frequently broke into disorder, usually petty in nature, but occasionally serious. Perhaps one or two had been drinking at the tavern and returning tied a calf in the pulpit of the Prayer Hall; perhaps some youngster stole the dinner trumpet and sounded a few blasts in the hallways; perhaps two quick-tempered boys got into a fight; perhaps some material was burned in the hallway to create a disagreeable smell,[59] perhaps a small outbuilding was overturned. How the unwise or tactless handling of some of these of-

---

[57] *Princeton Library MSS*, AM 2164.    [58] *Ibid.*, AM 2074.
[59] *Faculty Minutes*, I, Dec. 31, 1801; Feb. 28, 1804, etc.

fenses led to grave consequences we gather from an incident which occurred in February 1800. "The mornings being very cold this winter and the tutors praying very long" in the unheated Prayer Hall, "some of the students fell into a practice of scraping and disturbing them." Thereupon the faculty summoned three seniors to Doctor Smith's office and after securing admissions that they had been concerned in the disorder immediately suspended them. This punishment the student body thought too severe for a minor offense, in which half the college had participated, and so vented their wrath in a serious riot. For several days Nassau Hall resounded to the report of pistols, the crash of brickbats against walls and doors, and the rolling of barrels of stones along the hallways. President Smith made an appeal for order and all was quiet for a fortnight. Then one of the suspended students who had remained in town nursing his grievance started things off again. He induced one of his friends to roll a three-pound cannonball down the hallway. When, as was the intention, it drew from his room one of the tutors whom he blamed for his troubles, he pounced on him and gave him a beating. "This again stirred up the students, and for about three days the college re-echoed with stones." The president called the students into the Prayer Hall to expostulate and plead, but not until he threatened to "shut up college till a board of trustees met," did the disturbance cease.[60]

It was most unfortunate that the onerous task of preserving order and of reporting infringements of the regulations fell to the tutors. Selected for their piety and scholarly ability, egged on by the faculty and trustees, often inexperienced and tactless, they were resented and sometimes hated by the students. On one occasion, when a youth named Mayo was suspended for some minor offense, there was such great resentment against the tutor who reported him that he narrowly escaped from a crowd armed with tongs, sticks, and brickbats.[61]

---

[60] Elias Ellmaker to Nathaniel Ellmaker, Feb. 28, 1800, *Princeton Library MSS*, AM 11887.
[61] *Faculty Minutes*, I, March 8, 1809.

At the next meeting of the trustees Mayo made "acknowledg-ments where he had been wrong, but showed a manly spirit of opposition to the ill treatment he had received from the tutor." Believing that what he needed was "gentle and steady, not rigid discipline," the board restored him. Thereupon the tutor, and his colleague with him, handed in their resignations, declaring "they could do no good in an institution where their authority was not supported."[62]

One suspects that life in Nassau Hall would have been more orderly had a part of each afternoon been devoted to some form of athletics. The impulse to vent youthful spirits in rioting would not have been so strong had the students flocked in to supper, happy and tired after an hour or so of cricket, shinny, skating, or football. But the faculty frowned on "frivolity" of this kind. When the young boys indulged in a game with balls and sticks on "the back common of the college," they put a stop to it, as "low and unbecoming gen-tlemen and students." Moreover, they said, it is "attended with great danger to the health by sudden and alternate heats and colds."[63] A regulation forbidding sleigh-riding was habit-ually broken. "Almost every night during the continuance of the snow there are numbers of sleighs out filled with students going to either Trenton or some other of the neighboring towns," James Iredell tells us.[64]

In March 1807 came the great rebellion. Three students were suspended, one for "being in a tavern" where he "in-toxicated himself with strong liquor" and "cursing and in-sulting some of the peaceable and orderly inhabitants of the town"; one for cursing and insulting one of the tutors; the other for insolence to Professor Maclean, frequenting taverns, and "bringing strong liquor into college."[65] How far these charges were justified we have no means of determining. Some of the students afterwards declared that the faculty had accepted prejudiced evidence against the accused boys,

[62] Letter of Joshua M. Wallace, April 12, 1809, Virginia Historical Society.
[63] *Faculty Minutes*, I, Nov. 26, 1787.
[64] *Letters of James Iredell*, Jan. 7, 1805, transcript, Princeton Library.
[65] *Faculty Minutes*, I, March 25, 1807; March 30, 1807.

while refusing to credit their denials, backed by the word of their friends in college. At all events, there was an indignant consultation among some of the most prominent undergraduates, which resulted in the drawing up of a remonstrance to the faculty and in visits to every room in Nassau Hall to secure the united support of the student body.

The next day a committee of about ten appeared before the faculty with this paper. A vigorous document it was. It expressed the opinion that the faculty had acted precipitately and contrary to the "principles of justice" in suspending the three students, and the student body respectfully requested their reinstatement. An immediate answer would be appreciated as their further proceedings would depend upon the decision. Moreover, they asked the members of the faculty to retract certain expressions tending to "the destruction of their reputations individually, such expressions being in their opinion destitute of the stamp of truth."[66]

President Smith and the faculty stared at the excited students in astonishment. Why, this was open rebellion! The rules of the college expressly forbade the forming of combinations to resist the authority of the faculty and trustees, and here were these young men making demands in disrespectful language under a poorly veiled threat of united action in case of refusal. After a pause the committee was told that their "petition" would not be considered, and the boys withdrew.

Had the faculty now mixed a little tact and good judgment with firmness, it is probable that this crisis might have been safely passed. Young William Meade, afterwards Bishop of Virginia, stated that he and many others had been imposed upon and had signed the offensive document without giving it serious consideration,[67] thinking that nothing more was intended than a respectful petition.[68] All save a few would certainly have withdrawn their names had the president read

[66] *Faculty Minutes*, I, March 31, 1807.
[67] Quoted in John Maclean, *History of the College of New Jersey*, II, p. 76.
[68] *Trenton True American*, May 11, 1807.

the "petition" to the student body, explained that the faculty could not yield without surrendering their authority and forfeiting the respect of the students themselves, and then given them time to think the matter over. Instead, in somewhat of a panic they called in Richard Stockton, the only trustee in town, and after an earnest consultation decided to act immediately.

That evening when the boys filed into the Prayer Hall tense with excitement, they found President Smith and Mr. Stockton waiting in the pulpit to address them. After prayers the president rose and with his usual calm dignity tried to convince them that their complaints were unfounded and their act in breaking the regulation against "combinations" productive of ruin and chaos. Mr. Stockton followed with a speech of considerable length. But the determined young faces which looked up at them, together with the constant scraping of feet on the floor, made the speakers painfully aware that their listeners were unconvinced. At last it was announced that the roll would be called and every student who refused to withdraw his name from the offensive paper would be suspended immediately. But before the first name was called one of the leaders rose and, after stating that the students were united and firm in their determination to retract nothing, left the room. No fewer than a hundred and twenty-five rushed out after him "shouting and yelling," and leaving only thirty or forty behind. After this remnant had withdrawn their names from the petition, Dr. Smith declared the others suspended and the momentous meeting came to a close.[69]

That night Nassau Hall reverberated to the sound of crashing windows and doors, and the shouts of excited young voices. The faculty, fearing serious injury to the building, appealed to the people of the village to come to their assistance. But when some of them appeared at the doors with arms in their hands, they found them guarded by determined

[69] *Faculty Minutes,* I, March 31, 1807; *Trenton True American,* May 11, 1807.

students armed with the banisters of the stairways, "who menaced all who should molest them." At this juncture, the president, realizing that the situation had got entirely out of hand, dismissed college until after the approaching five weeks' spring vacation and waited anxiously for the next meeting of the trustees.

A very stern group of men it was who gathered at Princeton on April 8. After going over the details of the riot, they gave their sanction to all the faculty had done, but in their hearts they blamed Smith, not for severity in matters of discipline, but for not rooting out irreligion and dissipation with a sterner hand. "We mean to make the Faculty do their duty by execut-ing the laws," one trustee wrote a few days later. "And if they do not we shall in the fall proceed to employ men who have the firmness and ability to do better."[70] As for the rebel-lious students, it would be an excellent thing for the college to get rid of them, and with them the spirit of infidelity and hostility to orderly society. It did not matter that among the number were many youths of splendid promise, or that by their severity they were building up many enemies for the college. Better that the institution should close its doors forever, they said, than to compromise with insubordination, dissipation, and infidelity.

So when a committee of six, representing the suspended students, appeared before the board with a paper justifying their conduct, it was returned to them unread. If the indi-vidual members wished to present any grievances in their own cases, they would be heard, the trustees told them, but they would not treat with any combination. Thereupon a number of students, who in the meanwhile had heard from home, came in, made their submission, and were readmitted.[71] But Abel P. Upshur, who afterwards became Secretary of State under President Tyler, undismayed by the circle of stern faces, not only refused to yield but made a fine "display of argument and eloquence" in behalf of himself and his com-

---

[70] John Rhea to Joshua L. Howell, *Princeton Library MSS*, AM 9530.
[71] *Trenton True American*, May 11, 1807; *Trustees Minutes*, II, p. 194.

rades."[72] Of the one hundred and twenty-five students who had been suspended, fifty-five were ultimately readmitted,[73] though according to young William Meade, "the finest young men" refused to return.

The trustees drew up and published in the newspapers an account of the whole affair, laying the blame upon the "pernicious principles and loose morals of some vicious youths" among the students and to "the almost unlimited allowance of money or credit given to many others." They blamed also that "false but plausible principle that to give testimony against a fellow student, however gross his vices . . . was in the highest degree dishonorable." But whatever the cause, the action of the students, in erecting themselves into a tribunal to rejudge the decisions of the faculty, made it impossible to yield. "We must either govern our own college or resign it to the government of inconsiderate boys or passionate young men," they added.[74] They then wrote to the other American colleges, requesting them to cooperate with Princeton by refusing to admit any of the suspended students.

The replies show that the trouble was not local but national in scope. From Harvard President Samuel Webber wrote, giving his ready assent. "About the time of your disturbances," he added, "a serious and alarming opposition to government also arose in this seminary . . . and twenty-nine students . . . have been dismissed."[75] Had Princeton not been firm, said President Nott, of Union, "the youths in other seminaries, emboldened by a successful experiment, would have been easily excited to a similar combination."[76] "The cause in which the governors of the college of New Jersey are engaged is the common cause of all colleges," wrote President Timothy Dwight of Yale, who hoped that Princeton's firmness would "ultimately serve to strengthen the bonds of discipline and to put down that impatience of control

[72] *William and Mary Quarterly*, XVI, pp. 119-121.
[73] *Faculty Minutes*, I, March 31, 1807.
[74] *Trenton True American*, May 11, 1807.
[75] *Princeton Library MSS*, AM 4267.
[76] *Princeton Library MSS*, AM 4272.

which we also lament as a strong characteristic of the rising generation."[77]

The college presidents, almost all of whom were ordained ministers, would have been even more deeply concerned had they realized that the epidemic of student disorder was part of that vast movement to secularize education which was rapidly gaining momentum throughout the nation. They were ready enough to call attention to the service they were doing by developing leadership in all spheres of activity but they insisted upon rendering this service in their own way. Education had from the first been under the control of religious men and it was right and proper that it should remain so. When the Princeton students demanded that their rights be respected, the trustees informed them that they had only the right of obedience or the right to withdraw. The college was the property of the trustees, they pointed out, and the students resided in it only by permission and during good behavior.[78] They did not stop to reflect that the colleges could not exist without public patronage and that the time might come when in return the public would demand a voice in their control. A college which was to keep step with the age must broaden its perspective, constantly recast its courses to meet new needs, embrace in its sympathies all types of society, all religious beliefs. To hold rigidly to the ideals of a past era meant stagnation.

And stagnation was the lot of Princeton for the next few decades. The injury done by the riot of 1807 can hardly be overestimated. It aired before the public the hostility between students and trustees, created an unfavorable and on the whole unjust impression of the type of young men who came to the college, converted into enemies many who should have been stanch supporters, steeled the trustees for greater and greater severity in matters of discipline where there should have been more understanding and tact, cut down the

[77] *Ibid.*, AM 4271. Only the University of Pennsylvania refused to cooperate. The expelled students had been sufficiently punished, they said, and they thought it unjust to blast their future and deprive the nation of their services.

[78] *Trenton True American*, May 11, 1807.

enrollment radically and with it the income for running expenses, forced a reduction in the teaching staff, increased the tension between faculty and trustees.

"We will probably have fewer students, but a few under discipline is better than a mob without any," wrote one of the trustees after the riot.[79] In the end it was found that numbers had been lost without permanent improvement in order. In the winter session of 1806-1807 matriculation had approached the 200 mark; in May, President Smith could count but 112. The numbers remained fairly constant during 1808 and 1809 but the next year they dropped beneath the hundred mark. As the students were the chief source of revenue, this proved disastrous. In September 1806 the total income derived from room rent, entrance fees, and board was about $11,500;[80] in 1808 it could not have exceeded $6,500, and in 1812, despite a considerable increase in rates, it was about $8,500.[81]

Obviously retrenchment in the one large item of the college budget—expenditures for teaching—was now necessary. Already the faculty had been reduced by one, when Professor Kollock resigned in 1806 to accept a call to the Presbyterian Church of Savannah, and now both Thompson and Hunter were dropped. "When five years ago I received an invitation to this place, I came under the impression that I was to end my days here," Thompson wrote one of the trustees. "Providence, it appears, has determined otherwise," since he was to be dismissed and "turned once more upon the world under an almost overwhelming load of infirmities to earn an uncertain subsistence for my family."[82] As he was "charged with no fault," he was permitted to resign, with ill health as the ostensible reason,[83] retained his house and was granted a pension of $262.66 for five years.[84] At the same meeting of the trustees the resignation of Professor Hunter was accepted,

[79] *Princeton Library MSS*, AM 9530.
[80] *Trustees Minutes*, II, p. 189.
[81] *Princeton Library MSS*, AM 4212.
[82] *Princeton Library MSS*, AM 2171.
[83] *Princeton Library MSS*, AM 4260.
[84] *Trustees Minutes*, II, p. 225.

leaving the chair of mathematics and astronomy vacant. So all the gains of the past decade were cast overboard, and the president and Maclean, with the assistance of two tutors, took up the almost impossible task of instructing a hundred or more young men in the languages and the various sciences.

The loss of confidence in the college was even more pronounced within the Presbyterian church than with the general public. There was much shaking of heads at the meetings of presbyteries and synods and the general assembly, many expressions of sorrow that the institution founded by such good and holy men as Dickinson and Burr should have fallen on evil days. After the riot of 1807 the Reverend Samuel Miller, of the New York Presbyterian Church, wrote to the Reverend E. D. Griffin: "Have you heard the terrible news from Princeton? What is the great Head of the Church about to do with that seminary? Is it about to be purged and elevated, or totally destroyed? God grant that the latter may not be the case."[85]

President Smith had long been concerned over the falling off in divinity students, which was no doubt the result of a growing belief that Nassau Hall was no longer the proper habitat for pious young men. A few entered every year, to take advantage of scholarships, but they were strangely out of place among the sons of wealthy planters and merchants. "I would leave most cordially," wrote William R. Weeks in 1808, were I not "under obligations to those who have supported me here."[86] Thus at a time when Presbyterian doctrines were spreading rapidly throughout the expanding west, and when hundreds of pulpits were vacant, the college which had been founded chiefly to meet just such a need was turning out annually a mere handful of candidates for the ministry.

The appointment of Professor Kollock to the chair of theology, it had been hoped, would attract students and renew the days when the Presbyterian general assembly was packed with Princeton graduates. A house was purchased and fitted up as a dormitory for students of theology, which long bore

[85] Samuel Miller, *Life of Samuel Miller*, I, p. 228.
[86] *Princeton Library MSS*, AM 11456b.

the name of Divinity Hall.[87] But the old appeal of Burr, Davies, and Witherspoon had been lost, and Kollock resigned on the ground that he did not have enough students to occupy his time. His duties were taken over by the overworked president, who was able to report in 1806 that the college was still training "some pious and worthy men" destined for the ministry, having graduated not fewer than twenty-six in the past four years.[88]

The concern of the president and trustees over this matter was heightened by the possibility that the general assembly, despairing of the college, might establish a theological seminary. Many ministers had long lamented the lack of such an institution, and were deeply concerned when they saw young men inadequately trained in literature and science, often after only twelve or eighteen months' study of theology, filling important pulpits. Other denominations—"the Dutch Reformed Church, the Associated Reformed Church and the descendants of the venerable Puritans of New England"— were founding seminaries, and unless the Presbyterians followed suit their church would fall behind in the race for converts. They had been invited to participate in endowing and utilizing the Congregationalist seminary at Andover but this they declined, preferring to have an institution of their own, controlled by their general assembly. Such an institution must come within a few years, wrote Samuel Miller, "unless Princeton College should be placed on a better footing," a contingency which he considered remote.[89]

President Smith in 1805 tried to stem the tide by drawing up a statement of the facilities of the college for training in divinity, which was read before the general assembly. He dwelt upon the opportunity of his students to study "any branch of science," upon the large collection of theological books in the library, upon the funds available to aid pious youths, upon the courses in divinity, ecclesiastical history,

[87] John Maclean, *History of the College of New Jersey*, II, p. 63; *Princeton Library MSS*, AM 2170.

[88] *Princeton Library MSS*, AM 4234.

[89] Samuel Miller, *Life of Samuel Miller*, I, p. 232.

church government, and Hebrew.[90] But the effect was disappointing, and Samuel Miller, Ashbel Green, and others continued to press their plans for a seminary. "Every member of the Assembly ought to have a fire kindled in his mind," Miller declared.[91]

Accordingly, in his opening sermon before the general assembly of 1808, Archibald Alexander brought the matter squarely before the church, at the same time voicing the widespread distrust of the College of New Jersey. It was to be doubted whether the courses pursued in the college were suited for young men who were preparing for the ministry, because of "the great extension of the physical sciences,"[92] so that the need for a separate institution was apparent. Following this lead, the presbytery of Philadelphia the next year made a definite proposal for the establishment of a theological seminary, which was favorably received by the church as a whole.[93] Some months later a committee, headed by Ashbel Green, met in New York at the residence of Samuel Miller and drew up a plan or constitution for the proposed institution which later was adopted with minor changes.[94]

The trustees of the college were by this time thoroughly alarmed. They would have turned the institution over to the general assembly, giving it the right to appoint the teaching staff, shape the courses and direct its policies, had their charter permitted them to do so. As it was, they made a proposal designed to circumvent the wording of the charter, and to place the college in fact, if not technically, under the control of the church. "The College of New Jersey was instituted originally by members of the Presbyterian denomination and principally with a view to promoting the general interests of religion and chiefly within the Presbyterian Church," they said. Therefore they suggested that the general assembly establish, not a separate theological seminary but a divinity

[90] *Ibid.*, p. 202.
[91] *Ibid.*, p. 194.
[92] John Maclean, *History of the College of New Jersey*, II, p. 131.
[93] Samuel Miller, *Life of Samuel Miller*, I, pp. 280, 281.
[94] Ashbel Green, *Life of Ashbel Green*, p. 334.

school in the college, thus taking advantage of its library, dining hall, buildings, and faculty. In return they suggested "that the principal direction of the college in its instruction, government, and discipline, be gradually turned to promote the objects of the theological institution, in proportion as the funds can be so augmented as to complete it on the most enlarged scale."[95]

The trustees expressed great surprise when this startling proposal, apparently so favorable to the church, was decisively defeated on the floor of the assembly. Yet had they consulted two of their own number, Samuel Miller and Ashbel Green, this result could have been anticipated. Three years earlier Miller had written Green giving his reasons for favoring a separate seminary. "Nothing can be done at Princeton at present and perhaps not for ten years. I doubt whether a divinity school there . . . could be made, in the present state of the college, to command the confidence of the Presbyterian church. . . . I fear the theological students would not be the better for habitual intercourse with the students in the arts." Considering how many questions of doctrine and discipline would arise "none but ministers and elders of our Church," and not the trustees of the college, must govern. "In short, if it be desired to have the divinity school uncontaminated by the college, to have its government unfettered and its orthodoxy and purity perpetual," establishment of a completely independent seminary was necessary.[96]

Having failed in their efforts to incorporate the divinity school in the college, the trustees now bent their efforts toward having the seminary located at Princeton. In this they were successful, but at the cost of an agreement every advantage of which accrued to the seminary and none to the college. The students of the new institution were to have permission to use the college library, reside in Nassau Hall, and have their meals in the dining hall until their own buildings were ready to receive them; the college was not to establish a professor-

[95] *Princeton Library MSS*, AM 4234.
[96] Samuel Miller, *Life of Samuel Miller*, pp. 241-242.

ship of theology as long as the seminary remained at Princeton—and most remarkable of all—the directors of the seminary were permitted "to erect on the grounds belonging to the College such buildings" as they thought proper.[97] That the directors did not avail themselves of the last privilege was no doubt due to their desire to have their students at such a distance from the college as to render the danger of contamination less acute.

Henceforth the theological seminary became the pride and hope of the church, the college its wayward stepchild. We catch the spirit with which the new institution was founded from the election in the general assembly of its first professor. "Silently and prayerfully these guardians of the Church began to prepare their votes. . . . Not a word was spoken, not a whisper heard, as the teller passed around to collect the result. The votes were counted, the result declared and Reverend Dr. Alexander was pronounced elected."[98] A few months later the seminary opened with three students, who lodged, recited, and had their meals in the college, but the foundation for the first building was not laid down until 1815.

The establishing of the theological seminary was, on the whole, a good thing for the college. It is true that the contributions of those who wished to aid religion, which in the past had been a main source of revenue, were now diverted to the new institution. But the college had in large part already forfeited this asset. On the other hand, the giving up of the plan for a professorship of divinity and the frank acknowledgment that Princeton henceforth would be purely an arts college, might legitimately have entitled it to a wider patronage from the nation as a whole. Could not the trustees, following in the path laid down by Witherspoon, and capitalizing on the services of the college as a nursery of statesmen, appeal to all denominations and all sections for the funds necessary for new professorships, a greater library, new scientific equipment, new dormitories?

[97] *Trustees Minutes*, II, pp. 377-380.
[98] Samuel Miller, *Life of Samuel Miller*, I, p. 333.

Unfortunately, the establishment of the theological seminary in no wise altered the determination of the church to retain its control of the college, and for decades the by-law requiring that at least twelve of the twenty-seven trustees should be clergymen was strictly enforced. Most of these gentlemen were also connected with the seminary, no fewer than thirty-six, in the period from 1812 to 1868, being either directors, trustees, or professors of the sister institution.[99] Thus the seminary dominated the college and dictated its policies.

The key-word of the new regime which the trustees now envisaged for the college was reform. There was to be no yielding to the trend of the times; Princeton must be filled once more with pious youths, must be the scene of religious revivals, the faculty must purge the irreligious, must reestablish the stern discipline that was so good for men's souls, must beware of heresy, must close their ears to scientific discoveries which might weaken belief in revealed religion. As the present faculty had so signally failed to attain these ideals, it would be wise to remove them and place men in charge who had the complete confidence of the church.

The first step was to inform the able, popular Professor Maclean that the trustees would welcome his resignation, to take effect in September 1812.[100] In this case Princeton's loss was William and Mary's gain. "An unexpected appointment renders it necessary for me to request that I may have leave of absence for remainder of this session," Maclean wrote to the trustees on August 13, 1812.[101] A few days later, as he was preparing to leave for Virginia, he received a communication which must have warmed his heart. "It is with sentiments of the most sincere and unfeigned regret that the members of the Junior Class receive the official notice of the resignation of their esteemed and ever to be remembered professor."

[99] Varnum Lansing Collins, *Princeton* (Oxford University Press, 1914), p. 123.

[100] There is no mention of this action in the *Trustees Minutes*, but Maclean's letter to the trustees, dated Aug. 13, 1812, states specifically that his resignation was desired. *Maclean MSS*, Princeton Library.

[101] *Trustees Minutes*, II, p. 335.

They regretted deeply that they had to part "from one, for whom they entertained sentiments of the most profound reverence, esteem and affection, and under whose able instruction and friendly care they would have completed their collegiate course with pride and pleasure."[102]

The case of President Smith had to be handled more tactfully. The state of his health was used as an excuse for creating the office of vice-president, whose incumbent was to take over all responsibility for matters of discipline. The next day a committee of the trustees called on Doctor Smith, and "had a free and friendly conversation" with him. To the elderly president it must have been obvious that the trustees were taking the reins from his hands and that the vice-president henceforth would be the real head of the college. He therefore sent in his immediate resignation. What part his poor health and his desire "to enjoy the short remainder" of his "life in quiet retirement" played in this matter we cannot say, but the resignation was clearly forced.[103] The board were generous, however, in giving him a life annuity, and in providing a residence and purchasing his library in order to assist him in paying his debts.

With the retirement of Samuel Stanhope Smith, the college lost a truly able president, a man who, under more favorable circumstances, would have ranked with Witherspoon and McCosh. Had he been permitted to work out his own policies and put them into effect there is reason to believe that the college would have made rapid progress in the two decades of his administration. But he was caught between the changing spirit of the age manifested in the student body and the spirit of reaction which characterized the trustees. He might have been a great educational leader had the trustees permitted him to lead; he might have solved the perplexing problem of discipline had they left matters of discipline in his hands. Forced to carry out unwise policies, with which he was not in

---

[102] *Maclean MSS*, Aug. 17, 1812, Princeton Library.
[103] *Trustees Minutes*, II, pp. 338-340.

sympathy, he cannot be held responsible for the decline in teaching efficiency, the rebellious spirit of the student body, the failure to keep pace with the advance in science, the restricted enrollment, the loss of prestige within the Presbyterian church and throughout the nation as a whole.

# CHAPTER V

## Princeton's Nadir

HE first step in reforming the college was the selection of a president in full sympathy with the policies of the trustees. Ashbel Green was obviously the man. He was one of the most prominent and influential ministers in the Presbyterian church, he had served as tutor and professor with marked success, in the autumn and winter of 1802 he had been acting president, he had been outspoken in criticizing the "laxness" of Smith's administration. At a meeting of the board on August 13, 1812, when one of the members hinted to Green that their choice might fall on him, he answered that he would "instantly and absolutely refuse." "We shall do what we think right and you will do the same," was the reply.[1] Green later found that his friend, Samuel Miller, had gone from one member to another arguing for his election, so he was not surprised when at the meeting the following morning he received a unanimous vote.[2] At first he hesitated but when he found that his congregation, though not glad to part with him, was prepared to acquiesce, he accepted.

Despite the confidence which the board reposed in their new president, they did not take the trouble to consult him about the selection of the faculty over which he was to preside. "With respect to a vice-president, we have chosen one who probably was not at all in your list of candidates," Miller wrote him in October 1812. "It is a Mr. Slack, principal of the Trenton Academy, a licentiate of the New Brunswick presbytery, and about twenty-eight or thirty years of age. He is said to be pious, prudent and highly respectable, and one of the best mathematicians and natural philosophers in the country." The board elected as senior tutor Philip Lindsley, and junior tutor John F. Clark.[3]

[1] Ashbel Green, *Life of Ashbel Green*, p. 339.
[2] *Trustees Minutes*, II, p. 341.      [3] *Princeton Library MSS*, AM 3598.

After the session of 1812-1813 had opened, the faculty had set aside a day of prayer for guidance in their duties, and Green had installed his family in the charming old President's House on Nassau Street, many doubts and fears assailed him. It had been easy to criticize his predecessor but he had now to prove that he would be more successful. Could he maintain discipline among the students? Could he restore the finances of the college? Could he regain for the institution its old reputation in the Presbyterian church? "I knew before I left my pastoral charge that the college was in a most deplorable state," he wrote. "I went with the resolution to reform it or to fall under the attempt."

So, as he paced back and forth in his study, he outlined his plans and his educational policies. He resolved to pray to God to make the institution "what its pious founders intended it to be"; to conduct himself with "humble fortitude and firmness, dignity and meekness, decision and caution, courtesy and reserve, piety unfeigned; to treat the students with tenderness and freedom," but never to permit them to treat him with familiarity; in all cases of discipline to act with "great coolness, caution and deliberation, and having done this, to fear no consequences."[4] Perhaps Green was unconscious that he was trying to pattern himself upon Witherspoon, but the figure of the great president under whom he had studied and taught was ever present in his mind. He forgot that in the quarter of a century since Witherspoon's day the times had changed, that new problems confronted the college, that the nation's needs required new educational policies, that it was incumbent on him to be a leader, not a mere imitator.

It was Green's great hope that Nassau Hall might become the seat of a series of religious revivals which would transform the worldly and the vicious into meek, pious youths, some of whom would go forth to preach the Gospel. Then would the college be carrying out the intention of its founders, then all troubles from insubordination would vanish. But if it should chance that he could not reform the students, he was deter-

[4] Ashbel Green, *Life of Ashbel Green*, pp. 343-344.

mined to rule them. There must be no relaxing of discipline. To make strictness more palatable, however, he tried to mingle with it a touch of paternal interest and kindness. "My general plan was to give the students more indulgences of a lawful kind than they had ever had before that I might with more propriety counteract all unlawful practices," he tells us. "I got cards of invitation printed to bring them by companies of eight at a time to my table." But, he adds sadly, "I found that it had but little effect in reclaiming the vicious."[5]

It was a misfortune for Green that his old friend Miller was called to Princeton as a member of the faculty of the theological seminary, because his fellow advocate of "reform," and the man who secured for him the presidency, was always at his elbow to see that there was no yielding to the "degeneracy of the times," no laxity in discipline. If Miller caught a group of boys loitering at the tavern, or if reports came to him of disorders in Nassau Hall or of a spirit of irreligion among the undergraduates, Green was sure to hear from him. Had it not been for this, the president might have learned from experience, might not have repeated the same mistakes over and over until the college was brought to the verge of ruin.

The session of 1812-1813 was but a few weeks old when Green's theories concerning discipline were put to the test. "Every kind of insubordination" the students could devise was indulged in. "I bore it for a short time in the hope that the offenders would be reclaimed without extreme measures," he wrote, "but at length it became insufferable."[6] After an explosion of gunpowder in Nassau Hall, the faculty dismissed three students, not because they had proof that they were concerned in this particular offense, but because their "general character and conduct" had been in a "high degree culpable." A month later, when a mischievous student forced open the door of the belfry and began ringing

[5] Ashbel Green, *Life of Ashbel Green*, p. 345.
[6] Ashbel Green, *Life of Ashbel Green*, p. 346.

the bell at three o'clock in the morning, the faculty members tumbled out of bed to hold a meeting on the spot and dismiss him.[7] This was followed by an act of "flagitious impiety" when one of the boys forced a window of the Prayer Hall and cut through the leaves and cover of the Bible to form a cavity into which he inserted a pack of playing cards.[8]

The following session opened auspiciously and for a fortnight there was perfect order. "The system I had been trying to establish seemed to have gone into complete effect," wrote the president. "I was saying to myself 'this is all I could wish.' On a sudden, without any known cause disorder commenced and there was a series of attempts in every imaginable form to promote mischief." Crackers were fired, the walls were scrawled on, there was clapping, hissing, and screaming in the refectory. This culminated on the night of January 9, 1814, with the tremendous explosion of the "big cracker." The cracker, consisting of a hollow log charged with two pounds of gunpowder, was set off behind the central door of Nassau Hall. The discharge cracked the adjacent walls from top to bottom, broke windowpanes in all parts of the building, and hurled a fragment of the log through the door of the Prayer Hall. "The merciful providence of God preserved the lives and limbs" of several persons, who had just passed that way.[9]

For two days the faculty had no clue to the perpetrators of this outrage, but at last they received word that two former students, residing in town, were concerned in making the "infernal machine." One was let off because of youth and comparative innocence and the other held for trial in the civil courts. But their seizure was the signal for further disorders, especially in the dark hallways, when the boys were on their way to or from supper. One evening Green took a lighted candle and stationed himself where he could see every student as he left the refectory. "They passed me in perfect silence and respect," he said, "but as soon as they

---

[7] *Faculty Minutes*, 1812-1820, p. 26.    [8] *Ibid.*, p. 32.
[9] Ashbel Green, *Life of Ashbel Green*, p. 361.

had got out of sight" some of them "began the usual yell."
Vice-President Slack "ran through the crowd and seized
one of the small rogues in the very act of clapping and
hallooing, took him up in his arms, brought him through
the whole corps and set him down before me." Seizing this
opportunity, Green addressed the crowd at some length, "to
try to reason, to shame and to intimidate them out of their
folly."[10]

It was a time of distress and anxiety for the president. The
discovery and punishment of those implicated in the explosion of the big cracker and the maintenance of discipline
during this time of excitement required all his ingenuity
and taxed his strength and patience. In all, eleven students
were found guilty, of whom five were expelled and the
others pardoned on promise of good behavior. "There were
crackers in the institution today, and the evening was a most
painful one to me," Green wrote in his diary on April 5.
"We met in Faculty in the room of one of the tutors and
determined to dismiss two or three of the students." "This
morning the Faculty admonished four students and dismissed
two," he wrote the next day. "I took the examination of the
senior class on belles lettres and wrote letters to the parents
of the two dismissed students. The Faculty met in the evening and a pistol was fired at the door of one of the tutors.
I ought to be very thankful to God for his support this
day."[11]

The diary continues: "April 7. Attended examination. We
had a cracker in college today and in the evening a company
of students in the front campus behaved in a very improper
manner.

"April 11. Met the Faculty and wrote a sentence for the
criminal students for tomorrow morning. This day and evening my mind has been burdened almost beyond endurance.

"April 12. I slept but little last night. Rose early, prayed
and prepared for the important business of the day. Called

[10] Ashbel Green, *Life of Ashbel Green*, p. 363.
[11] *Ibid.*, p. 373.

up and dismissed a student for writing an insolent letter to a trustee of the college.

"April 14. The students who were under discipline were called before the trustees and the board caused to be read certain resolutions. . . . The Faculty met in my study and dismissed two of the number. The remaining six called before the board and required to renounce their insubordinate principles."[12]

To any university president of today Green's handling of the problems of discipline and order would certainly seem reactionary and unenlightened. Yet he was not greatly out of step with his age. Harvard, Yale, Dartmouth, and even the progressive University of Virginia, all had their troubles from the spirit of insubordination. At Harvard the class of 1823 won notoriety for rowdyism, and its last year in college was marked by explosions in the Yard, the scraping of feet in classroom and chapel, and the drenching of tutors with buckets of ink and water. When one of the class was expelled, a group met under the Rebellion Tree and swore that they would leave college until he was reinstated, for which forty-three were dismissed on the eve of commencement.[13]

At the University of Virginia, Thomas Jefferson inaugurated an enlightened and progressive policy. "We studiously avoid too much government," he said. We treat the students "as men and gentlemen, under the guidance mainly of their own discretion." Yet in October 1825 a group of fourteen, "animated with wine" and masked to escape detection, staged a riot on the Lawn. When two professors came out of their residences to interfere they were greeted with insults and brick-bats. After this the Board of Visitors found it advisable to "add much to the strictness of their system."[14]

It is regrettable that Jefferson's policy, despite this setback, was not continued, for clearly it marked the path of

[12] Ashbel Green, *Life of Ashbel Green*, pp. 374, 375.
[13] S. E. Morison, *Three Centuries of Harvard*, pp. 230, 231.
[14] A. E. Bergh, *Writings of Thomas Jefferson*, XVIII, pp. 341-345.

future progress. But in this, as in so many other things, the Sage of Monticello was far in advance of his age. The faculties of the colleges had built up the reputation of being petty tyrants, "unfeeling, little-minded, arbitrary pedants," who delighted in imposing severe burdens and undeserved punishments on innocent youths. So, as Philip Lindsley pointed out, the students "came to college after having fought their way through the preparatory schools and acquired a reasonable share of adroitness in evading law and plaguing their teachers, anticipating a system of vigilant espionage and religious discipline, and fully prepared from the first to regard the Faculty as their enemies."[15] Obviously reform lay in removing petty restrictions, placing the burden of discipline more and more on the students themselves, and filling in the idle hours with wholesome recreation, after which it would be easy to convince the undergraduates that the professors were their friends. Unfortunately for Princeton, neither President Green nor the trustees grasped these facts, and the college continued to suffer from riots, explosions, and legal prosecutions.

Profound changes in American education were under way in the first decades of the nineteenth century, changes which were to affect the political as well as intellectual life of the people, but the trustees of the College of New Jersey either were ignorant of them, or opposed them with all their might. They were unsparing in their condemnation of Thomas Jefferson for his efforts to wrest education from the control of the religious denominations, and spoke of the University of Virginia as a center of atheism designed "to crush the institutions of religion in the state." The election of John T. Kirkland, a Unitarian, as president of Harvard, they regarded as an act of treachery to Calvinism, which bore its inevitable fruit some years later when in the faculty and administration of that old center of Puritanism there were six Unitarians, three Roman Catholics, one Lutheran, one

[15] Philip Lindsley, *An Address*, etc. (Nashville, 1825), p. 40.

Episcopalian, one Quaker, one Sandemanian, and only one Calvinist.[16]

In an age when the old intellectual springs were drying up, when teaching was becoming stereotyped and lifeless, Princeton turned its back on the new sources of inspiration coming from the German universities. It was in 1815 that Edward Everett was made professor of Greek literature at Harvard and sent to Göttingen for two years of study, in company with the brilliant young George Ticknor. Here a new world opened to the two Americans. They were impressed by the boundless erudition and critical acumen of the German scholars, by the flexibility of the curriculum, by the freedom of inquiry. There were visits to Weimar, to Paris, to Rome, to Venice; interviews with Goethe, Madame de Staël, Sir Walter Scott, Lord Byron. On returning to Harvard they were brimful of enthusiasm, eager to share with students and friends their new interests and discoveries. Emerson went so far as to say that Everett's influence at Cambridge was "comparable to that of Pericles at Athens."[17] But the trustees and president of Princeton looked only to Burr, Davies, and Witherspoon for their models, forgetting that these men had drawn their inspiration largely from Europe and that they had all been innovators who had not been afraid to break with the past.

It is true that in 1825 the board appointed to the chair of languages Robert B. Patton, a graduate of Göttingen, and a man of high scholarly attainments. Imbued with the German methods, his first step was to organize the Nassau Hall Philological Society to which he turned over his private library, which James W. Alexander declared the finest he had ever seen. "He has the best editions ancient and modern of all the classics . . . a uniform edition of the whole range of Italian literature and all of the German writers of eminence. His collection of atlases and plates is noble indeed."[18]

[16] S. E. Morison, *Three Centuries of Harvard*, pp. 196, 197, 257.
[17] *Ibid.*, pp. 226-227.
[18] John Hall, *Familiar Letters of James W. Alexander*, p. 88.

The meetings of the society for discussion, criticism, lectures, and illustration created a new "tone of literary excitement," which broke like a ray of light upon the usual round of classes. It was Patton who inspired the senior class to prepare an edition of the *Seven Against Thebes*, which was published by the local printer. But this awakening was short-lived. The trustees lowered the salaries of the professors, Patton resigned to take charge of Edgehill, the preparatory school at Princeton, and once more dullness settled over the atmosphere of Nassau Hall.[19]

As for the curriculum, it remained a hodgepodge of poorly related subjects—Greek, Latin, astronomy, belles-lettres, navigation, logic, geography, mathematics, physics, philosophy, chemistry, religious history—which every student had to take regardless of his tastes, desires, and future career. This was at a time when Thomas Jefferson had pointed the way to better things by inaugurating the elective system at the University of Virginia. "We shall certainly vary from the practice of holding the students to one prescribed course of reading and disallowing exclusive application to those branches only which are to qualify them for the particular vocations to which they are destined," he wrote George Ticknor. "We shall, on the contrary, allow them uncontrolled choice in the lectures they shall choose to attend."[20]

At Princeton as elsewhere there was urgent need for the raising of standards. Although the youths who sought admission were often only thirteen or fourteen years of age, most of them went directly into the sophomore class. In the class of 1825, out of a student body of 107 there were only six freshmen. "Boys are sent too early to college," wrote James W. Alexander. "I think boys should leave school about the same age that they usually leave college, i.e. about eighteen. . . . Let the standard of college attainments be elevated far above the present degree. Let the servile work of learning

[19] John Maclean, *History of the College of New Jersey*, II, p. 277.
[20] Thomas Jefferson, *Writings*, XV, p. 455.

to read Latin and Greek be kept to the schools. . . . I would have the students learn in college the higher branches of education—the higher mathematics if his taste let him pursue it, the philosophy of the mind, ethics, natural law, political economy and the classics."[21] Unfortunately, the faculty dared not follow this advice, for they feared an advance in standards might bring a reduction in attendance and thereby enhance the already acute financial problem.

In this period of retrogression, when the president and trustees seemed either blind to the needs of the college or incapable of meeting them—a larger endowment, more professorships, better teaching, better equipment, fresh intellectual springs, national rather than denominational control, a saner policy in maintaining discipline—there was among the faculty members one of the most progressive and ablest educational thinkers in the country. Philip Lindsley, the son of an Englishman of a distinguished family, studied under Robert Finley, graduated from Princeton when eighteen, became a tutor in 1807, studied theology under Samuel Stanhope Smith, and in 1817 became vice-president of the college.[22] Despite his sensitiveness and nervous temperament, he was an interesting teacher and profound scholar. Amidst all the tumults in Nassau Hall, all the harsh repressive measures of the faculty and trustees, the students always respected Lindsley as their friend and trusted adviser.

Such was the man who drew up for the colleges a program which, had they followed it, would have advanced American higher education by decades. Let us borrow some ideas from the new Swiss schools, he wrote, something from the ancient Greeks and Romans, something from our military academies at Norwich and West Point, something from the pages of Locke, Milton, and other writers, something from common sense, from old and existing institutions. From the ancients he drew his ideas on college athletics. Their schools were centers of sports and games, he pointed out. "Inured to labor,

[21] John Hall, *Familiar Letters of James W. Alexander*, p. 9.
[22] John Maclean, *History of the College of New Jersey*, II, pp. 239-243.

to athletic exercises, to temperance, to study, to every species of bodily and mental effort, their youth entered upon the duties of manhood . . . with the strength of Hercules and wisdom of Minerva." In contrast, the modern colleges cultivated only the mind and neglected the body. Consequently, our youth were becoming so "delicate" and "bookish" as to be ill-equipped for life.

It was this, Lindsley thought, which was largely responsible for the disorderly conduct of the undergraduates. They could not spend their entire time in study, yet they were left to devise their own amusements. So their spare moments were often wasted in lounging, talking, smoking, and sedentary games, if not in dissipation, drinking, and gaming. The colleges, he thought, should provide "complete employment of a proper kind for all the time of every individual. Keep your youth busy and you keep them out of harm's way." Lindsley did not state what form of athletics he advocated, but he obviously had in mind running, jumping, wrestling, and other sports practiced by the Greeks and Romans.[23]

Even more remarkable was his suggestion of student self-help. The poor at a college could supply their needs by labor in the shop, the field, the garden, he said. This would not lead to a neglect of studies, for the poor lad would learn more in half his time than the rich in all of his. Nor would the plan degrade the poor, for they would learn to despise the *petits maîtres* who might affect to be their superiors. They would be the fashion. They would conform to established usage. And they would be respectable just in proportion to their modest, fearless, independent conformity to their actual condition. How much more truly respectable and republican would be their condition while thus laboring for the food of body and mind.[24] It would have been gratifying to Lindsley could he have foreseen that this suggestion would one day be adopted by practically every college in the country

[23] Philip Lindsley, *Inauguration Address* (Nashville, 1825), pp. 24, 25.
[24] *Ibid.*, pp. 27-30.

and become one of the distinguishing features of American education.

Lindsley saw clearly that the American colleges could make little progress so long as they were hampered by lack of funds, their equipment inadequate, the professors over-worked, giving most of their vitality to the dull routine of classwork and to spying on the students. The time would come, he predicted, when they would have "such an array of able professors, such libraries and apparatus, such cabinets of curiosities and of natural history, such botanical gardens, astronomical observatories and chemical laboratories as to vie with the oldest and noblest European universities." Then it would be possible for the teacher to drink anew at the fountain of learning, then the student would find fresh inspiration aside from the assigned reading and regular lectures. There should be easy access to every species of information, the pupils should breathe an intellectual atmosphere, live in a learned society, witness new experiments, share with the professors their enthusiasms, their thirst for knowledge. Then how liberal and enlarged would be their views, how widened their horizon! Then the college would have attained its purpose—the purpose of imparting quickness in investigation, patience in research, strength to grapple with difficulties, accuracy in thought, refinement in taste, vivid perception of beauty.[25]

To what extent Lindsley discussed his educational policies with President Green or the trustees we do not know. It is remarkable that they should have this advanced educational thinker at their elbows for years and profit so little from his advice. His inaugural address as president of the University of Nashville, in which he embodied his ideas, remained in the Princeton library more than a century before its pages were cut. But Green was not interested in Lindsley's theories. His hopes were centered on restoring the atmosphere of piety which once had prevailed in Nassau Hall; in organizing Sunday schools, Bible societies, and tract societies.

[25] *Ibid.*, pp. 34-37.

During the winter of 1814-1815, to Green's great joy, a wave of religious sentiment swept through the college. "The divine influence seemed to descend like the silent dew of heaven," he wrote, "and in about four weeks there were few individuals in the college edifice who were not deeply impressed with a sense of the importance of spiritual and eternal things." In many a chamber, where formerly mischievous youths plotted to burn an outhouse or to set off crackers in the lecture rooms, there was now earnest prayer or anxious discussions of religious matters. The students of divinity, usually despised and snubbed by their classmates, were sought after and requested to lead in prayer-meetings. The president happened to be ill at the time and could not stand in the pulpit, so that he was forced to deliver his sermons while seated, but the professors of the theological seminary assisted him with repeated sermons, exhortations and private conferences. "It was a period never to be forgotten by those who witnessed its remarkable impressions and transformations." Green reported that more than forty students had become "the subjects of renewing grace" and that twelve or fifteen more had received "promising impressions of religion." Of the remainder a large proportion showed a hopeful "tenderness of conscience" and a deep "regard to religious duties." "I believe there were never such times in Nassau Hall before," wrote a visitor, "the old college is literally a Bethel."[26]

Green ascribed the revival to the Bible studies which he had introduced in the curriculum two years previously; to the moral discipline of Nassau Hall "vigorously and vigilantly maintained" which had "preserved the youth generally" from those "vicious indulgences" which counteract all serious religious impressions; to the influence of a few pious students who spoke "privately and tenderly" to their friends on the subject of religion.[27] But the impulse seems to

[26] *Princeton Library MSS*, AM 8791.
[27] Ashbel Green, *Report on the Revival of Religion*, 1815 (Philadelphia, 1815).

have come from without as part of a widespread religious movement among undergraduates in the American colleges. In addition to "the revival of religion at Yale college, Dartmouth and Andover have also been visited with a season of refreshing," wrote Daniel Baker of the class of 1815. "I am informed that a society has been formed amongst the students in Yale with the express and specific object of praying for a revival in Cambridge."[28]

To Green it seemed that his fondest hopes had been realized, that his policies had been justified, that all his problems of discipline had vanished. "Through the last session your officers have indeed enjoyed halcyon days," he reported triumphantly to the trustees at the end of the session. "They have experienced no ordinary pleasure in directing the studies and conduct of liberal-minded youth, who have emulated each other in seeking their own improvement, in giving pleasure to their teachers, in obedience to the laws. I consider the youth who form our present charge as decidedly the most amiable and exemplary that I have ever seen. The public sentiment of the College, so far from being hostile to discipline, had called for it."[29] When some "spiteful youth," to show his opposition to religion, fired a cracker, it filled the student body with "abhorrence and detestation."[30]

But Nassau Hall did not remain long under the influence of the religious reawakening. In September 1815 a large number of the converts graduated, others had dropped out because of bad health, still others because they could not keep up in their work; and of the new admissions Green considered many "bad in morals and religion."[31] Before the new session had been under way many weeks as many crackers were going off as in the old evil days. A ray of hope appeared in mid-winter, when "almost every member of the house, profane as well as the pious, seemed to be held in still and solemn suspense, waiting for and expecting another religious revival."

[28] *Princeton Library MSS*, AM 11292.
[29] Ashbel Green, *Life of Ashbel Green*, p. 379.
[30] *Ibid.*, pp. 379-380.          [31] *Ibid.*, p. 385.

But the clouds gathered again, the revival failed to material-
ize, and the students returned to the old provoking disorders.

In January 1817 this culminated in one of the most serious riots in the turbulent history of Nassau Hall. The students, considering their assigned reading too long, showed
their resentment in the traditional violent way. On Sunday,
January 19, in the early hours of the morning they nailed up
all entrances to the building together with the doors of the
chambers of the tutors and the religious students. Then
rushing up to the top floor, yelling "Rebellion! Rebellion!
Fire! Fire," they broke windowpanes, rang the bell inces-
santly and created a scene of the wildest disorder. Vice-
President Slack rushed across the campus and, finding every
door secure, broke out several panes in one of the basement
windows, crawled through and ran upstairs. One of the
rioters hurled a "flint glass decanter" at his head but he
hastened on his way with the remark: "Ah! You missed your
aim!" As he appeared among them the boys blew out their
candles and fled, but not before he had jotted down the
names of a dozen or more.[32]

But every student who was summoned before the faculty
protested his innocence. "We were awakened by the noise
and ran out of our rooms to see what was the matter," they
said, "but we had no part in the mischief." Green was non-
plused until a student, no doubt one of his favorite pious
youths, came to his study and, going over the roll of the
college, "pointed out all that were disaffected."[33] Against
these Green decided to proceed, acting on the principle that
since the students were adamant in refusing to testify against
their fellows, the interests of the institution demanded that
in some cases punishment had to be meted out "without
formal proof." Hearing that plans were afoot for another
riot "which should cast entirely into shade all that had been
done" before, he decided to anticipate the trouble. So, call-

[32] *Princeton Library MSS*, BF 561, AM 494.
[33] Ashbel Green, *Life of Ashbel Green*, p. 392.

ing "the most criminal" before him one by one, he dismissed no fewer than fourteen.[34]

This aroused the entire student body to a vigorous protest. Forcing open the door of the Prayer Hall the boys crowded in, elected a chairman, and passed resolutions demanding a rehearing for the dismissed students in which only "regular testimony" was to be considered in determining their fate. When the faculty remained firm, bedlam broke forth. The college resounded with yells, interspersed with the reports of pistols and the crash of glass, doors were broken down, the walls were scrawled with charcoal, the pulpit in the Prayer Hall was partly demolished, the hallways were barricaded with firewood. At intervals the students could be seen jumping out of the windows to march around in the college yard, brandishing their clubs and dirks. Expecting an attack from a posse of citizens, they prepared to defend themselves by hurling firewood from the windows.[35] Vice-President Slack, whom they found stalking up and down on the first floor of Nassau Hall with a club in his hands, they drove before them to one of the doors and pushed him out. President Green, after a piece of ice had been thrown on his head from an upper window, took refuge on his study steps, where he stood shaking his cane at the rioters. At this moment Professor Lindsley appeared on the scene, "and he being very much respected by them, they all collected about him to hear what he had to say." But even he could not persuade them to submit to the faculty ruling and return quietly to work.[36]

As residence in Nassau Hall became more and more uncomfortable "the virtuous students" one by one got permission to leave, until the building was deserted by almost all save the principal rioters. Of these seven were arrested and held for trial in the courts. How unwise this was is shown by the letter of an irate parent, whose son was saved from prison "only through the kindness of a stranger." The boy

[34] *Princeton Library MSS*, BF 561.    [35] *Ibid.*
[36] *Princeton Library MSS*, AM 493.

had been detected in the act of yelling in Nassau Hall and President Green had concluded from this that he "belonged to the combination of rioters." Yet the court dismissed him for lack of any real evidence. This was such a manifest breach of authority by the president as might be a subject of inquiry in a court of law, said the father. "Certainly parents do not anticipate when sending their children to a seminary of learning, to find stern and rigid accusers and judges in place of friends and protectors."[37]

"The true causes of all these enormities are to be found nowhere else but in the fixed, irreconcilable and deadly hostility . . . to the whole system established in this college by its chartered legislators and guardians," wrote President Green, "a system of diligent study, of guarded moral conduct and of reasonable attention to religious duty. . . . The more carefully such a system is administered, the more offensive it will be rendered to such youth. A perfect administration will be the most offensive of all. . . . The tornado which has struck us, though it was violent and in passing shook us rudely, yet has carried away in its sweep much of the concealed taint of moral pestilence and left us a purer atmosphere."[38]

This was at a time when other long-established institutions were forging ahead with enlarged faculties, better equipment, and increased student bodies, and when new colleges were springing up in regions from which Princeton had drawn many of her undergraduates. "People are asking why is the college at Princeton on the decline," one writer asked. "Why are the students less numerous and the state of her finances less flourishing than in years that are past? By some it is attributed solely to the character of those into whose hands the government and instruction of the institution has fallen; by others to the expense of living; by others to the disorders and irregularities of the students."[39] Some there

[37] J. R. Cox to the Board of Trustees, 1817, *Maclean MSS*, Princeton Library.
[38] *Princeton Library MSS*, BF 561.
[39] *Princeton Library MSS*, AM 2564.

must have been who realized that deeper still lay the drying up of sources of financial support because of the strict denominational control of the college, the alienation of its friends by the outmoded system of discipline, the stagnation of both teaching and scholarship because of the reactionary educational policies, the making of religion rather than education the chief aim of the institution.

It is significant that in 1817 Green spent most of the autumn vacation in Philadelphia soliciting funds, not for the college of which he was president, but for the theological seminary. The $4,400 which he succeeded in raising would have been a godsend to the institution which paid his salary and to which his chief allegiance was due.[40] It is true that during the following summer he renewed the old attempt to secure aid from the New Jersey legislature, making several visits to Trenton, attending the sessions, buttonholing delegates, dining with the governor and presenting the old arguments. But the politicians still remembered "the kicking out" of those who voted for the $4,800 appropriation of 1796, and "from a desire to retain their places refused to patronize the college."[41]

So once more hope of new professorships, new buildings, better scientific apparatus had to be abandoned. At this time the general fund yielded about $200 a year, the vice-president's fund about $500, the fund for the education of poor and pious youths about $775, tuition and room rent about $6,500, or a total income of about $8,500, less than $8,000 of which was available for salaries and current expenses.[42] A very small sum, this, on which to run a college, so much too small that there could be little hope of expansion and growth until it had been tripled or quadrupled.

Throughout most of Green's administration the faculty consisted of a president, vice-president, one professor, and two tutors. In 1817, when word came to Mr. Slack's ears that he had been sharply criticized by certain trustees follow-

[40] Ashbel Green, *Life of Ashbel Green*, p. 403.     [41] *Ibid.*, p. 423.
[42] *Maclean MSS*, 1813, Princeton Library; *Trustees Minutes*, II, p. 351.

ing his undignified antics during the riot, he handed in his resignation. Thereupon the board made Lindsley vice-president and called in Henry Vethake, of Queen's College, as professor of natural philosophy and chemistry. The next year, encouraged by an increase in the number of students they created the chair of experimental philosophy, chemistry, and natural history and invited the president's son, Jacob Green, to fill it.

In 1821 Professor Vethake resigned to accept an appointment at Dickinson College. Vethake was an able teacher and scholar and President Green would perhaps have insisted upon his remaining at Princeton had he not been offended by what he considered a personal slight. At the time he little realized that he was paving the way for his own retirement. When the board took up the matter of filling Vethake's chair, they decided to reduce expenses by combining it with Jacob Green's chair to form the professorship of mathematics and natural philosophy. Since Green was not prepared to teach mathematics, this action was tantamount to his dismissal. President Green protested. He told the trustees "respectfully but plainly" that if there was any objection to his son to set him aside at once, but not to destroy the professorship. The college could not prosper "unless the elements of chemistry, now become an important and favored science, should be a part of the system of education and unless experiments should be made in illustration of the several parts of natural philosophy." When the board persisted in their course, the president decided to resign. "I cannot remain responsible for the college when my views are overruled," he said.[43]

The usual amenities followed. "I am conscious of having endeavored for ten years past to discharge my duties with fidelity and often with anxieties and exertions, which I ought never to recollect without lively gratitude to God that he sustained me under them," Green wrote the board. In reply the board expressed their respect for his "ministerial character," his unwearied exertions to promote the best interests of

---

[43] Ashbel Green, *Life of Ashbel Green*, pp. 427, 428.

the students, and thanked him for the "zeal, fidelity and wisdom" of his administration. Yet it is obvious that Green's resignation was not only acceptable to the board, but was actually forced.

His administration had been a failure. Appointed to the presidency to "reform" the college, to restore the old atmosphere of piety and its reputation in the church, his efforts had resulted only in antagonizing the students and bringing the institution into further disrepute. During his regime the disorders in Nassau Hall reached their zenith; scholarship and teaching their nadir. It was a deep humiliation to Green that the man who had been chiefly responsible for his appointment should witness his failure. "Dr. Miller made a communication to me in regard to the state of the college which alarmed me and affected me much," he wrote in his diary in August 1818.[44]

Ashbel Green was a man of many fine qualities. John Maclean, who knew him well, says: "He was a truly great, good, humble and devout man. . . . He was conscientious and upright, free from deceit and even from the appearance of it."[45] Samuel Miller spoke of him as "a sincere, ardent, faithful friend," a man of unfeigned piety.[46] But his selection as president of the college was a mistake. At a time when there was need for new educational policies to meet the requirements of the rapidly changing nation, he had nothing to offer, and at his retirement the fortunes of the college had sunk so low that for several years it was feared by many of its friends that it would have to close its doors.

With the going of Green a great opportunity opened to the trustees. The logical choice was Vice-President Lindsley, whose election would have placed the college under the leadership of one of the ablest educators in America. But Lindsley had incurred the hostility of several members of the board by an address in which he stigmatized as narrow and

[44] *Ibid.*, p. 418.
[45] John Maclean, *History of the College of New Jersey*, II, p. 226.
[46] *Princeton Library MSS*, AM 3522.

dogmatic the minister who had not been to a theological school but had been privately trained. "With a little smattering of letters and with abundant self-complacency he marches forth . . . and continues through life the same opinionated, bigoted creature that he was at the beginning."[47] He could hardly have had any of the trustees in mind when he wrote this but he struck so near home with several of them that they never forgave him. So, when he intimated that he did not wish his name to be placed in nomination for the presidency, the board, with a sigh of relief, cast a unanimous vote for the Reverend John H. Rice of Richmond, Virginia.

But Rice declined, declaring that he was unfitted by disposition, habits, and attainment to govern a college and that he believed that he could be most useful in the south.[48] This threw the responsibility of the administration on Lindsley's shoulders for the session of 1822-1823, without the prestige or authority of the president's office, with not a single professor to advise him, aided in his teaching only by four tutors —John Maclean, Jr., Samuel K. Talmage, Alfred A. Sowers and George Bush—most of them young and inexperienced. Yet his ability as a teacher, his enthusiasm and, most of all, his popularity with the students carried him through triumphantly. An address to the undergraduates at the opening of the session had an especially happy influence and even the usually rowdy winter term went by without disorder, so that he "gained universal approbation."[49]

When the trustees assembled on April 8, 1823, Lindsley's claims could no longer be ignored. The friends of the college, the students, and the tutors were singing his praises; his reputation as a teacher and scholar had spread to all parts of the country, he had just been invited to assume the presidency of the University of Nashville. Lindsley himself thought that he "stood on high ground."[50] So, with only a few irrecon-

[47] Philip Lindsley, *A Plea for the Theological Seminary*, p. 15.
[48] John Maclean, *History of the College of New Jersey*, II, p. 228.
[49] John Hall, *Familiar Letters of James W. Alexander*, p. 21.
[50] *Princeton Library MSS*, AM 2157.

cilables voting against him, the board yielded and elected him president. But Lindsley hesitated. The task of bringing the college out of the depths to which it had sunk, of raising funds, expanding the faculty, inspiring the lifeless teaching, putting an end to the disorders which by this time had taken on the strength of tradition—all this in itself was a tremendously difficult task; it might be impossible with a group of trustees ready to criticize him and render his efforts futile.

What he had to expect is shown by the report of a committee of the trustees that during the session he had been acting president students had been seen clustering about tavern doors, drinking, and sitting up late at night. Against this charge John Maclean, who "knew more of the state of the college at that time than did any one or all the members of the committee," long afterward made a flat denial. He would not say that the author of the report was influenced by personal hostility to the acting president, but he intimated that such was the case.[51]

Since Lindsley asked for time to make up his mind, the board adjourned until May 12 and then sent a committee to demand his final answer. They found him still undecided, anxious to accept, yet fearing that he was not really wanted. A word of encouragement, an assurance that he would have the united support of the trustees would have decided him and given Princeton a truly great president. But the committee did nothing to aid him and, when he finally declined, accepted his decision with alacrity. Lindsley was bitter. "Is it possible that the Board should ever have really wished me to be the President of Nassau Hall, and yet to allow me only four weeks . . . to decide?" he wrote. "Could they unite last fall . . . in the choice of a man wholly unknown to most of them, while in regard to me who had been all my life in their service and who had at least for one year governed the college, they could not make up their minds hastily and when in a sort made up, demand an answer, yes or no, off hand? And when 'no' is in

[51] John Maclean, *History of the College of New Jersey*, II, pp. 234, 235.

a measure extorted, to seize upon it with an eagerness which has no parallel."[52]

The next year Lindsley left Princeton to accept the presidency of the University of Nashville, where he remained twenty-six years, playing a notable role in the educational life of the south. In 1826 he wrote Robert Baird: "Our college is flourishing in every respect far beyond my anticipations. . . . I honestly think that in matters of instruction and government we are already far ahead of dear old Alma Mater."[53] Perhaps no other man in the history of the United States has been offered the presidency of so many colleges as Philip Lindsley, for he was elected twice by Transylvania, three times by the University of Nashville, twice by the University of Alabama, once each by the University of Pennsylvania,[54] Washington College,[55] Dickinson, the College of Louisiana, South Alabama College, and Princeton.[56]

On May 12, 1823, when the trustees received word that Lindsley had declined to accept the presidency, they unanimously elected the Reverend James Carnahan of Georgetown, D.C.[57] Carnahan was an amiable, honest, unassuming man, a successful preacher and teacher. After years as pastor in western New York he resigned because of ill health and later opened a classical school at Georgetown. To the invitation of the trustees he replied: "With much trembling I have determined to accept the high and responsible office. . . . I will devote to the interests of that institution whatever abilities I possess."[58] This promise he kept faithfully and for thirty-one years he remained the titular head of the college, during which time marked and important advances were made. Yet he was not an able administrator, not an inspiring educational leader, and his chief merit was his ready acceptance of constructive measures when they were suggested by others.

[52] *Princeton Library MSS*, AM 2157.
[53] *Princeton Library MSS*, AM 2158.
[54] Elected Provost.     [55] Now Washington and Lee.
[56] John Maclean, *History of the College of New Jersey*, II, p. 243.
[57] *Princeton Library MSS*, AM 8433.
[58] John Maclean, *History of the College of New Jersey*, II, p. 247.

Carnahan's administration opened auspiciously, for the students showed their good will by marching in a body several miles out of town to meet him and escort him to Princeton. To assist and advise him during his first year he had not only Vice-President Lindsley but also John Maclean, who had just been made professor of mathematics, Talmage and Sowers, the two tutors, and the Reverend Luther Halsey, who taught natural philosophy, chemistry, and natural history during the first term. But Carnahan was not long in discovering that his path was not to be smooth. He had been led to believe that he would have the united support of the trustees, but he found such "conflicting views and interests of certain parties" that he was tempted to resign and return to Georgetown.[59] As for the old spirit of insubordination among the students, his first session was but a few weeks old when it became as manifest as ever.

It was in December 1823 that Nassau Hall was alarmed by the explosion of a large cracker. Rushing out of their rooms into the hallway the tutors found a student shouting "at the top of his voice." Thereupon the faculty convened and, without giving the youth a hearing, suspended him. When the president called him in to announce this decision, the boy was greatly surprised. He had had no part in preparing and firing the cracker, he insisted, and his shouting was meant as an expression not of approval but of disapproval and indignation.[60] Unpleasant repercussions followed. The undergraduates called a meeting, drew up a remonstrance, and demanded the restoration of their fellow student. When told that no communication "respecting any act of discipline could be received from a committee of the college," they met again to voice their indignation. In the midst of great excitement Professor Maclean entered the room and ordered the chairman to leave his seat. But he refused to budge, and his fellow students voted that the meeting would support him and "share his fate." So when he and two others were suspended many declared themselves bound in honor to leave college. The

[59] *Ibid.*, p. 396.    [60] *Ibid.*, p. 252.

faculty gave them permission to go and remitted part of their board and room rent, but most of them were promptly returned by their parents.[61] "I cannot but regard the meeting that took place with the students in order to dictate to the faculty as an act of rebellion that ought to have been severely punished," wrote one father. "The fact is simply and plainly this—that a parcel of young lads of the ages of sixteen to eighteen, well clothed, well fed and money in their pockets cannot be managed in any other way than by the most decided measures."[62] Yet President Carnahan later admitted that the student "suspended for hallooing" had had no part in exploding the cracker and that to punish him without a hearing was unjust and unwise. He determined, then, that he would never again agree to suspend a student without affording him an opportunity to be heard.

The incident proved even more injurious to the college than some of the more violent riots which preceded it. The public began to believe that the students of Nassau Hall were incorrigible, that it was impossible to maintain order no matter who was president. "I feel much concerned for the reputation of my beloved Alma Mater," wrote John Lador of King George County, Virginia. "Various stories are circulated throughout this State by those students who have arrived from Princeton in consequence of the late unhappy affair calculated to injure the interests of the college."[63]

It was with alarm that the trustees, the president and the faculty noted the gradual falling off in the number of students. In 1825 the catalogue showed 107 matriculates; during the winter session of 1827-1828 the highest number was seventy-one. When two youngsters went to a "frolic in the suburbs" and remained out until one o'clock in the morning, they were merely fined five dollars apiece, since "the faculty felt somewhat averse to suspend, from a view of the present diminished

[61] *Faculty Minutes*, 1820-1835, pp. 80, 81.
[62] Edward Thompson to John Maclean, December 16, 1823, *Maclean MSS*, Princeton Library.
[63] *Maclean MSS*, 1824, Princeton Library.

numbers."[64] The founding and rapid growth of colleges in the south no doubt accounted for a part of the decline, but it could not explain why at the opening of the academic year coach after coach rolled through Princeton laden with youths from Virginia, South Carolina, or Georgia heading for Yale or Harvard.

"The friends of the college are now anxious to extend its patronage by all fair means," wrote Isaac V. Brown of the class of 1802 to a friend in Savannah. "You probably know that the southern interest and especially the Georgian has been of late pretty much withdrawn from Princeton. Could you not . . . do something to restore to us the attention of gentlemen in Savannah and the surrounding towns and country? They ought not wholly to neglect their own state institutions, but since they continue sending their sons to the North, they cannot commit them to a government more worthy of their confidence than that of Nassau Hall. Cambridge is full of contagion and Yale overrun with numbers."[65]

It was unfortunate that Princeton had acquired the reputation of being a rich man's college where expenses were excessive, and though the board had been at some pains to refute this impression, it influenced many fathers to send their sons elsewhere. So in 1827 the trustees decided to reduce board to two dollars a week and tuition to $20 a year. The loss of revenue which this entailed would be more than offset, so it was hoped, by a large increase in numbers.[66]

But, far from increasing, the number of matriculates continued its steady decline, the maximum for the summer term, 1827, being eighty and for the session of 1827-1828 only seventy-one. The total receipts in 1826-1827 were about $6,575 and expenses $6,900, leaving a deficit of about $325. The next year matters were worse, and when income dropped to about $6,147 and the deficit mounted to $753, the trustees

[64] *Faculty Minutes*, 1820-1835, p. 171.

[65] *Princeton Library MSS*, AM 9783: There were forty-one Southerners in a student body of 107 at Princeton in 1824-1825, of whom two were from Georgia.

[66] John Maclean, *History of the College of New Jersey*, II, p. 272.

became seriously alarmed. They considered it unwise to persist in a course which would "speedily exhaust the little fund accumulated with so much care and difficulty and deemed of so much importance to the prosperity and even permanence of the college." In this dilemma they decided, most reluctantly, to reduce salaries, by which means they effected a saving of $1,130. This balanced the budget temporarily, but it wrecked the faculty, for both Professors Patton and Halsey resigned. It was with profound regret that Patton gave up his stimulating teaching and his philological society, but he could not support his family on his reduced income.[67] Thus Princeton lost one of the ablest scholars and teachers in the country, one whose contagious enthusiasm was desperately needed in the humdrum life of Nassau Hall.

At this critical juncture, when it seemed that the end was close at hand, it was fortunate that there was one member of the faculty who had enough vision and initiative to point out the road to recovery. While the trustees were at their wits' end and President Carnahan was content to let matters drift, John Maclean drew up and submitted a plan for the replacement of Patton and Halsey so that the instruction could go on with the essential courses in the hands of competent scholars and teachers. This plan, which after some modifications was adopted, called for the reengagement of Henry Vethake, who was now willing to return from Dickinson to conduct the courses in mathematics; the appointment of Albert Baldwin Dod, a brilliant young scholar who was serving as tutor, as teacher of natural philosophy; the employment of Professor John Torrey of the Medical College of New York, as lecturer on chemistry, and of Lewis Hargous as teacher of modern languages. To make this arrangement possible Maclean himself agreed to transfer his field from mathematics to ancient languages and literature.[68]

When Maclean presented this plan to President Carnahan he gave his hearty assent. The trustees, on the other hand,

[67] Patton to Trustees, August 11, 1829, *Maclean MSS*, Princeton Library.
[68] John Maclean, *History of the College of New Jersey*, II, pp. 278-282.

hesitated because of the additional expense involved, and several of the most influential were in favor of reuniting the chairs of mathematics, natural philosophy, and chemistry. But Maclean, believing that this was the counsel of despair which would lead to a further reduction in numbers, refused to consent to it, and both he and Carnahan resolved to resign should it be insisted upon. Fortunately, the trustees, humbled by the complete failure of their own policies, yielded and the appointments were made. After this, Maclean points out with justifiable pride, "the number of students rapidly increased . . . until in the academic year of 1860-61 it reached 314."[69]

Helpful as was this recasting of the faculty and the appointment of such distinguished scholars as Vethake, Dod, and Torrey, it was not, as Maclean intimates, the turning point in the history of the college. This could come only with the utilization of some new source of support, some means of building up the small endowment. The cost of educating each student was much greater than the $52 a year paid for tuition and room rent, so that when every room in Nassau Hall had been occupied and the courses filled to capacity, additional matriculates became a liability rather than an asset. To construct new buildings, add needed volumes to the library, create additional professorships, purchase scientific apparatus, assistance from some outside source was urgently needed.

This, it came to be recognized, must come from the alumni. Despite the frequent disorders, the occasional bitterness against the faculty, the dullness of courses, the monotony of life in Nassau Hall, the student took away with him from college many close friendships, many happy recollections. The pranks which seemed so serious to the president or the trustees were usually fun to the undergraduates. In after days, when two or more got together, they loved to bring up these incidents and to boast how they had outwitted "Old Johnny" Maclean or "Boss" Carnahan. The

[69] *Ibid.*, p. 280.

close association of students in an institution where they all
ate together, attended prayers together twice a day, roomed
in the same building, went to classes together, built up a spirit
of camaraderie which persisted throughout life.

"My jovial hours at Nassau Hall . . . I shall always consider my happiest," wrote James W. Alexander. "I often
recall a merry circle of careless college blades seated about
'the witching time of night' around a Nassau fire, by the way
a preeminently good one, enveloped in fragrant clouds, en-
joying all that flow of youthful hilarity and good humor
which a release from irksome duty engenders. . . . In my
hours of twilight musing and castle-building I often read
in a bed of glowing coals the almost faded story of these old
times and picture to myself the future various destinies of
my old friends and classmates."

Commencement had already taken on the character of a
reunion in which classmates greeted each other, swapped
news of old friends and lived again the experiences of college days. "My old college friends and our family acquaint-
ances are already pouring in," wrote one alumnus in 1823.
"It is gratifying to meet after the lapse of two or three
years even those companions in study who were never intimates or confidants. Some of my friends . . . have already
begun to fill some space in the public eye."[70]

It was a momentous event in the history of Princeton
when a group of alumni assembled during the commencement of 1826 and organized the Alumni Association of
Nassau Hall. With the Honorable Henry W. Edwards,
United States senator from Connecticut, in the chair and
with Professor Maclean as secretary, the meeting proceeded
to draw up a constitution and elect officers. The object of the
association was declared to be "to promote the interests of
the college and the friendly intercourse of its graduates,"
and meetings were to be held annually in the Prayer Hall
on commencement day. They then elected James Madison
president, and instructed the secretary to write a circular

[70] John Hall, *Familiar Letters of James W. Alexander*, p. 19.

letter to the alumni, announcing the formation of the association and requesting their cooperation.[71]

At last, after eighty years, the alumni had been organized and steps had been taken to capitalize the college's greatest asset—the love and loyalty of its sons. Before the formation of the alumni association individual alumni had made gifts to the college, and many had contributed generously to the rebuilding of Nassau Hall in 1802. But there had been no coordinated effort, no organized campaign for the endowment of professorships or the erection of buildings. And even though the first efforts of the association to raise funds were not very successful, it was vitally important that a beginning had been made.

Important, also, was the fact that in measure as they contributed to the upbuilding of the college, the alumni demanded a voice in its management and its educational policies. This influence they used, on the whole, wisely. It was the alumni who brought about the secularizing of Princeton, the gradual weakening of denominational control. Slowly, almost imperceptibly, the needs of the nation rather than those of the church received consideration in the curriculum and teaching. The change did not take place without opposition. John Maclean, who himself had been so instrumental in creating the alumni association, expressed the earnest wish that it might "not be a hindrance to our venerable and beloved college," but aid the trustees to make it more and more useful, "especially to the Church of God for whose special interest it was originally established."[72]

Despite all the blunders of the period from 1812 to 1829, despite the opportunities which were missed, despite the disorders, the ill-formed curriculum, the dullness of the teaching, the falling off in the number of students, the lack of vision by trustees and faculty, the period was by no means sterile, for the college continued to send out men who won distinction in every line of endeavor. Of the 356 graduates

[71] *Princeton Library MSS*, AM 795.
[72] John Maclean, *History of the College of New Jersey*, II, p. 364.

during Green's administration, twenty became college presidents, four United States Senators, eleven United States Representatives, one a cabinet officer, one a minister in the diplomatic service, one a major-general, four governors of states, twelve federal or state judges, sixteen distinguished ministers of the Gospel.

# CHAPTER VI

# Life in Nassau Hall
## 1790-1830

**I**T was an eventful day for the entering freshman, especially if he lived in a state remote from Princeton, when he told his father and mother goodbye, turned his back on home, and set out to begin his college career. In the family coach with him was his chest, filled with clothing, a few books, and perhaps a box of delicacies; in his pocket a letter to Dr. Witherspoon, or Samuel Stanhope Smith, or Ashbel Green. A journey of hundreds of miles might lie before him, marked by changes from stage wagon to stage boat and back again to stage coach, by dangerous ferry trips over great rivers, by nights in uncomfortable wayside taverns. But however fearful the youngster was at heart he kept a brave face befitting a young man of fifteen. Traveling was full of interest, and he gazed wide-eyed as he passed woods and fields and villages, or as the coach stopped to change horses, or to take on passengers. Yet it was usually a tired and homesick boy who arrived at Princeton and engaged a bed for the night at the Sign of the College.

The next morning the freshman had to gather all his courage to cross the street to the President's House, present his letter and face the professors and tutors for the ordeal of entrance examinations. These over, he hastened out with a burden lifted from his soul to secure a room, bring over his chest and await his future roommate, who would be his closest companion and who might make or mar his college career. When the roommate had made his appearance and the two young men had greeted each other, they went to a store on Nassau Street to make their purchases—two cots, with a single mattress each, a washstand, a table, a few chairs, a book-shelf, shovel and tongs.[1]

To the newcomer Nassau Hall seemed impressive with its great stone walls pierced by long rows of windows, its hall-ways running the entire length of the building, its many bedrooms and studies, its Prayer Hall, its classrooms, its cupola. He was interested in the library, the cabinet of curi-osities, the orrery, the scientific apparatus. But he now had to purchase books, secure a seat in the refectory, go over to the bank to pay his tuition fee and room rent, unpack his clothes. If he happened to be from the south he found, when he strolled out on the campus, that his broad-brimmed hat, bobtailed coat, baggy breeches, and high-heeled boots sub-jected him to good natured raillery,[2] even though there were scores of other southern boys in college to keep him in coun-tenance.

With the ringing of the bell in the cupola the freshman turned toward the refectory to join the stream of boys who were pouring into the hallways and down the steps for supper. In the early days of the college meals had been served in a room in the basement, but later a separate building had been constructed and connected with Nassau Hall by a covered passage. This, in turn, had given way to a room on the first floor of the stone building later known as the Philosophical Hall, opposite Stanhope Hall. The students waited at the door until a servant opened it, and then entered and looked for their seats. They were arranged by classes at three long tables and stood at attention until the tutor took his place and said grace. They then sat down on the benches and ate their supper.

To many an incoming freshman the supper seemed un-usually simple, almost mean, consisting as it did only of bread and butter, with milk. He was soon to learn that breakfast was similar, with bread and butter, and occasionally radishes, served with coffee. At dinner the food, both in quantity and variety, was more in keeping with the appetites of growing

[1] *Princeton Library MSS*, AM 9976.    [2] *Ibid.*, AM 11815.

boys—ham, veal, beef or some other meat, with potatoes and fresh vegetables in season, for dessert, if any, apple pie or chocolate cake. On festive occasions, of course, the meals were more elaborate. "Our dinner was composed of chickens and pigs, not alive or with knives in their mouths crying 'come and eat me,' vegetables, pies, puddings, porter, lemonade, wine, raisins and figs," wrote William B. Clymer, of the Fourth of July celebration of 1819.[3]

The boys did not expect a banquet every day and were satisfied with their usual plain fare so long as it was wholesome and of good quality. But when the steward neglected his work, or tried to gain a few dollars at their expense, the letters to father or mother were full of complaints. "We eat rye bread half dough and as black as it possibly can be, old oniony butter and sometimes dry bread and thick coffee for breakfast," said one boy in 1781, "a little milk or cyder and bread and sometimes meagre chocolate for supper; very indifferent dinners such as lean, tough boiled fresh beef with dry potatoes. . . . We may be said to exist and not to live as it becomes persons of good extraction."[4] On one occasion, when the butter was bad, some of the boys carved it into an image of the steward and hung it up by the neck in the dining room.[5]

The presence of a professor or tutor, while a restraining force, did not necessarily assure good order at meals, and we find a record of one youngster who had a long argument with a friend at breakfast over the propriety of snatching bread and butter before grace was over.[6] A few days later when no tutor appeared at the opening of the door of the refectory, the same boy was bowled over by the mob who stormed the room. When he had disentangled himself from those who had fallen on top of him and had taken his seat, he found that the meat pie had been swept off, some of the lads seizing near one-third of the whole. Usually restlessness or dis-

[3] *Ibid.,* AM 10230.  [4] *Ibid.,* AM 8797.
[5] *Philip Vickers Fithian, Journal and Letters,* John R. Williams, ed., p. 34.
[6] "Journal at Nassau Hall, *Princeton Library MSS,* AM 10841.

approval of the food or dislike of the tutor was expressed by the scraping of feet on the floor under the table. This practice was especially annoying since it was so difficult to detect, and anyone whom the tutor suspected was promptly ordered to leave the room.

Although the regulations at first forbade the student "to make any treat or entertainment" in the chambers or "have any private meals," this rule in time was modified, so that the boys were "indulged to make a dish of tea" after evening prayers. And it was found impossible to prevent them from purchasing a watermelon in season and inviting their friends in for a feast, or from opening a box of delicacies from home, or from stripping a nearby cherry tree. One student relates that he bought some whortleberries from country people who were peddling them, but when he got into a scuffle with a classmate, most of them were crushed in his pocket.[7]

The living conditions in Nassau Hall were even plainer than the food, and the sons of the wealthy could not help contrasting them with those in their own residences. Instead of hardwood floors they found the hallways paved with brick and those of the rooms covered with simple planking; instead of paneled or papered walls, bare plastering often smudged with candle smoke or marred by crude drawings; instead of Chippendale chairs or Sheraton tables, the cheapest and plainest furniture.

The rooms from Number 1 to Number 16, situated in the basement, were extremely undesirable because of the dampness, which even the digging of the so-called moat had by no means eliminated. As there were no gutters to the building, water from the roof poured into this ditch whenever it rained and, seeping into the massive stone walls, gave a permanent chill to the entire lower floor. Not infrequently parents wrote to the president demanding that their sons be transferred from these "damp, unhealthy" rooms to more wholesome quarters under threat of taking them out of college.[8] When

[7] *Ibid.*

[8] Philip Stuart to Ashbel Green, June 19, 1814, *Maclean MSS*, Princeton Library.

an epidemic of dysentery swept through the student body in late May and June 1813, President Green ordered the steward to keep fires going in every basement room. "The 'entry' was so damp that I certainly would not have permitted a son of mine to lodge in it without keeping a fire constantly in his room,"[9] he said. Later, with the erection of other dormitories, the lower floor of Nassau Hall was abandoned.

Upon ascending the stairs to the upper floors the student found the rooms far more pleasant. Not only were they dry and well lighted, but their occupants, when they lifted their eyes from their textbooks, might look out over the charming, peaceful New Jersey countryside, toward Tusculum on the north, or the woods and fields beyond Stony Brook on the south. Yet this beautiful view could be enjoyed only in mild weather, for when the windows were closed, one could not see through the thick, rough, greenish little panes. Every room had its washstand with basin and pitcher filled from the college well.

In the corner of bedrooms or studies, or in the hallways were stacks of wood. Even in November the air was sharp and fires were going in many of the chambers and lecture rooms. Each student paid for his own wood, the three cords which he consumed during the year costing him on the average about $14.[10] In 1802 President Smith made a contract with one Oliver Hunt "to supply wood for the college and engaged John Green to cut and carry it into the students' rooms."[11] With the opening of the Pennsylvania mines, the thoughts of the college turned to coal as a substitute for firewood, and the trustees directed President Carnahan to investigate the new fuel.[12] They were interested, no doubt, not only in the cheapness and heating capacity of coal, but also in whether it offered rioting students a less dangerous weapon than wood. At all events, it eventually came into universal use, together with the picturesque Franklin stove.

[9] President's Report, Sept. 1813, ibid.
[10] Princeton Library MSS, AM 9976.
[11] Faculty Minutes, I, Dec. 10, 1802.
[12] John Maclean, History of the College of New Jersey, II, p. 282.

The freshman's sleep during his first night in college was apt to be troubled by dreams of bespectacled professors, of long assignments in Livy and algebra, and of innumerable strange faces. At five in the morning, when it was still quite dark, he woke with a start at the blowing outside his door of a horn which sounded like the last trumpet.[13] It was the servant whose duty it was to rouse the students for morning prayers. In earlier days all sleep was supposed to stop with the ringing of the old bell in the cupola, and when this proved ineffectual, the rouser went through the hallways and knocked on every door. This, in turn, was superseded by the blast of the horn. At its summons the student hustled out of bed, lit his candle, washed his face and hands, got into his clothes and joined the stream of boys on the way to the Prayer Hall.[14] Those from the two upper stories entered the gallery while the others filed in at the lower door and took their seats on the main floor. On the opening day it was the president who conducted morning prayers. He mounted the pulpit in the south end of the room, the roll was called, and all united in singing a psalm, after which he made a brief talk, expressing the hope that the students would improve their time by hard study, observe all the laws of the college, and open their hearts to the influence of religion. It was only on special occasions that the president graced either morning or evening prayers, for it usually fell to the lot of the tutors to conduct these services. The students as a rule preserved order in the Prayer Hall, because they realized that any disrespect to religion would bring speedy and severe punishment.[15]

It was the bitter cold of winter mornings as well as the earliness of the hour which made prayers so unpopular. "I huddle on my clothes anyhow and push into the hall all open and unbuttoned, tho' by far the coldest morning of the season, and escape being tardy," wrote one boy in his diary in 1786.[16]

[13] *Faculty Minutes,* I, Dec. 10, 1802.
[14] *Princeton Library MSS,* AM 10841.
[15] *An Account of the College,* p. 27; *Trustees Minutes,* I, p. 14.
[16] "Journal at Nassau Hall," *Princeton Library MSS,* AM 10841.

What made the matter worse was the removal, in the interest of better ventilation, of the sashes from the hallway windows so that often when the student stepped out of his door he was greeted by an icy blast. Nor was there any hope of getting warm during prayers since the hall seems to have been devoid of fireplace or stove.

After breakfast, when the newly-arrived freshman wandered out on the campus to join a group of older students, he found some of them chewing tobacco, others smoking cigars.[17] Their conversation was puzzling at first, for they made free use of college slang, much of it peculiar to Princeton. But he was not long in discovering that to "fizzle" meant to recite poorly in class; "to get a fat" meant a letter from home containing money; to "poll" was to study hard; to "cut at" was to make a sarcastic remark; that President Carnahan was the "Boss," Professor Maclean "Old Johnny," Professor Topping was "Top." Perhaps one or two of the boys, after looking around carefully to be certain no tutor was near, produced a pistol and handed it around for the admiring inspection of the group.

The conversation might turn to the street fight several years before when the apprentices and journeymen of the village attacked a group of students and stabbed one of them.[18] There would be boasting of how the tutors were outwitted, of how one boy rode a mule up and down in the hallway of Nassau Hall, of how another exploded a cracker on the "Boss's" doorstep, of how another slipped out of his window for a night sleighride. The tutors, of course, came in for a generous share of criticism and ridicule. This one was puffed up by his own importance; that one hated the students and delighted in reporting them so that they would be punished; another did not know his subject and was a poor teacher.[19]

But at heart the boys knew that the tutors were not such bad fellows. They were usually recent graduates, only a few

[17] *Trustees Minutes*, I, p. 63.
[18] *Faculty Minutes*, 1812-1820, Aug. 12, 1820.
[19] John Hall, *Familiar Letters of James W. Alexander*, p. 56.

years older than the students whom they taught and for whose conduct they were responsible. No boy could leave the campus during study hours, or have a meal in his room, or take his seat at dinner if he got in after grace, or go to the post office on Sunday without their permission. It was the tutors' duty not only to hold classes but to aid the students in preparing for them, to visit each room once a day, to preside in the refectory and at prayers, to detect and report breaches of discipline. Perhaps the boys would have been more charitable had they realized that beneath a dignified and firm exterior, these young men were often timid and apprehensive. "It requires all the effrontery which I can assume to fill my gown with any kind of effect," said one, "to sit in the focal point of vision before one hundred carping young gentlemen, to march through the congregation to the foot of the refectory steps . . . and sit in state at the upper end of the long college table."[20] Nor was it an easy matter to maintain discipline without being harsh, to be friendly without sacrificing dignity, to distinguish between harmless pranks and real defiance of authority. The difficulty was increased by the short tenure of the tutors, for they usually served but two or three years and then left to study theology or take up a profession. It was rare indeed when one of them won promotion and made teaching his life work.

The students at times were provoked by the inefficiency and laziness of the college servants, but they admired their strong individualism and homely philosophy. If one spoke to Jemmy McCarrier of the difficulty of his work, he would say: "Wid patience and perseverance a man may open an oyster, my dear, wi' a rolling-pin."[21] It was the duty of the servants to make the fires and fill the pitchers in each bedroom before morning prayers, to black the students' shoes and boots before breakfast, to sweep every room and make up the beds before noon, to take the soiled linen into the dining room and there deliver it to the washerwomen, to ring the college bell and sound the

[20] John Hall, *Familiar Letters of James W. Alexander*, p. 51.
[21] *Ibid.*, p. 52.

rouser, to eject from Nassau Hall all venders of apples, nuts, etc. They were permitted to earn an extra penny by running errands provided they did not connive with the boys to break the regulations.[22] Servants received on an average from each student forty-four cents a month or $4.40 for the ten months' session.[23]

For one to keep pace with boys from well-to-do families it was necessary to spend considerable sums on clothing. When it became apparent to the trustees and the president that Princeton had acquired the reputation of being a rich man's college they were seriously disturbed. How could they attract pious youths to the institution if they were to be snubbed by a campus aristocracy? Even though the son of the sturdy New Jersey farmer or the theological student probably looked on with more disgust than envy as the barber plied his curling irons to give a graceful ear-lock to some youthful orator before his appearance on the rostrum, there was a feeling of resentment, perhaps of inferiority. Even William Paterson tells us that he was "confounded jealous of the dressy college fellows." Matters must have been bad indeed when a youth could spend all the afternoon dressing, or consider it unpardonable to deliver an oration unless the barber had worked for an hour on his hair.[24]

It was this kind of thing which gave the public the impression that expenses at Princeton were higher than in other colleges. The trustees, although they could not exclude a boy merely because his pockets were full of cash, several times sent circular letters to parents urging them to limit the spending money of their sons. "Many young men, aiming at too much ostentation in their appearance, are apt to incur heavy and unnecessary debts for clothing, barbers and horses," wrote President Smith in 1799, "but these are wholly in the power of parents to restrain by limiting their children to a certain sum." "The greatest dangers of idle or vicious habits in any

[22] *Faculty Minutes,* I, Dec. 10, 1802.
[23] *Princeton Library MSS,* AM 10353.
[24] "Journal at Nassau Hall," *Princeton Library MSS,* AM 10841.

of the young gentlemen we have always found arise from . . .
allowing them too large supplies of money," he reiterated in
1804. "There are always designing people . . . ready to take
advantage of the indiscretions of youth."[25] The necessary
expenses he estimated at $171.23, of which $94.50 went for
board, $41.33 for the entrance fee, tuition, room-rent and the
use of the library, $12 for washing, $14 for firewood, $4.40
for servants' wages and $5 for candles.[26] Many students from
well-to-do families spent in addition from $100 to $200 for
clothing and other personal wants, while some went as high
as $500, $1,000 or even $1,500 a year.[27] It is difficult to un-
derstand how a boy could squander such sums while living
under the Spartan regime of Nassau Hall, for in those days
even a fine broadcloth coat could be had for as little as $10.
We know, for instance, that when Robert Sanders' clothing
was burned in the fire of 1802, his wardrobe was replenished
for $26.50.[28] In 1831 the college tried the experiment of
running two tables in the dining hall, one for the well-to-do
students as $82 a year, the other for those who found economy
necessary, at $61.[29] But this merely emphasized class distinc-
tions and intensified the very evils it was designed to eliminate. For, although there was never a group at Princeton
comparable to the Oxford servitors or the Cambridge sizars,
this "poor man's table" put a certain stigma of social inferiority on those who sat at it.

The students were free to take walks or play games after
breakfast until nine, after dinner until two, and between
afternoon prayers and supper. Of course intercollegiate athletics were unknown. For Princeton to send a team to New
Haven by stage coach and ferry would have required a week
or more and the cost would have been prohibitive; one might
as well have suggested a trip to the moon as a visit to Cambridge. Had the faculty been wise enough to follow Philip
Lindsley's advice, they would have encouraged interclass ath-

---

[25] *Princeton Library MSS*, AM 2114.
[26] *Ibid.*, AM 9976.       [27] *Ibid.*, AM 11420.
[28] *Ibid.*, AM 1163.       [29] *Ibid.*, AM 10353.

letics, or perhaps a series of cricket, bandy, or track games between the two literary societies. This would have worked wonders in keeping the boys contented and in developing their bodies.

What athletics there were at Princeton were unorganized, the spontaneous effort of a group of boys seeking fun and exercise. Two or three young men might run a race around the campus while their fellows stuck their heads out of the windows to shout encouragement. They might indulge in a game of quoits, or bounce balls against the gable-end of the President's House, or take a turn at bandy, or even roll hoops in the basement hallway.[30] Apparently there was no football and no cricket, although some of the younger boys played some kind of game with a ball and sticks.[31]

In the winter when the weather was cold and the ice firm the student might tuck his skates under his arm and set out for Stony Brook or the Millstone River. If he were from the north and so at home on the ice, he often joined the other boys in a game played with a ball, possibly hockey.[32] He would not go sleighriding, however, as it had been prohibited after some students had taken advantage of this sport to visit neighboring towns. In mild weather those who owned or hired horses could indulge in riding, while relief was sought from the heat of summer by swimming.

Many enjoyed taking a walk over the countryside, especially on crisp autumn days, or in the spring when the leaves and buds were first appearing in woods and fields. Sometimes they made their way through lanes and meadows and marshes to Pretty Brook, to sit beside the stream and read, sometimes they headed for Morgan's Quarry. In after days the graduate looked back upon these excursions as one of the most pleasant features of student life. "In the walks around our venerable abode how enchanting were the prospects," wrote one. "Those

[30] *Ibid.*, AM 9487; "Journal at Nassau Hall," *Princeton Library MSS*, AM 10841; *Trustees Minutes*, I, p. 92.

[31] *Faculty Minutes*, I, Nov. 26, 1787.

[32] *Letters of James Iredell*, Jan. 7, 1805, transcript, Princeton Library; "Journal at Nassau Hall," Jan. 1, 1786, *Princeton Library MSS*, AM 10841.

lovely fields are fresh in my recollection; as I behold them thro' the tears of affliction, verdure assumes a softer tint."[33]

Sometimes the walk led to inspiration as well as reflection. When George Strawbridge dropped from near the head of his class to near the bottom upon entering the junior, or mathematical year, he found the key to his trouble one morning while walking in the woods. "A flash of light crossed my brain and I saw the force of demonstration," he says. "I had nothing to commit to memory, the mathematical figures made that unnecessary. After this I took my station in the class able to understand and sure to get on."[34]

Perhaps the most unpopular of undergraduates was the college loafer who insisted upon calling upon others who wanted to study or to read, and taking up their time with idle conversation. Often several would come together and a general "bicker session" would ensue. "Why must I be interrupted by these triflers, who come in to lounge upon me whenever they are tired of themselves,"[35] James Iredell wrote home in disgust.

The average freshman was too young to take an interest in the belles of Princeton when he first came to college, but before he had reached his sophomore year he was calling at Morven dressed in his best broadcloth coat, or perhaps turning his partner at an informal dance. The Princeton beauties were famous in the annals of the college, and many are the references to charming Betsey Stockton, to Laura Lee, Nancy Lawrence, and others. "We have a number of pretty girls here now, a new race of beauties," wrote William Paterson, in 1772. "Were you here I could give you a description of some of the girls and a character of some of their lovers, and private anecdotes of both."[36] Unfortunately the belle of today became the "college widow" of tomorrow, for with young

[33] John Hall, *Familiar Letters of James W. Alexander*, p. 81; *Princeton Library MSS*, AM 11456a.

[34] *Memoirs of George Strawbridge*, transcript, Princeton Library.

[35] *Letters of James Iredell*, Jan. 13, 1806, transcript, Princeton Library.

[36] W. Jay Mills, *Glimpses of Colonial Society and the Life at Princeton College, 1766-1773.*

men of Nassau Hall a woman of eighteen was passé, one of twenty a hopeless old maid. The young lady, in turn, even the incomparable Miss Stockton, could find little of interest in the conversation of fourteen-year-old freshmen. "The pigmy race of students which at present fill the college are not at all suited to a lady whose mind is deeply tinctured with the principles of science," wrote one senior loftily.[37]

It was with frowns of disapproval that the trustees learned in 1783 that a French dancing master had come to Princeton and was giving lessons at one of the taverns. This they thought useless, the students "being generally past that period of youth in which manners are formed," injurious to the reputation of the college, and "unfriendly to order and good government." So it was unanimously resolved that henceforth attendance at the dancing master's salon be strictly forbidden to the students.[38] That this action was applauded by some of the undergraduates themselves we know from a letter of Zadock Squire. "I believe it would be better for us if these Frenchmen were all where they came from, for a republic cannot subsist by such useless accomplishments, it must subsist only by simplicity and frugality."[39]

Though the trustees sent the dancing master on his way, they did not deem it wise to put an absolute ban on dancing itself, and custom fixed the annual ball as an important part of every commencement. This formal function, held in one of the village taverns, was graced not only by Princeton girls but by fair guests from nearby cities. Most of the boys enjoyed the dances thoroughly, but one lad, who obviously preferred the Virginia reel to the minuet or the cotillion, complained that there was too much formality and ceremony.[40] John Melish thought the ladies' costumes "showy but not neat" and remarked on their "Cupid's chariot wheels," or huge earrings three inches in diameter.[41] At two o'clock in the morning the ladies retired and the gentlemen, after seeing

---

[37] *Letters of James Iredell*, July 16, 1809, transcript, Princeton Library.
[38] *Trustees Minutes*, I, p. 238.   [39] *Princeton Library MSS*, AM 11288.
[40] *Letters of James Iredell*, July 7, 1804, transcript, Princeton Library.
[41] John Melish, *Travels in United States* (Philadelphia, 1812), p. 142.

them home, returned for a supper which often continued until daybreak. When the boys got back to Nassau Hall very few were in condition to tell what they had been doing the night before.[42] Several times the students asked permission to hold the ball in the college refectory, where they might "mingle in the dance," free from the bustle and dissipation of the public house, but the trustees invariably withheld their consent.[43]

In an age when the theater was looked upon with suspicion as tending to immorality it is strange that the trustees and faculty of Princeton should have permitted the students to stage plays. Yet Ezra Stiles tells us that when he attended the commencement of 1754 at Newark, two young gentlemen of the college acted *Tamerlane and Bajazet*.[44] In 1782 the students presented the tragedy *Ormisinda and Alonzo*, in which the "rich and elegant" costumes excited admiration and the acting was so real "that it caused the tears to flow from many a compassionate mind and made them feel for the characters in distress."[45] This was followed the next year by the *Rival Queens, or Alexander the Great*, acted before a very large and enthusiastic audience. Ashbel Green, who took the part of Alexander, was showered with praise and "gained almost immortal honor."[46] In 1801 a movement was started by a number of prominent citizens of Princeton to erect a theater, but support was lacking and they were forced to drop the matter.[47]

Although the interest in dramatics was sporadic in Nassau Hall, music held a permanent, if not very prominent, place in student life. The study of singing was a regular part of the work when the college was at Newark, and at the commencement of 1754 "anthems were sung very melodiously by a chorus of men and women in the gallery."[48] Soon after the

---

[42] *Letters of James Iredell*, July 7, 1804, transcript, Princeton Library.
[43] *Maclean MSS*, April 9, 1824, Princeton Library.
[44] "Diary of Ezra Stiles," *Princeton College Bulletin*, IV, no. 3.
[45] *Princeton Library MSS*, AM 8796.
[46] *Ibid.*, AM 11288.     [47] *Ibid.*, AM 11803.
[48] "Diary of Ezra Stiles," *Princeton College Bulletin*, IV, no. 3.

erection of Nassau Hall the trustees gave additional evidence of their approval of music as a part of religious exercises by placing an organ in the Prayer Hall. This Ezra Stiles thought "an innovation of ill consequence," of which they soon became a "little sick." He rejoiced that it had "been disused for sundry years and never was much used."[49] When the organ was destroyed during the Revolution, it was not replaced. Psalmody was more and more emphasized in religious services, however, and in 1783 a Mr. Poor was giving instruction in singing to about thirty students.[50] In 1812 a "school for improvement in psalmody" was opened by Backus Wilbur, a member of the senior class, at the request of the people of the village.[51]

As early as 1791 there was a student orchestra. We do not know what instruments it included, but that its numbers were small is indicated by the fact that at the celebration of the marriage of President Witherspoon they played in the restricted space of the belfry. The existence of the orchestra was not continuous, periods of interest alternating with years when it was allowed to lapse. "There are several of the students who play on different musical instruments and who have lately formed themselves into a society which they call the harmony society," wrote Samuel Howell in 1806. "They meet every Saturday evening for the purpose of amusing themselves and at the same time of improving themselves in the art."[52] In 1819 the student orchestra, then called the Orphean Society, played patriotic music in a very acceptable way at the Fourth of July celebration.[53]

For the students Sunday was a day of neither rest nor recreation. They were awakened by the rouser at the usual hour to attend morning prayers, after which they studied Bible lessons until breakfast. Later in the morning they donned academic gown and fell in for the procession to the Presby-

[49] *The Literary Diary of Ezra Stiles*, 1, p. 58.
[50] "Journal at Nassau Hall," *Princeton Library MSS*, AM 10841.
[51] *Faculty Minutes*, 1812-1820, p. 7.
[52] *Princeton Library MSS*, AM 9505.
[53] *Ibid.*, AM 10230.

terian Church where the north half of the front gallery and the whole of the north gallery were reserved for them. Here they listened to a sermon by Ashbel Green which one of them described as well reasoned but delivered with a bit of affectation. After dinner they recited to the president on five chapters in the Bible, and then went directly to the Prayer Hall for another sermon, possibly by Dr. Green, possibly by Dr. Miller of the seminary. Under no circumstances were they to leave the college grounds except when they went to church. Altogether it was a rather dull day for the youths who were not deeply religious by nature, and many dreaded it.[54]

To those students who lived in New Jersey or an adjacent state the advent of spring vacation early in April was hailed with joy, but to the boy from South Carolina or Mississippi, for whom a visit home was impracticable, it was often a dreary occasion. He would stand disconsolately in front of the tavern as one friend after another clambered aboard the stage coach or started home on horseback. Then, returning to his room, he would pack up his belongings and take them over to Mr. Knox's or some other boarding house. Yet, with reading and rambles and visits to his friends the time usually passed so pleasantly that he was sorry in turn when the bell in the cupola announced that the summer session had begun.[55]

Despite the lack of an "infirmatory," despite the ill balanced fare of the refectory, the dampness and chill of some of the chambers of Nassau Hall, and the backwardness of the medical profession, the health of the students seemed usually to have been good. The trustees never tired of advertising the fact that Princeton, situated as it was upon a high ridge, was the most healthful spot in New Jersey. Yet one wonders why typhoid fever did not sweep the college when one considers that drinking water was drawn from a well on the campus. An inkling of what this was like is gained from a

[54] *Philip Vickers Fithian, Journal and Letters,* John R. Williams, ed., pp. 6-10; "Journal at Nassau Hall," June 25, 1786, *Princeton Library MSS,* AM 10841.
[55] *Letters of James Iredell,* Oct. 1, 1804, transcript, Princeton Library; *Princeton Library MSS,* AM 7685.

letter written by James W. Alexander. "A mineral spring has been discovered; that is, as in similar cases, a hole in the mud has been discovered which possesses rather more nastiness than the common water which tastes like a gunwashing, like a blacksmith's tub, like a what not."[56]

The isolation of the college and the difficulty of communication gave a degree of protection against epidemics. But when once a contagious disease had got a foothold in Nassau Hall it was very difficult to stop, because the students came into such constant contact with each other at prayers, meals, and in the classroom. "I have had the influenza which is extremely disagreeable and a complaint which while it lasts renders you totally unfit for any employment," wrote one student. "It prevails very much in college, two-thirds of the students have it."[57]

In 1813 an epidemic of dysentery swept through the college. President Green reported that in his thirty years' intimate acquaintance with the institution he had never known so much illness. In most cases, however, the complaints were "slight and short," there were no deaths, and not more than one case which appeared dangerous. Three or four of the sick boys had been removed from Nassau Hall, and in these cases he was persuaded it was "with no advantage." One of the theological students, Henry Blackford, placed the whole college under lasting obligation by his unceasing and kindly attention to the ill. "Without his aid I know not the extent of the inconvenience which the college must have suffered," the president added. The steward was obliging in making soup, while Green himself and Samuel Stanhope Smith sent many delicacies from their own tables. As the epidemic subsided Professor Slack prepared a "chemical fumigation" from a formula in a foreign scientific magazine "which had a most wonderful, speedy and happy effect in purifying the atmosphere."[58]

[56] John Hall, *Familiar Letters of James W. Alexander*, p. 108.
[57] *Princeton Library MSS*, AM 9493.
[58] President's Report, 1813, *Maclean MSS*, Princeton Library.

Of great importance in the life of the undergraduates were the Cliosophic and Whig literary societies. It was late in President Finley's administration that two organizations had been founded—the Well Meaning Club and the Plain Dealing Club. But their careers under these names were short, since in 1768 they incurred the displeasure of the trustees and were suppressed. The next year, however, the Plain Dealers were permitted to reorganize under the name of the American Whig Society and, in 1770, the Well Meaning Club came to life as the Cliosophic Society. The two were rivals, their activities were conducted in secrecy and their meetings and debates absorbed a large part of the time and interest of the students.

Freshmen little suspected that during their first four or five weeks in college they were being subjected to close scrutiny by the members of the societies, and their manners, habits, standing in the class and general conduct put into the balance for or against them. Unlucky was the youth who was excluded, for he was cut off from the most pleasant, perhaps the most valuable part of college life, and made an outcast in the little world of Nassau Hall. But even when a boy missed the first initiation, he might be admitted later, for neither society would run the risk of having its rival snap up a bright student who might some day become a valedictorian or a salutatorian. Although it was tacitly understood that there should be no pressure on prospective candidates to influence their choice, there were frequent charges of "hoaxing." "Please write to little Skinner and advise him to be proposed to Whig," James Booth wrote to James Iredell in 1807. But the Clios had already caught young Skinner's interest. Although he had intended entering Whig, they had placed him in a Clio room and in two weeks he was to be proposed to their society.[59]

The societies exercised a disciplinary influence upon the students even before they were admitted to membership. Shortly after George Strawbridge of the class of 1802 entered college

[59] *Letters of James Iredell*, Dec. 1, 1807, transcript, Princeton Library.

he commenced an habitual prank which might have had disastrous results for his college career. It happened that one day
as he was standing on the campus in front of Nassau Hall,
someone emptied a pitcher of water on his head from a window above. Although he could not discover the culprit, he
accepted this as an established custom, and so took revenge
on anyone who came under his own window. He always succeeded in escaping detection, but he was strongly suspected.
As a result, when he made application for admission to the
American Whig Society, some of his victims were for excluding him and only his good scholastic standing and the pleas
of one or two newly made friends overcame their objections.[60]

When the day for the initiation arrived, the candidate was
escorted to the library building[61] and, upon mounting the
stairs, found a number of other boys waiting in the upper hall.
They were excited and nervous, for though most of them had
been in college only a few weeks, they had learned to regard
the society halls as places of mystery, never entered by any
save members, and with their secrets closely guarded. When
the door was opened, they filed in and stood for a moment
behind a red curtain which had been hung across the east end
of the room. At a signal the curtain was drawn aside and the
initiates now could see that they were in a large blue room,
which was given a circular appearance by concave book cases
in the corners. Facing them, at the opposite end of the hall,
were the officers seated on a stage each behind a desk—the
moderator elevated above the rest, with the censor, the clerk,
and the treasurer grouped around him. On either side of the
room, seated on chairs and settees were the other members
of the society. There was no levity, no suppressed snicker;
all was serious.

The members now rose and the moderator proceeded to
address them. "Gentlemen, in admitting you as members of
the society we expect your most solemn promise . . . to obey its
constitution and laws, and endeavor by every laudable means

---

[60] *Memoirs of George Strawbridge*, transcript, Princeton Library.
[61] Now Stanhope Hall.

to promote its honor and advance its interests. . . . We trust you will act as becomes so exalted a character. . . . Our object is the promotion of literature, friendship and morality. The venerable institution to which we belong numbers in her catalogue many of the most illustrious citizens of our country, and the society has been the school in which a large portion of them laid the foundation of whatever distinction they have since acquired. Whether, sirs, you will attain similar eminence depends in a great measure upon your own exertions. Remember, you no longer act in a private capacity, but that the honor of this institution is connected with your every action. . . . You should, then, endeavor to live in the bonds of fellowship and love with your fellow members; to render strict obedience to the laws of the college; and ever cultivate that spirit of virtue and honor which is so bright an ornament of character."[62]

The moderator was speaking advisedly when he claimed that the societies had laid the foundation for the distinction won in after life by so many of their members. The boy who entered either Whig or Clio found himself a citizen of a little republic, whose benefits and responsibilities he shared. In his society he could exercise his own judgment, have a part in making regulations and shaping policies, strive for honors without the interference of the faculty, express his opinions from the floor, sharpen his wit by debates with other members, learn to cooperate for the good of the society, to feel the stimulus which comes from rivalry. In comparison with the intellectual life in Whig and Clio, regular college courses seemed dull and uninspiring.

"I seriously pronounce the Whig Society to have been the best society I ever had anything to do with," said one alumnus. "It was worth more as a part of education than the college itself, not only in a literary point of view, but in manners and morals. It did more to remove boyish habits and make men of us, and men of sound and correct principles for society in after

[62] Jacob N. Beam, *The American Whig Society* (Princeton, 1933), pp. 109, 110.

life, than all the reasoning and lecturing, moral or religious, that ever was uttered. It was a practical school unequalled within my knowledge."[63] "Here you have no Faculty to tease," pointed out another graduate, "no tutor to alarm, no companion to bore.[64] When you cross the threshold of this retreat you enter it in a different capacity; from the mere college student, you enter as a citizen of a community on whom depends a portion of its happiness, whose respect you should esteem, whose honor you must hold dear."[65]

The discipline exercised by the societies over their members was not only very real but was apt to be more efficient than that imposed by the faculty and trustees. The society censor kept a constant vigil and anyone who neglected his work, or loitered at the tavern, or acted in a way unbecoming a gentleman might be admonished or even suspended. On one occasion the moderator himself was punished, when he became irritated at the levity of a member whom he was swearing into office and hit him on the head with a copy of the constitution. Usually, however, improper deportment in the halls consisted of nothing more serious than "laying about under the settees," or standing before the fire more than three minutes, or "smoking segars."[66]

The importance of the societies in upholding discipline in the turbulent early years of the nineteenth century, and also the folly of interference with their affairs by the faculty, are well shown by an incident which occurred in 1806. It seems that William Hamilton, a member of Whig, had been suspended from college for "gross and repeated insolence" to Professor Thompson.[67] Thereupon a member of the faculty sent for the censor, told him what had happened, and advised the society to expel the culprit.

Accordingly, a meeting was called and the censor and council recommended that Hamilton be suspended. A warm debate

[63] *Memoirs of George Strawbridge*, transcript, Princeton Library.
[64] In college slang to bore meant to tease.
[65] Jacob N. Beam, *The American Whig Society* (Princeton, 1933), p. 78.
[66] *Ibid.*, p. 145.
[67] *Faculty Minutes*, I, Jan. 6, 1806.

followed. It was argued on the one hand that to suspend him before the action of the faculty was announced would prevent a disgrace to the society, and that moreover his fault made him unworthy of being a member of Whig; on the other hand, that stigma could not be avoided by an eleventh-hour suspension, that they should not be guided by the decisions of the faculty, but should consider the case on its own merits, and that the punishment was too severe, since suspension should not be inflicted for such "a comparatively trivial offense as mere impertinence to a professor." In the end it was voted to admonish Hamilton but not to suspend him. "I opposed especially because the report of the censor and council was made at the instigation of a member of the faculty," one member stated afterwards. "We should show them that we had the independence to think and act for ourselves."[68]

The student of the time of Samuel Stanhope Smith or Ashbel Green or of "Boss" Carnahan took as much interest in the debates in Clio and Whig as the student of a later generation in football. Not only were these exercises preparing him for the day when he might have to defend the honor of his society against the champions of its traditional rival, but the training they gave him proved valuable throughout life. They widened his field of information, sharpened his wits, taught him to think on his feet, improved his diction, gave him a good delivery. They also forced him to keep abreast of current events and to form intelligent opinions concerning them. He might have to argue on questions such as: Ought freedom of thought to be granted to all men? Is it probable that the states of Europe will relapse into their ancient state of barbarism? Is the theater prejudicial to public morals? Which tends more to relieve a female of celibacy, wealth or a beautiful face? Is unrestrained immigration harmful? Do the talents of man deteriorate in the Western Hemisphere?[69]

[68] *Letters of James Iredell*, Jan. 13, 1806, transcript, Princeton Library.
[69] Jacob N. Beam, *The American Whig Society* (Princeton, 1933), pp. 129-133.

The rivalry between Whig and Clio was so intense that it permeated every phase of college life. The inhabitants of Nassau Hall, although living in intimate contact with each other every day at meals, at prayers, in the classroom, were divided into two rival camps. Whigs made their close friendships with Whigs, Clios with Clios. One young diarist thought it an incident worthy of note that when he visited a neighboring room he found it crowded with "Whigs and Clios promiscuously."[70] When the son of an alumnus entered college, it was taken for granted that he would join his father's society, and certain families were affiliated with one or the other for several generations. On the rolls of Whig one finds no fewer than twenty-four Stocktons of the Morven family, including Annis, wife of Richard Stockton, the only woman member of the society; thirty-seven Alexanders; fourteen Breckinridges; nine Livingstons; eight Imbries; eight Scribners.[71]

Even before the Revolution the two societies had taken on a sectional character which continued until modern times, a majority of the southern students entering Whig, Clio becoming the usual choice for northerners. As early as 1771 the Whigs were deriding their rivals as New Englanders, and a century later Clio stigmatized Whig Hall as a nest of rebels and copperheads. In the sixty-one years from 1800 to 1860 southerners had a majority in Whig forty times, in Clio only eleven times. Not only did the sectional quarrel over slavery intensify the rivalry between the societies, but it frequently led to divisions and disputes within the Halls themselves. Only too often the debates were heated and the retorts acrimonious when such subjects were proposed as: Is the emancipation of slaves politic? Should abolition of slavery be a condition of admitting states into the Union? Is W. L. Garrison benefiting the cause of the Negroes?[72]

[70] "Journal at Nassau Hall," March 18, 1786, *Princeton Library MSS*, AM 10841.
[71] Jacob N. Beam, *The American Whig Society* (Princeton, 1933), pp. 168-171.
[72] *Ibid.*, p. 132.

The two societies strove to excel each other in scholarship, conduct, and especially in oratory. How intense this rivalry was is shown in the letters of students and alumni, as well as in the Hall records. "I am glad . . . that you are so warm a Whig," wrote James C. Johnston to young James Iredell in 1804. "The honor of your society will be an additional stimulus to the many others which you have to incite you to industry and close application." Two years later, when Iredell had entered his senior year, a friend who had just graduated wrote him urging unity in the society as essential to victory over Clio. "In our class you remember we had as great superiority as possible when juniors, but at the end of the senior year in my opinion they had the advantage. In your class we always expected to excel and always did before you became seniors, but now you know it is expected that the first honors will be divided . . . so keep united."[73] "Rivals they were," wrote George Strawbridge of Clio and Whig, "and the standing of the society was supposed to be increased in proportion to the scholarship and general standing of its members, by the number of distinctions at their examinations, especially the list for degrees, and in the superiority of their speakers on all occasions of public exhibition."[74]

The great prizes for which the two societies contended were the Latin salutatory, the English salutatory, and the valedictory delivered at commencement. Weeks before the final awards were made Nassau Hall buzzed with excitement, and many were the predictions and many the claims for superiority for this or that champion. When one society won a decided victory by carrying off most of the honors, the members of the other often charged the faculty with partiality and threatened to withdraw from participation in the commencement exercises. This was a source of serious worry to the faculty for the desire to win honors was a great incentive to study, and in 1812 they sought a solution by leaving the awards to the vote of the senior class. But this led to greater dissatisfaction than

[73] *Letters of James Iredell*, Jan. 13, 1806, transcript, Princeton Library.
[74] *Memoirs of George Strawbridge*, transcript, Princeton Library.

ever since the Clios, who were more numerous than the Whigs, voted themselves both the Latin salutatory and the valedictory.[75] Another compromise tried in 1809 proved equally unsatisfactory. The faculty, after awarding the three major plums and appointing a Greek orator, placed the rest of the class on an equal footing. "It has raised a great tumult in college," wrote William Meade. "The injured have asked for a distribution and it has been refused. . . . It is a cruel affair; I fear its effect on the college. . . . I pity some of the studious and worthy who are now confounded with the lazy and insignificant."[76]

Occasionally society rivalry affected seriously the relationship of the students with their tutors, especially when the latter were recent graduates. In 1818 the appointment of John Maclean, Jr., a member of Clio, brought the charge of persecution from the Whigs. A few years later, when Maclean moved into the house directly south of Stanhope Hall and thus within possible earshot of the debates in Whig Hall, the censor directed that the adjacent windows be closed during meetings.[77]

It was his regard for the honor of his society that kept many a student from indulging in common breaches of discipline. The boy who hoped to be valedictorian set off no crackers, did not bring strong liquor to his room, refused to take a hand at cards when gambling was involved, even refrained from scraping his feet at prayers and never threw bread in the refectory. His indiscretions were limited to visiting the tavern occasionally, slipping out of Prayer Hall after roll call, perhaps drinking a bit too much wine at the Fourth of July dinner.[78]

But even the paragons welcomed enthusiastically any break in the monotony of life in Nassau Hall, the visit of some famous man, the Fourth of July celebration, commencement. When news of the XYZ Affair reached Princeton and it was

[75] Jacob N. Beam, *The American Whig Society* (Princeton, 1933), p. 158.
[76] *Princeton Library MSS*, AM 9517.
[77] Jacob N. Beam, *The American Whig Society* (Princeton, 1933), p. 159.
[78] *Faculty Minutes*, 1812-1820, pp. 284, 339, 340, 362.

thought that French insults to the United States would lead to war, the students were fired with a spirit of patriotism reminiscent of the days just prior to the Revolution. On May 15, 1798, they held a meeting in the Prayer Hall, elected Josiah Watson, Jr., chairman and drew up an address to President John Adams. The students of the College of New Jersey, deeply impressed by the threatening clouds, wished to offer their support, they said. Their lives were not worth preserving unless they enjoyed the independence of free men. They lamented the necessity of taking up arms but they were ready to do their part to repel the enemy. Although they had just arisen from their cradles when the French nation broke the scepter of despotism they had caught the flame of enthusiasm in their battle for liberty against a succession of tyrants. Now they were disappointed in seeing the French laying aside the principles of justice and aiming at universal empire. President Adams replied at length, thanking the students, and declaring that he saw no way of averting war, and that the nation was ready to dedicate itself to its fatigues and dangers.[79]

Nineteen years later the campus was stirred again to a fever of anger and patriotism by the attack of the *Leopard* upon the *Chesapeake*. Once more the only topic of conversation was the probability of war. A local patriot, to show his defiance of the British, drew the spike out of the old Revolutionary cannon, mounted the gun on a carriage and fired a salute almost every evening.[80]

A thrill went through college in September 1824 when the Marquis de Lafayette visited Princeton on his triumphal tour of the United States. A "Temple of Science," consisting of a circular canopy resting on white classic columns and set off by the Peale portrait of Washington, was erected near the central gate of the front campus. Here, before a great crowd of students, villagers, and country people, Richard Stockton delivered an address of welcome. Then President Carnahan presented the Marquis with the doctor-of-laws diploma,

[79] *Princeton Library MSS*, AM 2076, AM 2077.
[80] *Letters of James Iredell*, July 10, 1807, transcript, Princeton Library.

signed by Dr. Witherspoon, which the college had conferred upon him *in absentia* in 1790. Lafayette replied and the guests then retired to the gaily decorated refectory for a bountiful breakfast.[81]

Throughout the early decades of the century the Fourth of July celebration continued to be one of the bright spots in the college year, far more important than Christmas—which, to the disgust of the southerners, was practically ignored. In 1813 the whole front of the college and all the public rooms were decorated with green boughs and flowers on Independence Day. At eleven the faculty and students assembled in Prayer Hall for the reading of the Declaration of Independence, patriotic orations, and music; later all sat down to a sumptuous dinner; at four there were more orations; in the evening Nassau Hall was brilliantly illuminated until nine o'clock, when at the stroke of the bell every light was extinguished. Fearing that the excitement might end in disorders, President Green patrolled the college until a late hour, but to his great relief all remained quiet.[82]

The exercises of 1819 were equally interesting. "We met in the Prayer Hall at eleven o'clock A.M. and marched in procession with our gowns on to the church, accompanied by a small band of Princeton Blues, about twenty-five in number," wrote William B. Clymer, a sophomore. "They were in the van. The freshmen followed, then the sophomores and so on, the faculty closing the rear. We stopped at the door and the order being then changed the faculty went in first, then the seniors, etc. The Doctor opened the ceremony . . . with a prayer. Then a hymn was sung and the Declaration of Independence was read by Mr. F. Schroder, a Cliosophian, a patriotic tune was then played. . . . The first oration was delivered by Mr. A. Venable, a Whig of Virginia, the second by Mr. J. Stuart, of South Carolina. Between and after each oration the band played some patriotic tune."[83]

[81] *Princeton Press*, July 2, 1904.
[82] President's Report, 1813, *Maclean MSS*.
[83] *Princeton Library MSS*, AM 10230.

The freshman, when once he had got into the current of college life, found that time passed quickly and on the whole pleasantly. Often he himself did not realize that he was gradually changing from a boy to a young man, and that his studies, his experiences in Hall, his associations were shaping his character and leaving an indelible imprint. Before the first session was over he had made friendships which remained firm not only during his stay at Princeton but throughout life. With his chums he talked over his ambitions, his ideas of life; during vacation he often visited those who lived near Princeton; with them he corresponded after leaving college.

The summer session was always trying because of the heat, and for the senior it was full of hard work and excitement. It was difficult for him to keep his mind on his books when the thermometer went above ninety and the humidity was oppressive, and he rejoiced when the president announced that the students would be permitted to divest themselves of their heavy coats and attend classes in "slight clothing" or "morning gowns." Occasionally the boys would gather under one of the poplars on the campus to keep cool, but this was unsatisfactory because out-of-doors there was so much to divert their attention from their books.[84] Some had to devote themselves to writing orations which they would be called upon to deliver at commencement in case their standing was high enough.

When at last the fateful day of examinations drew near the boys often became panicky and asked for extra time in which to review the work. This the faculty usually refused. As soon as the test was over and the class had received the verdict from the president, they clattered downstairs from the examination room and out onto the campus to gather in excited groups, to express their dissatisfaction, and make the usual protests against the passing over of some student in the awards or the elevation of another.

The evening before commencement the faculty, alumni, and students assembled in the Presbyterian Church for the

[84] G. W. P. Custis to George Washington, *Virginia Magazine of History and Biography*, XX, pp. 297-304.

annual alumni address. The speaker, selected alternately by the two literary societies from among their alumni, held forth in florid language upon some live topic of the times or upon pleasant memories of college days. Typical was the address of Richard S. Coxe:

"When after the lapse of years, we revisit the scenes of our youth, endeared to our affections by a thousand attracting associations, memory awakens all the circumstances which gave interest and animation to that delightful period of life. Our former companions live again in our recollections; the objects which we had been accustomed to regard with veneration and respect once more reappear to claim our homage, and the interval of time which has elapsed since our separation seems like a fleeting shadow or a summer's dream. To one who was accustomed a quarter of a century since to tread the paths of Nassau Hall, to roam through the adjacent woods and valleys, this place is rich in recollections. He may retrace his favorite haunts, expecting at every turn to meet some old friend or venerable instructor.

"It was here that we formed our first acquaintance with man; that we learned to explore the motives by which he was governed, those virtues and talents which have since manifested themselves upon a more extended theatre. How rarely have we been disappointed in our estimates. The fond hopes of parents and teachers may be disappointed, but our judgment has been vindicated. Yet the hopes of youth are rarely realized. Buoyed up by youthful fancy we look forward to the busy scenes of life with sanguine feelings. The imagination throws a mellowing mist over the road and we see but a smooth and easy ascent to the pinnacle of our wishes. But arduous struggles await us, rude repulses are our portion, parents sink into the tomb and life becomes a sad and bitter struggle."[85]

At commencement the taverns were crowded with the families and friends of the graduating class and with trustees

[85] Richard S. Coxe, "An Address, etc.," *Princeton Pamphlets*, no. 23.

and alumni, while every residence had its visitors. The stages from New York and Philadelphia were jammed, and many persons came in private carriages or on horseback. For the people of the surrounding country it was a festive day, even though few could gain admission to the actual exercises. Nassau Street was filled with vehicles of all kinds and with hundreds of noisy men, women, and children, and with hucksters crying their wares. Here was a wagon in which a farmer and his wife quietly ate luncheon, here a crowd gathered around a fiddler, in this field they were baiting a bull, in that there was horse racing.[86]

But all this was a mere side show to the real business of the day. At the ringing of the bell the academic procession started from Nassau Hall to the Presbyterian Church, where the trustees, faculty, and distinguished guests took their seats on the rostrum and the students in the body of the building. The galleries were filled to overflowing with gaily dressed women, alumni, and townspeople. The president opened the ceremonies with a prayer, after which came the Latin salutatory, followed by the English salutatory. With a band from Philadelphia providing music in the intervals between orations, one speaker after another rose and delivered the address which he had been practicing assiduously for weeks. In quick succession came eloquent harangues on moral science, belles-lettres, military characters, the character of a statesman, etc. Often the youths, while awaiting their turn, were seized with panic as they looked around at the distinguished men on the platform, at their classmates, and the crowded floor and gallery; but once upon their feet their self-possession usually returned. The exercises concluded with the conferring of degrees, the valedictory oration, prayer and the benediction.[87]

As commencement was the greatest day of the session, so the following day was the saddest. Silently the seniors packed their chests, engaged their seats on the stage coaches, and told each other goodbye. There were tears in the eyes of some of

[86] John Maclean, *History of the College of New Jersey*, II, p. 101.
[87] *Ibid.*, pp. 160, 161.

the boys who, in those days before the advent of railways, believed it unlikely that they would ever see each other again.

For the family of the southern boy his return from college was a memorable event. They found that he had now grown into a young man whose bearing, clothing, and even accent had undergone a change, and who had lost something of the old provincialism, had become more cosmopolitan. Although still an ardent southerner, his sympathies were national rather than sectional. He had no patience with narrow prejudice against northerners, now that so many of them were his intimate friends; he could not be taken in by every partisan argument, since he had heard the other side presented in those heated debates in Hall. And though this proved a handicap in local politics, it made him a more useful citizen, and a wiser public servant.

Throughout life the graduate continued grateful to the college for the intellectual fields which it had opened to him. Perhaps he did not deserve the reputation for erudition which he enjoyed among his neighbors, for his scholarship was neither deep nor broad, but when tired out with the supervision of the plantation, or weary with the problems and conflicting interests of political life, he might turn again with a sigh of relief to his Homer or his Horace. The chief and the most lasting benefits of his studies at Princeton were the enriching of his character and mind, the introduction they gave him to Greek and Latin literature and art, to natural science, to philosophy and history.

CHAPTER VII

# The Alumni to the Rescue

ETWEEN ourselves, I could wish your worthy president were more known, but few in this part of the world seem to know at all who Dr. Carnahan is," wrote an alumnus from South Carolina to John Maclean.[1] The day had passed when the presidency of the college carried with it leadership in the Presbyterian Church, and Dr. Carnahan was not the man to win distinction through the mere possession of scholarship or intellect. He was a pious, inactive person, without much vision as an educator. When he stood before the undergraduates in the Prayer Hall to deliver a Sunday sermon, they found him dignified and respectable, but "ponderous in delivery and slow to speak," his prayer "almost always the same."[2] If they happened to meet him socially, he was kind, affable, and possessed a sense of humor, but when they visited his office to submit an oration or explain an absence, they found him unapproachable and cold. It never occurred to them to go to him for advice in time of trouble, or to ask a favor.[3]

Had the students been able to look beneath the stolid exterior of the "Boss," they would have found more of timidity than coldness or indifference. They did not realize, also, that he had for many years suffered from a disease of the throat which made public speaking difficult and painful, and which gradually sapped his strength. Yet the undergraduates considered him a clear and forceful teacher. When expounding Alexander's *Evidences of Christianity* or pointing out the errors of Paley's *Theology*, he could hold the attention of his listeners, and make telling points which "rang in their ears

[1] Undated letter of W. A. McDowell, *Maclean MSS*, Princeton Library.
[2] E. Shippen, *Notes About Princeton*, MSS, Princeton Library.
[3] *Journal of Job M. Allen*, 1837, p. 37, MSS, Princeton Library.

for half a century."[4] In his capacity of president, however, the best that can be said for him is that he never blocked progressive policies when others had formulated them and were trying to put them into effect. Throughout all of the thirty-one years of his administration he remained, as an alumnus expressed it, "a good deal of a figure head."

Yet at no time in the history of the college was leadership more urgently needed. It was a period of profound change throughout the nation. The population was increasing rapidly, the borders of the country were pushing out to embrace vast areas in the west and southwest, the shift from commerce and agriculture to industry was affecting the life of millions of people, the production of wealth had doubled and tripled, society was undergoing a leveling process under the influence of Jacksonian democracy, public schools and state colleges were springing up on all sides as symbols of the trend toward the secularizing and popularizing of education; the public was demanding that the colleges should not be monopolized by the rich and candidates for the ministry, but should open their doors to the sons of the farmer, the small merchant, and the mechanic, that there should be less time devoted to the classics, philosophy, and mathematics and more to English literature, history, and the practical sciences.

If the College of New Jersey was to live up to its great traditions of service to the nation, she could not close her eyes to the spirit of the age. Fortunately, she was not lacking in devoted sons who desired to see her take the lead in progressive educational policies and sought to supply her with the means to do so. Samuel L. Southard, in his commencement address of 1832, sounded the keynote. "I cannot err in believing that at the present moment in our country it is the duty of the scholar to direct his learning and to bend his efforts to that which shall be practically useful to the best purposes of life," he pointed out. "Our theory of government, which rests on general intelligence, our public prosperity, which depends on general virtue, our past history and our future

[4] *Reminiscences of T. W. Tallmadge*, MSS, Princeton Library.

hopes, all demand this at our hands. Every social element is in agitation in this extraordinary age." But to meet the challenge of the age Princeton must have an enlarged endowment. Amherst, Yale, and other colleges had recently received large sums, and Princeton's claims were as valid as theirs. "Do we love our Alma Mater less? Are we less devoted to the cause of science, religion and learning?"[5]

But already the alumni were coming to the rescue. In September 1830, when Mr. Southard himself, together with the Reverend John McDowell, had been authorized to raise $20,000 for the endowment of a professorship, the alumni, trustees, and even the faculty subscribed liberally. Unfortunately the entire project was endangered by the provision that unless $10,000 had been obtained by April 1, 1831, the whole subscription should be null and void. On February 1 the total was only $7,055 and McDowell began to worry; on March 16 it was about $7,500 and his nervousness increased. It was agreed that Maclean should go to Baltimore in a desperate effort to save the situation, but when March 30 dawned and McDowell had heard nothing from him, he "posted off to Newark through a torrent of rain and labored all day," vowing that never again would he be a partner "in begging with anybody in Princeton." Yet Maclean, too, had been hard at work, and a letter from him received on the fateful closing date sent the subscription over the top with a total of $10,200.[6]

A pathetically small sum this! Yet its importance is not to be measured in dollars and cents, for it was a beginning, an earnest of greater things to come. The alumni at last were awake to the needs of the college and to their responsibility toward it. At their annual meeting during the commencement of 1833 it was voted "to raise $100,000 for the extension and improvement of the college." The Reverend Daniel Newell was made agent for soliciting funds and a

[5] *College Mementos of Princeton,* 1831-1841.
[6] McDowell to Maclean, Feb. 1, March 16, 31, April 1, 1831, *Maclean MSS,* Princeton Library. The final report brought the gifts to $10,835 and expenses to $611.

circular letter was sent out to the alumni stating the claims of the college. "The whole of the available funds of the college ... little exceeds $2,000 per annum," it pointed out. "Only one professorship is partially endowed. The fluctuating and inadequate income from the students, therefore, is the only support for all the officers, both permanent and temporary."[7]

Throughout her career Princeton has suffered severely from great national disasters—her students were scattered and Nassau Hall wrecked by the Revolution, her rebuilding fund was almost wiped out by the inflation of the Continental currency, she lost a large part of her student body by the withdrawal of southern boys at the outbreak of the War Between the States. Now, her first real efforts to secure an endowment were doomed by the financial troubles of Jackson's second administration and the Panic of 1837. "When I was about to make an effort upon our community in the winter of 1833-34, lo! the Jackson times were upon us and it was not very safe for an agent to approach the pockets of the people," wrote a Mississippi alumnus in May 1835. "It was agreed on all hands that it would be better to defer operations to a future and more favorable opportunity."[8] But the future grew blacker and blacker. The removal of the deposits from the Bank of the United States was followed by wild speculation, wild speculation by the specie circular, the specie circular by the crash of 1837 and years of depression.

Despite all this, the endowment campaign failed of success only by a very narrow margin. The subscriptions were to be paid in five installments and all save the first were to be canceled should the total not reach $50,000 by January 1, 1836. The first response was encouraging, the Princeton community subscribing $10,000 and New York $15,000.[9] George Douglass, of New York, led the list with $5,000, Professor Maclean, James Lenox, and others followed with $1,000

[7] *Princeton Library MSS*, BF 752.
[8] J. Tyler to Maclean, May 19, 1835, *Maclean MSS*, Princeton Library.
[9] *Princeton Library MSS*, BF 752.

each, and many others with $500 or less.[10] In April Newell reported that from $30,000 to $40,000 had been subscribed and expressed confidence that the whole sum of $100,000 could be raised.[11] But soon unfavorable reports began to come in. William Forman of Baltimore wrote that he had "scraped the city" but had found all pockets "hermetically seal'd" and "the fountains of liberality dried up."[12] As the close of the campaign approached, great efforts were made to save the endowment, but when the sun set on the last day the fund was still a few thousand dollars short of the goal.

Yet the campaign had not been entirely in vain. Several thousand dollars had been collected,[13] of which $500 was spent for apparatus for Professor Joseph Henry, $420 for a "large" telescope, and $4,000 added to the endowment. More important was the placing of the needs and claims of the college before the alumni. Some who could not give in 1835 were more liberal after the return of prosperity, others made bequests in their wills. The venerable James Madison, former President of the United States and president of the alumni association, left the college $1,000 to be paid from the proceeds of the publication of his "report of the discussions and proceedings of the Convention," which was placed in trust for the library.[14] In 1837 the interest on invested funds was $3,835, a sum but slightly less than one-fourth of the annual income of the college and indispensable in meeting the necessary expenses.[15]

But the chief endowment of the college was the endowment of scholarship. One heard nothing of the conflict between investigation and teaching; there was no demand that the instructors devote all their attention to the students at the

[10] "Alumni Association of Nassau Hall," 1830-1839, *Maclean MSS*, Papers 2, Princeton Library.
[11] Newell to Trustees, April 15, 1835, *Maclean MSS*, Princeton Library.
[12] William Forman to Maclean, Nov. 21, 1835, *ibid.*
[13] "Alumni Association of Nassau Hall," 1830-1839, *Maclean MSS*, Papers 2, Princeton Library. The total was $8,920, of which $4,000 was paid to the agent.
[14] *Princeton Library MSS*, AM 5146, AM 503.
[15] *Maclean MSS*, 1837, Princeton Library.

cost of research. Research, it was clearly recognized, was essential to good teaching, for it constantly revived the professor's intellectual inspiration and gave him new enthusiasms, new ideas to pass on to his pupils. Thus scholarship was regarded not only as essential in upholding the reputation of the college but in preventing stagnation in the classroom.

This it was which gave to Princeton Joseph Henry, one of the great American scientists. When the chair of natural philosophy became vacant in 1832 through the resignation of Professor Vethake, the college turned its thoughts to the young master in the Albany Academy because of the reports of his scientific investigations. "I cheerfully comply with your request respecting the scientific character of Professor Henry of Albany," John Torrey wrote Maclean. "I have known this gentleman for several years and have marked with great satisfaction his course since he commenced his career as a cultivator of physical science. He gave promise from the first that he would be one of the foremost in pursuits of this kind; and he has already, though so young, gained a reputation that would do honor to grey hairs. I have no doubt should his health be spared a few years, but he will stand among the first philosophers of the country."[16]

From Professor Benjamin Silliman of Yale came similar assurances. "As a physical philosopher he has no superior in our country, certainly not among young men. . . . If placed in favorable circumstances I doubt not that he will add to the science of physics and bring forward other discoveries besides the brilliant ones which have already made him . . . known to the scientific world."[17] And as it was Henry's scholarly ability which made Princeton want his services, so it was the opportunities there for experimentation which induced him to come. "My only views at present are to secure a comfortable support for my family and next to establish and to deserve for myself the reputation of a man of science," he wrote Maclean. "I have determined to confine my attention principally to a course of study and investigation intermediate to pure mathe-

[16] *Princeton Library MSS*, AM 8377.      [17] *Ibid*.

matics, on the one hand, and to the more detailed parts of chemistry on the other. Any honorable situation in which it would be a part of my duty to teach these branches and which would afford me superior advantages to those I now possess for prosecuting them will be acceptable."[18]

In the selection of other members of the faculty there was the same regard for scholarship, and though it was not to be expected that all should approach the greatness of a Henry, each enjoyed a wide reputation in his field. When Professor John S. Hart received an offer from a school trebling his income, the fact that it would put a stop to his studies—and study he declared to be his "paramount earthly object"— made him reluctant to accept.[19] Professor Benedict Jaeger "was particularly devoted to natural science," and could boast of "extensive attainments in mineralogy, botany, zoology, etc." before he came to Princeton. Albert Baldwin Dod, John Torrey, James W. Alexander, Stephen Alexander, Matthew B. Hope, George M. Giger, Elias Loomis were all distinguished scholars.

One wonders how these men could continue their investigations so successfully in the limited time stolen from their teaching. Much was accomplished during the vacations, much by preparing advanced lectures for delivery to the senior class, much by subdividing the fields of instruction. The day had passed when there was but one professor of languages and one for mathematics, natural philosophy, and chemistry. In 1835 the faculty comprised, in addition to President Carnahan, John Maclean, professor of ancient languages and literature; Albert B. Dod, professor of mathematics; Joseph Henry, professor of natural philosophy; James W. Alexander, professor of belles-lettres; John Torrey, professor of chemistry; Samuel L. Howell, professor of anatomy and physiology; Louis Hargous, professor of French and Spanish; Benedict Jaeger, professor of German and Italian, and lecturer on natural history; John S. Hart, adjunct professor

---

[18] *Ibid.*
[19] *Maclean MSS*, July 19, 1836, Princeton Library.

of ancient languages; Stephen Alexander, adjunct professor of mathematics; and George Burrowes and Samuel Miller, Jr., tutors.[20]

As an investigator Henry was the most distinguished. Perhaps none of the students who crowded into the recitation room in the old Philosophical Hall to hear his brilliant lectures and witness his fascinating experiments realized that their favorite professor was explaining to them inventions of epoch-making significance. Yet from that very room Henry sent out wireless transmissions decades before Marconi was born, and made experiments in telegraphy which antedated the work of Morse and Vail. Before coming to Princeton he had invented the electromagnet in its present form, had constructed and operated an electromagnetic telegraph, had observed the induced electric current and had been the first to explain the current of self-induction.[21]

At Princeton he built a great magnet[22] and set up a telegraph line through the trees in front of Nassau Hall and used it to signal his residence when he wanted his luncheon.

To this day Henry has not received due credit for his work on the telegraph. He always claimed that Morse and Vail had treated him unjustly and even denounced them to his students. "Henry sticks it into Morse," young John R. Buhler jotted down in his diary on February 21, 1846. "Says Morse's assistant Vail has lately published a book purporting to be a history of the telegraph and hasn't mentioned him at all in it, although it was through communications and instructions . . . made by him that Morse's telegraphic scheme came to consummation."[23]

It was while making an extensive study of the induced current that Henry discovered that the inductive action could be transmitted for considerable distances. "A single spark from the prime conductor of the machine, of about an inch

---

[20] *Catalogue of the College of New Jersey*, 1834-1835.

[21] Dean W. F. Magie, and Joseph Henry, quoted in *Princeton Alumni Weekly*, April 29, 1914.

[22] Still preserved at Princeton.

[23] J. R. Buhler *Diary*, I, p. 120, MSS, Princeton Library.

long, thrown on the upper end of a circuit of wire in an upper room, produced an induction sufficiently powerful to magnetize needles in a parallel circuit of wire placed in the cellar beneath, at a perpendicular distance of thirty feet with two floors and ceilings, each fourteen inches thick, intervening." Later he announced that he had increased the distance to "more than two hundred and twenty feet," by discharging through his telegraph wire in front of Nassau Hall a battery of several Leyden jars, and so magnetizing needles by the induced current in a parallel wire set up on the back campus. In the words of Dean William F. Magie: "In these discoveries of Henry we have the essential features of wireless transmission."[24]

Such a man could not fail to be a great teacher. The boys listened eagerly as he explained the mysteries of electrodynamics, dynamic induction, galvanism, magnetoelectricity, of transmitted vibrations, the decomposition of light; or showed them "the appearances of the spark through perfect and partial conductors," or made his "huge magnet" lift a group of "sneezing and coughing" students "equivalent to 3,500 pounds," or tried the experiment of the enchanted lyre. "Henry . . . gets more and more interesting every time he lectures," said Buhler. "He is a great canal in constancy, uniformity, depth and majesty of flow."[25] Buhler's only regret at having been suspended for sleeping through morning prayers several times in succession was that it caused him to miss one of Henry's lectures.

No one knows better how to evaluate a teacher than an undergraduate, and the students of 1832 or 1846 respected Henry not only for his scholarly ability, but for his character as well. "He was an enthusiast of true science, preeminently an educator, all the students having for him an unbounded admiration and affection," wrote Stephen G. Dodd of the class of 1842. "He had large, lustrous, blue eyes and an ex-

[24] William F. Magie, "100 Years Ago," *Princeton Alumni Weekly*, Jan. 13, 1941.
[25] J. R. Buhler *Diary*, II, p. 97, MSS, Princeton Library.

pressive and winning countenance. As a lecturer and professor he was simple and natural, fond of being questioned by us in our recitations."[26] "He affects no superiority," agreed Buhler, "is free and familiar and social, but 'for a' that' there is that about him—an indescribable *Je ne sais quoi*, which excites within one an emotion akin to awe! I always feel as if I were in the presence of a superior being. . . . May a star ever shine on the head of Nassau's nobleman—the great and wise Henry."[27]

Like Henry, Albert B. Dod was universally respected and loved. A thin, sallow man, with "an eye which would look right through anything,"[28] his gentle, lovable nature, nonetheless, endeared him to faculty and students alike. "He was the admiration and marvel of the students, brilliant in thought and language, clothing the abstruse with charms, making plain the incomprehensible," wrote Stephen G. Dodd.[29] Joseph J. Halsey of the class of 1843 described him as "rather under size, middle aged yet withered in appearance, with his camlet coat like the one grandpa used to wear . . . the waist about four inches under his arm, his head bent forward and looking down, with a very careless step, you would think him the last man that could lay claim to *first* place among the mathematicians of the United States."[30]

He was remarkable for his versatility. An able mathematician, a brilliant preacher, a distinguished theologian, a clear teacher, giving courses in architecture and political economy, deeply interested in belles-lettres, it was an inspiration to sit at his feet in class or to listen to his conversation. Buhler thus describes one of his sermons: "Never heard such a sermon in my life, so magnificently grand, so solemnly awful. . . . Dod has hitherto confined himself to the delivery of gorgeous moral panoramas, of sublimely ornamented orations, of splendidly drawn pictures. He is a perfect Raphael or rather

[26] *Princeton Alumni Weekly*, Dec. 11, 1912.
[27] J. R. Buhler *Diary*, I, p. 136; II, p. 96, MSS, Princeton Library.
[28] E. Shippen, *Notes About Princeton*, MSS, Princeton Library.
[29] *Princeton Alumni Weekly*, Dec. 11, 1912.
[30] *Ibid.*, March 22, 1911.

Claude Lorraine . . . the harmonious blender of the lights and shades of eloquence."[31]

Dod's optional course on architecture, which he took over from Professor Henry, was very popular. Many years after graduation Edward Shippen asked a classmate what he remembered best of his work at college. "Professor Dod's voluntary lectures on architecture," was the reply.[32] John Maclean declared that as a teacher of mathematics this country had probably never produced his superior,[33] while young Theodore W. Tallmadge wrote that "he was, in the belief of all, the smartest man in the faculty." He was valued not only for his "enchanting manner in the pulpit," and his ability as a teacher, but for his private conversation, "the benefits of which were eagerly sought by every collegian."[34] It was not to be expected that one occupied with so many and such varied interests should produce a large volume of scholarly work, and Dod the mathematician, the teacher, the pulpit orator, has left little more than a series of articles in the *Biblical Repertory and Princeton Review*. When he died in the prime of life, in November 1845, however, it was regarded as a "tremendous blow to the college."

Less versatile than Dod, but one of the most distinguished scientists in the country was Stephen Alexander, whose sister had married Joseph Henry. Accompanying Henry to Princeton in 1832, he was made tutor in 1833, adjunct professor in 1834 and professor of astronomy in 1840. A small, dark, modest man, he was well liked by the students, who at once dubbed him "Stephy." Even though he seldom looked up from his notes when lecturing, the boys discovered that he was fully alive to each individual's attainments, foibles, or failures. In matters of discipline his chief reliance was an unfailing sense of humor. When, on one occasion, he found the

[31] J. R. Buhler *Diary*, 1, p. 82, MSS, Princeton Library.
[32] E. Shippen, *Notes About Princeton*, MSS, Princeton Library.
[33] *Biblical Repertory and Princeton Review*, vol. 18, pp. 350-351.
[34] Tallmadge to William Cox, Nov. 22, 1845, *Princeton Library MSS*, AM 1253.

benches of his recitation room coated with tar, he had the students go through the hour standing.

When young Buhler first entered Alexander's course in astronomy, he was critical of the teaching. "He is a very uninteresting and unimpressive lecturer," he complained. "It is surprising to think of how little substance comes out . . . of an hour's gab." But he soon revised this estimate. "Stephy gives a splendid lecture on nebulae," he wrote. "Speaking of starlight he said: 'This semi-transparent light which covered the face of the heavens like a veil, was woven of the scattered glory of a thousand suns.' Styled the stars 'jewels in the glorious diadem around the dark brow of night.' . . . 'Kepler,' he said, 'had written his name in sunbeams on the heavens.' "[35] It was a great treat for the boys when "Stephy" invited them to his residence to look through his telescope at Saturn and its rings or at Jupiter and its satellites, or perhaps at an eclipse of the moon.

Stephen Alexander continued in the faculty until 1877, when he retired after forty-four years of teaching and research. Some of his observations were published in the *American Journal of Science*, some in the *Proceedings* of the American Philosophical Society, some in the *Astronomical Journal*. In 1859 he became president of the American Association for the Advancement of Science and in 1862 was chosen as one of the fifty original members of the National Academy of Sciences.[36]

Nor were Henry, Dod, and Stephen Alexander lone stars in an otherwise somber sky. Henry Vethake was an able economist. John Torrey, who held the chair of chemistry and natural philosophy concurrently with a professorship at the College of Physicians and Surgeons in New York, enjoyed an international reputation as a botanist. He was elected to the Linnaean Society of London in 1839, to the American Academy of Arts and Sciences in 1841, and was a corporate member of the National Academy of Sciences.

[35] J. R. Buhler *Diary*, II, p. 28, MSS, Princeton Library.
[36] *Dictionary of American Biography.*

There was no more distinguished group of scientists in the country than was embraced by the Princeton faculty in the fourth and fifth decades of the century. Among the men who taught in the quaint old "philosophical" building nestling under the wing of Nassau Hall were four members of the National Academy of Sciences, three of them original members, two members of the American Philosophical Society, two members of the American Association for the Advancement of Science, and two members of the American Academy of Arts and Sciences.

The achievements of the faculty in scholarship may be explained in part by the acquisition of new and better equipment. Compared with the fine collections and apparatus of today in Guyot Hall, the Palmer Physical Laboratory, Frick Chemical Laboratory, and elsewhere, the "astronomical, philosophical and chemical apparatus," the mineralogical cabinet, and the museum of natural history housed on the first floor of the Philosophical Building seem pathetically meager. But they constituted a great advance over the past.

One wonders how the room set aside as the museum could have contained the whale which John Torrey wrote Maclean in 1830 was badly in need of disinfecting. Other specimens were not so bulky, and the stuffed birds and animals, the shells and the butterflies exhibited in cabinets excited the interest of all visitors. With the appointment of Benedict Jaeger to the faculty, the museum took on new life for he was not only a distinguished botanist but also an indefatigable collector. Jaeger it was who induced the trustees to secure a taxidermist to preserve the specimens from decay,[37] and he presented to the college a collection of about 150 animals, reptiles, and birds, together with about 2,000 insects.[38] The collection of minerals originally donated by Dr. David Hosack was enlarged in 1837 by nearly 600 specimens, the gift of Samuel Fowler of New York.[39]

[37] Jacob Green to Maclean, July 3, 1839, *Maclean MSS*, Princeton Library.
[38] B. Jaeger to Carnahan, April 8, 1839, *ibid*.
[39] Maclean to Carnahan, April 11, 1837, *ibid*.

It was in 1848 that a correspondent of the *Princeton Whig* pointed out that an observatory was urgently needed, and appealed to the generosity of some "friend to the college and to science" to present one as "a memorial more durable than brass and marble."[40] However, two decades were to pass before this suggestion was acted upon and the walls of the Halsted Observatory began to rise, and in the meanwhile Stephen Alexander had to make his observations with his own small telescope. Fortunately Joseph Henry was not so greatly handicapped in his work as was his brother-in-law, for in 1837 he visited Europe, where with the backing of the alumni association he laid out several thousand dollars in "philosophical apparatus."[41] Perhaps the men whose loyalty to Princeton made these purchases possible little realized the rich dividends which in the hands of Henry they were to yield to science and to civilization.

The library was entirely inadequate throughout Carnahan's administration, and there seems to have been no attempt to make the few thousand volumes housed in Stanhope Hall the tools for undergraduate work. Students were admitted twice a week to take out a book if they could find anything of interest among "the dusty tomes—mostly polemical and controversial."[42] The library was especially deficient in the field of belles-lettres, as James W. Alexander pointed out in 1835. He could not inspire interest in the undergraduates in the British poets, he said, when there was not a line in the library from Cowper, Moore, Wordsworth, Southey, Lamb, Coleridge, and many others.[43] The need for more books was recognized by the trustees, and in the endowment plan of 1835 the sum of $10,000 was set aside to meet it, but with the failure of Newell's efforts there was no money available for purchases.[44]

[40] November 3, 1848.
[41] "Alumni Association of Nassau Hall," Sept. 28, 1842, *Maclean MSS*, Papers 2, Princeton Library.
[42] E. Shippen, *Notes About Princeton*, MSS, Princeton Library.
[43] J. W. Alexander to Maclean, Sept. 21, 1835, *Maclean MSS*, Princeton Library.
[44] *Princeton Library MSS*, BF 752.

Fortunately, the boy who was discouraged by the shelf after shelf of theological works in the main library had only to climb the stairs to Clio Hall or Whig Hall to find more interesting reading. Here were hundreds of books which a boy could really enjoy. "A fine edition of Froissart was a revelation to me which set me reading other works about the times then described," Edward Shippen tells us. "To my recollection the Clio library was very fairly selected, and one of my great delights in college."[45]

One suspects that it was from his Hall library that young Job M. Allen secured the volumes which so enthralled him that he kept his lard lamp burning far into the night—Goldsmith's *Citizen of the World*, Middleton's *Life of Cicero*, Washington Irving's *Bracebridge Hall*, a *Life of Schiller*, and others. Shakespeare he found "one of the most interesting of all dramatic writers," and Sir Walter Scott "decidedly the best novel writer that ever lived," even though his portraiture was matched by that of Washington Irving.[46]

Although Princeton had neither the traditions of an English university nor the financial resources to imitate one, she did make at this time an attempt to expand along the lines of the American university. As early as 1824 a committee of the trustees recommended the establishment of professorships in law and medicine.[47] Six years later Samuel Ladd Howell was appointed professor of anatomy and physiology and during the winter term delivered lectures which seniors were required to attend. Unfortunately, when Professor Howell resigned in 1835, his chair remained vacant and the embryo medical school came to an untimely end.

The Law School, although it started with much brighter prospects, was equally unsuccessful. It was in 1835 that an effort was made to secure the famous Chancellor James Kent of New York to come to Princeton once a year and give a course of lectures. But Kent declined. "I am too far advanced

[45] E. Shippen, *Notes About Princeton*, MSS, Princeton Library.
[46] Job M. Allen, *Journal*, pp. 44, 61, 66, 74, Princeton Library.
[47] John Maclean, *History of the College of New Jersey*, II, p. 256.

in life to engage in new enterprises," he wrote Maclean. "I have as much as I can do at home."[48] Justice Smith Thompson of the Supreme Court also declined, as did Samuel L. Southard and Theodore Frelinghuysen, and the project for the moment was abandoned.[49]

In 1847, however, the prospect brightened when Chief Justice Joseph C. Hornblower of New Jersey and James S. Green and Richard S. Field, distinguished Princeton attorneys, accepted appointments as professors of law. The new school, it was announced, would give courses in "Public and Constitutional Law, Equity and Common Law," by means of "recitations, examinations, lectures and the preparation of legal forms and instruments," and a moot court. A three years' course was to lead to the degree of bachelor of law.[50] So interested was Mr. Field in the project that he erected at his own expense a suitable building on Mercer Street, now known as Ivy Hall.[51] It seemed especially auspicious that the opening of the Law School should coincide with the celebration of the college centennial. This celebration should rightly have been held on October 22, 1846, but when it was found that most of the Presbyterian synods would be in session on that date, it was decided to postpone it until June 1847.[52] The occasion was to be seized upon to emphasize both the services of Princeton's sons to the nation and the marked growth of recent years—the enlarged faculty, the contribution to scholarship, the building expansion, the increase in students. Some of the alumni, men of deeply religious lives, insisted, also, that it be pointed out that the founders had planned the institution as "a temple of piety."[53]

The Princeton community was all excitement on June 29, 1847, when the academic procession formed at the Law Build-

[48] *Maclean MSS*, March 7, 1835, Princeton Library.
[49] John Maclean, *History of the College of New Jersey*, II, p. 299.
[50] *Law School of the College of New Jersey*, Oct. 2, 1846, MSS, Princeton Library.
[51] J. F. Hageman, *History of Princeton*, I, p. 271.
[52] *Maclean MSS*, 1846, Princeton Library.
[53] John Sergeant to Dr. Samuel Miller, *Princeton Library MSS*, AM 3112.

ing and proceeding down Mercer Street into Nassau Street filed into the Presbyterian Church. The crowds who lined the streets saw a distinguished group—the governor of New Jersey, Chief Justice Henry W. Green, two United States senators, the faculty and many prominent alumni. In the church the students and guests who filled every available seat listened attentively while Justice Green delivered an address showing the need for a thoroughly educated bar. In the afternoon the beloved James W. Alexander spoke over two hours with such eloquence that the audience sat in rapt attention, missing not a single word.[54]

The next day dinner was served in a large tent set up on the campus back of the chapel. Here good food alternated with the drinking of toasts, the exchange of reminiscences and the singing of the centennial song.[55]

> Alma Mater, cherish'd mother,
> Hark! Thy sons their voices raise;
> Loving kindred, friend and brother,
> Meet again to hymn thy praise.

Toasts followed to Alma Mater, to the "Venerable President of Nassau Hall," to the "Founders and First Board of Trustees," to the "Long Line of Professors," to the Log College, etc. There were responses by James W. Alexander, Governor Pennington, Professor Olmstead of Yale, Vice-President Dallas, and others. Samuel Stanhope Smith and other leaders of Princeton were praised, and gratitude was expressed for "the numberless improvements" of recent years. When Edward Dickinson arose and proposed the toast "As long as the telegraph wires shall extend from Maine to Louisiana, may the name of Henry ever be prominent," there was enthusiastic applause. Altogether it was a most successful celebration, which not only emphasized the accomplishments of the first century of the college but promised greater things to come.[56]

[54] *Centennial Anniversary of the College of New Jersey*, pp. 4-7.
[55] Written by Matthias Ward, Class of 1833.
[56] *Centennial Anniversary of the College of New Jersey*, pp. 11-34.

Unfortunately the Law School, so auspiciously launched, lasted but a few years. The catalogue of 1847-1848 listed the three members of the law faculty, four attorneys at law attending the lectures and eight regular students. Since the fees were inadequate to compensate the professors for their time, and since the college could not afford to pay them salaries, the project was discontinued after nine years' trial.[57]

With its board of trustees controlled by Presbyterian ministers, with its faculty made up of deeply religious men, with hundreds of its alumni leaders in the church, it was inevitable that the college should enter the lists as a champion of fundamentalism in the battle of science and theology.

Princeton men for a century had contended that science, far from contradicting revealed truth, could only substantiate and buttress it, and they were not to be driven from this position by the reasoning of Louis Agassiz or Edward Hitchcock. A course on "Christian evidences" was required of all juniors, with William Paley's *Natural Theology* as the textbook. A new and realistic touch was introduced when Professor Hope, on being placed in charge of this course in 1847, included in it anatomy and physiology. So a manikin showing the "entire vascular, lymphatic, nervous and muscular systems," which could be taken to pieces just as one would dissect the real body, was purchased, at considerable expense, as an aid in displaying the wonders of nature and the evidences of a "planned" creation.[58]

Not content with this, faculty members, trustees and even alumni, in public address and in articles in the *Biblical Repertory and Princeton Review*, carried the battle to those who were attempting to deny the literal interpretation of the Biblical account of the creation. The study of geology should not be made an instrument to unsettle faith, a thing more precious than science itself, S. L. Southard pleaded in an address in 1837. "Properly investigated it furnishes satisfactory evidence that the Christian's God made the earth as

[57] John Maclean, *History of the College of New Jersey*, II, p. 319.
[58] *Maclean MSS*, 1846, Princeton Library.

he spread out the heavens." The earth, he contended, was a great laboratory whose teeming wonders, its mountains and vales, its oceans with their vast depths, the formation of minerals, the fires of the volcano, provided an answer more potent than miracles to "the atheist's crime and the sceptic's folly." As for the published works of "Voltaire, Hume, Paine and the whole host," they were so full of errors of fact and reasoning as to disgrace a college undergraduate.[59]

Eight years later the usually gentle Albert B. Dod, in a fifty-page review, delivered a frontal assault on the book by Robert Chambers, *Vestiges of the Natural History of Creation*. His acceptance of Laplace's nebular hypothesis, Dod declared, came from "a confused and imperfect comprehension of it," and the cumulative force of a number of theories, none of which possessed much weight of itself. "With most of our readers," Dod wrote, "we trust it would be deemed an ample refutation of any system to show clearly that it was atheistic in its essential character." The author, therefore, could never seduce him into the belief that we who stand at the head of creation have grown up from the simplest form of vegetation by successive translations of species. The only argument he could think of for believing that man may have come from the brute was that men existed capable of maintaining such a theory.[60]

There could be no better illustration of the stimulating effect of scholarship upon teaching than the eagerness with which the undergraduates looked forward to their senior year because of the privilege of hearing the lectures of Princeton's distinguished scientists. After the long grind of recitations in Greek, Latin, mathematics, and philosophy, it was a joy to listen to Henry, or Torrey, or Stephen Alexander, or to watch their experiments, or to go with them through the cabinet of natural history. Buhler might complain that Torrey had discoursed so long on vapor that his ideas "had all turned into gas" and that he had been in such intimate fellowship

[59] *Princeton Whig*, Dec. 8, 1837.
[60] *Biblical Repertory and Princeton Review*, XVII, pp. 505-557.

with metals that he had taken on "the dullness of lead," but he as well as the others thoroughly enjoyed his lectures.

With the irksome round of classroom recitations, essays, and examinations to which freshmen, sophomores, and juniors were subjected there was much dissatisfaction. Before them in unending array passed Livy, Xenophon, Horace, Demosthenes, Cicero, Homer, Euripides, and Sophocles, sandwiched in with Roman antiquities, algebra, geometry, trigonometry, surveying, navigation, elements of history, calculus, philosophy, "evidences of Christianity," and natural theology. That some of the teachers did little to enliven this formidable list of subjects or to inspire the student we gather from the recollections of Edward Shippen. "It was very funny to see Dr. J. Maclean, who was then Professor of Greek, in his recitation room, in the Library Building.[61] When we wished to, we could always prevent any regular recitation or construing, say in Homer, by someone rising . . . and saying: 'Professor Maclean, I have looked closely at this passage (quoting it) and I do not see that the significance of *de* in line twenty-three is very clear.' Then Johnny would dive down among his folios at the bottom of his desk and bring up Porson or some other authority, put his spectacles up on his forehead and go into the thing." In the meanwhile some member of the class would make a pretense of reciting. "At the end, he would announce that the meaning of the particle, in that connection, was doubtful and then, the hour ended, we went away."[62]

Had the teachers of Latin and Greek enlivened the routine of syntax and case relations with excursions into the beauties of classical literature, the students would have profited more by their courses. But they adhered strictly to the beaten paths of "mental discipline." When word reached Maclean that Professor Topping was teaching Greek literature rather than the Greek language, he at once called him to account. Topping replied that he used literature as a means to an end, in order

[61] Stanhope Hall.
[62] E. Shippen, *Notes About Princeton*, MSS, Princeton Library.

to interest the students in their work. After years of futile attempt in the familiar method of teaching, in which he was often interrupted "by groans and other wilful noises," he began to intersperse the translation and parsing with such comments on the passages as had attracted his own attention. The effect was immediate. From being notoriously unruly and apathetic, the students became docile and studious. "We must succeed, it seems to me, by interesting the understanding of the students," he concluded, "by rousing a manly interest of thought and then turning them back upon themselves."[63] That this was rank heresy we conclude from the fact that a few days later Topping's resignation was accepted by the trustees.

Despite the tedium of classwork, the students complained more of the rigidity of the curriculum and of the subjects included in it than of the teaching. Despite the talk about mental discipline, despite the pleas that one could not master English without knowing Latin, despite the beauty of ancient literature, they were skeptical about the value of the classics and of mathematics. But the trustees and the faculty clung to the old program. It had been basic in the days of Jonathan Dickinson and of Witherspoon; it must be basic now. The only concessions to the pleas of the undergraduates was the institution of elective courses, entirely outside the curriculum, and for these the students paid fees, and received no official credit. In this way French, German, Italian, English literature, architecture crept into Princeton as subjects to be tolerated—but they continued to be regarded with suspicion.

There is reason to believe that the first course in English literature given in the college came as a result of an article in the *Nassau Monthly*. Denouncing the fixed curriculum, the youthful writer declared that he knew nothing it so nearly resembled as the patent medicine which cured "with perfect indifference, fevers and colds, vertigo and indigestion, sickheadache and consumption, sciatica and the gout." To secure

[63] E. M. Topping to Maclean, June 22, 1846, *Maclean MSS*, Princeton Library.

very real benefits from Latin and Greek "we must be able to think in Latin and Greek," he argued, "and we never yet knew a senior in any college who could do that. . . . We have known young men graduate with considerable honor, who knew absolutely nothing of history and of Shakespeare and Milton, and Spenser and Dryden, of Swift, Addison and Johnson." Yet they "were supposed by their friends to have a finished education which fitted them for any employment within the grasp of the human intellect. Were they? . . . Their education is about as fit for the station they are to occupy through life as the military tactics of the Baron de Steuben for fighting the Blackfeet Indians among the passes and glens of the Rocky Mountains. . . . To graduate with honor it is necessary to become intimately acquainted with the prescribed college studies, but it were, we think, almost a compensation for the loss of health to know some things else beside these."[64]

The year following the publication of this article, Matthew Boyd Hope was added to the faculty as professor of belles-lettres. "New professor, Hope, is in town. Quite an excitement about it, of course," wrote Buhler in his diary. "He is a long, tall, snaky individual. . . . He carries his head, which is sandy, in a foppish kind of manner and has already acquired the professorial sling!"[65] Although Hope's course in English literature was announced in the catalogue of 1845-1846, it was not given until the following session, when at last the students could get their allotment of Chaucer, Shakespeare, and Milton. That these lectures were interesting and stimulating —though thin in content as compared with those of today—is inferred from an examination of several undergraduate books of notes on Hope's sister course in rhetoric.[66]

The trustees and the faculty were not blind to the need for better standards in the undergraduate courses. The time had come, it was admitted, when fathers wished "to see their sons elevated to the highest literary and scientific honors and be-

[64] *Nassau Monthly*, Sept., 1844.
[65] J. R. Buhler *Diary*, II, p. 26, MSS, Princeton Library.
[66] Notes of W. J. Magie, of D. L. Smith and of George E. Clymer, MSS, Princeton Library.

come thoroughly furnished for elevated stations in the learned professions."[67] Yet it was feared that to make drastic changes might frighten off would-be matriculates and so cut down the meager income of the college. As formerly, most newcomers went directly into the sophomore class, although many were but sixteen years old. In 1839-1840 the freshman class numbered but 16 boys, in 1840-1841 but 21, the next year 13, the next only 9, in 1850-1851 it rose to 42 and in 1852-1853 sank to 19.[68]

The system of examinations and grading also remained substantially unchanged during the fifth and sixth decades. The passing mark was fifty. "To obtain over ninety-five required very diligent application . . . and the student had not time for preparation for Hall duties and outdoor exercises," T. W. Tallmadge tells us. "Hence most of our bright fellows had a grade in the eighties. . . . The grade was averaged from all the studies and it was quite common for a student to have been very bright in some one or more . . . while a single study in which he did not give the required attention brought down his average grade."[69]

The final examinations were partly oral, partly written. Since it would have taken too much time to question each student on all phases of his work in a course, the class was divided by lottery into groups of ten or twelve, for examination on one book or one division of the subject. When Buhler found himself in the group to be quizzed on Alexander's *Evidences of Christianity*, though he was better acquainted with natural philosophy, he tried to effect a transfer, but "Boss wouldn't permit it," and he had to "sit up" and do his best. Fortunately he acquitted himself well.[70]

It is interesting to follow Buhler through one day of oral examinations. "Peirce pulls me out of bed at 6 o'clock. Johnny begins his examination at 6:30. Calls me up on Juvenal *Satires*.

[67] *Princeton Library MSS*, BF 752.
[68] *Princeton College Catalogues*, 1839-1856.
[69] *Reminiscences of T. W. Tallmadge*, MSS, Princeton Library.
[70] J. R. Buhler *Diary*, II, p. 74, MSS, Princeton Library.

. . . I rowl[71] like the very devil. Bullit Head[72] fizzling on the pronunciation of some word, was sarcastically asked by the old fellow 'for his principles of pronunciation,' and says he, 'If you get the Latin Salutatory, Mr. Depue, you won't be able to pronounce it even!' . . . I stand my examination on astronomy in the afternoon. I fizzle abominably. Stephy asked me one question concerning some one of the zones, which being unable to answer, Fid, who was just behind me prompts me in a whisper unfortunately too audible. 'Will you be kind enough to move further towards the center of the room, Mr. Buhler?' said the professor. Needless to say I felt mean as I had to shuffle off from Fid's vicinity. The worst of it was that one of the Trustees, old Shippen,[73] was present to witness the mortification."[74]

Apparently the undergraduates resented the intrusion of trustees at their examinations. "Boss Miller[75] came up today while Baltzell was being examined by Henry and opening his mouth, spoke after this fashion in his . . . rotundo, staccato style of orthoepy, 'Mr. Professor, I happen in this instance to be acquainted with Mr. Baltzell. But will you be so kind as to enunciate the name of each individual as he successively rises to recite?' Thinks I, that's perfectly uncalled for. . . . Old Shippen was seen to nod, whether from somnolency or acquiescence, it is doubtful."[76] At the Greek examination two trustees were present, "holding Greek books firmly in their hands and trying to affect familiarity with the contents, in a word to look knowing and critical. . . . Trustees are monstrous humbugs, as well as arrant bores."[77]

Yet there was no sham in the control the trustees exercised over the college. Whenever the charge of sectarianism was leveled at the institution there were indignant disclaimers.

[71] Make a good recitation.
[72] David A. Depue, of Belvidere, N.J., Judge New Jersey Supreme Court, 1866-1901.
[73] Dr. William Shippen, of Philadelphia.
[74] J. R. Buhler *Diary*, II, pp. 75, 76, MSS, Princeton Library.
[75] Rev. Samuel Miller.
[76] J. R. Buhler *Diary*, II, p. 76, MSS, Princeton Library.
[77] *Ibid.*, p. 78.

Men of various denominations were chosen trustees, it was pointed out. "Young men of all sects . . . are admissible as students. A student is permitted to attend that house of worship which his parent or guardian may prefer or direct. Jews as well as Christians will be found among the alumni of Nassau Hall; Catholics and dissenters of all denominations." Yet year after year, decade after decade, Presbyterian ministers constituted a majority in the board of trustees, leavened with a group of men distinguished in public life, such as Secretary of the Navy Samuel L. Southard, the Honorable Lucius Q. C. Elmer, James Lenox, Chancellor Henry W. Green and the Honorable Daniel Haines. Of the twenty-three listed in 1840, nine were trustees also of the Princeton Theological Seminary and three—Samuel Miller, Archibald Alexander, and John Breckinridge—members of its faculty.

Even in the selection of lay members of the board, the religious beliefs of the candidate were weighed carefully, and the ideal man was the Presbyterian giver. In 1845 Henry M. Alexander wrote Maclean, suggesting Dudley A. Gregory. "He is a man in the prime of life, of great wealth and liberality. . . . By appointing him I think you would secure for the college not only a warm but an efficient friend, and a person whose donations, which are not small, might be directed into channels which you gentlemen at Princeton consider best. He is a Presbyterian and a man of unimpeachable morals . . . the pillar of the Jersey City Presbyterian Church."[78]

With Presbyterian influence thus entrenched in the college, it was with astonishment and alarm that many good churchmen received the news that a cruciform chapel was being erected on the campus. What would Jonathan Dickinson, Aaron Burr, Jonathan Edwards, or Samuel Davies have thought of that? When the trustees met in June 1847 they discharged the committee which had been responsible for this blunder, and appointed a new committee headed by the Reverend Cortland Van Rensselaer, with power to alter the plans. At a special meeting of the trustees, in July 1847, attended by

[78] *Maclean MSS*, 1845, Princeton Library.

every minister on the board, this new committee made a report. "Cruciform architecture is so identified with popery that it becomes us to beware of adopting its insignia. . . . Far be it from us to assume a position of irreverence towards this sacred object. But the history of the Church proves that when the cross has been imitated externally in buildings and crucifixes it has tended to degrade religion. . . . Your committee think that the cross form ought not to have been selected for the chapel of our college. . . . Least of all ought such a building to be erected where the minds of the young can be easily familiarized with a form of architecture condemned by our Church."[79]

What was to be done! The walls were two-thirds up, all the stone had been purchased, a contract had been made with a builder. To demolish the completed work and start anew would be very expensive. So, with profound regret, the trustees voted that "the chapel be completed according to the plan of the architect," and since the new committee now washed their hands of the matter, the original committee was reappointed.[80]

But several of the trustees entered a protest to be placed in the minutes and one, the Reverend Isaac V. Brown, vented himself in a bitter letter to Maclean. Since the chapel had derived its form from the Dark Ages, its influence would be anti-Christian and as infectious as death, an indication that Princeton was going the way of Oxford and Carnahan the way of Cardinal Newman.[81]

And for many years the drab, inoffensive little building was regarded with aversion. "The bell tolls forth the hour of prayer," said William Paterson in an oration two decades later. "And here the change seems great indeed. As I look upon the cruciform building erected as a house of worship . . . it does appear as if it had been constructed by surpliced priests, where long robed prelates chant a service learned

[79] *Trustees Minutes*, III, pp. 483, 484.
[80] *Ibid.*, p. 484.
[81] *Maclean MSS*, June 27, 1847, Princeton Library.

by rote, not where the creed of that stern faith of love taught by Geneva's School is preached by plain robed men."[82]

Suspicion and dissatisfaction were increased when the students, of their own volition, started a subscription for an organ in the chapel. Organ music might be appropriate for an Episcopal church, but it was out of place with Presbyterian congregational singing. "I do not know that the Faculty have sanctioned it," Isaac V. Brown wrote to Samuel Miller, "but I do think they ought to arrest the measure instantly. . . . Are the Trustees cyphers and tools? . . . I think you will hear from others soon on the same subject."[83] Good Mr. Brown seems to have been unaware that the students two years before had organized a choir and orchestra for Sunday services, and had made the old chapel in Nassau Hall resound not only to the sound of young voices, but with an "abundance of wind and stringed instruments."[84]

In the minds of many good men there was ever present the danger that the college would forget its origins and throw off the guiding hand of the church. "The early presidents . . . were men who had devoted themselves to the service of religion. . . . This was the end and object of their lives." They sought to make the college "a temple of piety," a place where "a holy life was to be maintained and taught."[85] When Samuel Miller resigned from the trustees after forty-three years of service he made a solemn appeal that the college be "conducted on the strictest principles of intellectual and moral discipline."[86]

However, it was only too obvious that many of the students had strayed from the straight and narrow path the trustees had marked out for them. Dissipation was not general, but in every class there were a few wild fellows who were always causing trouble. Strong ale was to be had from Anthony's on Nassau Street opposite the campus. A colored boy would

[82] *Princeton Library MSS*, AM 11803.    [83] *Ibid.*, AM 2533.
[84] J. R. Buhler *Diary*, II, p. 4, MSS, Princeton Library.
[85] John Sergeant to Samuel Miller, July 29, 1847, *Princeton Library MSS*, AM 3112.
[86] *Princeton Library MSS*, AM 530.

hide a two or three gallon jug in the weeds and high grass in the front campus near the east gate, and the students would take the risk of smuggling it past Johnny Maclean's house and into Nassau Hall.[87]

Often the strong imbibers were as great a nuisance to their fellow students as to the faculty. "Go out on serenade tonight," wrote Buhler in his diary. "Turba, Tom, Tony on flute, Townsend on guitar, Key and Welsh voice. . . . The serenade is an awful fizzle. We afflict Mrs. Cook and daughters and two young ladies from Washington. The fizzle is occasioned by the intrusion and obstinate cooperation of Guerard and Howard beastly and vociferously noisy. Otherwise it would have been delightful."[88] Some of the trustees were inclined to blame the faculty for conduct such as this, not because they were not on the alert to detect and to punish it, but because several of them themselves served wine at their meals.[89]

The spirit of youth and recklessness occasionally took a dangerous turn. One dark evening Edward Shippen, in company with several other students, was passing President Carnahan's residence on his way to Nassau Hall. "There was a glass door into the study. . . . We were anxious to get back to our comfortable open fires in the Franklin fireplaces . . . when J. suddenly said: 'The Boss is sitting in there, I'll give him a shot!' . . . To our surprise he pulled out a pistol, and, with a very good aim, fired through the glass window, which was illuminated by the lard lamp within. It was proved afterwards that the ball had not missed the president by more than a foot or two. . . . J. was given three hours to get out of town."[90]

Usually the escapades were merely mischievous, intended to break the monotony of college life. It was so thrilling to awake to the cry, "Heads out! Heads out!" when a glare on

[87] E. Shippen, *Notes About Princeton*, MSS, Princeton Library.
[88] J. R. Buhler *Diary*, II, p. 58, MSS, Princeton Library.
[89] "Letters of David Magie," Sept. 3 and 5, 1839, *Maclean MSS*, Princeton Library.
[90] E. Shippen, *Notes About Princeton*, MSS, Princeton Library.

the back campus announced that an outhouse had been set on fire. It was such good fun to raid the village for signs, wagons, hen-houses, gates, and fences and deposit them around the cannon, or to bring a mule up to the third floor of Nassau Hall, or to place a stuffed raccoon behind the Bible in the Prayer Hall to peep out at the students and faculty when they assembled for services. Freshmen were usually too timid to take part in these escapades, seniors too dignified. Buhler not only would have nothing to do with the back campus burning of 1846, but he denounced it as "a d—d low trick without even the excuse of originality to compensate for its meanness."[91]

Of a different order was the invasion of the so-called "Cape Horn." As noted before, it was the custom for the rousers to ring the bell and blow a horn at five o'clock to awaken the students in time for morning prayers. In the summer of 1836 the boys smuggled fifteen or twenty horns into Nassau Hall, and the next morning assisted the servants with a thundering blast which caused the faculty as well as every student to jump out of bed. Late that night, when four or five horns were blown in the west end of the top story, two tutors rushed upstairs to confiscate them. Thereupon the miscreants threw the horns out of the window to accomplices beneath, who brought them back up one stairway while the tutors rushed down another. So while the tutors were searching, a triumphant blast from above announced that they had been tricked. "The tutors were so mad and ashamed they gave up the chase."[92]

Despite escapades such as this, the question of discipline assumed less importance than formerly.[93] The faculty at last were learning that it was wise to ignore much, to smile at much, and to depend upon a sense of humor rather than upon harsh repression. Joseph Henry, more than any of the others, seems to have understood the undergraduates and to have

[91] J. R. Buhler *Diary*, II, p. 11, MSS, Princeton Library.
[92] John McA. Eager to James Sears, *Princeton Library MSS*, AM 11816.
[93] *Reminiscences of T. W. Tallmadge*, MSS, Princeton Library.

commanded their respect. Whenever a fight with the village boys or some other serious riot was threatened, he would restore peace by convincing the students that he was on their side.

For the professor or tutor who incurred the dislike of the students life was hard indeed. Professor Hope was especially unpopular. He was "stamped at" when he entered chapel, his horse was taken from its stable and left in Nassau Hall, torpedoes were exploded against the walls during his lectures.[94] It was only with time that they learned to respect him as the kindly man and able teacher that he was. When the faculty, in 1853, placed a "freshman tutor" in charge of one of the sophomore courses, the boys "raised the very deuce in the recitation room," throwing eggs, letting off crackers, and filling the air with sulphureted hydrogen fumes.[95]

It was Maclean who took upon himself the task of upholding the former standards of discipline. So prompt was he in rushing from his residence, lantern in hand, at the first notice of trouble, that the students accused him of sleeping in his clothes. Although kind-hearted and a true friend of the boys, he always assumed an air of severity. "Very well, you can pack up your trunk and go tomorrow," he would say to some delinquent. But the student who knew Johnny did not pack up and probably never heard any more of it. When someone in Nassau Hall spied him rushing across the campus to Dr. Carnahan's residence, his winter cloak flying out behind him, the windows would go up and cries issue of "Hi, Johnny! Keep off the grass!"[96]

Maclean seems to have been unaware that his undignified conduct impaired his influence with the students and actually invited infringements of college discipline. Baiting dear old Johnny was a well-established tradition. On one occasion when two undergraduates were performing on musical instruments on the steps of Nassau Hall, Maclean ordered

[94] Robert Bolling to T. D. Davidson, Nov. 12, 1848, MSS, Princeton Library.
[95] J. C. Boyd to H. R. Slack, Nov. 8, 1853, MSS, Princeton Library.
[96] E. Shippen, *Notes About Princeton*, MSS, Princeton Library.

them to stop. "He was saluted from every window with groans, hisses, 'heads out' and imprecations of all sorts— hang him, pump him, shoot him!" One wit excited "immense applause by shouting out, 'Music hasn't any charms to soothe that savage!' "[97]

Carnahan's administration came and went, and still there were no organized athletics at Princeton. But there were walks to the canal, the woods, or around the "little triangle"[98] or the "big triangle";[99] swimming in Stony Brook or the canal in the summer and skating and sleighriding in the winter; playing old-fashioned football, shinny, wrestling, jumping, battles with snowballs, or hiking expeditions to Worth's Mill, followed by midnight feasts. "The old puerility of playing marbles is again arrived on the campus," wrote Buhler in April 1846. "I see squads of indiscriminate mixt seniors, juniors, sophomores and freshmen kneeling down to it."[100] Hunting, which was indulged in occasionally, proved fatal in one instance when young R. Stockton Boudinot shot himself. It was a sad event for the students as they gathered in hushed groups to discuss the accident or as they listened to Professor Dod's eloquent funeral sermon.[101]

Had it not been for the fact that some of the members of the faculty were themselves inveterate users of tobacco, it would seem strange that smoking was not prohibited. Theodore Tallmadge was in a classmate's room one evening when in dropped one by one a group of loafers, "their study caps as useless as their segars in their mouths. . . . The room was soon like those foggy mornings when you can only see to a certain limit."[102] On another occasion Buhler, upon spying one of his chums who had returned to college after a long absence, rushed up to him to kiss him and burnt his "cheek like the devil with his cigar."[103]

[97] J. R. Buhler *Diary*, II, pp. 74, 75.
[98] Stockton Street, Lovers' Lane, Mercer Street.
[99] Stockton Street, Stony Brook Road, Mercer Street.
[100] J. R. Buhler *Diary*, II, pp. 60, 61, MSS, Princeton Library.
[101] *Princeton Library MSS*, AM 11413.    [102] *Ibid.*
[103] J. R. Buhler *Diary*, I, p. 97, MSS, Princeton Library.

If passers-by on Nassau Street saw a cloud of smoke arising at the corner of the campus near the west gate, they knew that some idle students were perched on the top rail of the fence beside the President's House. Lazy Corner it was called. Some of the boys might be clad in outlandish ways, possibly in dressing gowns and top boots. Here was relayed all the gossip of college and town, here there were boasts of daring pranks and of outwitting the tutors, here some wit would repeat almost word for word Johnny's annual sermon on Shadrach, Meshach, and Abednego. No freshman was tolerated at Lazy Corner, and those who passed by were lucky if they escaped scoffing remarks.[104]

But while some of the students were wasting their time at Lazy Corner, others were knitting their brows over youthful literary attempts. "Today appeared that paper entitled the *Cameleon*," wrote William Paterson to his uncle, Andrew Bell. "Various conjectures as to who the editors are are afloat."[105] We do not know the exact character of this publication, since no copies have come down to us, but *The Tattler*, from December 1839 to August 1840 has been preserved in manuscript form, with its interesting collection of immature poetry, essays, editorials, and fiction. Now we are treated to a poem on the "Texas War of Independence," now to a "Tale of the Mountains," now to a serial entitled "The Young Lovers," now to an essay on "The Death of a Great Man," all written in the sentimental and stilted style so typical of the age.[106] In February 1840 selections from *The Tattler* were published in an eight-page magazine entitled *A Gem from Nassau's Casket*, of which three numbers have been preserved.

Two years later undergraduate literary ambitions found expression in the more pretentious publication *The Nassau Monthly*. The first number presented, in addition to the

---

[104] E. Shippen, *Notes About Princeton*, MSS, Princeton Library; *Princeton Library MSS*, AM 8418.
[105] *Princeton Library MSS*, AM 11803. The *Cameleon* appeared on Feb. 28, either in 1833, 1834 or 1835.
[106] *The Tattler*, MSS, Princeton Library.

"Editor's Table," "An Hour's Talk About History," "College Portraits" and a poem entitled "The Stranger Knight," essays on "Milton's *Cosmos*," on "Oaths," on "European Prose-Fiction" and on "Professor Wilson," the author of *Christopher North*.[107] The students were especially interested in "College Portraits," which satirized the "bore," the "clever fellow," and the first honor man, and continued in subsequent issues as "College Daguerreotypes." In March 1846 all the college was "thrown into convulsive throes of excitement" by the issuing by certain persons in the village of *The Rattler*, in which "several happy hits appear burlesquing certain pieces in the last *Monthly*." Immediately a notice was placed on the campus trees calling a meeting around the cannon to plan revenge for this invasion of college dignity, but we are not informed of what steps were taken.[108]

Living conditions in the dormitories were still primitive. Lard lamps had to some extent supplanted candles, but gas lights, which by 1852 had been installed in the village stores, several of the hotels, many private residences and the theological seminary, were conspicuously absent in the college buildings.[109] Whenever the weather turned cold, "the repercussive tones of hatchets, axes and all the implements of cleft resounded in loud echoes throughout the entries."[110] The typical room boasted of a clothes press, a bookcase, a washstand, a rocking chair, and a table, while the more luxurious students indulged in curtains and a carpet.[111] Students who dispensed with the attendance of servants had a reduction of three dollars a term from their bills, but even the poorest could not do his own laundry. Like the janitors, the washerwomen became "college characters," and there was great interest on the campus in 1846 when it was an-

[107] John Wilson, Professor of Philosophy and Rhetoric, University of Edinburgh.
[108] J. R. Buhler *Diary*, II, p. 28, MSS, Princeton Library.
[109] *The Princeton Whig*, May 7, 1852.
[110] J. R. Buhler *Diary*, II, p. 65, MSS, Princeton Library.
[111] A. D. Hollingsworth to J. Maclean, Nov. 25, 1836, *Maclean MSS*, Princeton Library.

nounced that "Sukey Soapsuds" was to be married to "S—
the Falstaff hackdriver."[112]

Visits of distinguished persons, now as formerly, were
greeted with joy by the students. In 1833, when President
Jackson arrived at Princeton, "the horsemen and infantry
of the town, and faculty and students of the college and
seminary, and citizens of the town went to meet him about
a mile out of town and escorted him to Joline's tavern."[113]
The next morning he attended prayers in Nassau Hall and
went over the college buildings.[114] Not to be outdone, his
great political rival, Henry Clay, not only visited the college,
but joined the Cliosophic Society.[115] On September 17, 1836,
the students crowded into Prayer Hall to attend funeral
services for Aaron Burr. Here President Carnahan preached
a sermon dwelling on the evils of dueling, which would have
been even more appropriate had the body before him been
that of Alexander Hamilton. Thereupon the solemn procession proceeded to the cemetery, where the former Vice-
President was laid to rest.[116]

Meanwhile, Princeton, because of the inception of the
railway era, was losing something of its old seclusion. Lying
directly between New York and Philadelphia, on the "waist-
line" of New Jersey, it was inevitable that the trunk railways
should pass near it. But the clatter of horses' hoofs and the
crack of the driver's whip continued to be heard on Nassau
Street for a few years yet as stage coaches left to meet the
trains at Rahway or New Brunswick or Trenton.[117] In 1837,
however, the rails of the Trenton and New Brunswick line
were laid on the banks of the canal at Princeton, and in
1839 through connection was established with Jersey City
and Philadelphia. When the puffing little engine with its
train of wooden cars pulled up at the station at the foot of

[112] J. R. Buhler *Diary*, II, p. 28, MSS, Princeton Library.
[113] Known also as Nassau Hotel. Parts of the building were incorporated in
the Nassau Inn.
[114] *Princeton Library MSS*, AM 11803.
[115] *Ibid.*, AM 9751.
[116] *Ibid.*, AM 1258.       [117] *Princeton Whig*, Dec. 29, 1837.

Canal Street,[118] passengers for Princeton stepped off, and climbing into Ross's hack, were driven to their residences, to the Mansion House, or to Nassau Hall Hotel.[119] In 1846, when the schedule was changed so that a train for the southwest left at 5:30 p.m., the boys noted with glee that it was now possible to slip down to Philadelphia in time for the theater.[120]

Commencement continued to be the big event of the year. Then it was that the countryside poured in its thousands to witness horse-racing and bull-baitings; that guests arrived from all parts of the country; that distinguished public men prepared to deliver their orations; that the Presbyterian Church was crowded to suffocation as oration followed oration and the students received their diplomas; that the "Fantasticals" paraded in fancy costumes; that the seniors held their annual ball; that the alumni, some of them dating back to Witherspoon, returned to greet former classmates and talk over old times.

It was in 1840 that Maclean suggested a change which affected college life profoundly. The time-honored custom of holding commencement late in September, he pointed out, was attended by many evils. It made it necessary for faculty and students to work through the scorching summer months; it threw the Fourth of July, Christmas, New Year's Day, and Washington's Birthday within the normal sessions and thus interrupted the work and invited dissipation; and it made it difficult for students who lived at a distance to visit their homes during the comparatively short vacations in October and April. Accordingly, the trustees decided that commencement, beginning with the year 1844, should be held on the last Wednesday of June, followed in sequence by a summer vacation of six weeks, a first term of nineteen weeks, a winter vacation, and a second or spring term of twenty-one weeks.[121]

---

[118] The present Alexander Street.
[119] *Princeton Whig*, Dec. 4, 1846.
[120] J. R. Buhler *Diary*, II, p. 8, MSS, Princeton Library.
[121] *Maclean MSS*, 1840, Princeton Library; *Princeton College Catalogues*, 1839-1856.

For the nearby farmers commencement was never the same after this. "Right pleasantly did the time-honored day pass off," said the *Princeton Whig* of June 27, 1845. "From a distance there were a good many in attendance, but from the surrounding country not near so many as when commencement was held in September. The time to the farmer, in the midst of hay and beginning of harvest, is too precious to give it up to a holiday. . . . But the change of season . . . has brought no change of routine in the college exercises."

Following the critical years after Carnahan's inauguration, when many feared that the college would have to close its doors, it was with relief, even with elation, that the trustees and faculty watched the number of matriculates slowly rise. From 150 in 1829-1830 it became successively 128, 139, 150, 191, 215, 227. Even the panic of 1837 did not suffice to halt this encouraging movement. "This venerable institution appears to be rapidly advancing in the estimation of the public," said the editor of the *Princeton Whig*. "The fall session . . . shows a much larger accession of new students than has ever joined this college at any one session. About seventy applicants have already been admitted and more are expected."[122] Eventually, however, the prolonged depression did have some effect and in 1841-1842 there was a slight decline. But the upward swing was resumed immediately, until in 1847-1848 the high point of Carnahan's long administration was reached, when no fewer than 270 students responded to the clang of the old college bell.[123]

But prosperity had its embarrassments. Nassau Hall was crowded to overflowing, even though some unfortunate boys were still housed in the dark and damp basement,[124] and many others were rooming at Mrs. Morford's, Mrs. Gaston's, Mrs. Ten Eyck's, and elsewhere in the village. These good women no doubt assumed some responsibility for the conduct

[122] Nov. 24, 1837.
[123] *Catalogue of the College of New Jersey.*
[124] *Ibid.*, June, 1833. C. H. Beale, of Norfolk, Virginia, was in No. 7; A. M. Jerome, Palmyra, New York, and R. M. Snowden, of Maryland, were in No. 2, etc.

of their lodgers, but the faculty thought their houses were too scattered and too remote from the watchful eye of Johnny Maclean. So, in 1833, the trustees authorized the erection of a new structure to cost $13,450,[125] to be placed southeast of Nassau Hall and facing the back campus. East College, the building was named, although it embraced merely bedrooms and studies, and not a separate dining hall, library, and recitation rooms as the English term "college" would seem to imply.

For the students it was a pleasant break in the round of studies to watch the masons and carpenters at their tasks. "The new college is progressing, the foundation is dug and masons are coming from New York tomorrow to begin it," wrote young William Paterson on June 17, 1833. "It is to be 100 feet long, 36 broad and to have 32 rooms in it."[126] The work progressed rapidly, and on January 4, 1834, some of the rooms were so far completed that the students moved in. "The walls are not yet thoroughly dry," one youth wrote his father, "and I should think it dangerous to stay in them. The other end will not be finished before next spring."[127]

But when, at the beginning of the winter term of 1834-1835 the entire building was occupied, the increase in the number of students was found to be so great that once more scores were forced to lodge in the village. Thus, while the campus was still littered with left-over materials from East College, the masons began constructing West College.[128] "The walls of the new college edifice, 112 by 32 feet, 4 stories high, are now going up, and the workmen are engaged in roofing it," stated the *Princeton Whig* on July 22, 1836. West College contained thirty-two studies, each with a double bedroom, and cost $13,000.

With the completion of these new dormitories, Nassau Hall itself acquired a new name, for students and faculty

[125] *Maclean MSS*, 1832, Princeton Library.
[126] *Princeton Library MSS*, AM 11803.
[127] D. L. Gardiner to his father, January 5, 1834, *ibid.*, AM 11205.
[128] Agreement with Eli F. Cooley, Dec., 1835, *Maclean MSS*, Princeton Library.

alike began to call it North College. And "Old North," although dingy and uncomfortable, was long considered the "swell residence."[129] Yet there seems to have been little real rivalry between dormitories, no athletic contests between teams of Easts or Wests or Norths. The student's loyalty, now as before, was reserved for his literary society and his class, or possibly for one of the newly established Greek-letter fraternities, not for the building in which he roomed.

And the literary societies took on enhanced importance with the erection of new halls. The two rooms in the upper floor of Stanhope Hall had long been too "confined and uncomfortable," and with the great increase in numbers were now "crowded to excess." So an appeal was sent out to the alumni for funds, and the distinguished Philadelphia architect, John Haviland, was engaged to draw the plans.[130] Unfortunately, instead of selecting the type of architecture established by Robert Smith for Nassau Hall and adhered to by the architects of Stanhope Hall, the Philosophical Hall, East College, and West College, Haviland designed two little Ionic temples in keeping with the current neo-classic style, and Princeton lost its opportunity for uniformity in its architecture. The halls were situated to the rear of North College and at the ends of the two walks which, starting from Nassau Street, pass that building on the right and left.

With these additions the campus assumed new dignity, for like Jefferson's University of Virginia, the buildings were so placed as to form a balanced plan.[131] The elms were attaining height and stateliness, an iron fence extended along Nassau Street, while paths were cut through the grass from one building to another. It was after the completion of the much discussed chapel that the old Prayer Hall, where a few treasured portraits had long looked down upon the youths who crowded in for services, was converted into a picture gallery.[132] A tract

[129] E. Shippen, *Notes About Princeton*, MSS, Princeton Library.
[130] John Maclean, *History of the College of New Jersey*, II, p. 305.
[131] *Princeton Library MSS*, AM 8110.
[132] *Ibid.*, AM 11413; John Maclean, *History of the College of New Jersey*, II, pp. 324-325.

of several acres to the south of the campus was purchased on which it was planned to erect "a gymnasium, a bathing establishment and wash-house."[133] Alumni returning for commencement remarked proudly, yet sadly, on the startling changes that had taken place since their college days, and found the places where they had dreamed their dreams and planned their future careers covered by new buildings.

In the last ten years of Carnahan's administration the faculty suffered a series of losses which deprived the college of some of its ablest scholars and teachers. On November 20, 1845, when Albert B. Dod died suddenly, the students gathered in groups to discuss the sad event and to express their sorrow. The trustees entrusted the classes in mathematics to Stephen Alexander and strengthened the faculty by appointing Matthew B. Hope professor of belles-lettres, but the well-loved Dod was greatly missed by both the faculty and the students.

A year later came the news that Joseph Henry had resigned to become the first director and secretary of the Smithsonian Institution. Henry was made professor emeritus of natural philosophy, and for years came back to Princeton to give a few lectures to eager groups of seniors.[134] However, the fact could not be disguised that the faculty had lost its most distinguished member. In 1853 the trustees made an effort to endow a professorship of applied science, with Henry as the incumbent. "You cannot but be aware of the earnest desire entertained by all the friends of the college that you should return to Princeton and again take an active part in the instruction of the youth here," Maclean wrote him. "We shall undertake to raise from the friends of the college the sum of $50,000 . . . the interest to be paid to you."[135] Regretfully Henry declined. "I have devoted nearly seven years of my life to the organization and development of the plan of the Smithsonian Institution," he wrote. "It has now

[133] *Princeton Whig*, June 29, 1849.
[134] *Catalogues of the College of New Jersey*, 1840-1867; *Princeton Library MSS*, AM 9903.
[135] *Hodge Papers*, Nov. 10, 1853, MSS, Princeton Library.

arrived at what I consider a crisis in its history and were I to signify my intention . . . to leave it I think the effect would be disastrous."[136]

Other losses followed. In 1844 the able James W. Alexander resigned the chair of belles-lettres to become the pastor of the Duane Street Presbyterian Church in New York.[137] In 1849 Elias Loomis, professor of natural philosophy, returned to King's College, and in 1854 the distinguished John Torrey left to accept a position with the United States Assay Office. Fortunately the trustees, insisting now as before upon scholarly promise in their faculty, were able to fill the ranks with a group of young men who were to bring new distinction to the college—James C. Moffat, professor of Greek and history; Lyman H. Atwater, professor of mental and moral philosophy; Arnold Guyot, professor of geology and physical geography; George Musgrave Giger, professor of Latin; John T. Duffield, professor of mathematics; J. Stillwell Schanck, curator of the museum and lecturer on zoology.

In June 1853 President Carnahan tendered his resignation to the trustees. "Having arrived at that period of life when freedom from the cares and labors of my present station is very desirable and when in my opinion the interests of the college require the services of a more active and efficient man, I beg leave . . . to resign the office of president. . . . During the past session the disease to which I have been subject more than half my life has been so severe that every attempt to speak in public has been attended and followed with great pain. . . . I have now held the office of president of this college for thirty years, which is four years longer than any of my predecessors."[138] At the request of the trustees Dr. Carnahan continued in office for another year so that there should be time to select his successor, and it was at the commencement of 1854 that he bade goodbye to his colleagues and the students.

[136] Henry to John Maclean and Charles Hodge, Dec. 19, 1853, *ibid.*
[137] John Maclean, *History of the College of New Jersey*, II, p. 311.
[138] Transcribed copy of Carnahan's letter of resignation, June 6, 1853, *Maclean MSS*, Princeton Library.

The alumni saw before them the same large, slow, timid man who had addressed them as undergraduates, some of them three decades ago, a man still sturdy and erect, but touched by the frosts of seventy-nine winters. He could state with pride that the college had made great strides during his administration, rising from its nadir to enter a period of growth and expanded usefulness. "Not less than $75,000 has been expended in the erection of new buildings, in the improvement of the college grounds, in the purchase of real estate and in increasing the philosophical and chemical apparatus and the library. Instead of two professors and two tutors as in 1823, we have now six professors, two assistant professors, three tutors and a teacher of modern languages. . . . For the harmony that has generally prevailed between the Trustees and the Faculty there is great cause of thankfulness. . . . How far the college has accomplished or failed in attaining the great end for which it was founded, viz., the glory of God and the best interests of men, will not be fully known until the books are opened on the last and great day."[139]

[139] *Ibid.*

# CHAPTER VIII

# Through Fire and War

OHN MACLEAN and his friends took for granted that he would be chosen to succeed President Carnahan. For thirty-five years he had served the college as tutor or professor or vice-president; he it was who had taken upon himself the chief responsibility for upholding discipline, who had formulated new educational policies, who had served as a link between the college and the Presbyterian church. Accordingly, surprise and resentment followed the discovery that a large faction in the board of trustees, consisting chiefly of laymen, was opposed to his election. These men seem to have considered Maclean lacking in dignity, a poor administrator, and a reactionary who set himself against the educational trends of the day. They wanted either a minister who was an acknowledged leader in the Presbyterian church, or a layman distinguished in the world of science.

In the summer of 1853 it became common knowledge that many were in favor of electing Joseph Henry. This, it was thought, would add prestige to the college, assure a vigorous administration, and emphasize the close harmony between science and religion. Thereupon, Maclean's brother, George M. Maclean, wrote heatedly to Henry demanding that he decline to be a candidate. Henry returned this missive to the writer "as unworthy of him or myself."[1] When Charles Hodge wrote John Maclean that there seemed to be "a general desire to see Professor Henry made president," he received in reply a twelve-page letter of protest. "If I have any reputation at all, I presume it is as a college officer. . . . I did imagine that my friends would feel some satisfaction in bearing . . . public testimony to the faithfulness of my services . . . not leaving it to be inferred from their passing me by that they were dissatisfied with my past course." To

[1] *Maclean MSS*, Aug. 8, 1853, Princeton Library.

elect a layman would be a dangerous reversal of policy. "Many years ago Mr. Southard observed that though the charter of our college did not require that the president should be a clergyman, it was evidently the design of the founders of the college that it should be so."[2]

In the meanwhile Henry wrote to different members of the board of trustees declining to be a candidate. "I could not think of accepting the office were I elected. . . . Were I a Trustee I would vote for Dr. Maclean. Though he may not possess popular or brilliant talents he is deficient in no essential qualification. He is a man of talents, of energy and of untiring devotion to the interest of the college. His views of education are of the most liberal character."[3]

Yet when the board met on August 30, the faction opposing Maclean was strong enough to force an adjournment without action. So throughout the autumn the rumors and heartburnings continued. Many thought that James W. Alexander would make a good president, but he was "as firm as a rock" for Maclean.[4] Finally the opposition fell back on David Magie, and one of the trustees wrote Maclean: "If you can get him out of the way it will be arranged at our next meeting." Magie flirted with the idea, but Maclean did get him out of the way by a rather pointed personal letter,[5] and on December 20, 1853, was elected.[6]

It was on June 28, 1854, in the presence of "a large assembly of the learning, beauty and fashion" of the entire region, that Justice Green administered the oath of office to the new president and delivered to him the keys of the college. Maclean replied with an address in which he outlined the policies of his administration. He would not aim at innovations, he said, his chief ambition being to expand, not to change, the system of instruction marked out by his prede-

---

[2] Maclean to Hodge, Aug. 24, 1853, *Maclean MSS*, Princeton Library.
[3] Henry to David Magie, Aug. 29, 1853. Copy in Maclean's handwriting in V. L. Collins's papers, Princeton Library.
[4] Hodge to Maclean, Aug. 31, 1853, *Maclean MSS*, Princeton Library.
[5] Maclean to Magie, Nov. 12, 1853, *ibid.*
[6] *Trustees Minutes*, IV, 1853.

cessors. "No chimerical experiments in education have ever had the least countenance here. . . . Mental discipline has been aimed at. . . . Nor has it ever been the aim . . . to make the college a collection of separate schools, and to permit the students here congregated to determine for themselves to what branches they will devote their time." He would adhere, therefore, to the time-honored plan of "having one course of study for all the students." In the curriculum the emphasis was to be placed upon religion, to which "every other part of education" was to be subordinated.

Within these limits he outlined several paths along which the college was destined to progress to new usefulness and distinction. Foreshadowing the preceptorial system, he declared that "the provisions for imparting instruction" must be in proportion to the number taught, for, even though the faculty might be made up of ripe scholars, the quality of teaching would deteriorate if the class sections were too large. It was imperative, he thought, to demand a more thorough preparation on the part of entering students, so that the college courses could be of an advanced character. He hoped, with a larger endowment, to establish new professorships. As for the matter of discipline, he did not expect the students to be angels, or to display the discretion of men of mature minds, and though they would be required to pay strict attention to the regulations, every reasonable indulgence would be granted.[7]

With the excitement of commencement and the inauguration over, and with the students dispersed for the summer vacation, Maclean might have hoped for a short respite from work. But there were multitudinous and varied tasks which crowded upon him and demanded consideration. The college president of his time assumed many of the functions of registrar, secretary, dean of admissions, proctor, superintendent of grounds, chaplain. As one goes through Maclean's voluminous correspondence one wonders how he found time for his many activities. Now he gives his opinion concerning an

[7] John Maclean, *History of the College of New Jersey*, II, pp. 412-435.

issue before the Presbyterian assembly, now he replies to an indigent minister's appeal for assistance, now he writes to the African Colonization Society, in which he was deeply interested. In his mail there were innumerable letters from parents asking his personal attention—to see to it that James had a warm room, to forward two albums of photographs which William left in Room 48 North College, to be sure that Albert secured a suit of warm underwear; or expressing grief and mortification that John had been suspended, or explaining that Francis has been detained at home by a swollen hand. Today, when the college president presides over a network of departments, schools, and administrative committees which carry on the various functions of the institution, it seems a far cry to the day when "Johnny" Maclean ran Princeton almost single-handed, knew every student by name, gave him personal advice or warnings, visited him when ill, perhaps prayed with him in his room.

Maclean's pride in his faculty was that of a father for a dutiful and promising family. Scholarship and teaching ability he considered indispensable, provided they could be found in a deeply religious man, preferably a Presbyterian. Of the group which gathered around him for his first faculty meeting, some were distinguished in the world of science, some were popular with the undergraduates, but all were Calvinists of the old school of orthodoxy.

Prominent was Stephen Alexander, still active despite his graying hair, still modest and retiring. Advancing years had brought him new honors among scientists, but it did not improve his teaching, for he was inclined to talk over the boys' heads and seldom paused to explain the points which gave them the greatest difficulty. Many a puzzled lad looked in despair at the huge blackboard filled with mathematical formulae which little Stephy used to illustrate his lectures.[8]

Matthew Hope, on the other hand, was considered a clear and interesting lecturer. It was the custom for the students

[8] "Reminiscences of A. A. Woodhull," II, p. 14, *Princeton Library MSS*, AM 9276.

to express their approval of a teacher by stamping when he entered the room. So whenever the tall, spare, blond, courteous, somewhat nervous man made his appearance, he received a noisy welcome. Hope, whose health had been undermined when he was a missionary at Singapore, did not relish this peculiar mark of favor, but his pleas for less noise and less dust were in vain. As a teacher he was as thorough as he was entertaining.[9] "He won't satisfy himself with an answer from the book; you must give him the why and the wherefore of everything you say," wrote one of his students.[10]

James C. Moffat, professor of Greek, was respected as a classicist, but he was not an inspiring instructor, and not apt in explaining the intricacies of the language to the lower grade of students. His lectures in history were more interesting, but when he became excited and spoke rapidly, his Scotch burr was so marked that it was difficult to follow him.[11] Arnold Guyot, a Swiss, also had trouble with his pronunciation, and a roar of laughter would greet him when he declared that the "yox were devil-upped," meaning that the rocks were developed. Yet the students respected him as a great scholar and an able teacher.[12] Guyot had won distinction before coming to America by his investigations of glacial motion, the structure of glaciers and the movement of morainic matter. In the United States the publication of *The Earth and Man* at once established his reputation as a geographer, while his plan of teaching geography, which he embodied in a series of books, greatly influenced instruction in the schools. His work in selecting and equipping weather observation stations was the genesis of the present system of the United States Weather Bureau.

George Musgrave Giger, professor of Latin, a small, delicate, dark man, with piercing eyes and long flowing hair,

[9] *Ibid.*, II, p. 8.
[10] J. C. Boyd to H. R. Slack, Nov. 8, 1853, *Princeton Library MSS*, AM 9604.
[11] "Reminiscences of A. A. Woodhull," II, p. 13, *Princeton Library MSS*, AM 9276.
[12] *Ibid.*, p. 11.

very neat in dress and polished in manner, was popular with the students, possibly because of his great interest in the Cliosophic Society. When he first came to Princeton as a tutor, the disdainful young Buhler criticized his lectures as full "of trite similies and weather worn metaphors," with too many allusions to "clouds, storms, stars, skies, flowers, etc."[13] But Maclean says he was "an accurate scholar, a/ successful teacher, a faithful college officer, and a man greatly respected by his colleagues and his pupils."[14] The students in time of need came to him for encouragement, sympathy and aid, and were never disappointed.[15]

The newly appointed professor of mathematics, John T. Duffield, was a dignified man, with thinning hair, prominent nose, whose heavy eyebrows and firm mouth gave an impression of sternness. But not even Maclean was possessed of a kinder heart. It is said that if a freshman on entering college could not find a room in one of the hotels, Duffield would take him into his own house for the night.[16] As a teacher of mathematics he ranked with the leaders.

Lyman H. Atwater, professor of mental and moral philosophy, concluded this interesting group. A ponderous man in aspect and speech, with rotund face, double chin showing above a clerical collar, and long hair hanging over his shoulders, he was not popular with the students. His fondness for words derived from Latin seemed to them an effort to appear erudite. They respected him, however, as one who had won distinction as logician and theologian.[17]

Maclean had been president less than a year when disaster struck the college. It was at 8:30 on a stormy March night in 1855, when most of the students in Nassau Hall were hard at work in their rooms, that the silence was broken by the cry of "Fire! Fire!" Apparently an ember had fallen

---

[13] J. R. Buhler *Diary*, ii, p. 42, MSS, Princeton Library.

[14] John Maclean, *History of the College of New Jersey*, ii, p. 321.

[15] *Nassau Herald*, June, 1866.

[16] A. A. Schank, *Princeton and Thereafter*, p. 8.

[17] "Reminiscences of A. A. Woodhull," ii, p. 10, *Princeton Library MSS*, AM 9276.

from the grate in Room 33-A, on the second floor near the northeast corner, and in the absence of the occupant, Samuel W. Oliver of Mobile, the flames had gained considerable headway before the warning signal was sounded.[18] In a moment all was confusion—students making desperate efforts to save their belongings, firemen shouting, professors giving directions, hundreds of the villagers looking up from the campus in awed silence. Students and firemen worked manfully side by side and when they stretched the hose to the second story and began to pour a stream upon the fire they had hope of success. But the supply of water failed and a few minutes later the old building was a roaring furnace. Attracted by the glare, which was visible for many miles, crowds flocked in from the country to see the spectacle. By midnight nothing was left of the structure save the massive stone walls, which were thrown into strong relief by the glowing embers within.[19]

In the general confusion it was impossible to bring furniture and clothing from the upper stories, so that many of the students suffered heavy losses. But Professor Cameron and others had the presence of mind to take down the portraits hanging in the old chapel and carry them to a place of safety.[20] The head of Homer, which is said to have been brought from England to adorn the flat arch of the main door when the building was erected, and which had long been an object of veneration to the students, was—amid the cheers of the crowd—chiseled out of its position. But the bell, which had been recast after the fire of 1802, and for half a century had summoned the students to prayers and meals and classes, was melted beyond reclamation.[21] During the early hours of the morning some of the dispossessed students consoled themselves uproariously at Joline's and with the dawn sought new

---

[18] *Princeton Alumni Weekly*, Jan. 17, 1903.

[19] *New York Weekly Times*, March 17, 1855; *Newark Daily Advertiser*, March 12, 1855; *Princeton Press*, March 15, 1855; Account by G. Wilcox '56, *Princeton Alumni Weekly*, March 31, 1915.

[20] *New York Weekly Times*, March 17, 1855.

[21] *Princeton Library MSS*, AM 9604.

lodgings in the village or with friends in East College and West College.

President Maclean immediately made an appeal for funds with which to rebuild "Old North." "The insurance was only $12,000," he said, "and we shall need at least $20,000 in addition. In this emergency we must look to our friends and especially to the alumni of the college for aid to restore a building around which cluster so many pleasing associations." So confident was he of success that plans were made for an immediate restoration within the original walls.[22]

The first step was to secure an architect, and for the third time Princeton turned to a distinguished Philadelphian. John Notman, designer of St. Mark's, the Church of the Holy Trinity, St. Clement, and many residences, including "Prospect" and "Guernsey Hall" in Princeton, was a devotee of the Florentine school of architecture so popular in the fifth and sixth decades of the century. After Queen Victoria's palace, "Osborne," had set the style, the square towers, stone balconies, rounded arches of doors and windows, low roofs and quoins became familiar both in England and America.

Notman could not resist the temptation to remodel Nassau Hall in conformity with this mode. Fortunately he was restrained by the necessity of using the old walls, but within these limits he did his best to convert Old North into an Italian villa. The central Georgian doorway and the window above it gave way to an arched Florentine entrance. Above this was placed a stone balcony with an arched window reaching up through the cornice into the central pediment. At either end Notman erected square towers, similar to the one on "Prospect," rising a full story above the roof line and throwing the entire structure out of proportion. The whole was surmounted by a cupola, graceful in design, but much larger than its predecessors. No doubt Notman realized that the new cupola must dominate not a single building, as had Robert Smith's, but a group of buildings. Yet the result was

[22] *Maclean MSS*, March 29, 1855, Princeton Library.

to dwarf Nassau Hall itself and rob it of the impressiveness which had been so noticeable in former days.[23]

The interior, too, was greatly altered. The old staircases were replaced by winding red-stone steps in the two new towers; partitions were placed across the east and west hallways to debar the students from the historic custom of rolling cannonballs along them and to discourage riots; the old cross hallways were united with adjacent rooms to create single chambers, the picture gallery was enlarged by an addition on the south for use as the library. So far as possible the building was made fireproof—the iron roof frame was covered with slate, the cornice was of galvanized iron, the hallways were paved with brick, in place of joists were railway rails spaced three feet apart, supporting brick arches.[24]

Reconstruction went on somewhat slowly, and it was not until August 7, 1856, that the work had progressed far enough for the students to move in.[25] This they did with enthusiasm, even though the campus was littered with piles of stone and other building material and the masons and carpenters were still at work. Although interested and delighted with the innovation of central heating, they complained that the rooms were cold when the janitor paid more attention to the bottle than to the furnaces.[26] From their windows they could watch the artisans who either were bringing up stone (quarried from a lot recently purchased by the college from Professor Halsey) which was intended for the walls of the new library,[27] or else were working on the main doorway and steps.

The library was not completed until 1860. With its tiled

[23] Robert Kerr, *The Gentleman's House*; Joseph Jackson, *Early Philadelphia Architects and Engineers*, pp. 213-225; Report of the Building Committee, Dec. 18, 1855, *Maclean MSS*, Princeton Library; Notman to Maclean, March 22, 1855, *ibid.*

[24] Report of Building Committee, June 21, 1855, *Maclean MSS*, Princeton Library.

[25] *Ibid.*, Dec. 16, 1856.

[26] J. H. Muse, *Correspondence With My Son*, p. 170; "Justice" to Maclean, Feb. 11, 1858, *Maclean MSS*, Princeton Library.

[27] Report of Building Committee, Dec. 18, 1855, *ibid.*

floor, its shelves projecting into the room at right angles with the walls, its lofty arched triple windows, its central table and desk from which Professor Giger dispensed books to the undergraduates, it was a distinct improvement upon the former cramped quarters in Stanhope Hall.[28] As the number of volumes was only 10,400 and growth was slow, there promised to be ample space for expansion. The portraits of Princeton's former great were brought back, Peale's Washington being hung over the door at the north end of the room, while some of the other pictures were propped against the walls on top of the bookshelves. But there were no student desks and the room was open only on Mondays and Tuesdays, serving more as a storeroom for books than an intellectual workshop.

Nassau Hall had hardly been restored when the college was shaken by the rumblings of approaching war. With dismay Maclean witnessed the breach between northern and southern Presbyterians. In November 1860 he wrote the *Central Presbyterian*, protesting against its incendiary policy. "Instead of endeavoring to allay the unhappy excitement existing in some of the Southern States, you publish the most offensive articles you can find. . . . This surely is not the duty of ministers of Christ, who should ever study the things which make for peace."[29] But though Maclean sought to pour oil on the troubled waters, he was himself unalterably opposed to slavery and quick to resent injustice to the Negroes in the north. When a Black Code, depriving them of many civil rights, was introduced in the New Jersey Legislature, he opposed it violently. "To treat with cruelty, under any pretext whatever, the poor slaves who . . . may become free, I regard as barbarous and wicked."[30]

Although the number of students from the south had gradually lessened during the sixth decade of the century, a third of them were as yet from slave-holding states when

[28] Eleazer Jones to Maclean, Dec. 23, 1859, *ibid.*
[29] *Ibid.*, Nov. 20, 1860.
[30] Maclean to J. E. Scudder, May 21, 1863, *Maclean MSS*, Princeton Library.

the session of 1860-1861 opened. These boys were liked by their fellow classmen, took a prominent part in college life, and gave to the institution a decidedly southern flavor. It is not true, however, as has often been stated, that some of them brought slaves with them as personal servants, from whom certain Princeton Negro families are descended. In the Spartan life of Nassau Hall, slave valets would have been useless, even had their presence not been prohibited by New Jersey law.

Despite the warm friendships between southern and northern boys, sectional spirit ran high as the Dred Scott decision was followed by the John Brown raid, the raid by the election of Lincoln, the election of Lincoln by secession. "Political opinions or prejudices went off at hair-trigger touch," stated J. M. Ludlow of the class of 1861, "and from the excited tones of the self-appointed protagonists in the melee, one might have thought that the Civil War began on the Princeton campus instead of Charleston harbor."[31]

Yet when the southern boys, in December 3, 1859, made a noisy protest against abolitionist agitation, they were joined by many from the north. A procession marched up Nassau Street in the early evening holding aloft transparencies and banners with such inscriptions as "Down with Seward," "John Brown, the horse thief, murderer and martyr," or "Down with Henry Ward Beecher." When Maclean rushed out to order the boys to their rooms, they dispersed. But later they reassembled in front of Nassau Hall, where effigies of Beecher and Seward were consigned to the flames amid groans, cheers, and harangues.[32]

But all demonstrations ceased for the moment when news arrived that the war had actually commenced. "There was a closer grip of the arm as we sauntered to Jug Town[33] or Rocky Hill, there were many sad scenes at the railroad station by the canal, as our Northern groups gave the farewell—generally

---

[31] J. M. Ludlow, *Reminiscences of Princeton*, MSS, Princeton Library.
[32] *Baltimore American and Commercial Advertiser*, Dec. 5, 1859.
[33] The site of a pottery on Nassau Street.

a hug—as the . . . train creaked its fatal echo of goodbye."[34] Theodore W. Hunt tells us that when he came to Princeton in June 1861 for his entrance examination, he was moved by the sight of a group of seniors "assembled at the east end of Nassau Hall, bidding one another an affectionate farewell," pathetically conscious that they might soon be facing each other as mortal enemies in the great clash of armies.[35]

Personal friendships did not prevent the northern boys, in April 1861, from showing their loyalty to the Union by raising the national flag over the cupola of Nassau Hall. When the faculty removed it, as a rebuke to insubordination, there was great indignation not only among the undergraduates but throughout the north. A few days later Captain H. Margerum risked his life by climbing to the dome and restoring the Stars and Stripes to its place upon the weather vane, amid the cheers of the students on the campus below. This time the faculty allowed it to remain. It is said that the weight of the flag, fluttering in the wind, bent the vane so that it became fixed with its point to the north,[36] where it remained throughout the war.

The students, though tolerant of the views of the southerners, were bitter against their fellow northerners with southern sympathies. One youth who had been outspoken in justifying secession was dragged from his bed and held under the pump "until the fire of disunion was pretty well quenched in his breast." Although the faculty secretly approved of this "water cure," they decided to suspend three of the ringleaders in order to uphold college discipline. Immediately the delinquents became heroes and martyrs. When the three left town the students seated them in a carriage decorated with American flags and drew them to the railway station through streets lined with cheering people. Here, while awaiting the train, prominent undergraduates addressed the throng to the

---

[34] J. M. Ludlow, *Reminiscences of Princeton*, MSS, Princeton Library.
[35] *Princeton Alumni Weekly*, May 23, 1917.
[36] John F. Hageman, *Princeton and Its Institutions*, I, p. 292.

accompaniment of cheers and the waving of flags, lauding the young patriots and denouncing the faculty.[37]

When accounts of this affair were published, the press of the north rallied to the support of the students. "I am by every acquaintance I meet congratulated on account of my son's participation in this transaction," one father wrote Maclean. "I regret the occurrence very much on my son's account and on account of the effect that is produced on the minds of the public in regard to the institution."[38]

The war brought deep sorrow to the faculty. Loyal to the Union, they could not forget their former pupils from the south, so many of whom were fighting under Lee or Jackson. When Maclean received a letter from south of the Potomac, couched in affectionate terms, wishing Old Nassau "a long prosperous life in spite of the troubles which agitate the outer world,"[39] or when word came that a youth who recently had sat before him in chapel or in his course on religion had been mortally wounded in battle,[40] it was not to be expected that he should join the usual denunciations of all southerners as rebels and traitors. Maclean's album of photographs, preserved in the Princeton University Library, is revealing of the breadth of his sympathies, for side by side with portraits of Grant and Farragut is one of Robert E. Lee.

But public opinion in the north did not understand or sympathize with the position of the Princeton faculty. The removal of the flag from Nassau Hall, the punishing of the students concerned in the ducking of the Copperhead, and the failure of professors to join in the usual violent denunciations of the south led to the belief that the college was lukewarm in its support of the Union and of Lincoln's war efforts. This Maclean denied. "On the one hand, the Faculty will allow no mobs among the students; and on the other hand,

[37] *Princeton Alumni Weekly*, Oct. 20, 1933; Oct. 25, 1916.
[38] John F. Hageman, *Princeton and Its Institutions*, I, p. 293; S. C. Huey to Maclean, Sept. 19, 1861, *Maclean MSS*, Princeton Library.
[39] E. M. Burruss to Maclean, Jan. 21, 1861, *Maclean MSS*, Princeton Library.
[40] C. H. Earl to Maclean, Sept. 2, 1863, *ibid.*

they will not permit the utterance of sentiments denunciatory
of those who are engaged in efforts to maintain the integrity
of the national government; nor will they allow of any
public expression of sympathy with those who are endeavoring to destroy that government."[41]

Nonetheless, suspicion remained so widespread even after
the close of the war that the trustees thought it necessary to
ask Joseph T. Duryea to make a strongly patriotic address
at the commencement of 1866. "I know such an oration is
needed to satisfy warm friends of the college," wrote S. H.
Pennington to Maclean. "You gentlemen at Princeton, in
your comparative seclusion, . . . have very little idea of the
extent of the distrust which has arisen in the minds of alumni
and others in consequence of occurrences in the College during
the rebellion, and the alleged absence of patriotic demonstrat-
ing there on public occasions."[42] Although some faculty members thought it unwise, the address was duly delivered and
published. But it proved mild, indeed, merely a justification
of the Union cause, a denunciation of slavery, and a eulogy
of the men who fell under the Stars and Stripes. It was an
address which would have been approved by Lincoln, but
must have stirred resentment in Thaddeus Stevens and
Charles Sumner if it ever came to their notice.[43]

There would have been less talk of Princeton's lukewarm-
ness in the Union cause had the critics been present at the
celebration of the capture of Richmond. The news was received with wild rejoicings. "The bells of the Seminary and
College pealed out 'good news,' the national colors were run
out . . . floating from windows and housetops; men of all
shades of opinion grasped each other by the hand in congratulatory joy." There were addresses by Professor Cameron and
others; in the evening a large bonfire was kindled around the
cannon back of Nassau Hall; fireworks were sent up; a grand

---

[41] J. F. Hageman, *Princeton and Its Institutions*, I, p. 293.
[42] *Maclean MSS*, April 7, 1866, Princeton Library.
[43] J. T. Duryea, *An Oration Commemorative of the Restoration of the
Union* (Philadelphia, 1866).

procession marched through the village streets, while every home was illuminated. "Flags flying, handkerchiefs waving, windows blazing, torchlights burning, fireworks flying through the air, everyone shouting, horns sounding—who ever beheld such a time in the usually quiet, serene Princeton."[44]

Many Princeton men won distinction in the war, some in the service of the Union, some in the Confederate army. Even during the commencement of 1861 the graduating class were saddened by reports of fatalities among their classmates. One had been shot by a sentry by mistake. "Another distinguished himself at Great Bethel, being in the thickest of the fight, in which the buttons of his coat were shot off. He has gained himself the name of 'the fighting chaplain.' "[45] In all, Princeton gave to the Confederacy at least eight brigadier generals, fourteen colonels, and many lesser officers;[46] to the Union General William W. Belknap, General Frank Preston Blair, General J. Tilford Boyle, General Horatio P. Van Cleve, and many others of like prominence. Engraved on the marble walls of the beautiful Memorial Room in Nassau Hall are the names of seventy Princeton men who gave their lives for the Union or the Confederacy.

It was with no little apprehension that President Maclean regarded the withdrawal of the southern students and the occasional enlistment in the Union army of northern students. Of the eighty-eight members of the class of 1861 who entered college in the autumn of 1860, only forty-five remained to take the final examinations.[47] The total enrollment in 1861 had been 314, in 1862 it was only 221. But there were some who drew a measure of comfort from the situation. "The expected absence of students from the States which are waging war to overthrow the Union, will greatly increase the interest of the free States in this institution," prophesied *The Princeton Standard*. "We know that not a few parents at the North

---

[44] *Princeton Standard*, April 7, 1865.      [45] *Ibid.*, June 28, 1861.
[46] Varnum Lansing Collins, *Princeton*, p. 161.
[47] Petition of Class of 1861, *Maclean MSS*, Princeton Library.

and West have heretofore withheld their sons from this college because of the predominating influence of Southern students here."[48] But Maclean missed the bright faces and soft accents of the southern boys, and the loss of revenue from tuition fees produced a serious financial problem.

The president met the situation by renewed efforts to secure an adequate endowment. Long before this, even prior to Carnahan's retirement, he had set on foot a project to raise $100,000 for the founding of one hundred scholarships, each to yield $60. It occurred to him, he tells us, that this would make it possible to remit tuition fees for a large number of able students and at the same time assure a fixed yearly income for the college.[49] However reactionary Maclean may have been in some matters, his initiative in inaugurating a plan which has since been widely adopted and which has had a profound influence upon education in the United States stamps him as a far-sighted educational leader. At Princeton it made possible more careful selections in admissions, elevated the standards of work, enlarged the faculty, and was influential in preserving the old personal methods of teaching.

The trustees gave their approval and in 1853 appointed Maclean and Hope to carry the scholarship plan into effect. Roswell L. Colt of Paterson made the first contribution by endowing one scholarship unconditionally and offering two others should fifty be secured.[50] There now followed weeks and months of soliciting. By January 27, 1854, half of the number of scholarships had been promised, James Lenox of New York endowing five, Silas Holmes of New York five, President Maclean and his brother, George Maclean, one, Professor Giger one, the First Presbyterian Church of Trenton one. Before the campaign ended $60,000 had been raised, providing free tuition for sixty students.[51]

Encouraged by this success, Maclean next devised a plan to secure a new professorship and at the same time bind the

[48] August 9, 1861.
[49] John Maclean, *History of the College of New Jersey*, II, pp. 330-335.
[50] *Princeton Whig*, Jan. 27, 1854.
[51] John Maclean, *History of the College of New Jersey*, II, pp. 438, 439.

college more closely to the Presbyterian church. So he sent out appeals to devout men asking them to endow a chair of applied science for the purpose of defending Christianity and "the doctrines of revealed truth in general from the assaults of infidels." As a double attraction, he hoped that Joseph Henry could be lured away from the Smithsonian Institution to become the first incumbent. "Could you do more for the interests of religion and science combined than to secure for our institution here the services of such a man as Professor Henry, who beyond dispute stands at the head of the scientific men in this country?" he wrote one prospective donor. "No gentleman of wealth could, in a more honorable way, obtain for himself and family a lasting reputation as a patron of learning united with religion."[52]

Before the end of the year 1855 the necessary $50,000 had been promised, though on the condition that Henry accept the professorship. Henry hesitated, not only because of his obligations to the Smithsonian Institution, but because he was interested in science for science's sake and did not wish to devote his energies to reconciling it with the theologian's idea of "revealed truth." At this point things took a different turn when a benefactor was discovered in the person of C. H. Shipman of Newark who gave Hope reason to think that he might donate the entire amount—not, however, for a chair devoted to harmonizing science and religion, but for applying science to industry. "What he is after is that besides the prosecution of science, for the sake of science, the opportunity should be thrown open to persons wishing to apply science to the practical specialties of life, whereby money can be made and good done, such as engineering, mining, surveying and the like, without making it a condition in all cases that the persons seeking such advantages should have had a classical training."[53]

Thus without warning the college was confronted with one of the most difficult problems with which higher education

[52] Letter dated Feb. 17, 1854, *Maclean MSS*, Princeton Library.
[53] M. B. Hope to Maclean, May 18, 1856, *ibid*.

had to deal in the second half of the nineteenth century. Should the curriculum remain entirely academic? Should a new school of engineering be founded which would be in part at least professional in character? Professor Hope, however, did not foresee any great difficulty. "All we require is to guard any depreciation of thorough scholarship into narrow specialties merely for utilitarian or money making uses," he wrote Maclean. "Against that result we may, I think, consider ourselves abundantly strong. . . . The tendency of power in our day is to become practical. Men of science and education must not allow it to pass out of their hands by ignoring or despising that tendency, but hold it in a firmer grasp by showing the relation of art (applied power) to science."[54] But once more Henry blocked the plan, for he was no more inclined to make concessions to the utilitarian point of view or to shackle pure science with money-making aims than to subordinate it to theology. When he and Shipman met for a personal exchange of views, the two men were not long in finding that they were entirely at variance. Professor Hope, who was in Europe at the time, was confident that when he returned he could reconcile them, but he was mistaken, and the professorship was not established until many years later when it appeared under its original guise as the "Chair of the Harmony of Science and Revealed Religion."[55]

Maclean and Hope were consoled by the launching of two other professorships, one of mental and moral philosophy and the other of geology and natural history. The real founder of the first was Mrs. Susan Dod Brown of Princeton. "Mrs. Brown has authorized me to say that she will furnish $1,000 a year while she lives toward securing a Professor of Mental Science if we will erect a separate department," Hope wrote Maclean in June 1854. "Though she has given no promise to continue it after her death, yet this would give us time to try our wings. . . . My impression is that the Trustees . . . would erect a department that would do honor to the college and to you and would offset the heavy preponderance to our

[54] *Ibid.*    [55] *Ibid.*

scientific side."[56] It was to this chair that the board called Lyman H. Atwater. At the same time they elected Arnold Guyot professor of geology and physical geography, trusting that so distinguished an incumbent would attract donors to endow his chair.

The press aided the campaign by calling on the wealthy to contribute. One editor declared that they were neglecting their duty to education, their entire donations in the whole United States being less than $2,000,000, "a sum inferior to the fortune made by some private individuals within the last ten years by trade with California."[57] The response at first was heartening, and Professor Hope could report that Silas Holmes of New York had given $30,000; Daniel Price of Newark had promised the interest on $25,000; Mr. Shipman had promised $10,000; R. L. Stuart and A. Stuart of New York $5,000; Thomas U. Smith of New York $5,000; and James Lenox of New York $5,000.[58] But now things began to go badly. Hope became ill, the rebuilding of Nassau Hall diverted funds from the permanent endowment, the country entered upon a period of "hard times."[59] With the advent of the War Between the States, with all the financial difficulties entailed for the country and the college, it seemed that the consummation of Maclean's plans must be postponed indefinitely.

But when the trustees saw that many persons were reaping rich profits from the war and were indulging in extravagant and lavish expenses, they decided to make another attempt.[60] On April 11, 1863, the alumni of the New York area, meeting in the Presbyterian church at Fifth Avenue and Nineteenth Street, with Honorable William C. Alexander in the chair, launched the campaign by calling upon the friends of the college to raise $100,000.[61] When the meeting requested Maclean to submit a statement of the college finances, the

[56] *Ibid.*, June 17, 1854.
[57] *Princeton Press*, Aug. 31, 1855.    [58] *Trustees Minutes*, Dec. 22, 1857.
[59] Report of M. B. Hope, Dec. 19, 1854, *Maclean MSS*, Princeton Library.
[60] W. W. Phillips to Maclean, Nov. 5, 1862, *ibid.*
[61] *Princeton Standard*, April 24, 1863.

president replied that the invested funds totaled less than $70,000, of which $38,000 was for salaries, $20,000 for scholarships and $8,800 to aid pious young men in preparing for the ministry. The number of students had diminished very nearly one-third, he said, entailing a loss in revenue of $6,000 a year, and unless the alumni came to the rescue it would be necessary either to incur a burdensome debt or lower the standard of teaching by reducing the number of instructors.[62]

Success followed quickly. A month after the New York meeting, Professor Atwater announced at commencement that $35,000 had already been raised, principally in New York and Brooklyn,[63] and that the donations were continuing. "Money is subscribed by hundreds and thousands," announced *The Princeton Standard* in November. "Within the last few days one of our young farmers, Joseph H. Bruere, has set a noble example, by giving $500." Success was assured when John I. Blair gave $30,000 to endow the chair of geology and physical geography occupied by Guyot.[64] When the alumni gathered in the Presbyterian Church for the commencement of 1864, they received enthusiastically the announcement that the full $100,000 had been paid in and that more had been promised.[65] Thus, in the midst of the war, which many thought might prove as disastrous as the Revolution, the college completed the most successful endowment campaign since Tennent and Davies made their memorable voyage to Great Britain more than a century earlier.

This timely assistance made it possible for the college to maintain its standards of teaching, not only by retaining its most distinguished professors, but by relieving them from some of the strain of holding recitations and of grading papers. In the session of 1860-1861 the ratio of instructors to students was one to eighteen, in 1863-1864 it was one to sixteen. The faculty was fully alive to the threat to teaching in the gradual increase in student enrollment. In Witherspoon's day, when a

[62] *Maclean MSS*, May 26, 1863, Princeton Library.
[63] *Princeton Standard*, June 26, 1863.     [64] *Ibid.*, Nov. 20, 1863.
[65] *Ibid.*, June 24, 1864.

class might number no more than twenty or thirty, the instructor not only knew every student's weaknesses and could strive to rectify them, but quizzing was general and the class meetings informal. But when classes grew to eighty or ninety, the effectiveness of teaching declined. As early as 1852 the faculty had recommended that "the classes be divided for recitation, so as to ensure, so far as possible, that every student shall recite at least once daily."[66]

The dangers and difficulties of the situation were explained by Professor Hope in a report to the trustees. "The size of the classes during the junior and senior years is such as to render instruction from textbooks in the ordinary way exceedingly inefficient. Not more than one-sixth part of the class can be called upon to recite . . . and it is easy to see that no skill can enable the teacher to hold the undivided attention of all the remaining five-sixths. . . . To remedy this evil . . . [I] adopted the method of teaching by lectures. . . . The attention of the whole class was held to the subject, partly by the style of personal address, and principally by requiring every member of the class to write out the substance of the lecture and submit it." When this too proved ineffectual, Hope "allowed those who preferred . . . to form themselves into a separate class" with instruction wholly from textbooks, with "double the number of recitations and also double the number of original compositions."[67] But this caused a "rebellion" among the students, and was discarded in favor of lectures and essays to be submitted every three weeks.

We gain an insight into the teaching methods of this period through the diaries of students and the reminiscences of alumni. "Instead of entering a cellar through a window as [do] the Sophomores, the Juniors walk up the steps of the Library Building,[68] and thence ascend by a winding staircase to their recitation room situated above the Library. . . . Rows of semi-circular benches, rising above each other as in the

[66] *Maclean MSS*, Sept., 1852, Princeton Library.
[67] Report of M. B. Hope, June 24, 1851, *Maclean MSS*, Princeton Library.
[68] Stanhope Hall.

other rooms, face a semi-circular desk. . . . Light is admitted into the room through a skylight, which is situated almost directly above the desk. The blackboard which is of slate-stone, is divided into three squares." The senior classroom was on the same floor on the north side of the building, the freshman and sophomore rooms in the basement.[69]

"The two lower classes were taught by the tutors and adjunct professors and the instruction was by recitation from text-books," A. A. Woodhull tells us. "The upper classes were taught by similar recitations and also by lectures. When, as in the case of the juniors by Professor Hope, the lectures were in the classrooms, they were necessarily repeated for both sections. The Philosophical Hall . . . had a large room on each of its two floors in which the entire class met when required. On the first floor Professor Atwater lectured on logic, Professor Guyot on physical geography, Dr. Schanck on chemistry and Professor Moffat on history; on the second floor Professor Stephen Alexander lectured on mechanics and astronomy, and Professor Henry, who came on from Washington, gave a short course on magnetism and electricity. . . . In the matter of recitations pure and simple, in my judgment, there was little teaching except by Professor Duffield in mathematics."[70]

Meanwhile the American colleges, a quarter of a century after Philip Lindsley had pointed the way in his brilliant inaugural address at Nashville, began slowly to awaken to the need for organized physical culture. In this, as in many other progressive measures, the initiative came from the students. "It is a pity that this college does not, like some other similar institutions, possess a gymnasium where students could take exercise during rainy weather," complained young Scharff and Henry in 1853.[71] Five years later the undergraduates requested permission to erect a building and were over-

[69] C. H. Scharff and J. B. Henry, *College As It Is*, pp. 160, 161, 167, 170, MSS, Princeton Library.
[70] "Reminiscences of A. A. Woodhull," *Princeton Library MSS*, AM 9276.
[71] C. H. Scharff and J. B. Henry, *College As It Is*, p. 181, MSS, Princeton Library.

joyed when the trustees consented and Maclean and other faculty members pledged themselves to pay half the cost of $984.31.[72] Thus, in the spring of 1859, the boys looked on eagerly as a crude frame structure, 70 feet by 30, arose in the northwest corner of the ball and cricket field near the site of present-day Witherspoon Hall.[73] They elected two superintendents from the junior class, purchased apparatus from a New York dealer and set on foot the first officially sanctioned athletics in Princeton.[74] A strange contrast this barnlike structure presents to the massive gymnasium of a later day, but the students were well satisfied. And all winter long, with the wind sweeping in through the loose boards, a few enthusiasts could be seen at work on the parallel bars, the trapeze, or the flying rings. But their pleasure was short-lived, for in 1865, when a report spread that a tramp suffering from yellow fever had been sleeping there, someone applied the torch and the building burned to the ground.[75]

Back of Nassau Hall the students on crisp autumn afternoons continued to work off their youthful energy with spirited games of shinny. But this resulted in so many bruised legs and bleeding heads that Maclean became alarmed lest some serious accident should result and planted that portion of the campus with trees.[76] The trees, however, did not prevent the boys from indulging in football. When the ball was set up in the middle, and the cry of "A to M on this side" was heard, often more than half the college lined up. The big rush through the trees or a scrimmage in front of one of the goals was strenuous indeed, and every quick run or long kick was hailed with loud applause.[77] Later the faculty set aside a field adjoining the old railway station and here the boys were un-

[72] *Maclean MSS*, Dec. 21, 1858, Princeton Library; *Trustees Minutes*, IV, p. 142.

[73] *Nassau Literary Magazine*, XIX, p. 252.

[74] J. W. Alexander to Maclean, Oct. 29, 1861, *Maclean MSS*, Princeton Library.

[75] *Princeton Book* (1879), p. 268.

[76] "Reminiscences of A. A. Woodhull," *Princeton Library MSS*, AM 9276, Part I, p. 12.

[77] *Princeton Book*, p. 386.

restricted in their enjoyment of handball, football, shinny, and baseball.

Baseball seems to have been first introduced to Princeton in 1858, when three freshmen organized a nine. Its popularity was instantaneous, and within a year or two various classes, the halls, and boarding clubs were contending on the diamond. In 1860 the college nine, or the "Nassaus" as they were called, went to Orange where they played a tie game, while two years later they won the championship of New Jersey by defeating the Stars of New Brunswick.[78] Even more successful was the 1863 season, when the Nassaus defeated the Athletics of Philadelphia "handsomely," and then triumphed over three Brooklyn clubs. But the Atlantics of Bedford, the second strongest club in the country, won from them by the score of 18 to 13.[79] Altogether, it was an auspicious beginning for Princeton's long career on the diamond.

The last barring-out in Nassau Hall took place a few months prior to the fire of 1855. The practice of barricading the upper stairs with firewood so as to bar admission to the tutors, and then shouting, blowing on horns, and ringing the bell, had long tormented the faculty. But with the dividing of the halls by a partition in the building, as it was reconstructed after the fire, the practice died out.[80] However, horn-sprees, the tarring of benches in the classrooms, and clashes with village youths continued. In March 1864 some daring youth climbed up on the outside of the cupola and made off with the bell clapper. This made it necessary for the janitor to ascend by means of a ladder and strike the bell with a hammer for classes and prayers, until a new tongue could be ordered.[81] In subsequent years the feat of stealing the clapper fell to the lot of the freshmen and became so frequent an occurrence that the college had to keep a supply of extra clappers on hand.

[78] *Ibid.*, p. 418.    [79] *Princeton Standard*, Oct. 23, 1863.
[80] *Princeton Alumni Weekly*, Jan. 17, 1903; "Reminiscences of A. A. Woodhull," *Princeton Library MSS*, AM 9276, Part II, p. 20.
[81] *Princeton Standard*, March 11, 1864.

Maclean's promotion to the presidency did not in the least alter his rather undignified manner of searching out delinquent students and trying to maintain order when mischief was afoot. On one occasion, when several students ran a big baggage van over the campus and down the street, he ran after it and leaped aboard. "The midnight ride of Paul Revere was not more exciting" as he was jolted over "sidewalks and curb stones." Finally, in desperation, he called to the driver: "If you'll let me out, I'll go straight to me office."[82] More serious was an affair on the front steps of Philosophical Hall. Joseph Henry still came back to Princeton each year for a series of lectures, and many underclassmen had been in the habit of attending them, often appropriating seats which of right belonged to the seniors. When Maclean found that some of the seniors had taken a stand at the door to keep out the interlopers, he mounted the steps to forestall trouble. Unfortunately, he turned his head for a moment and the crowd took the opportunity to rush up past him. He lost his hat and his famous cape in the melee and was not a little bruised and battered.[83]

The so-called horn-sprees were a source of great annoyance. Typical was the spree of March 9, 1864. When the sound of the horn summoned the students to assemble on the campus, a riotous procession moved into the streets of the village, shouting, breaking windows, and making off with fences and gates. "The martial music of the tin horn and the martial orders of the leaders commanding the fellows to close in," aroused the villagers from bed to be indignant witnesses of the destruction of their property. The spree ended with a giant bonfire.[84]

Deep was President Maclean's concern when he discovered that several Greek-letter fraternities had established chapters in the college. In former days the literary societies had served as social clubs, binding their members together in friendship

---

[82] J. M. Ludlow, *Reminiscences of Princeton*, MSS, Princeton Library.
[83] Letter of W. S. Nichols, *Princeton Library MSS*, AM 11289.
[84] *Princeton Standard*, March 11, 1864.

and guarding their secrets jealously. But with the great increase of numbers in the mid-century, many students formed
smaller and more intimate circles within or even beyond the
bonds of Whig or Clio. The soil was thus prepared for the
fraternities when they sought admission to the campus. First
came Beta Theta Pi in 1843, followed by Delta Kappa Epsilon, Zeta Psi, Delta Psi, Chi Phi, Kappa Alpha, Phi Kappa
Sigma, Sigma Phi, Chi Psi, and Delta Phi.[85] The chapters
were very small, seldom including more than ten men, and
the members met at not very frequent intervals in their
bedrooms.

Maclean, fearing that the fraternities would undermine
college discipline and prove injurious to the literary societies,
declared open war. So, in 1855, the faculty and the trustees
passed resolutions requiring all entering students to take a
solemn pledge not to join any secret society, and at the opening of college Maclean announced to the assembled student
body that he had been instructed by the trustees to dismiss
anyone known to be a member. The youthful "Greeks" were
deeply aroused. In many a midnight conclave they discussed
the prohibition, debating whether it was dishonorable to break
a forced pledge, and meditating open rebellion. Both Whig
and Clio protested to the trustees that the fraternities had not
tended to wean their members from the two societies but, on
the contrary, had greatly mitigated sectional animosities
within their ranks.

Nonetheless, in 1852 Zeta Psi disbanded, followed in 1853
by Delta Psi, and in 1856 by Kappa Alpha.[86] "I wish I could
say as much for the others," wrote Maclean. "They still exist
by the admission of youth who have broken their solemn
promise. . . . They exist in defiance of the college authorities."[87] When one boy told him that there were no fewer than
one hundred members still active in Princeton, he was deeply
discouraged.[88] But when disclosures of the names were made

[85] W. P. Baird, *Manual of American College Fraternities.*
[86] *Princeton Library MSS*, AM 10868.
[87] *Maclean MSS*, Dec. 20, 1856, Princeton Library.
[88] Statement of H. P. Ross, *ibid.*

and dismissals seemed imminent, most of the remaining chapters disbanded—Chi Phi, Delta Kappa Epsilon, Sigma Phi, Chi Psi, and others. By 1864 the president claimed triumphantly that so far as he knew no secret society remained at Princeton.[89]

He would have been less complacent had he realized that new social organizations of a fraternal nature were growing up with the express sanction of the college. As early as 1846 the catalogue announced that "select associations" of students had been formed as eating clubs, which was a perfectly satisfactory arrangement "and by some preferred to every other." With the permanent closing of the refectory in 1856, these clubs took on new significance. In 1864 they numbered twelve, rejoicing in the names of Old Hickory, The Society, The Autocrats, Sprinklings of Ceres, Pi-etas, Old Bourbon, Maryland, Hole in the Wall, '66, Sepoy, Gideon's Band, and Shucks. These little circles around the table, where "sympathy in taste and singleness of purpose evolve from many hearts," even in Maclean's day were becoming important units of college life.[90]

Maclean's administration was not marked by the erection of many new buildings, for the funds which might have gone into dormitories or laboratories or lecture halls were absorbed in the restoration of Nassau Hall, the founding of scholarships, and the endowment of professorships. Yet to him fell the honor of initiating, with the erection of the Halsted Observatory in 1867, the great period of construction which culminated under McCosh.

For decades Stephen Alexander, working with the small and totally inadequate telescope in his residence on Potter's Lane, had dreamed of an observatory at Princeton equipped with the largest telescope science could devise. Great was his delight, then, when General N. N. Halsted donated a sum

[89] Letter of March 30, 1864, *Maclean MSS*, Princeton Library. He seems to have been mistaken, for there is evidence to show that a chapter of Theta Delta Chi was in existence in Princeton at this date.

[90] *Nassau Herald*, June, 1864.

for the purpose, and construction got under way. Alexander himself drew the plans which were later perfected by the architect.[91] So a massive stone structure slowly arose on University Place, with a central octagonal building capped with a revolving dome and flanked by two smaller octagonal wings. Perhaps it was the proudest and the happiest day in Alexander's long life when he made the address in March 1867 at the laying of the cornerstone, with his usual "combination of eloquence, poetry and science."[92] Unfortunately, he had to wait another fifteen years before the telescope was installed and, at last, as an elderly and infirm man, he could take a look at Venus or Jupiter through the fine twenty-three inch glass.

As the years passed and Maclean approached the age when he would be forced to resign the presidency, he became more and more opposed to change, more and more apprehensive that the Presbyterian church might be forced to relinquish its hold upon the college. This became startlingly clear in 1866 when it was necessary to fill the chair of Latin made vacant by the death of Professor Giger. Maclean was in favor of John S. Hart, who had formerly served as tutor and adjunct professor of Greek, was now lecturer on English literature, and was a stanch Presbyterian. Since, however, he was not a Latin scholar, Maclean proposed to make him professor of Roman and English literature and to bring in the Reverend Samuel Stanhope Orris to teach Latin. When Orris accepted a call to a Presbyterian church in Philadelphia, he was at a loss what to propose.

When the trustees took matters in their own hands by electing Charles A. Aiken of Dartmouth, Maclean was so outspoken in opposition that some of them accused him of discourtesy. His objections were not of a personal character, he said, but from a belief that to appoint one who was not a Presbyterian minister but a "Congregationalist from New England" would be distasteful to many graduates.[93] For the

[91] *Princeton Library MSS*, AM 11445.
[92] *Princeton Standard*, March 22, 1867.
[93] Maclean to Pennington, March 8, 1866, *Maclean MSS*, Princeton Library.

moment the good doctor forgot that the college had been founded by men of New England descent and education, who were at least as much Congregationalist as Presbyterian in their beliefs.

Before taking final action, the trustees requested S. H. Pennington to visit New England and investigate Aiken's career and religious views. At Portland he asked a friend: "Can we make a good Presbyterian of him?" "No doubt of it, sir! No doubt of it!" was the emphatic reply. Wherever Pennington went he had good reports of Aiken's "scholarship, gentlemanly and affable manners and his theological soundness." "Nor is there any reason to fear in regard to his substantial accord with Princeton in theological sentiment," he wrote Maclean. "He is by inheritance a Presbyterian, his connection with the Congregational Church being purely accidental. His father and mother are both descendants from the Scotch-Irish, who left the north of Ireland in the Londonderry troubles and established the Presbyterian Church in New Hampshire."[94] Maclean, making the best of the situation, wrote Aiken assuring him of a hearty welcome, though he did so with grave misgivings. But five years later he must have realized that all these fears had been needless because Aiken was called to the chair of Christian ethics and apologetics at that fountainhead of Presbyterianism, the Princeton Theological Seminary.

While Maclean was protesting against any breach in the solid ranks of the Presbyterians in the college, he became even more deeply concerned over the defense of what he considered the very foundations of Christianity itself involved in still another addition to the faculty. Charles Woodruff Shields of the class of 1844, the scholarly minister of the Second Presbyterian Church of Philadelphia, published in 1861 a little book entitled *Philosophia Ultima*. In it he called for a resurvey of the entire field of science and the entire field of Christian theology, so that all apparent conflict might be reconciled. So great was the interest aroused by this suggestion

[94] Pennington to Maclean, March 7, 1866, *ibid.*

that wealthy friends raised a fund for a professorship at Princeton on the harmony of science and religion, so that he could pursue the subject further.[95]

Maclean was pleased. He would have preferred Joseph Henry as the incumbent, but his chief concern was to have Princeton take the lead in proving to the world that the discoveries of geologists and astronomers in no way conflicted with the literal interpretation of the Bible. At Shields' introductory lecture to his class Maclean was an interested and apparently approving listener. But when the lecture was printed and he had had the opportunity to study it in detail, grave misgivings began to trouble him. Had Shields conceded too much? Would he, in his course and his subsequent writings, bring theology into line with science, rather than explain away any doubts as to "revealed truth"?[96] However, Shields took pains to reassure him. He had understood that the trustees had in view when creating the department "a systematic illustration of the harmony of Biblical and scientific truth, involving an argument for the divine authority of the Holy Scriptures and the Christian religion." At least that had been his purpose in accepting the chair.[97]

But there were many who continued to say openly that the trustees had blundered. In his address Shields had explained that he was to be "a mediator or umpire" in adjusting the boundaries of science and theology, "settle their border feuds and check their raids upon each other's territory." "We confess that we fail to appreciate fully . . . the wisdom . . . of establishing a chair with such exalted prerogatives and supreme jurisdiction," said an article in the *Princeton Standard*.[98] "We believe that all truth is harmonious with itself; that truths of revealed religion are in unity with all the discovered facts of science; that no discovered truth in physics or metaphysics can be in conflict with divine Revelation. This is the

[95] *Dictionary of American Biography*, XVII, p. 104.
[96] Shields to Maclean, April 12, 1866, *Maclean MSS*, Princeton Library; letter of Charles Hodge, April 26, 1866, MSS, Princeton Library.
[97] *Ibid.*, June 25, 1866.
[98] April 20, 1866.

faith of the most learned theologians and of the most religious scientists . . . whose duty requires them to teach the people that the Bible is sustained and not overthrown by the discoveries of science, as is done by the creation of this new chair —this pure, impartial umpire." Poor Shields could only explain that his intention had been to eliminate, not to create doubts, and that he came as a champion, not as an enemy of the Bible. But many years were to pass before suspicion was allayed.

Maclean was now advancing in years, and though still vigorous and in good health, he thought it wise in December 1867 to submit his resignation. As Charles Hodge read his letter to the trustees, they listened with deep emotion. Maclean had been connected with the college for half a century, as tutor, professor, vice-president, and president, and all realized that his passing meant the end of the old era. In accepting his resignation they thanked him for his faithful and self-sacrificing devotion to the college, his parental interest in the students, his long and valuable services in the cause of Christian learning.[99]

On Sunday, June 22, 1868, Maclean delivered his final baccalaureate sermon to the students who crowded into the chapel to receive his advice and blessing. The following Wednesday he presided at the regular commencement exercises, listening attentively to one young orator after another and conferring the degrees upon the graduating class. He was touched when the class of 1865, who had assembled for their third reunion, passed resolutions expressing their respect and affection for him. "We hereby tender him our earnest thanks for his uniform kindness and courtesy," they said, "and our warmest wishes for his future good fortune and prosperity."[100] Thus did John Maclean relinquish the post of pilot for the college which he had held officially for fourteen years and in all but name for three decades.

Princeton owes much to John Maclean. In the days of ad-

[99] *Princeton Standard*, Dec. 20, 1867; *Trustees Minutes*, IV, pp. 457-459.
[100] *Princeton Standard*, June 26, 1868.

versity, when the very existence of the college was at stake, he was strong and steadfast. He it was who rallied the alumni to the rescue when student enrollment fell beneath a hundred, when Nassau Hall went up in flames, when the War Between the States produced serious financial problems. His administration was marked by the building up of the first really adequate endowment in the history of Princeton, a movement which was to assume startling proportions under McCosh. The establishing of a number of scholarships to cover tuition costs proved of incalculable service in securing the best type of students, raising standards, and bettering teaching.

On the other hand, Maclean was himself largely responsible for the failure of his faculty to maintain the remarkable standards of scholarly attainment which had characterized their predecessors of the fifth decade of the century, since he insisted upon filling each vacancy with a devout Presbyterian. If he could find an able scholar who was a Presbyterian, he would try to get him; if no such man was available, he would secure a Presbyterian who was not an able scholar. Of the ten professors in his faculty on the date of his retirement, no fewer than seven were ministers, and all were ardent Calvinists. But with the exception of Guyot and the aging Stephen Alexander, none of them had acquired a wide reputation for scholarship.

Both Maclean and his faculty strongly resisted the growing pressure for a modified curriculum, in which the elective system should have some part. Not only did they insist that they, and not the students, were best qualified to select the courses to be pursued, but that they could draft a program suitable for all. It mattered not whether the student intended to become a minister, a lawyer, a doctor, or a farmer, he had to go through the standard course of study. As the importance of previously neglected subjects became more fully recognized, the faculty began to yield to the pressure and included them in the curriculum, apparently unconscious that breadth was being gained at the cost of thoroughness. At the close of Maclean's administration the junior and senior courses must have seemed to the students like a moving panorama, giving them hasty glimpses of logic, calculus, Latin, Greek, history, philosophy, mechanics, physics, rhetoric, theology, geography, astronomy, chemistry, geology, botany, architecture, constitutional law, economics, zoology, etc.

Unfortunate also was the rapid change from a national to a sectional college which marked Maclean's administration. Princeton from the very outset had drawn her students from widely separated districts—from New England as well as New Jersey, from the valley of Virginia as well as from western Pennsylvania. When the healing of the breach between New Lights and Old Side in New England cost the college most of its patronage in that section, there came ample compensation in the winning of hundreds of students from the planter class of the south. With the War Between the States, not only was this planter group alienated, but also the formerly intensely loyal Presbyterians of Virginia, North Carolina, Tennessee, and Kentucky. In the years following the war it was to New Jersey, Pennsylvania, and New York that Princeton had to look for most of her students, and not until the twentieth century did she regain her national character.

At commencement in 1886 the alumni were having their annual dinner in University Hall, at the corner of Nassau Street and Railroad Avenue.[101] Suddenly there was a tremendous burst of applause. The alumni seemed to go mad with excitement, clapping, stamping, jumping, waving hats, while the *siss, boom, ah* of the Princeton cheer rang out again and again. Slowly Dr. Maclean, his accustomed cape over his shoulders despite the heat, his gray locks hanging below his black velvet cap, moved down the aisle, leaning on the arm of Professor Schanck. Too feeble to deliver an address, the former president had written a short message to the alumni, which he requested Professor Cameron to read. It conveyed his blessing upon the institution to which he had devoted his life, and an earnest appeal that in her efforts to advance

[101] Now University Place.

secular education she should continue to carry out the purpose of the founders in training young men for the gospel of Christ.

The reading being ended, Dr. Maclean moved out of the hall, while the great crowd rose and stood in respectful silence. As he passed along he was stopped again and again by this alumnus or that who grasped his hand and expressed once more loyalty and affection. It was John Maclean's farewell to Princeton. He died a few weeks later at his residence on Canal Street,[102] in his eighty-seventh year, and his body was interred in the Princeton Cemetery, where he rests beside Aaron Burr, Senior, Jonathan Edwards, Samuel Davies, and John Witherspoon.

[102] Now Alexander Street.

## CHAPTER IX

# The Birth of a University

T HE selection of Maclean's successor was a matter of grave concern for the trustees. American education was entering a new epoch. Under the stimulus of increased endowments the leading colleges were enlarging their faculties, erecting new buildings, adding to their scientific equipment, broadening their curricula to include art, engineering, economics, and other neglected fields of study, bettering the methods of teaching, seeking to arouse the intellectual curiosity of their students. It was a time when educational leadership was at a premium, and when a mistake in selecting a president might prove disastrous. There was rejoicing among the friends of Princeton, then, when it was announced that the board had chosen the Reverend William Henry Green, a nephew of Chancellor H. W. Green, and a member of the faculty of Princeton Theological Seminary. A distinguished scholar, a remarkable linguist, an eminent divine, he seemed in every way fitted for the post.[1] Joseph Henry was gratified that the choice had been "so judiciously made" and hastened to write Dr. Green urging him to accept.[2] None the less Green declined and the board was forced to canvass the field anew.

Some of them recalled that it was just a century before that John Witherspoon had come to Princeton and suggested that Scotland once more might produce a great president for the college. In the summer of 1866 the Reverend James McCosh, professor of logic and metaphysics in Queen's College, Belfast, had come to the United States and had visited many of the colleges, where his learning, piety and personality had made a most favorable impression. Perhaps he would be the

[1] *Princeton Standard*, April 10, 1868.
[2] Henry to Maclean, April 9, 1868, *Maclean MSS*, Princeton Library.

man to lead Princeton into a new epoch of growth and prosperity. On April 29, 1868, he was elected.

McCosh had won distinction for his part in the secession
of the Free Church of Scotland from the established church
and in the disestablishment of the Irish Church, for his leadership in the evangelistic movements of his country, for his
scholarly works, *The Method of the Divine Government,
Physical and Moral* and *An Examination of Mill's Philosophy*, and for his success as a teacher and disciplinarian. "I
shall never forget Dr. McCosh's opening lecture," wrote one
of his Queen's College students. "From that time forth I was
an enthusiast in all the exercises of the class. He had the
power of inspiring in the minds of his students not merely
a love for the mental sciences but a profound respect for
himself."[3]

Of first importance to Princeton was McCosh's wide acquaintance with the universities of the Old World. A graduate of two Scottish universities, he had visited Oxford and
Cambridge where he formed friendships with some of their
most distinguished men, had inspected many of the leading
German universities and several in Switzerland and Holland.
In the period of educational expansion which lay ahead for
the American colleges he was splendidly equipped to bring to
Princeton the best from European systems.

It had taken several weeks for the news to reach Witherspoon when he was elected president, but the invitation to
McCosh went by "ocean telegraph," which had been established only two years before. The announcement that he had
accepted was received with joy in Princeton. And when, five
months later, he arrived off Sandy Hook on the *Tripoli*,
the students prepared to give him a rousing reception. "As
the hands of the clock crept around to four, there arose from
the college a shout. . . . Then there was a rushing to the
depot, and a marshalling of the students. Soon the shrill
whistle, and after, the 'down brakes' announced that he had
come—announced the arrival of McCosh. Of course, there

[3] *Princeton Standard,* May 8, 1868.

was cheering again, the old cheer of the Nassaus, and the procession moved towards the President's house. . . . Arrived at the house, the students formed in a semi-circle about the front, when Dr. Atwater, Acting President, introduced to them their real president."[4] That night the campus resounded to the tread of marching columns and to the cheers of the students, while the sky was lit up with rockets and the glare of a huge bonfire.

A week later McCosh was installed in office before a gathering of statesmen, college presidents, alumni, students, and other guests. As he arose to deliver his inaugural address the assemblage saw a man of fifty-seven, large of stature, but with somewhat rounded shoulders, a splendid head sparsely covered with gray hair, blue eyes, the finely cut features expressive of spiritual thought. His nervous temperament was revealed by a rapid passing of the hand from the top of the head down across the broad forehead to the tip of the nose.[5]

With a broad Scottish burr he proceeded to outline his theories of education and the policies he intended to pursue. He held that the highest end of a college was to educate, that is, draw out and improve innate faculties. The next aim, but subordinate to the first, should be to impart knowledge, such knowledge as would be useful in future life. He warned against forcing students to do "dull and crabbed work" merely for the sake of mental discipline, lest it weary and disgust them and give them a distaste for study. It was right to give professional instruction, but only in the scientific spirit that subordinated preparation for ordinary vocations to inventing new instruments and making improvements.[6]

Scholarly attainment by the faculty he thought vital to successful teaching. "Those who are placed in the offices of a university should aim at something more than being merely the teachers of a restricted body of young men. The youths who are under them and who look up to them will be greatly

---

[4] Geo. R. Wallace, *Princeton Sketches*, p. 109.
[5] *Princeton Standard*, May 8, 1868.
[6] *Inauguration of James McCosh*, p. 45.

[ 292 ]

stimulated to study by the very circumstance that their professor is a man of wide sympathies and connections with the literature or science of the country."[7] Yet he considered the glory of every alma mater her children, and her ambition was to send forth a host of able ministers, lawyers, physicians, businessmen.[8]

After saying a word for Latin and Greek, modern languages, mathematics, the physical sciences, the mental sciences, and the social sciences, he struck a shattering blow at the inflexible curriculum to which Princeton had adhered for so many decades. "I say, if you are to admit, as you must in justice as well as in expediency, the new branches without excluding the old, then you must allow a choice. If our years were as many as those of the antediluvians, one might require all of every student, but to do so in a four year course, would give but a smattering of all without a real knowledge of any."[9] The solution he proposed was a groundwork of required courses, with a superstructure of electives for training in special fields. Theological students might properly concentrate on Greek and philosophy, medical students on chemistry and physiology, law students on political economy. But he warned against too much specialization. "Let the student first be taken, as it were, to an eminence, whence he may behold the whole country, with its connected hills, vales and streams lying below him, and then be encouraged to dive down into some special place, seen and selected from the height, that he may linger in it, and explore it minutely and thoroughly."[10]

The time had come, he thought, to create a new intellectual atmosphere at Princeton. The influence of Oxford and Cambridge upon their students was to be explained by the memory of the great men who had been there, by their distinguished scholars, by the quiet life in the colleges, by the societies and university meetings, by the museums, the manuscripts, the

[7] *Ibid.*, p. 50.
[8] *Ibid.*, p. 51.
[9] *Ibid.*, p. 70.
[10] *Ibid.*, p. 75.

old books. Princeton must create such an atmosphere. "We have grand names in the past and need only like men in the present: by accessions to our apparatus and our library and encouragements to our students to go on to higher learning and by the founding of new chairs of literature and science."[11]

It must have been with mixed emotions that the trustees and faculty listened to this frank statement of policy. To some, especially among the older professors, it seemed revolutionary, a rash attempt to engraft European ideas upon an American college. Was it wise to introduce the elective system, to establish new courses to vie with the classics, mathematics, science, and philosophy? In the expansion of secular instruction was there not danger of forgetting that the college was a religious foundation? But the doubting Thomases, as they viewed the strength and resolution revealed in every feature of the new president, realized that they had no choice but to assent. And even they must have caught some of the enthusiasm with which the students and younger alumni hailed the advent of the new era.

McCosh was fortunate in having at hand a group of generous and far-sighted benefactors. John C. Green of New York, brother of Chancellor Green, together with his residuary legatees, gave no less than $1,500,000, while Robert Bonner, H. G. Marquand, Robert L. Stuart, Alexander Stuart, William Libbey, William Osborn, James Lenox, John S. Kennedy, and others contributed liberally. In all, donations of nearly $3,000,000 were received during the twenty years of McCosh's administration.[12]

In his first report to the trustees the president dwelt upon the need for new buildings. "The state of most of the recitation rooms is very unsatisfactory. . . . If there is any prospect of an increase of students, there must be farther accommodations provided for them. . . . The museum and scientific apparatus of the college are in a very defective state. No one

[11] *Ibid.*, p. 89.
[12] James McCosh, *Twenty Years of Princeton*, pp. 9-14.

will present us with scientific specimens so long as there is not a fit place in which to exhibit them."[13]

The response was immediate. Robert Bonner and H. G. Marquand, impressed with the need for more physical education, made an offer of $10,000 each for the erection of a gymnasium.[14] So a lot was purchased just west of the site of Alexander Hall, and there the masons set to work rearing a stone building whose octagonal corner towers topped with spires, sharply rising roof lines, and closely set dormers gave the impression of a French chateau.[15] To the undergraduates of today the building would seem small and poorly planned, but at the time it was a source of pride as well as a stimulus to healthful exercise.

It was the generous John C. Green who gave the money for the new recitation hall. "I should be much gratified," he wrote McCosh in June 1870, "if the ground which I have given to the college were cleared of the unsightly objects now upon it, and graded and suitably embellished. . . . The expenses of every kind, on the building, the furniture and equipment and the regulation and ornamentation of the ground, I am prepared to pay."[16] So Dickinson Hall, with its stone walls, its eight recitation rooms, its large examination room, its entrances on four fronts, arose east of Nassau Hall, across William Street from the site of the present chapel and about three hundred feet northwest of the building on Washington Road which now bears its name. McCosh watched its progress with deep satisfaction, for the building was a necessary adjunct to his elective system, since there could be no expansion of courses without a corresponding multiplication of classrooms. As for the need for more dormi-

[13] James McCosh, *Reports to Board of Trustees*, Dec. 16, 1868. From Dec. 16, 1868, to June 26, 1876, the reports appear in manuscript form in Dr. McCosh's handwriting; from Nov. 9, 1876, to Feb. 9, 1888, they were printed on loose sheets. The whole, bound under one cover, was presented to Princeton University by Dr. McCosh in July, 1891.

[14] *Princeton College*, published by Princeton Alumni Association of Philadelphia, p. 12.

[15] James McCosh, *Reports to Board of Trustees*, Dec. 22, 1869.

[16] June 25, 1870, *Princeton Library MSS*, AM 10775.

tory space, it was met by the erection of a building between West College and Stanhope Hall, named Reunion Hall in celebration of the reuniting of the Old and New School branches of the Presbyterian church.

But the pride of the college was the new library building, donated by John C. Green, and named, for his brother, the Chancellor Green Library. So solicitous was the chancellor that it should be the most convenient and up-to-date library in the country that he sent out a circular to faculty members and others, asking their advice as to building materials, reading rooms, light, ventilation, heating, shelving, etc.[17] Professor C. W. Shields suggested a round building topped by a dome, with the books deposited in alcoves and with two wings for reading rooms, faculty room, and trustees room. "A tasteful architect might give such a structure a highly ornate expression by means of columns, pilasters, etc. with the dome as the striking feature."[18] Professor Cameron thought the building should be but one story with a gallery erected of stone and iron, lighted by means of lancet-shaped windows and a skylight and fitted with reading room, research room, etc. It was vital that it should be capable of enlargement although it would take fifty years to build up a collection as large as the Astor Library with its 137,000 volumes. But he did not favor adding volumes indefinitely, which might become "useless just by reason of the great number."[19] McCosh, himself, rather favored a rectangular building similar to the library at Queen's College, Belfast.[20]

Out of the plethora of advice grew an octagonal building of stone, each side capped by a pediment and pierced by slender windows, with a skylight above and two wings connected with the main structure by ornate doors. So proud were the trustees of this building that they insisted upon its being on the front campus, even though that necessitated destruction of Philosophical Hall made famous by Joseph Henry's epoch-making discoveries. "It is so situated as to make North Col-

[17] *Princeton Library MSS*, AM 9310.　　[18] *Ibid.*, AM 9314.
[19] *Ibid.*, AM 11895.　　[20] *Ibid.*, AM 9317, 9318.

lege and Dickinson Hall appear the wings of it," wrote Dr. McCosh.[21] The work of construction was completed in 1873 and the library books moved into it from the old room in Nassau Hall under the supervision of the new librarian, Frederick Vinton.[22]

Even before the Chancellor Green Library was completed the foundation was laid for the School of Science building, at the corner of William Street and Washington Road. Two years later the structure was completed and the scientific faculty abandoned their old cramped quarters to avail themselves of its large lecture rooms, laboratories, museums, offices, and photographing room.[23]

It is unfortunate that the greatest era of college expansion in the United States should have coincided with a period of poor architectural taste. Not only at Princeton but at scores of other colleges, early American traditions were discarded in favor of ornate towers, steep roofs set off by varicolored slate, broken façades and Romanesque doors and windows. But at the time the new Princeton structures were heralded as models of beauty. McCosh spoke proudly of "the stately structure of Dickinson Hall," while he considered the library "the most beautiful in the country."[24] He seems to have had no appreciation of the quiet charm and dignity of Nassau Hall and it did not occur to him that it might be used as a theme for a homogeneous and unique group of buildings.

If McCosh thought that the erection of so many buildings would win universal praise for himself and for Princeton, he was doomed to disappointment. Why is it, asked the *New York Tribune*,[25] that Princeton is throwing all its resources into buildings rather than into a scholarly faculty? "Every college finds that its able men, its recognized scholars, are its most productive wealth. Princeton needs them. . . . Not half of our college presidents are competent to recognize a scholar.

[21] *Ibid.*, AM 11678.
[22] James McCosh, *Reports to Board of Trustees*, Dec. 17, 1873.
[23] *Ibid.*, Dec. 18, 1872, June 22, 1874.
[24] James McCosh, *Twenty Years of Princeton*, p. 10.
[25] Dec. 2, 1876.

. . . In science Princeton needs to strengthen her teaching force. Prof. Alexander is old, Prof. Guyot feeble." This was but one of a long series of attacks on Princeton which turned many against the college and cost it large sums in gifts and legacies. One prominent New York alumnus declared that he would not give a cent to Princeton while McCosh retained the presidency.[26]

These attacks were unjust. One can erect a dormitory or a gymnasium in fifteen or eighteen months; it takes many years to build a faculty. McCosh in his very first report to the trustees had emphasized the need of new professorships and warned that without them Princeton would be outstripped by other colleges.[27] When the chair of belles-lettres became vacant in 1874, he insisted that it should be filled by a man of literary eminence. "This would tend more than anything else to bring young men of bright parts to us and keep our students from leaving us. . . . On the other hand, nothing would injure our college so much as the appointment to any vacant chair of a respectable, dull, lifeless man merely because he is ortho-dox."[28] If he chanced to be an alumnus and a Presbyterian, so much the better, but neither was essential if he was "a Christian man and likely to exercise a good influence on students."

McCosh inherited his faculty from Maclean. He could not dismiss men who had given many years of their life to the service of the college; he could not transform them immediately into profound scholars and inspiring teachers. But he could fill vacancies with the ablest men to be found; he could establish new chairs; he could bring in promising young men as assistant professors and tutors; he could lighten the heavy burden of teaching; he could provide a better library and more scientific equipment; he could stimulate intellectual activity by introducing advanced courses; he could increase salaries. But all this would require time, and it is to the clos-

[26] William B. Scott, *Materials for an Autobiography*, I, p. 157, MSS.
[27] James McCosh, *Reports to Board of Trustees*, Dec. 16, 1868.
[28] *Ibid.*, Dec. 16, 1874.

ing years of his administration, not its beginning, that one must look for final results.

McCosh added to his staff William Alfred Packard of Dartmouth as professor of Latin; General Joseph Kargé as Woodhull professor of continental languages and literatures; Cyrus F. Brackett, of Bowdoin College as Henry professor of physics; the Reverend James O. Murray of the Brick Church, New York, as Holmes professor of belles-lettres and English language and literature; Charles A. Young of Dartmouth as professor of astronomy; Charles G. Rockwood of Rutgers as professor of mathematics; S. Stanhope Orris of Marietta College as Ewing professor of Greek language and literature, and others equally distinguished. But his especial pride was what he termed "his bright young men"—Theodore W. Hunt, William M. Sloane, William Libbey, Samuel R. Winans, William B. Scott, Henry F. Osborn, Allan Marquand, Henry B. Fine, William F. Magie. Upon them in large measure, he thought the future of Princeton depended.

Some of these men, old as well as young, fully justified McCosh in their selection. Professor Young was one of the most distinguished astronomers in the country, his work *The Sun* and his articles in scientific journals winning wide acclaim. Professor Orris was recognized as a keen critic of literary expression and philosophic thought. His best known work was the translation of *The Teaching of the Twelve Apostles*. Theodore W. Hunt, known to thousands of Princetonians as "Granny" Hunt, was a pioneer in the introduction of old English studies in American colleges, and a penetrating literary critic. His works include *The Principles of Written Discourse, Studies in Literature and Style, American Meditative Lyrics*, and *Literature, Its Principles and Problems*. Scott won wide distinction in geology, Marquand in art, Fine in mathematics, Magie in physics. By 1875, McCosh was able to declare it his firm conviction that Princeton had as able a body of teachers as any college in the country.[29] He boasted,

[29] James McCosh, *Reports to Board of Trustees*, June 28, 1875.

also, of the rapid increase in their number. When he came to Princeton there had been but ten professors and seven associate professors and tutors; when he retired in 1888 the number had tripled.

Despite the enormous expansion of the budget which this entailed McCosh constantly urged on the board the need for an increase in salaries. The cost of living had gone up since the war, he pointed out, and some of the professors had suffered serious hardship and embarrassment—one having had to mortgage his library. Princeton could not expect to attract and hold eminent scholars and teachers under such circumstances. When no benefactor volunteered to meet this need, he launched a campaign to raise $60,000.[30] A bequest to the college of $26,000 by Mrs. S. A. Kirkpatrick was allocated to this purpose, Dr. Maclean gave $5,000, and other smaller gifts were added until in 1872 the total was $48,000, and in 1874 $63,000.[31] When McCosh became president the professors received $2,100 and a house rent free, but this new endowment raised the maximum salary to $3,400 or $3,000 and house. In 1883 the salary budget totaled $63,700,[32] a sum which would have seemed fantastic in the days of Carnahan, or even of Maclean.

But no one was more aware than McCosh that in order to have an able faculty, distinguished as teachers as well as scholars, it was necessary to create an intellectual atmosphere on the campus. It would be futile to bring in able men if they were to be overworked with undergraduate teaching, denied adequate laboratory and library facilities, and isolated from other minds interested in their fields of study, for in time they would lose their enthusiasm for research and become dull and uninspiring. So in Princeton's new buildings there must be a new intellectual life, induced by informal meetings of professors and students for the discussion of scholarly problems, by advanced courses for graduate students, by the founding

[30] James McCosh, *Reports to Board of Trustees*, Dec. 20, 1871.
[31] *Ibid.*, June 22, 1874.
[32] *Ibid.*, Feb. 8, 1883.

of fellowships, by scientific expeditions, by the expansion and greater use of the library, by the purchase of needed scientific equipment.

The president showed the way by organizing what he called library meetings. Every two weeks a group of graduates, professors, seniors, and juniors met in his library to hear a paper on some topic in literature, science, or philosophy, followed by an informal debate. It was a challenge to the professors, old and young alike, to have their views and findings subjected to the criticism of keen undergraduates, and for the undergraduates it was as though they had gained admission to the very sanctum of scholarship. The debates on Paul van Dyke's paper on the "Ethics of George Eliot," or G. B. Roddy's "The Philosophy of Cicero," must have been animated indeed.

Equally stimulating was the Natural History Society which met once a fortnight. This group it was which initiated the series of expeditions to the west to search for flora, fauna, fossils, and minerals. The first of these, led by the picturesque General Kargé, included William Libbey, Henry F. Osborn, William B. Scott, and others who were to attain distinction as scientists. For these young men it was a thrilling experience in which the excavation of animal fossils and the collecting of rare plants alternated with long rides on mule-back, visits to boom towns, and camping in the open.[33] It was with a sense of triumph that they returned to Princeton with their specimens of rock, animals, and fossils.

There was excitement among the highest standing students when it was announced in 1869 that three fellowships had been established for advanced study, open to members of the senior class, to be awarded under competitive examination. When the fellowship in mathematics fell to Theodoric B. Pryor, the fellowship in classical literature to George H. Hooper, and the fellowship in mental science to William D. Thomas, these young men became the envy of the entire student body. The next year five awards were made, two for

[33] W. B. Scott, *Materials for an Autobiography*, I, pp. 164-212, MSS.

study at the University of Berlin, one at Edinburgh University, one at the School of Mines of Columbia University, and one at the Princeton Theological Seminary. McCosh was elated. "The influence for good of these Fellowships in producing a higher scholarship is felt not merely by the successful candidates, but by all the better students; and not merely in the Senior year, but both in the Junior and Sophomore years," he reported to the trustees.[34] Other colleges were quick to grasp the importance of what he had done, and Harvard in particular was exerting herself to outstrip the field in endowing fellowships.[35]

When young William D. Thomas chose to remain at Princeton to pursue advanced work under President McCosh, he little realized that he was making a decision of vital importance for the college. There had been graduate students in Princeton before. James Madison, it will be recalled, remained to continue his studies under Witherspoon after receiving the bachelor's degree. But these had been isolated cases which led to no important changes in the life and academic structure of the college. When Thomas sought out the president or Professor Atwater to discuss with them his readings in Plato or the modern philosophers he became the entering wedge for a graduate school and so for the conversion of the college into a university.[36]

In 1873-1874 there were three fellows studying at Princeton, in 1877-1878 seven, in 1881-1882 eight. "With the additional and learned teachers we now have, arrangements should be made to have postgraduate courses," McCosh advised in 1877. "Already we have had this to a small extent in philosophy and certain departments of physical science. . . . I suggest that the Committee on the Curriculum prepare a scheme for postgraduate courses."[37] The trustees gave their assent, and at the next meeting the president announced that his most sanguine hopes had been exceeded and that no fewer

[34] James McCosh, *Reports to Board of Trustees*, June, 1870.
[35] *Ibid.*, Dec. 22, 1875.  [36] *Ibid.*, June 26, 1871.
[37] *Ibid.*, June, 1877.

than forty-two graduates had enrolled themselves in advanced courses, most of them in philosophy and physics.[38] Four years later the number had risen to fifty-six, among them Henry B. Fine, William F. Magie, Allan Marquand, and Paul van Dyke, all of whom were to play important roles in the Princeton of the future.[39]

McCosh was fully satisfied with the results. "There is more study and more intellectual life among a large body of the students than there used to be," he reported. "Our postgraduate courses are greatly stimulating the professors who give the instruction, and are drawing able youths to Princeton from various colleges. . . . Much stimulus is given to the whole college by its teachers' delivering lectures on such high branches as contemporaneous philosophy, Plato and his philosophy, Kant's philosophy, Early English, Anglo-Saxon, Sanskrit and the higher problems of physics. By this method we are seeking to gain some of the peculiar advantages of the German universities without their disadvantages. . . . The primary aim of a college should be to give instruction, but it should not neglect the other end; and the two ends may help each other. Knowledge will be most effectually advanced by those who are engaged in teaching, while not burdened with it; and a great stimulus is given to pupils when their instructors are engaged in special investigation."[40]

When McCosh came to Princeton he had no intention of converting it into a university; in fact he had no clear realization of the difference between an American college and a university. He planned to make Princeton "equal to any college in America, and, in the end, to any in Europe." But in striving toward this end he found he had created a university. It remained for his successor to secure official recognition of the new status, but it was he who worked the transformation. McCosh realized from the first that intellectual curiosity, the urge to make new discoveries, enthusiasm for constructive

[38] *Ibid.*, Nov. 8, 1877.
[39] *Catalogue of the College of New Jersey*, 1881-1882, pp. 11, 12.
[40] James McCosh, *Reports to Board of Trustees*, June 17, 1878.

work are necessary in the making of inspiring teachers; that an atmosphere of intellectual apathy in the faculty leads to apathy in the student body. He wanted to arouse the men around him, by his library meetings, by the scientific society, by the western expeditions, by fellowships, by graduate courses, by the multiplication of electives. "I think every educated man will allow that in all this we have a *studium generale* which is the essence of a university," he announced in 1887.[41]

McCosh had been president but a few months when the old unbending curriculum was superseded by the elective system. To undergraduates of today it would have seemed rigid and narrow, for freshmen and sophomores were allowed no electives, and juniors and seniors were required to study logic, psychology, mechanics, physics, natural theology, physical geography, rhetoric, astronomy, chemistry, English literature, economics, and moral philosophy. But at the time the changes were considered revolutionary. "In Junior year we had for the first time considerable freedom in the choice of our subjects of study," says William B. Scott of the class of 1878. "The complete change of atmosphere from the lower class years was most acceptable and I seemed to be entering new and more spacious worlds when I took up physics with Dr. Brackett, psychology with Dr. McCosh, logic with Dr. Atwater, geology with Dr. Guyot, and, above all, English literature with Dr. Murray. This latter subject was a revelation to me. . . . I was not content merely to hear and read about the great writers; so far as my very busy life permitted, I read their works, which, of course, made the lectures doubly interesting."[42]

From time to time, as new courses were added, the list of senior elections was lengthened, so that it was possible to choose from Latin, Greek, mathematics, astronomy, physics, history, chemistry, history of philosophy, French and Ger-

[41] *Ibid.*, Feb. 10, 1887.
[42] W. B. Scott, *Materials for an Autobiography*, I, pp. 135, 136, MSS.

man, political science, and museum work.[43] Of these, political science, taught by the aging but interesting Atwater, was the most popular, with chemistry and the history of philosophy following closely behind. The faculty, not always in accord with McCosh, were practically unanimous in supporting his recommendation that Greek be retained as a requirement for the bachelor's degree. They considered Greek the noblest language of antiquity, valuable not only as a training for the mind but for opening the door to a literature unsurpassed for its beauty. "If our colleges discard Latin and Greek," warned McCosh, "the whole ancient world with its thoughts and deeds will remain very much unknown even to our educated men."[44]

The president was criticized in the first years of his administration by the more conservative alumni for introducing the elective system, but he was criticized later in certain quarters for not carrying it far enough. Why, it was asked, does Princeton refuse elections to freshmen and sophomores? Why insist upon so many required courses in junior and senior year? Harvard had thrown most restrictions overboard and Princeton should do likewise.

This controversy culminated in a dramatic debate between President Eliot of Harvard and Dr. McCosh, under the auspices of the Nineteenth Century Club, at the residence of Mr. Courtlandt Palmer in New York. The distinguished group which crowded into the handsome parlors listened to a remarkable discussion which pointed out divergent paths along one of which American higher education must advance. After Dr. Eliot had pleaded for a wide extension of the elective system and expressed his confidence in the ability of young men to make wise selections, Dr. McCosh arose, not only to defend the plan in practice at Princeton but to criticize the wide liberty granted by Harvard.

He held that there are fundamental branches of learning that have stood the test of time in calling forth the higher

---

[43] *Catalogue of the College of New Jersey*, 1881-1882, p. 31.
[44] James McCosh, *Reports to Board of Trustees*, Nov. 13, 1884.

faculties of the mind, and that these should be required of every student. Such were Latin and Greek, certain European languages, mathematics, physics, philosophy, etc. Of especial importance, he thought, are the mental sciences, for young men should be taught to know themselves as well as the outside world. He would prefer a man who had received training in the fundamental subjects to one who had frittered away four years at Harvard studying music, art, and French plays. "From the close of Freshman year on it is perfectly practicable for a student to pass through Harvard and receive the degree of Bachelor of Arts without taking any course in Latin, Greek, mathematics, chemistry, physics, astronomy, geology, logic, psychology, ethics, political economy, German or even English!

"I hold that in a college with the variety there should be unity. The circle of the sciences should have a wide circumference but also a fixed centre. . . . In a college there may be, there should be, specialists, but not mere specialists, who are sure to be narrow, partial, malformed, one-sided and are apt to be conceited, prejudiced and intolerant. The other day a gymnast showed me his upper arm with the muscle large and hard as a mill-stone. It is a picture of the mental monstrosities produced by certain kinds of education. . . . I believe that comparatively few young men know what their powers are when they enter college. . . . Fatal mistakes may arise from a youth of sixteen or eighteen committing himself to a narrow-gauge line of study, and he finds when it is too late that he should have taken a broader road.

"I am glad things have come to a crisis. . . . Tell it not in Berlin or Oxford that the once most illustrious university in America no longer requires its graduates to know the most perfect language, the grandest literature, the most elevated thinking of all antiquity. Tell it not in Paris, tell it not in Cambridge in England, tell it not in Dublin, that Cambridge in America does not make mathematics obligatory on its students. Let not Edinburgh and Scotland and the Puritans in England know that a student may pass through the once Puritan college of America without having taken a single class of philosophy or lesson in religion."[45]

This celebrated debate was discussed from one end of the country to another and loosed a flood of letters to the newspapers. The consensus supported McCosh. It was misleading, wrote one correspondent, to compare American colleges with German universities, which were really clusters of professional schools, for which students had been prepared in the gymnasia by a fixed course embracing Latin, Greek, and other fundamental subjects. "When Harvard college becomes a university like that of Berlin or Bonn, and when it ceases to do the work of the German gymnasium and when that work is done by schools, then, and not before, the freedom of choice of studies permitted in German universities may be pleaded in support of the recent changes at Harvard."[46] Dr. Eliot was undoubtedly showing the way which American education was ultimately to follow, but for the moment his horse was too far ahead of the wagon, and it was only after the great advances made by the preparatory schools that his system worked to good advantage.

One of the most important achievements of McCosh's administration had its inception several years before he came to Princeton. It was in 1864 that the faculty recommended to the trustees the founding of a school of applied science, with a suitable building and additional professors. The time had come, they thought, to make special provision for those who were to make science the business of life by becoming analytical chemists or metallurgists, who could advise in chemical manufactures, or estimate the value of ore beds, or erect furnaces, or make discoveries in agriculture. A three-year course was outlined, embracing chemistry, physics, civil engineering, mineralogy, surveying, applied mechanics, metallurgy, etc.[47] The trustees gave their approval, but the plan

[45] James McCosh, *The New Departure in College Education* (New York, 1885).
[46] D. H. Chamberlain, in *New York Times*, Feb. 25, 1885.
[47] *Trustees Minutes*, IV, pp. 307-310.

was held in abeyance because the funds necessary to put it into operation were not forthcoming.

The matter was placed before McCosh soon after his arrival, but he decided that it must yield precedence to the revision and expansion of the academic work. However, in December 1871 he recommended the founding of a school of science, which he thought necessary if Princeton was to "keep up with the other great colleges of the country."[48] A committee was appointed to draw up a new plan and in June 1872 John C. Green gave $200,000 to put it into operation. So the masons and carpenters set to work to erect the School of Science building, professors were appointed, thirteen students enrolled, and the new school got under way. A three-year course including mathematics, chemistry, mineralogy, botany, anatomy, English, mechanics, physics, modern languages, drawing, astronomy, quantitative analysis, biology, geology, ethics, and political economy led to the bachelor of science degree. McCosh was well satisfied with the work of the new professors, Cyrus F. Brackett and Henry B. Cornwall, whom he thought men of "high ability" and successful teachers. That the number of entering students was not larger he attributed to the fact that Latin was required for admission.[49]

It was in November 1874 that Dr. McCosh paid a visit to John C. Green, in his New York residence. After he had gone Mr. Green wrote to Caleb S. Green: "If he is not mistaken in his opinion as to your views and those of the other Trustees in regard to the importance of an addition now of a department of engineering to the School of Science . . . I wish to say to you that I am willing to make the needed endowment of the new professorship."[50] This was the inception of Princeton's School of Engineering, with its various departments, its buildings, its libraries, its laboratories, its faculty. "I have not seen the members [trustees] so moved on any other oc-

[48] James McCosh, *Reports to Board of Trustees*, Dec. 20, 1871.
[49] *Ibid.*, Dec. 17, 1873.
[50] Letter of Nov. 10, 1874, MSS, Princeton Library.

casion as they were when your brother intimated your generous intention," McCosh wrote Green. "The disposition of the money is the wisest that could be made for the benefit of the School of Science."[51] So Charles McMillan was appointed professor of civil engineering and applied mathematics, and a four-year course leading to graduation was instituted.

In 1882 Dr. W. C. Prime offered to give Princeton his collection of porcelain and pottery, considered by many the finest in the country, on condition that a building be provided for it.[52] Although several years elapsed before the art museum was erected, this offer gave the impetus for the organization of a School of Art. Frederick Marquand donated $60,000,[53] a board of directors was appointed, and a program of courses outlined with lectures by McCosh on aesthetics, by Dr. Prime on the history of art, by Allan Marquand on painting in ancient times, and by Frothingham on Italian painting. McCosh then appealed to the alumni for funds for the museum. "Works of art are the only trustworthy record of, not alone the history, but the tastes, the mental character, and the manners and customs of various peoples in various ages. . . . Certainly Princeton may look with confidence to her sons . . . for contributions in this department."

It must not be supposed that McCosh carried through his revolutionary changes without opposition. "When he came to Princeton in 1868 he found both Faculty and Board of Trustees so full of hidebound conservatives that he could carry out his reforms only by playing off Board and faculty against each other and coercing one body by threats of what the other would do," says Professor W. B. Scott. "Does Dr. McCosh crack the Board over the Faculty's head the way he cracks the Faculty over our heads?" one of the trustees once asked Professor Sloane.[54] When the president proposed some progressive measure to the faculty, one reactionary professor

[51] Letter of Jan. 4, 1875, MSS, Princeton Library.
[52] James McCosh, *Reports to Board of Trustees*, June 19, 1882.
[53] *Ibid.*, June 18, 1883.
[54] W. B. Scott, *Materials for an Autobiography*, I, pp. 453, 454, MSS.

was very apt to rise and oppose it with the remark: "Change is not progress." Thereupon McCosh would pretend to be deeply offended and threaten to take the matter to the trustees. On one occasion, when young John B. McMaster confidently expected the faculty to show its independence, he was disgusted when they submitted. "Would you believe it, the old fogies took in their horns and backed down!"[55]

When McCosh first came to Princeton he was shocked at the condition of the library, which he found "insufficiently supplied with books and open only once a week and for one hour." "This seems very strange to one coming from a country where college libraries are open each lawful day of the week for five or six hours."[56] He considered that the library should be the heart of a college, a place of activity for both professors and students. How could his faculty acquire distinction without access to books beyond their private means? How could there be a truly intellectual life among the undergraduates if their reading was confined to textbooks? Books are the tools of scholars, from the oldest to the youngest; the library should be their workshop. So long as the pitiably inadequate collection was kept under lock and key in the library room in Nassau Hall—with Professor Cameron somewhat grudgingly opening it each Monday to hand out a few volumes—there would not be much intellectual life on the campus.

It seemed a revolutionary change when McCosh engaged one of the tutors to open the library every day except Sunday, a change which was so greatly appreciated by the students that the number of volumes taken out doubled and tripled. But even more important was the engagement of a professional librarian, Frederick Vinton of the Library of Congress, who brought with him long experience and a wide acquaintance with books. With the completion of the new building and the transfer of the books from Nassau Hall, Mr. Vinton set to work to arrange, classify, and catalogue them. At first

[55] Eric F. Goldman, *John Bach McMaster*, p. 24.
[56] James McCosh, *Reports to Board of Trustees*, Dec. 16, 1868.

there were many empty shelves, but with the establishment of the Elizabeth Foundation for the purchase of books, the library began to fill up rapidly. Mr. Vinton made many trips to New York to visit dealers; 12,000 valuable volumes were added by the purchase of the library of Professor Trendelenburg of the University of Berlin;[57] John A. Pierson presented about 1,000 books on the War Between the States; Professor Alexander gathered rare works of presidents, professors, and alumni for a Princeton collection. The number of volumes, which in 1868 had been 14,000, mounted to 25,000 in 1873, to 60,000 in 1883, and to 81,000 in 1884. When McCosh retired Princeton ranked second among the college libraries of the country.

Great was the surprise and consternation among conservative Presbyterians when it was announced that McCosh had accepted the theory of evolution. For years many Princeton men had been denouncing Darwin, had proclaimed that his theories were in direct variance with the Bible, that if evolution were accepted Christianity would fall. Yet here was the new president, himself a leading minister, calmly proclaiming that Darwin was right. "Ours is an age in which there is a fierce attack on Christianity," he said, "and not a little infidelity in many of the colleges of Europe and America. I am happy to report that there is little disposition in this college towards scepticism or scoffing. I do my best to guard against these. But I do this not by keeping the young men ignorant of prevailing errors, or by an empty denunciation of them— from a large observation I am able to say that this is the most effective of all means to produce infidelity. I encourage freedom of thought and expression among the students and seek to guide it aright. I state the errors of the day and then show the students how to meet them."[58]

But the time had come to give up the old literal interpreta-

---

[57] James McCosh, *Reports to Board of Trustees*, Dec. 18, 1872; *Princeton Library MSS*, AM 8506.

[58] James McCosh, *Reports to Board of Trustees*, Dec. 17, 1873; June 22, 1874.

tion of Genesis and to reread what it taught in the light of scientific discoveries. Nothing was to be gained by a dogged denial of scientific truth and much might be lost. "My first position is the certainty of evolution. . . . There is a general progression in nature. The theory that the world was once a vapor from which the earth evolved is not inconsistent with the Scriptures, for they speak of its being 'void without form.' The natural struggle for existence led to the survival of the fittest, a most benevolent law, and also in accordance with the Scriptures. . . . I have regretted for years that certain defenders of religion have been injuring the cause . . . by indiscriminately attacking development, instead of seeking to ascertain what the process is and turning it to religious use. They have acted as injudiciously as those who in Newton's day described the law of gravitation as atheistic."[59] His views were set forth in detail in his Bedell lecture, on "The Religious Aspect of Evolution," which was published in 1888. But the president indignantly repudiated Henry Ward Beecher's claim of theological kinship. In an interview in Louisville, he was quoted as saying: "If Mr. Beecher intends by claiming me as a representative Presbyterian evolutionist to pledge me as a believer in his religious theories, he has neither reason nor warrant. I don't believe Beecher has any theology and what little he has I don't believe in."[60]

In his eclecticism McCosh had the support of his great professor of geology, Arnold Guyot. Adding his own researches to the speculations of Laplace and Alexander, this great scientist drew a vast picture of creation through its cosmogonic eras, exhibiting during the first three Biblical days the formation of the heavens with their suns and planets, and during the second three days that of the earth, with its flora and fauna. But Professor Shields, after years of study and reflection, repudiated all such forced harmony, which he considered specious, illogical, premature, and vague. "We must therefore grant that the two interests, as now related, cannot at

[59] *Moses Taylor Pyne Scrap Book*, V, p. 79.
[60] *Ibid.*, p. 8.

once be brought into a just, safe and lasting union."[61] It was his view that science and theology should declare a truce until such time as new discoveries would bring all into perfect harmony and all narrow denominational differences would vanish.

Shields was regarded as a visionary by some of his colleagues, but those who read his works admired the scope and breadth of his philosophy. "He followed two magnificent ideals; to unite all sciences in a philosophy truly Christian and to unite all Churches . . . into one truly Christian Church," said Dean Andrew F. West. "If these two ideals are visionary they are at least the best ever offered to promote the real welfare of science and religion. . . . I believe he possessed the most comprehensive mind of any man that ever taught in Princeton."[62] Nevertheless, it was a long cry from the days when the founders of Princeton expressed their sublime faith that scientific discoveries could not conflict with revealed truth to those of McCosh and Guyot with their broadened interpretation of the Bible and of Shields with his belief that the future would explain all apparent contradictions and show the grand harmony of things material and divine.

The increasing enrollment, which rose from 281 in 1868 to 379 in 1871, was a source of deep satisfaction to McCosh. "It is evident that the public are ready to support the Trustees in their efforts to make the college advance with the times," he said. "I am still more pleased with the character than with the number of the new students. They belong to all classes of society, rich and poor, are intended for all professions."[63] But when, in 1872, there was a slight decline, he immediately became alarmed and began to inquire into the reasons. "One undoubtedly is that we are gradually raising our standard both of scholarship and moral conduct," he reported. Even more important, he thought, was the lack of "feeding schools" in the middle states. "In New England the colleges draw the

[61] Chas. W. Shields, *The Final Philosophy* (New York, 1877), pp. 396-398.
[62] *Princeton Library MSS*, AM 10213.
[63] James McCosh, *Reports to Board of Trustees*, Dec. 22, 1869.

majority of their students from schools endowed by the States, or by the towns, or by private benevolence. We have no such schools in New Jersey, in Pennsylvania, in Maryland, in Delaware." Thus a father in this region, in looking around for a preparatory school for his son, was attracted by the famous New England schools and sent him to one of them, to fit him perhaps for Princeton. "But from the day the youth enters the school he hears of no other college but Harvard, of its professors, of its students, of its games and generally of its vast superiority over all other colleges. It would require more courage than can be expected of a boy to resist this influence, and in nine cases out of ten the boy destined for Princeton goes to a New England college, where the religion of his father's household is entirely ignored."[64] So important did McCosh consider this matter that he gave it as his opinion that the friends of Princeton could do the college no greater service than to endow one or more preparatory schools.[65]

The first result was a gift from Henry G. Marquand to found a preparatory school in Princeton under the control of the college. So a building was purchased and Virginius Dabney, an experienced and able teacher from the Loudoun School in Virginia, was made principal. The school opened with a large enrollment,[66] but unfortunately the promise of success was not fulfilled. Mr. Dabney resigned, the number of pupils fell off, and eventually the college disposed of its holdings. Yet disappointment at this result was forgotten when it was announced that the trustees of the John C. Green estate had endowed the Lawrenceville School. James C. Mackenzie was made principal, a large building with library and recitation rooms was erected, the residential house plan was adopted, and an advanced curriculum adopted. It was a noble gift to the school Mr. Green had attended, in the town where he was born; a gift which bore rich fruit for education in the middle states and for Princeton in particular. "The magnificent endowment at Lawrenceville is the most im-

---

[64] *Ibid.*, Feb. 12, 1880.    [65] *Ibid.*, June, 1872.
[66] *Catalogue of the College of New Jersey*, 1873-1874, p. 46.

portant contribution that has been given to our college of late years," McCosh pointed out.[67] Two years later he was able to report that no fewer than twenty Lawrenceville boys had come to Princeton in the entering class.

McCosh appealed to the alumni in all parts of the country, but especially in the middle west, to hunt out promising youths to send to Princeton. "I mail a catalogue for you," he wrote C. L. Murray in December 1878. "You will confer a great favor on us if you will get it and the college noticed in the Louisville papers. I have marked some of the passages in the catalogue. We must persevere in our efforts to get students from your region. . . . Mr. Ballard[68] has won us great reputation as captain of the football team which has beaten both Harvard and Yale."[69] The president himself made repeated and extensive trips west of the Appalachians. In April 1880 he visited Detroit, Dayton, Cincinnati, St. Louis, Chicago, Frankfort, and Lexington, addressing the alumni, explaining the changes at Princeton, and receiving "favorable notices" from the public press.[70] He was deeply troubled when, despite all his efforts, the enrollment fell from 552 in 1882 to 492 in 1885, but he had the satisfaction of seeing a sharp upturn which brought the number of students to 603 before his retirement.

McCosh had been accustomed to student disorders at Belfast, but he was somewhat surprised and baffled by the unique American brand—hazing, rakes, midnight bonfires—or what he termed "debasing, corrupting old customs." But he made up his mind from the first to put an end to hazing, cost what it would. One morning at prayers he noted among the hundreds of young faces one shining, hairless pate. The night before a group of students had entered a freshman's room, and after gagging him and shaving his head, had taken him out to duck him under the pump. The president laid the

[67] James McCosh, *Reports to Board of Trustees*, Feb. 18, 1884.
[68] Bland Ballard, '80.
[69] *Princeton Library MSS*, AM 10613-5.
[70] James McCosh, *Reports to Board of Trustees*, June 22, 1880.

matter before Chancellor Green, who was "the head of the law in New Jersey,"[71] and proposed that he start a criminal process. Thereupon McCosh sent for one of the supposed culprits and told him that the chancellor was engaging the attorney general as prosecutor, and that if the guilty boys did not send him an apology within forty-eight hours they would all be in prison. A humble letter, signed by about a dozen students confessing their guilt, was the result. At prayers the next morning, amid an atmosphere of suppressed excitement, McCosh read the paper aloud, until he came to the signatures, when he put it in his pocket with the remark: "I accept the apology."[72]

The president was hampered in his fight against hazing by the refusal of the students to inform on each other. On one occasion upon hearing that Philip Ashton Rollins, then a freshman, had been thrown into the canal by a group of sophomores, McCosh summoned him to his library. "Me boy, I hear you have been hazed," he said. "Now tell me who did it."

"I am sorry, Dr. McCosh, I cannot tell you."

"What! You are not going to tell me?"

"No, sir."

"Then get out of me college."

The lad had gone but a few steps when he was called back.

"Is it true that your father gave a chapel to Dartmouth college?" he asked.

"Yes, sir, it is."

"Then come back into me college."[73]

McCosh, naturally a kindly man who liked and understood young men, often assumed a stern, even terrifying, exterior toward them. Giving them a bit of a fright, he called it. When a certain delinquent was sent to him by the faculty for reprimand, he stormed at him, cataloguing his enormities and concluded as follows: "You've disgraced yourself, sir; you've

[71] *Princeton Library MSS*, AM 11902.
[72] James McCosh, *Twenty Years of Princeton*, p. 39.
[73] Told to the author by Mr. Rollins.

disgraced your family; you've disgraced your college; and tomorrow it will all be in the New York papers and the next day in the Philadelphia papers."[74]

In fact, the most harmful part of the disorders resulting from hazing were the lurid and grossly exaggerated accounts sent to the newspapers. It was in 1878 that a group of sophomores hazed a number of freshmen who, in revenge, caught two of them and shaved their heads. Later in the evening there was a scuffle in the street, accompanied by the firing of blank cartridges, and by one real pistol shot which struck a sophomore in the leg and inflicted a superficial flesh wound. The next day the reporters swarmed into town and some of the boys thought it would be fun to "stuff" them with wild tales of hazing outrages, with the result that for days the newspapers rang with the horror of student life at Princeton. Some of the accounts were copied in England and even in Germany. McCosh took no notice of these stories until the faculty had investigated the whole affair and had punished the offenders. Thereupon the two upper classes passed resolutions condemning hazing and public sentiment slowly swung round to the side of the faculty.[75]

McCosh never wearied in his denunciation of college pranks, and each year in his reports to the trustees had a new and more vehement term to express his indignation. They were "old hereditary vicious habits," or "old and degrading college customs," or "corrupting old customs," or "barbarous customs," or "the old vices," or "the wretched customs of American colleges." But he realized the futility of spying on the boys in order to catch them in some infringement of the regulations, and wished to place the discipline of the college on a higher basis. "In a number of American colleges the discipline consists solely in detecting and punishing breaches of college law and no attempt whatever is made to bring any

---

[74] W. B. Scott, *Materials for an Autobiography*, I, pp. 217, 218, MSS.
[75] *Ibid.*, p. 219; James McCosh, *Reports to Board of Trustees*, June 17, 1878; *New York Tribune*, Feb. 20, 1878. One paper headed its article, "Hazing Almost Murder," another, "Bloodshed at Princeton."

moral or religious considerations to bear on the young man," he said. "We have been acting in a different manner in this college. When we see a student going wrong, we speak to him in a friendly manner.... My aim is not to devise a means for punishing crime. My object is to prevent evil by kindness, by fatherly care, by religion."[76]

No doubt a chief cause of the gradual decline in disorders at Princeton was the president's tact mingled with firmness, but even more important was the disinclination of the younger members of the faculty to keep an eye upon the students and report minor infringements of the rules. In other words, in the old conflict of tutor and student, the tutor refused to play the game and this spoiled the fun for the boys. But Mc-Cosh was dubious of this policy. "I abhor and discourage the spy system under any form," he explained, "but every one must keep his eyes and ears open and realize that he has a charge to endeavor by friendly means to secure the confidence of the students and to save them when they are exposed to temptation."[77]

At times McCosh was encouraged by the absence of disorders and would report joyfully to the trustees that the college had enjoyed extraordinary quiet for a term or perhaps an entire session. Then youthful spirits would burst out in some unexpected riot which would trouble and alarm him. Such was the horn-spree of December 21, 1881, when a number of freshmen marched through the streets of the village, blowing horns, breaking street lamps, overturning barrels, removing the swinging shop signs, and even stoning professors' houses. This was going too far, and the mayor of Princeton haled twenty-three of the rioters into court.[78] A few days later Judge Beasley delivered a severe reprimand to the thoroughly alarmed boys, and after fining each of them $20, dismissed them. To this punishment the faculty added a suspension of four weeks. The *New York Tribune* made light of the affair. "Exuberance of youthful spirits in the college

[76] James McCosh, *Reports to Board of Trustees*, June 19, 1882.
[77] *Ibid.*
[78] *Ibid.*, Feb. 9, 1882.

student has strange ways of manifesting itself. That is, they seem strange, almost unaccountable, to us old fellows, who long ago passed out of the period of sap and bounce, and have almost forgotten that twenty, thirty or forty years ago we were doing the same ridiculous and mischievous things, and thinking they were funny and smart. Yes, and even now, when we get together and talk over our college days, they seem the same. . . . And let us confess still further that perhaps these youngsters would not now be breaking street-lamps, carrying off signs and gates and making night hideous with their howling, if they had not heard their elders revel in the memories of just such absurd performances."[79]

It was on the morning of April 27, 1875, that the alarming news came that the little cannon had been dug up from its position between Whig and Clio Halls during the night and carted away. The report spread like wildfire through the campus. In their retreat after the battle of Princeton in 1777 the British abandoned several pieces of artillery, which Washington spiked and left behind because horses were lacking to draw them off. One of these, a large cannon bearing the mark of the British crown, lay for years on the campus where it served as the "bucking-place" for the students when they played bandy.[80] During the War of 1812 it was removed to New Brunswick to aid in the defense of that town against an anticipated attack, and there it remained for about twenty years. On the night of July 3, 1835, sixteen members of the Princeton Blues removed it under cover of darkness and headed back to Princeton, the cannon in one creaking wagon, the militiamen in another. When they had reached Queenston, near the present Evelyn Place, the weight proved too much for the vehicle, which "got out of kelter," and the cannon was abandoned in a field near the road.[81]

[79] December, 1881.
[80] H. C. Cameron, *Old Princeton* (1884), p. 10.
[81] *Princeton Library MSS*, AM 9775. The return from New Brunswick seems to have been on the night of July 3, 1835, not July 3, 1836 as stated in several accounts. J. C. Moffat tells us he saw it lying in the field near Queenston, which he could not have done later than the fall of 1835, when he left Princeton.

There it remained until the summer of 1838, when a large group of students, under the leadership of Leonard W. Jerome,[82] securing a wagon from one Gulick, brought it back to the campus and deposited it in front of Nassau Hall. As the cannon fell to the ground John Maclean was seen rushing out from his residence in dressing gown and slippers, and the students vanished, leaving Mr. Gulick alone to face the vice-president.[83] "Pick that thing up and take it off," commanded Maclean. "As it has taken a hundred men two hours to load it, I don't see exactly how I am to load it up again all by myself," Gulick replied. So the cannon remained where it was for two years, when it was moved to the back campus and, with appropriate ceremonies, planted in the center of the quadrangle.[84]

In the meanwhile another, and smaller, cannon had for years remained on the campus, doing duty on the Fourth of July and other days of patriotic celebration. At last pronounced unsafe, it was planted at the west corner of Nassau and Witherspoon Streets, apparently to protect the curb from sharp turns by teamsters. In 1858 fifteen members of the class of 1859 brought it back and sank it between Whig and Clio Halls.[85]

Here it would have remained indefinitely had not a tradition grown up that it had once lodged on the Rutgers campus whence Princeton students had taken it. When Rutgers men came to Princeton they were greeted with the taunt: "Why don't you come and get your gun?" Accordingly, on the night of April 26, 1875, nine Rutgers students, armed with ropes, shovels, pickaxes, and a crowbar, drove to Princeton, dug up the cannon, and returned triumphantly with it to New Brunswick.[86]

The next morning, when the Princeton boys discovered what had happened, they were prepared to march in a body

[82] Grandfather of The Hon. Winston Churchill.
[83] L. W. Jerome in *New York Times*, May 7, 1875.
[84] *Faculty Minutes*, May 15, 1875. H. C. Cameron, *Old Princeton*, pp. 9, 10.
[85] *Ibid.*, p. 11.
[86] *Princeton Alumni Weekly*, Dec. 1, 1933.

to recover the prized relic, and it was with difficulty that President McCosh restrained them. In fact, a raiding party actually made their way to New Brunswick and, failing to find the cannon, carried off a number of muskets from the Rutgers museum. Peace was restored only when a joint committee of the two faculties, meeting to weigh the historic evidence, decided that Rutgers had no legitimate claim to the cannon and ordered its restitution.[87]

A few days later a buggy with the New Brunswick chief of police, closely followed by a wagon in which reposed the cannon, drove into Princeton and headed for the campus. With shouts of triumph the students poured out of their rooms to surround the cavalcade. When McCosh appeared, rubbing his hands gleefully, and repeating: "I told you so! I told you so!" he was greeted with deafening cheers. In a short address he said that the rape of the cannon—which reminded him of the Trojan war and the conflict for Helen—ought to be immortalized by a new *Iliad*. Thus ended happily the celebrated cannon war.[88]

When McCosh told the trustees that he abhorred the spy system, he did not mean that he would remove the proctors from the examination rooms. That, he thought, would be going too far. Yet the very spirit of honor which he was doing his best to bring out in the students, was a better guarantee against cheating than the most thorough system of supervision, for many of the students, especially those from the south, resented the presence of the proctors. When the students held a mass meeting in 1872 and passed resolutions condemning cheating in emphatic terms, McCosh should have responded with a resolution in the faculty, removing watchers from the examination rooms and placing all responsibility upon the students themselves.

But he made the mistake of coupling his appeals to the students' sense of honor with greater alertness in spying upon them. "We have had evidence of late of a considerable amount

[87] *Faculty Minutes*, May 15, 1879.
[88] *Princeton Press*, May 22, 1875.

of trickery and deceit at testing examinations," he reported in June 1883. "I know of no practice which has a more demoralizing influence on the mind of students than this. The habit of cheating learned at college goes up into the business of life and continues with the man all his days. The Faculty has taken up the subject, and has subjected the examinations to a more careful watching, hoping all the while to induce the students voluntarily to pledge themselves against deceit."[89] This the students were prepared to do, and the *Princetonian* even threatened to expose delinquents in its columns. Some members of the faculty, wiser than their colleagues, took full advantage of this opportunity by withdrawing from the examination room after giving out the questions and refusing the service of proctors.[90] But the president failed to give them his support, and the beginning of the honor system was postponed for another decade.

Possibly McCosh might have been more far-seeing in this matter, if it had not been for his experience with the Greek-letter fraternities. Despite Maclean's efforts to suppress these societies, and despite the pledge required of entering students not to join them, they continued to exist and to give trouble. When McCosh first came to the United States he took pains to question other college presidents concerning the fraternities and discovered that the secret societies were considered very harmful, dividing the student bodies into factions, interfering with discipline, combining to monopolize college honors, and in some cases encouraging dissipation. McCosh made up his mind to drive them out of Princeton. "I felt that if I could not conquer the evil I would have to resign my office," he confessed years later.[91]

But it was not an easy task. Salving their consciences with the plea that a forced pledge was not binding, many of the most prominent students had joined the fraternities with the full sanction and even the encouragement of their parents.

[89] James McCosh, *Reports to Board of Trustees*, June 18, 1883.
[90] *New York Evening Post*, June 11, 1883.
[91] James McCosh, *Reports to Board of Trustees*, Dec. 22, 1875.

Every year just before the opening of college certain alumni would appear on the campus to induce new students to join this chapter or that. McCosh was convinced that the fraternities made a conscious effort to "lay hold of the sons and relatives of Trustees and of our benefactors in New York, in order, as they thought, to keep the Board from meddling with them."[92]

The climax came in the autumn of 1875. In the spring of that year the faculty had appointed a committee to get evidence—a task which they found difficult, delicate, and odious. Finally, however, group photographs of some of the chapters fell into their hands, and McCosh thought the time had come for decisive action. The offending youths were summoned before the faculty, faced with the evidence and then suspended. They were readmitted, however, when they gave their solemn pledge to have no further connection with any of the prohibited fraternities. Student sentiment seems to have been with the faculty in suppressing these sub rosa societies, some of the members themselves declaring that they were glad to be rid of the whole troublesome question.[93]

Some of the alumni did not submit so readily. At a meeting at Delmonico's in New York, one fiery speech followed another, praising the fraternities and condemning the action of the faculty. There was no valid reason, these alumni said, why a boy should not be allowed to enter his father's college and there unite with his father's fraternity. Yet the faculty had such a "gigantic misconception" of the real character of these societies, that the student could not join without violating a pledge and running the risk of expulsion. And with only one dissenting voice, the group passed a resolution appointing a committee to confer with the trustees in order to persuade them to remove the prohibition on fraternities and give them their blessing. But the trustees upheld the action of the faculty, and the Princeton Greeks went down to defeat.

[92] *Ibid.*
[93] James McCosh, *Twenty Years of Princeton*, p. 44; *Presbyterian*, Dec. 4, 1875.

But the faculty, though winning out over the fraternities, once more gave the eating clubs a clean bill of health. In 1877 the restoration of the old dining hall system had proved a failure. The students for a short while had found the commons an attractive novelty, but they soon tired of the confusion, the clatter, and the monotonous food. So many returned to the club system, fourteen or fifteen in a group, securing a room in town and agreeing upon the price of board with the landlord. The friendships formed around the table proved lasting, and the entry into the proper club often became of vital importance to the student's life on the campus.[94] But these organizations were temporary, some lasting four years, others only one.

The club situation assumed a new aspect in the autumn of 1879, however, when a group of upper classmen rented Ivy Hall, engaged their own steward and servants and launched a permanent organization. After several years they applied to the faculty for permission to incorporate and erect a building of their own. This precipitated a lively debate. Some of the older professors sensed trouble, but the "progressives" contended that the absence of secrecy, and the limitation of membership to the two upper classes made the eating clubs unobjectionable. Why should the students not form social clubs if they wanted to? So the permission was granted with the proviso that the club should elect three honorary members from the faculty to serve as a committee of supervision. Thereupon the group bought a lot on Prospect Avenue, on the site now occupied by the east end of the Colonial Club, and erected a small frame building. Thus began the Princeton "club system" as it became known later.[95]

Even more than the clubs the rapid development of athletics was destined to produce revolutionary changes in undergraduate life. McCosh was enthusiastic about the gymnasium, which he thought greatly improved the health of

[94] *New York Tribune*, April 5, 1878.
[95] W. B. Scott, *Materials for an Autobiography*, II, pp. 578-580, MSS. Dean W. F. Magie states that permission to incorporate was granted, not by the Faculty, but the Trustees.

the students without producing any of the abuses attendant upon intercollegiate contests. Occasionally he would look on as George Goldie took his place on the springboard and, after calling the roll, led the class in Indian club exercises. Or he would watch, with a pleased expression, as the more skillful performed on the flying trapeze or the horizontal bar, or gave an impromptu exhibition of tumbling. Goldie himself was a noted gymnast, having held the Caledonian championship in Canada and the United States for many years, and his pupils acquired a proficiency which, it was claimed, might have done credit to Barnum and Bailey's circus.[96]

Baseball continued to grow in popularity. In 1867 the sophomore team went to New Haven and defeated the Yale sophomores 58 to 52. Yale returned the visit, and despite a royal welcome, retaliated by winning by a similarly large score. In those days when the pitcher bowled the ball slowly with an extended arm the fielders were kept busy chasing flies, and the procession around the bases was almost continuous.[97] But with the introduction of speed and curves, the pitching became more effective and the scores were lower. The catcher had a punishing task, for he wore no gloves, and although he stood far back from the batter when there was no one on bases and received the pitch on the bounce, his hands often became so sore that he could not continue.[98]

It was on November 6, 1869, that the primitive game of football, which for many years the students had played on the back campus, was dignified by an intercollegiate match. A challenge had come in from Rutgers, the Princeton team had elected William S. Gummere (later Chief Justice of New Jersey) as captain and he had formulated a set of rules. The grounds were to be 360 feet by 225, each side was to have 25 players, there must be no throwing or running with the ball, no tripping or holding the players, goals were to be eight paces wide, the ball was to be advanced by kicking or

[96] W. B. Scott, *Materials for an Autobiography*, I, p. 98, MSS; *Moses Taylor Pyne Scrap Book*, IV, pp. 8, 9.
[97] A. A. Schanck, *Princeton and Thereafter*, p. 13.
[98] W. B. Scott, *Materials for an Autobiography*, I, p. 94, MSS.

by batting with the clenched fist—in other words, a game
something like soccer. The jerky little train which pulled out
of Princeton at nine o'clock was crowded with eager students
who, upon their arrival at New Brunswick, were greeted by
the Rutgers men en masse. The game started at three o'clock,
with the spectators seated on the ground or perched on the
top rail of a fence. The players laid aside their hats, coats, and
vests—the Rutgers men donning red turbans—and took their
designated positions, and the first intercollegiate football
game in the United States began.[99]

The Princeton kickoff against the wind glanced to one side
and a group of Rutgers men, pouncing upon it like hounds,
drove it down the field and through the goal posts for the
first score. The boys from Princeton were at first baffled by
the "mass play" or "blocking," of their opponents and it was
only when J. E. Michael, or "Big Mike" as he was called,
began charging in to scatter the players, that they turned the
tide. So the play surged from one part of the field to another,
each Rutgers score being matched by a score for Princeton.
In the midst of the excitement occurred a "grandstand disaster." Large, of Rutgers, and Michael, seeing the ball bounce
along the ground and come to a standstill against the fence,
charged down on it so fiercely that the fence gave way with a
crash, bringing down with it a whole line of spectators. But
there were no casualties. Despite all the efforts of the Princeton players Rutgers scored six goals to four and so left the
field in triumph. That evening the players of both teams sat
around the supper table to enjoy roast game, to recount the
many thrilling plays, to deliver impromptu speeches, and to
sing college songs.

Other intercollege football games followed, with the
regulations changing from time to time. The Princeton boys
adopted a uniform consisting of an orange jersey adorned
with a black "P," black knee breeches and orange stockings,
and a small close-fitting black cap. The sport in those days

[99] *Princeton Alumni Weekly*, Dec. 15, 1909.

was unorganized and informal, there being, of course, not only no coach and no training table but even very little practice.[100] In one of the games with Columbia, when it was found that each team had one man "not feeling well" it was agreed to play fourteen men on a side instead of the fifteen usual at that time. It is safe to say, however, that the boys enjoyed the game fully as much as the members of the highly trained, machinelike teams of a later time.

In the fall of 1876 the team had begun what gave promise of being a very successful season, having defeated Columbia at Hoboken and the University of Pennsylvania at Philadelphia. But in the midst of their preparation for Harvard and Yale, they received messages from those colleges stating that they had abandoned the old game for a modified form of Rugby and that if Princeton wished to meet them they must follow their example. In consternation the students called a mass meeting, and after speeches pro and con, decided to comply. Princeton's makeshift team lost both games, but by the following year the players had had time to master the fine points of American Rugby and, after defeating Harvard and Columbia, played a tie game with Yale. Although Princeton did not introduce Rugby she played an important role in its development by calling an intercollegiate conference to draw up a uniform system of rules. With the reduction of the players to eleven and the substitution of "downs" for the scrum of the English game, American football took on a character of its own.[101]

In rowing Princeton was hopelessly handicapped, for it was before the days of Lake Carnegie. None the less, the students organized their crew, worked diligently at Goldie's rowing-machine in the gymnasium in the winter, and with the coming of spring launched a six-oared shell on the canal to dispute the right of way with canal boats and tow-mules. McCosh warned them that they had no hope of competing successfully with the crews of colleges situated on lakes or

[100] W. B. Scott, *Materials for an Autobiography*, I, pp. 151, 152, MSS.
[101] Parke H. Davis, *Football*, pp. 66, 67, 76.

navigable rivers, but they insisted upon entering the Saratoga regatta.[102] Year after year they trailed the other boats and it was considered a triumph in 1884 when they tied for second place.[103] After this, intercollegiate rowing was temporarily abandoned.

As athletics began to absorb more and more of the students' interest, McCosh became concerned, and there were many anxious conferences of faculty and trustees. The hero of the class was no longer the best orator or the leader in literature or science, but the most successful kicker or pitcher. The excessive time spent by athletes in training was affecting their studies adversely, and it was rare indeed that any of them stood high in their classes; the trips to the cities, when large numbers of undergraduates accompanied the teams, were not only expensive but brought unusual temptations; the keen desire to win was leading to unfair competition, overemphasis, and professionalism.

As early as 1874 the president proposed that a set of rules be drawn up to lessen these abuses, and in time he secured the support not only of the faculty but of certain other colleges and of some of the leading newspapers. "The Faculty has found it necessary, in consequence of students' devoting a large portion of their time, day and night, to enjoin that there be no exercises in the campus or the gymnasium during study hours," he reported in 1881. To his appeals to other college presidents for cooperation in suppressing abuses, he received a sympathetic response from some, but a discouraging refusal from others. "The public press, as a whole, are telling the colleges very plainly that they are going to excess in sports; let them encourage those colleges that are seeking to lay restraints on the evil," he said with some heat. "Some colleges are refusing to join in the exertions we are making, not to stop sports, but to keep them within due bounds. . . . It may come to this, that we have to refuse to allow our students to play

[102] James McCosh, *Reports to Board of Trustees*, Feb. 12, 1885.
[103] W. B. Scott, *Materials for an Autobiography*, I, p. 99, MSS.

with those colleges which lay no restraint on the time devoted to games."[104]

The president and many members of the faculty were genuinely interested in the success of the teams. Professor W. B. Scott tells us that when he received the news of a football victory one day while on horseback, he cheered so loudly that the horse became frightened and ran away with him.[105] Some even hinted that McCosh never complained of overemphasis on athletics save when Princeton met defeat. The president tried to make his position clear, insisting that he himself enjoyed the games and objected only when they began to overshadow scholastic attainment. But he was rudely shocked when one youth told a professor that he had come to Princeton not to study but to play football.[106]

There can be no doubt that before the end of McCosh's administration the enthusiasm for athletics was beginning to undermine the two literary societies. As early as 1876 the president was troubled because a very considerable number of the new students had not entered either Whig or Clio. This he attributed to the growing belief that with one society's membership numbering 175 and the other 181, the Halls were so crowded that many got no benefit from either. Therefore the time had come, he thought, to consider the propriety of founding other literary societies, for the prosecution of particular studies, literary, scientific, or philosophic. The formal orations on commonplace subjects in the Halls were good as far as they went, but they did not call forth some of the highest qualities of oratory. This might be rectified by holding debates two or three times a year on important national questions which would be open to the entire college.[107]

Yet the two societies remained, as they had been for a century, vitally important factors in campus life. "The secrecy of their proceedings was sacredly maintained and no attempt

[104] James McCosh, *Reports to Board of Trustees*, June 22, Dec. 16, 1874; June 18, 1883.
[105] W. B. Scott, *Materials for an Autobiography*, II, p. 573, MSS.
[106] James McCosh, *Reports to Board of Trustees*, June 18, 1883.
[107] *Ibid.*, Dec. 22, 1875.

was ever made to penetrate these mysteries on the part of outsiders," says Professor W. B. Scott. "The Hall spirit and rivalry entered into every department of college life. The Junior Orations and the Lynde Debate were held before crowded audiences and the prizes were among the most coveted honors. The announcement of the names of the prizewinners was made on commencement day and was received with the wildest enthusiasm and storms of cheering from the members of the victorious Hall." Within the Halls themselves the extempore debate, open to juniors and seniors, gave excellent training in parliamentary law and practice in thinking on one's feet. Often the room resounded with oratory as the youthful contestants fought the War Between the States over again and lauded the generalship of Grant or Lee, or threshed out the constitutionality of secession.[108]

Commencement continued to be the day of days for alumni and students alike. June 19, 1883, was typical, even to the humidity and heat. On the campus could be seen groups talking over old times, while from out the various improvised dining rooms in the University Hotel (at the corner of Nassau Street and University Place) came shouts of laughter and snatches of college songs. On the broad porches of the residences along Nassau Street out-of-town guests watched the almost continuous procession of gay youths, pretty girls, alumni, and of the stylish equipages of some of the wealthy undergraduates. In the morning the crowd directed itself to the gymnasium to witness the acrobatic exhibition, even McCosh escaping from the trustees' meeting to see his favorite sport. "The events included the use of the parallel bars, the horizontal bar, pegpole and Indian clubs, double rings and the double trapeze. Then the flying trapeze on which the two brightest students in Dr. McCosh's favorite topic of logical psychology, Messrs. Haskins and Murdoch, went flying from one end of the gymnasium to the other as if in defiance of the mere law of gravitation."[109]

[108] W. B. Scott, *Materials for an Autobiography*, I, pp. 86-88, MSS.
[109] *Moses Taylor Pyne Scrap Book*, V, p. 62.

At the alumni luncheon in the University Hotel, there were speeches by McCosh, the venerable Maclean, and others. One alumnus got up and in no uncertain terms declared that the college was going to the dogs. It was becoming a rich man's college, where young men sought to display their athletic prowess and make a show of their wealth with costly clothes, luxurious rooms, and expensive carriages. It had not been so in the Spartan days of the 'forties. So McCosh had to rush to the defense, and, after showing that there were many poor boys in Princeton, declared that one could go through on as little as $200 a year. Later in the afternoon, in the Presbyterian Church, an assemblage of proud fathers, mothers, and sisters heard a discussion of the Irish Land Act of 1881, while in the evening the Sophomore Ball attracted "scores of the prettiest young ladies from Philadelphia, New York and Trenton and the enjoyment in the finely decorated hall ran on till a very late hour."[110]

Although McCosh resented the charge that Princeton had become a rich man's college, in his private reports to the trustees he admitted that the proportion of wealthy students had greatly increased. This he blamed in part upon the rising cost of living and in part upon the heavy expense entailed by sending a boy to a preparatory school. To check the decline in the number of students preparing for the ministry he wrote many letters to Presbyterian ministers, especially in the south, assuring them that an education need be no more expensive at Princeton than at other colleges. When he discovered that one-third of the freshman class in 1879-1880 were Episcopalians, he decided that things had gone far enough. So he built a new dormitory (Edwards Hall) back of Clio Hall, "which, while neat and comfortable, well aired and heated," would be cheaply furnished and "let at a moderate cost."[111]

But the decline in the number of religious students was merely a symptom of the revolutionary change going on in

[110] *Ibid.*

[111] Edwards Hall; James McCosh, *Reports to Board of Trustees*, Nov. 13, 1879; Feb. 14, 1884.

Princeton, a change which was to transfer the ultimate control of the college from the Presbyterian church to the alumni. The aging Maclean saw what was happening and lifted his voice against it. No doubt McCosh saw it too, but he was convinced either that the change was desirable or that he was powerless to stop it. More and more he was turning to the alumni for financial support—to erect dormitories, lecture halls, laboratories, to found new chairs, to endow fellowships, to provide books, scientific apparatus, specimens for the museums. It was inevitable, therefore, that the alumni should demand a greater voice in determining the policies of the college.

So he was not surprised when the Chicago graduates began agitating for alumni representation on the board. They pointed out that twenty-three successive classes had taken their degrees and started on their life work without having any of their number elected. Some of the older trustees were far too conservative, they said, and there was need for able, progressive men, of the stamp of young Moses Taylor Pyne of the class of 1877. In November 1889 the trustees took the hint. "We have unanimously elected you a member of our Board of Trustees," McCosh wrote Pyne. "This is done in accordance with the wish of the younger alumni of our college. I did all that man could honorably do to carry it."[112] Thus it was that Pyne began his four decades of devoted service on the board, and that the power of the alumni began to assert itself in the control of college policies.

It was no doubt to give the alumni further outlet for their interest in the college without launching a bitter and perhaps destructive battle in the board that McCosh proposed the establishment of an alumni council. "After much thought and consultation with our younger alumni I venture to say that the time has now come to consider whether there should not be instituted an Advisory Council of Alumni," he reported in 1878, "with power to watch over the requirements for degrees and the state of learning in the college and to offer recom-

[112] *Moses Taylor Pyne Scrap Book*, VI, p. 3.

mendations to the Board of Trustees, but with no power to pass laws or to interfere with the college funds. This might give a legitimate outlet to the desire felt by so many of our graduates to have some share in the management of the college, with the view of promoting its best interests."[113] Had the trustees accepted this suggestion the actual establishment of the Graduate Council would have been anticipated by thirty-one years.

In visiting cities in various parts of the country to establish alumni associations, stimulate interest in the college, explain changes, and raise money, McCosh was indefatigable. In 1879-1880 alone he paid three visits to places in Pennsylvania and then, after a brief trip to Washington, traveled nearly three thousand miles in a "swing around the circuit" including Detroit, Dayton, Cincinnati, St. Louis, Chicago, Frankfort, and Lexington. Everywhere he was entertained lavishly, everywhere he found evidence of loyalty to Princeton.[114] At Frankfort he addressed the Kentucky legislature by special request. In numerous cities McCosh established alumni associations, and where they already existed he urged them on to greater activity, especially in sending desirable boys to Princeton. By 1886 there were no fewer than seventeen alumni associations in existence, with several others in the process of organization.

Intensely proud of "me college," proud of the great advances made under his leadership, McCosh was quick to resent any slurs by the press or by sister institutions. In November 1886 Harvard celebrated the two hundred and fiftieth anniversary of its founding with academic processions, class reunions, orations, athletic contests, and complimentary addresses by delegates from foreign universities. President McCosh, who represented Princeton, listened with impatience as some of the speakers gave to Harvard a position of preeminence among American colleges, and his feelings rose to anger when of no fewer than forty-two honorary

[113] James McCosh, *Reports to Board of Trustees*, June 17, 1878.
[114] *Ibid.*, June 22, 1880.

degrees conferred, not one went to Princeton. But the crowning blow came when Oliver Wendell Holmes read one of his occasion poems, including the lines:

> As once of old from Ida's lofty height
> The flaming signal flashed across the night,
> So Harvard's beacon sheds its unspent rays
> Till every watch-tower shows its kindling blaze.
> Caught from a spark and fanned by every gale,
> A brighter radiance gilds the roots of Yale;
> Amherst and Williams bid their flambeaus shine,
> And Bowdoin answers through her groves of pine;
> O'er Princeton's sands the far reflections steal,
> Where mighty Edwards stamped his iron heel:
> Nay, on the hill where old beliefs were bound
> Fast as if Styx had girt them nine times round,
> Bursts such a light that trembling souls inquire
> If the whole Church of Calvin is on fire!
> Well may they ask, for what so brightly burns
> As a dry creed that nothing ever learns?

Offended at what he considered a slighting reference to Princeton, and an attack on Calvinism, McCosh quietly withdrew and took the next train back to Princeton. There he penned a letter to the Secretary of the Committee of Arrangements, expressing his indignation at "treatment that could not possibly by any chance have happened to a Harvard representative at Princeton."[115]

This letter brought a prompt reply from President Eliot. "The Secretary has handed me your note of yesterday. I need not say that its contents give me great concern. Dr. Holmes said something regrettable about a dry creed; but I thought he referred to the Andover creed, against which he has often pointed his lance. I did not catch a word directed against Princeton. . . . I am sure you will not hold me, or the university, accountable for anything which either Dr. Lowell or Dr. Holmes said. . . . I am sorry that you left Cambridge under a sense of annoyance and injury and wish very much

[115] *Moses Taylor Pyne Scrap Book*, VI, p. 138.

that I could have had opportunity of talking with you before you went away."[116]

The repercussions of this affair were long in dying out. From one end of the country to the other, wherever Princeton men met, it was discussed and McCosh was lauded. They thought that the light which shone on "Princeton's sands"—granting that there were sands at Princeton—was not a mere reflection from Harvard, but a torch which had been lit by Dickinson and Burr and Davies, had been burning for nearly a century and a half, and had burst into new brilliance in the hands of McCosh. One alumnus went so far as to reply to Dr. Holmes in his own medium:

> But Princeton waves the bright delusion hence;
> Her sacred memories prove a sure defense.
> Thus the deceptive light from Harvard's ray,
> Burns for its glorious self; then dies away.[117]

In the meanwhile the college, ignoring the old criticism that it had overemphasized the importance of buildings, experienced a new era of construction. The year 1877 saw the opening of Witherspoon Hall, a five-story dormitory, considered at the time an imposing and beautiful example of the Victorian Gothic. With its forty single rooms and its suites of two bedrooms and study, it at once became the most popular dormitory on the campus.[118] Aristocratic Witherspoon was offset by Edwards Hall, McCosh's poor man's dormitory. At the same time arose Murray Hall, devoted to the religious interests of the campus. Among the students who graduated in June 1873 was a young man honored for his seriousness and piety, Hamilton Murray. By a tragic turn of fate he was lost at sea five months later upon the ill-fated steamer *Ville de Havre*. When his will was opened it was found that he had bequeathed $20,000 to Princeton for the building which bears his name.[119]

---

[116] *Princeton Library MSS*, AM 11529.
[117] *Moses Taylor Pyne Scrap Book*, VI, p. 138.
[118] *Harpers Weekly*, June 18, 1887, p. 439.
[119] *Moses Taylor Pyne Scrap Book*, VII, p. 97.

Although nothing could overshadow the devotion and loyalty which produced it, the building itself was soon overshadowed by the erection close by of the Marquand Chapel. It was in June 1882 that the new building was crowded with trustees, faculty, alumni, and students for the dedication and the baccalaureate sermon by Dr. McCosh. Without, they saw a brown stone structure, with triple Romanesque doors, and high tower with cone-shaped dome; within, an arched ceiling of carved pine, wainscoting of ash, apse set off by columns of polished granite. "This temple has been built for two ends," said the president. "One, as a piece of art, it is meant to refine the minds of those who meet here daily. But after all this is subordinate to a higher end, which is to lift the thoughts and the heart to God. Here art is consecrated to religion."[120]

In the meanwhile McCosh's dream of a museum of historic art in which to house the great Prime collections of pottery and books was approaching realization. Subscriptions by Mrs. R. L. Stuart, the Hon. John S. Blair, T. H. Garrett, and others brought the total funds in hand in 1887 to $31,000, and on June 21 of that year ground was broken.[121] The crowd cheered as Mrs. McCosh turned over the first sod with a spade decorated with orange and black ribbons, and the glee club sang "Old Nassau." Then, after a brief address by President McCosh, Henry van Dyke delivered an oration. "The erection of this museum asserts the definite value of the study of art in a complete system of education," he said. "It has been said that history is philosophy teaching by example; we may add that art is history teaching by pictures."[122]

For the first ten years of his administration McCosh occupied the old President's House on Nassau Street, where Burr, Davies, Witherspoon, and others of Princeton's great had preceded him. The last ten years he spent at Prospect,

[120] *Ibid.*, v, p. 10.
[121] James McCosh, *Reports to Board of Trustees*, Feb. 10, 1887.
[122] *Moses Taylor Pyne Scrap Book*, VII, p. 42.

the dignified Potter mansion, purchased by Robert L. Stuart and A. Stuart and presented to the college. This building, occupying the site of the Colonel George Morgan house, was a handsome country residence surrounded by spacious grounds. It was designed by John Notman in the Florentine style so popular in the 1850's, with its square towers, arched windows and doors, and stone balconies. "I hope that during the few years I may live in the house, I may make it pleasant both for the students and the friends of the college," McCosh told the trustees. Dean Murray moved into the old President's House, which thereafter became the residence of the dean of the faculty.[123]

The acquisition of Prospect was doubly welcome to Mc-Cosh, for it seconded materially his efforts to enlarge and beautify the campus. When he came to Princeton he found the college hemmed in on both sides by privately owned residences which marred the beauty of the grounds and occupied sites needed for new buildings. One by one these were taken over, some by purchase from college funds, others by the gifts of benefactors, in one case of the Pennsylvania Railroad.[124] So the campus, which even in 1877 had embraced only twenty acres had grown to seventy by the time McCosh retired.

It was in 1869 that McCosh suggested to the trustees that they engage a landscape gardener "to furnish a plan for the improvement of the college" which was to be followed "piece by piece" as funds permitted. And when the plan was drawn, which he insisted should be done in imitation of the English nobleman's park, "usually reckoned the highest model of landscape gardening,"[125] he himself, whenever time permitted, aided in its execution. Often students on their way to and from classes would see his tall form, his arms full of shoots and cuttings, as he walked from one place to another to decide where to plant them, or stopped to direct

---

[123] James McCosh, *Reports to Board of Trustees*, Feb. 13, 1879.
[124] *Ibid.*, Dec. 22, 1869; June, 1872; June 22, 1874.
[125] *Ibid.*, June 28, 1875.

the workmen in removing deformed trees or shrubs or in planting new ones.[126] With the putting down of walks, the laying out of rose beds, the grading of the grounds, the care of the grass, the Princeton campus became one of the most beautiful in the country.

Although McCosh introduced some of the best features of European universities, he had no sympathy with the European neglect of the student outside the classroom. It was the duty of the professors, he insisted, to set an example of right living to the young men entrusted to their care, to win their friendship and confidence, and to interest themselves in undergraduate affairs. His promise to throw open Prospect to the students was faithfully kept. "Many an alumnus cherished in his memory a picture of that tea-table, a few students around it, the Doctor at the head, leading the conversation with his strong, cheery voice and slight Scotch accent; his wife Isabella, 'the mother of the students,' opposite him, pouring tea."[127]

Isabella McCosh was a remarkable woman, peculiarly suited to be the wife of a college president. Hers was a life of self-forgetful absorption in doing good with gentleness and perseverance. "Its center was her home, but its circumference was the outmost bound of the circle of persons she could benefit," says Dean West. "It was this which made her home a constant source of actively good influences. And she was ever interesting—never dull, never at a loss, never monotonous, never lacking distinction and never failing in the little offices of friendliness. . . . It will never be known how many times in the twenty years of her husband's presidency she toiled up the dormitory stairs to visit one and another sick student, bearing in her own hands the neat little basket of home-made delicacies."[128]

On one occasion a sophomore had injured his ankle so severely that the surgeons decided that an amputation was

---

[126] Geo. R. Wallace, *Princeton Sketches*, pp. 115, 116.
[127] *Ibid.*, p. 119.
[128] *Princeton Alumni Weekly*, Nov. 24, 1909.

necessary. The boy was lying in his room trying to adjust himself to this disaster, when there came a gentle rap at the door, accompanied by "May I come in?" It was Mrs. Mc-Cosh. "Young man, I understand they're thinking of taking off your foot. Let me see it." Whisking back the sheet, she gave one intensive look. "They'll nae do it. There's a surgeon in Philadelphia. He's Doctor Agnew. I'll telegraph him. You're going to him tomorrow and you leave on the mid-morning train. He'll save you." He did. And Mrs. McCosh won another of those friendships which lasted through the years.[129]

And now the president began to consider the advisability of resigning. He was still full of vigor, his hold upon the trustees and faculty was as strong as ever, but there was a hesitancy in the former firm tread, the thinning hair was white, there were deep wrinkles on the broad brow and around the firm mouth. McCosh had led a very active life, full of hard work and conflict, and his seventy-four years were beginning to tell on him. But before handing on his office to his successor he wished to consolidate and perpetuate what he had done by having official sanction for Princeton's change from a college to a university. He wished, also, to use this sanction as a springboard for further expansion—enlargement of the faculty, institution of new departments, acquisition of new equipment.

McCosh launched his campaign in an address at Woodstock, Connecticut, on "What an American University Should Be." "A college is a teaching body; a university something higher; it embraces a number and variety of departments, it may be a number of colleges—Oxford has twenty-two—combined in a unity of government and aim, which is generally to promote a higher learning." He thought that a college well equipped and devoting itself to its work was preferable to a university which, professing to teach everything, taught nothing effectively. There were many institutions, with one-third the number of Princeton's students and one-fourth the num-

[129] Philip Ashton Rollins, *Reminiscences of Mrs. McCosh*, p. 10.

ber of instructors, which called themselves universities. "I will not name them," he added sarcastically, "as their grand title proclaims their fame."[130] The obvious implication that Princeton was in fact a university and should so declare itself precipitated a general and at times bitter debate among Princeton men. There was much opposition. Was the institution to turn its back on all its traditions? Already it was losing sight of religion as its chief aim. Would this accelerate the tendency? Would it not lead to the introduction of schools of law and medicine? Would it not put an end to the old intimate relation of teacher and student, undermine the literary societies, and change completely undergraduate life? At every meeting of the alumni associations the matter was argued, some of the older graduates opposing the change, the younger men arguing for it. But as usual the majority stood behind the president, and by 1886 the associations of Washington, Philadelphia, San Francisco, St. Louis, Chicago, Cincinnati, and Central Pennsylvania had voted their approval.

Still the trustees hung back, and in 1887 McCosh urged it upon them again. "I think every educated man will allow that we have a *studium generale* which is the essence of a university," he argued. "True, we have not medicine nor law, but professional schools are not necessary to a university which is a place of learning and not of the practical arts." Princeton with its graduate students, its advanced courses in literature, science and philosophy, its higher degrees, its School of Science, its School of Art, should proclaim itself a university in order to consolidate and seal the whole. Many rival institutions—Harvard, Johns Hopkins, Pennsylvania, and more recently Yale—had led the way, and Princeton must either follow suit, or fall to the rank of a second-rate college. He cherished the hope that it might be the opening of a new era, an era of expansion and prosperity. The trustees still refused to act, however, and a year later, when McCosh retired, the institution which he had served so well still retained the official title of college.

[130] *Moses Taylor Pyne Scrap Book*, VI, p. 67.

To what extent this disappointment influenced McCosh in handing in his resignation, we do not know. But he was now an old man, approaching his seventy-seventh birthday, and he began to fear that by continuing in office he might retard the progress of the college. "Having been in your service for upwards of nineteen years, and being several years above the three-score and ten," he told the trustees, "I see it clearly to be my duty to ask the Board to accept my resignation and to appoint a successor."[131] With deep regret the trustees accepted the resignation.

The news was received with general regret throughout the country and there were many newspaper editorials on the services of the Scotch divine, not only to Princeton, but to the cause of education throughout the country. "His eye is not dim and his natural force hardly, if at all, abated," said the *New York World*.[132] "He lays down the sceptre which he has so long and so well wielded over Princeton college entirely of his own accord and with the expressed regrets of students, graduates and friends of the college, and also of the public at large, who, although they have not known him save as a public character, have grown to admire as those who have known him have grown to love and almost worship the sturdy old Scotchman. . . . One of the ablest of living philosophers, one of the profoundest thinkers in America today, his fame has spread far beyond Princeton college."

The Princeton which McCosh handed on to his successor was very different from the Princeton which he had found in 1868. The physical growth had been remarkable. The alumni who returned for their twentieth reunion were at home only in the old quadrangle enclosed by Nassau Hall, West College, East College, and the two Halls. On all sides save to the north the grounds had been expanded and new buildings had arisen—the Library, Dickinson Hall, the Marquand Chapel, the School of Science Building and many others. The alumni wondered how the students, now that they numbered over

---

[131] James McCosh, *Reports to Board of Trustees*, Nov. 10, 1887.
[132] Feb. 12, 1888.

six hundred, could learn to know each other, or crowd into Whig and Clio, and they were surprised to find that instead of the ten professors of their day there were now thirty-seven.

But some realized that there were even more profound developments than these physical changes. There had been an intellectual awakening, a new spirit of inquiry, an eagerness on the part of the students to learn, which had been lacking in their day. There were still young men who tried to get through college with as little work as possible but the proportion of those who did their work with zest as an exciting adventure was much greater. Moreover, the students seemed more mature, more self-reliant, more interested in the serious side of college life. The *Princetonian*, the undergraduate newspaper, did not hesitate to pronounce on such weighty matters as the elective system, new methods of teaching, the introduction of new courses, the honor system in examinations. There were still some hazing, occasional horn-sprees, disorders in the classroom, but the undergraduate of 1888 looked down upon many of the pranks of former days as beneath his dignity. On the other hand, the overshadowing of the literary societies by athletics seemed deplorable to the alumnus, and he could hardly credit it when his son told him that the class valedictorian was less the campus hero than the most skillful player in this newfangled football game.

As one reviews the changes under McCosh, they fit themselves into one pattern—the transformation of a college into a university. The building program, the creation of a real library, the founding of schools of science and art, the elective system, the giving of graduate courses and the building up of a body of graduate students, the encouragement of research, the acquisition of new scientific equipment, the arousing of the intellectual curiosity of the undergraduates, the raising of the entrance requirements, the offering of fellowships—all pointed in the same direction.

McCosh came to Princeton at a time when the country was in the midst of a tremendous industrial expansion, accompanied by the creation of vast fortunes. The railways which be-

fore the War Between the States had reached out to and beyond the Mississippi, now cleared the Rockies to link the
Atlantic with the Pacific coast. The standard of living rose
rapidly as the use of more efficient machinery in the factories
not only lowered the cost of many essential articles, but increased the output per worker and so made possible higher
wages. The din of the factory, the roar of the locomotive, the
dust of the coal mine, mingled with the clink of dollars.

Princeton must keep pace with this development or find
itself hopelessly antiquated and out of step with the times. It
could not go on educating young men for the ante-bellum age
after that age had ceased to exist. If Princeton stood still there
were other colleges to take the lead—Harvard, Yale, Columbia, Cornell, Michigan, Johns Hopkins. So it was fortunate
that she had found a leader who not only realized the opportunity for the college but knew how to take advantage of it.
Had McCosh contented himself with preserving old traditions, splendid though many of them were, had he rejected
the elective system, frowned on expansion, insisted on rigid
Presbyterian control, denounced the theory of evolution,
maintained the old tutorial supervision, Princeton would have
missed its golden opportunity, might have remained con-
tentedly dreaming of the days of Witherspoon and Maclean,
out of step with the times, performing a task of limited usefulness to the pulsing life of modern America.

CHAPTER X

## Expansion and Inaction

T HE conservative group in the board of trustees insisted that McCosh's successor should be a Presbyterian minister. Since the days of Jonathan Dickinson there had been an unbroken line of ministers at the head of the college; was it wise to disregard tradition? On the other hand the alumni, to whom the institution had been turning more and more for financial support and who were demanding some share in its control,[1] wanted an experienced administrator, one who was not only an educational leader but also a businessman. There was deep disappointment among the graduates, then, when it was announced that the trustees had elected Francis Landey Patton, who held professorships in both the college and the Princeton Theological Seminary.

This seemed a step backward. With new currents of thought sweeping over the nation, why choose a man around whom hung an atmosphere of ecclesiasticism, "a man with a white lawn tie, a black frock coat, side whiskers and the pallor of a medieval monk"?[2] Patton was known chiefly for his part in the David Swing trial for heresy before the Chicago presbytery in 1874, a trial which drove an influential minister out of the Presbyterian church and offended thousands of sincere Christians throughout the nation. It was objected, also, that Patton was not a graduate of Princeton and not even a citizen of the United States.

But sentiment changed when the alumni had had a chance to see and hear the president-elect. Patton was a brilliant speaker, and it was almost impossible to resist the sharp but kindly wit, the cleverly worded phrases, the display of scholarship, to which the rasping intonation somehow added telling force. On March 15, 1888, when he addressed the New

[1] *Christian Intelligencer*, Feb. 29, 1888.
[2] *Princeton Alumni Weekly*, April 25, 1930.

[ 344 ]

York alumni, he arose amid an atmosphere of cold hostility. As he took up the objections made to him one by one without appearing to do so, and in the most skillful way answered them, his audience began to melt. "When I think of Witherspoon and McCosh," he said, "I am compelled to believe that there is more joy among the alumni over the one president who is naturalized than over the ninety and nine who need no naturalization." Before he had finished he had won over the audience completely, and "his enemies were standing on tables, waving napkins and yelling in a frenzy of enthusiasm."[3]

With the undergraduates, also, Patton had to win his way. When "the appalling rumor got around" that he was indifferent if not actually hostile to athletics, he put an end to it by occasionally attending football practice. There were smiles of satisfaction when he appeared on the field, "pale of face, in his tightly buttoned frock coat," to be "jostled by the throng of corduroy-trousered and besweatered students," and to applaud "with thin hands a goal kick from the 35-yard line." "His head was carried high, as much through necessity as pride," for his "poke collar" constantly jostled him under the chin. But in time Patton changed. "The collar came down in height, the more secular black tie supplanted the white tie for business wear. The austere whiskers were shorn away. His thin cheeks filled out and traces of "tan were discernible on his pallid countenance."[4]

On the afternoon of June 20, 1888, the academic procession formed in front of Nassau Hall and marched across the campus to the Presbyterian Church. Governor Robert S. Green and Dr. McCosh led the way, followed by Dr. Patton, the trustees, the faculty, the trustees and faculty of the Princeton Theological Seminary, invited guests, alumni, and undergraduates. When all had been seated, Dr. T. L. Cuyler made the opening prayer and Dean Murray and Dr. Henry van Dyke delivered brief addresses. Chancellor A. T. McGill

[3] W. B. Scott, *Materials for an Autobiography*, III, pp. 673, 674, MSS.
[4] *Princeton Alumni Weekly*, April 25, 1930.

then administered the oath of office to Dr. Patton, and Dr. McCosh handed over the college charter and keys.[5]

When the undergraduates had vented their enthusiasm with the college cheer, the new president began his inaugural address. To the alumni and faculty who listened intently, the outline of policies for the new administration was full of promise. One after the other the great educational problems of the day were marshaled before them with a clarity, an understanding, a forcefulness which brought the conviction that McCosh's scepter had fallen into worthy hands. This was no narrow theologian, no bigot, no impractical recluse, but a far-sighted leader who would keep the college abreast of the times.[6]

The age-old problem of the relationship of scholarship and teaching was defined and clarified. "The university is meant to be a place of research," he pointed out. "It is a hive as well as a home. We have not yet reached the full stage of productive activity that is desirable in this land because our professors as a rule are overworked in the classroom. We have not fully learned the difference between a professor and a pedagogue, and that while the one may hear lessons, the other should inspire with thirst for knowledge and speak with authority. But we are coming to this position. We are finding that the professor who has ceased to learn is unfit to teach, and that the man who sees nothing before him to kindle his own enthusiasm will chill the little enthusiasm the student may carry into his lecture-room. There is no necessary antagonism between man's work as a teacher and his work as an investigator. It is the man who is making contributions to his department whom the students wish to hear. None know this better than Princeton men who remember Professor Henry as the prince of teachers, and who at the same time know that he was the father of telegraphy and that it is his genius that has enabled us to whisper round the world."[7]

[5] *Moses Taylor Pyne Scrap Book*, VIII, pp. 6, 7.    [6] *Ibid.*
[7] *Inauguration of Francis Landey Patton*, pp. 19, 20.

The new president struck a responsive cord when he proclaimed his faith in the ability of American youth themselves to solve the problem of college discipline. "Self-government is ideal government," he said. He feared, however, that it would take at least another administration to bring the Princeton undergraduate up to that standard.[8] Similarly farseeing were his views on alumni participation in the conduct of college affairs. "Some think that . . . the graduates ought to have their interest stimulated through more tangible ideas than filial piety and love of Alma Mater." Much would be gained if there were more frequent interchanges of ideas among trustees, faculty and students, for "college administration is a business in which Trustees are partners, professors the salesmen and students the customers."[9]

With remarkable insight into the future trend of higher education he predicted the development of the social sciences and outlined the channels which they should follow. "It is manifest that as our life grows more complex new questions will arise; and new problems requiring profound investigation. . . . In the interests of national integrity it is important that they shall be dealt with in our colleges. . . . It is from the experience of the past that we are to gather the canons of to-day. History in this way takes its place in a group of studies which we may call the Science of Politics. As in ethics we deal with human conduct with reference to the individual, so in politics we consider it with reference to society. I think that the first thing to be done in the development of Princeton College is the full equipment of the department of politics."[10]

The years of Patton's administration were marked by great building activity. In February 1889 the president announced to the trustees that Mrs. David Brown had provided funds for a new dormitory, to be named for her brother, the beloved Albert B. Dod.[11] Constructed in the most substantial manner of sandstone from Bull's Island,

[8] *Ibid.*, p. 28.      [9] *Ibid.*, p. 29.      [10] *Ibid.*, pp. 34, 35.
[11] *Trustees Minutes*, Feb. 14, 1889.

near Trenton, and provided with suites consisting of a study and one or two bedrooms, roomy and well-lighted, it became very popular with the students.[12] But the somber façade, set off by a central Romanesque doorway, two arched side doors and two semicircular towers, the low roof, the wide windows, the bristling chimneys robbed the structure of architectural charm.

It was a thing of beauty, however, when compared to David Brown Hall, the next monument to Mrs. Brown's generosity. Built around a court, the two lower stories of Quincy granite, the two upper stories of Pompeian brick, it was "modeled exteriorly after one of the palaces of ancient Florence." But the completed building with its heavy lines, its bleak façades, its long rows of windows, had little of the charm of Italian architecture. The *Princeton College Bulletin*, however, thought it a model of convenience. "The day is past when it was considered necessary that the student should live in a dungeon or with surroundings which reminded him of a poor-house." Yet to the students of today Brown Hall would have seemed cheerless indeed, for the rooms were heated by open grates, supplied from coal-lockers in the hallways,[13] and there were no bathrooms.

The trustees had frequently expressed the hope that some benefactor of the college would provide funds for the erection of a commencement hall, for with the growth of numbers the Presbyterian Church had become inadequate. It was customary to erect a platform for the trustees, faculty and guests, and this so encroached on the main floor as to leave insufficient room for the students, who often resorted to scuffling to obtain seats for themselves and their "fair visitors."[14] So there was rejoicing when President Patton announced in November 1890 that Mrs. Charles B. Alexander had provided funds for a large auditorium.[15] Alex-

[12] *Princeton College Bulletin*, III, p. 51, June, 1891.
[13] *Ibid.*, IV, p. 69, November, 1892.
[14] *Moses Taylor Pyne Scrap Book*, IX, p. 59.
[15] *Trustees Minutes*, Nov. 13, 1890.

ander Hall, designed by William A. Potter, a member of
the Richardson school of architecture, differed radically from
any other building on the campus. Princetonians could have
overlooked this, had it not been overornate, heavy and ill-
proportioned. There was high praise for the exterior sculp-
tures by J. Massey Rhind and the interior mosaics by J. A.
Holzer illustrating the Homeric story, but the heavy
Romanesque arches of the ambulatory, the round dunce-cap
towers, the expanse of rounded roof, the bands of red free-
stone robbed the structure of all grace and proportion.

Less pretentious, but even more urgently needed, was the
infirmary. President McCosh, urged on by Mrs. McCosh,
had repeatedly presented this matter to the trustees, and
now, with the steady increase in numbers, it could no longer
be delayed. A dormitory room with its lack of quiet, the
absence of medical equipment, and because of the impossibility of securing nurses, was no place for a sick boy. In 1891
Dean Murray reported that a faculty subcommittee upon its
own initiative had launched a campaign for funds, had selected a site on Washington Road "just below the barn on
the President's premises," and had induced Surgeon General
John Shaw Billings of the United States Army, an expert
on hospital construction, to visit Princeton and supervise the
drawing of the plans. By February 1892, the sum of $26,475
had been subscribed, with I. V. Brokaw and Mrs. R. L.
Stuart heading the list with $5,000 each. The Isabella Mc-
Cosh Infirmary, the building was to be called, in memory of
the woman whose loving care and sympathy had meant so
much to many a sick lad in the days gone by.[16]

So a two-story brick structure arose on the slope back of
Prospect. In the basement were to be laundry, drying room,
boiler room, and two bedrooms; on the first floor a ward
designed for four beds, two single rooms, a reception room,
an operating room, pharmacy, bathroom with movable tubs,
and kitchen and pantry; on the second floor another ward,
a double room, two single rooms, a nurse's room, and nurses'

[16] *Trustees Minutes*, June 8, Nov. 12, 1891, Feb. 11, 1892.

kitchen. Attached to the two wards were sun-parlors which looked out to the south over the lovely New Jersey landscape. The cornerstone was laid with appropriate ceremonies at the commencement of 1892, and the building was ready for occupancy in April of the following year.[17]

In the meanwhile revolutionary changes were taking place in the library which were transforming it from a storage place for books to the heart of the college, a center for undergraduate study and faculty research. It became necessary to add more reading tables, card files, shelves. The students, no longer content to depend entirely upon textbooks for their reading, were making ever increasing demands for volumes on literature, history, philosophy, etc. In 1888-1889 the circulation was 16,939, three years later 20,442, in 1893-1894 it was 22,271. The experiment of opening the library from eight in the morning until dark proved so successful that Dr. Richardson, the new librarian, predicted that if lights were installed students would come in even in the evening.[18]

"No one who knows the history of the last twenty years can fail to perceive that Princeton has changed," the *College Bulletin* pointed out in 1890. "We are no longer the old-fashioned small American college and we cannot go back to the outgrown past. And our library must be as high in its ideals and as broad in its scope as the aims and the horizon of the institution of which it is the center. . . . It is impossible for most professors to depend for their necessary tools on their private libraries. . . . If we want our professors to represent us amid the learned discussions of the world—we must supply them with a library. . . . If one as wise as Cicero were to be asked what is the first essential to a university library, he would answer Books, and the second? Books, and the third? Books."[19]

But books soon became a source of embarrassment. As the volumes poured in, the shelving space in the Chancellor Green

[17] *Princeton College Bulletin*, v, p. 49, July, 1893.
[18] *Trustees Minutes*, Nov. 12, 1891.
[19] *Princeton College Bulletin*, II, p. 12, January, 1890.

became inadequate and the librarian was forced to remove thousands of volumes to the cellar, although, as he pointed out, they not only suffered there from the dampness but were practically out of reach for the undergraduates.[20] By 1893 even this resource failed, for the basement shelves were crowded and the staff was at its "wits end for room."[21] It was suggested that the old chapel, which at the time was used as a lecture hall, be converted into a wing of the library, and that a similar wing be constructed on the north,[22] but the trustees thought that this would be both unsatisfactory and wasteful. It would be better to have "an additional building, planned to hold 500,000 volumes and capable of future extension, to be placed back of the Chancellor Green Library and joined to it."[23]

On April 10, 1896, Moses Taylor Pyne announced to the trustees that "certain friends, acting through him," were prepared to erect "a large convenient, handsome, fire-proof library building." They had taken the liberty of having the plans drawn in advance, and as the group gathered round he spread the architect's drawings before them.[24] Amid the general rejoicing, there was regret that the new building seemed to doom both the old chapel of 1847 and East College. Would not the generations of alumni who had roomed in East College resent its passing? Would it not destroy the harmony of the south quadrangle as the removal of the Philosophical Hall had destroyed that of the north? And when, in the summer of 1897 East College was actually torn down, and the class of 1897 used the doors and other woodwork for their graduation bonfire, there was deep regret among the alumni and many outspoken criticisms. The "Crime of 'Ninety-Six," they called it.

Yet all Princetonians rejoiced in the new library. The Chancellor Green was retained as a reading room, to which was attached a new quadrangle 160 feet square built around

[20] *Trustees Minutes*, Nov. 12, 1891.     [21] *Ibid.*, Feb. 9, 1893.
[22] *Ibid.*, June 11, 1894.                [23] *Ibid.*, Feb. 14, 1895.
[24] *Ibid.*, April 10, 1896.

a court. Here were placed the stacks, the exhibition room, administration rooms, seminars, storerooms, etc. In the ligature joining the two structures were the main entrances, the delivery desk, and the card catalogue. The combined buildings could house no fewer than 1,250,000 volumes, so that at the existing rate of increase it would take two centuries or more to fill the shelves.[25] Ground was broken in the spring of 1896, and by November 1897 the work of construction was nearing completion and most of the books had been transferred to the stacks.

The trustees were now surprised and not a little disconcerted to find that with the erection of the new building new problems of organization and administration presented themselves. The "factory of education" which they had created would not function without its trained staff and its machinery for handling books. Slowly they came to a realization that the finest building in the United States, the largest collection of volumes would not constitute a real library unless the volumes were made available to the reader.

Dr. Richardson pointed out in 1899 that the system of "fixed location" in use in the old library, in which each book was assigned to a definite shelf, must give way to the "modern relative system," under which each volume was classified in such a way as to allow indefinite expansion and adjustment.[26] This entailed recataloguing at a very heavy expense. The difficulty was heightened by the rapid increase in accessions. In the year ending August 1, 1898, about 6,000 new titles had been added. The following year the number rose to 12,077, in 1899-1900 to 23,763, and only by the most rigid economy was the library "kept from anarchy."

The pride of Princeton men in the remarkable expansion of building in the last decades of the century was tempered by regret that there was such striking lack of unity in the architecture. The campus, itself beautiful with its great trees, its vines and shrubs, had become a hodgepodge, the Georgian

25 *Alumni Princetonian*, Nov. 11, 1897.
26 *Trustees Minutes*, Dec. 14, 1899.

of Nassau Hall contrasting strangely with the Florentine of
Prospect, the Romanesque of Alexander Hall with the
Grecian of Whig and Clio Halls. Why should the college
be swayed by every passing style, it was asked, why not adopt
some suitable architecture and adhere to it in all future
buildings?

It was Professor Andrew Fleming West who won Princeton
over to the Tudor Gothic architecture, of which the new
library was an example. West had visited both Oxford and
Cambridge, bringing away a keen appreciation of the beauty
of the buildings and the cultural influence they exerted on
both students and faculty. Later, when several Gothic buildings arose on the Bryn Mawr campus, designed by the brilliant architects Walter Cope and John Stewardson, proving
that the style could be adapted to the needs of American
colleges, West realized that the time to act was at hand. It
was an easy matter to win over Moses Taylor Pyne, chairman
of the Trustees Committee on Grounds and Buildings—who
likewise had seen and admired the English university buildings—and through him to gain the support of the board.[27] It
must have been difficult for William A. Potter to turn from
the Romanesque as expressed in Alexander Hall to the Gothic
of the new library. But for Cope and Stewardson, to whom
the college turned next, the designing of a dormitory presented by John I. Blair was a work of love. The pointed
arches, the battlements, the leaded panes, the bay windows,
the ornate carving of Blair Hall gave it immediate rank as one
of the most beautiful college buildings in America. Nor was
it a mere slavish imitation of the English Gothic. "It is rather
the spirit of Oxford and Cambridge architecture reproduced
in new forms by the most wonderfully sympathetic understanding of changed architectural conditions," said President
M. Carey Thomas of Bryn Mawr.[28]

Six years later Woodrow Wilson, then president of Princeton, declared that the adoption of Gothic architecture had

[27] I have these facts from Dean West himself.
[28] *Princeton Alumni Weekly*, Nov. 15, 1902.

added a thousand years to the history of the university, had pointed every man's imagination to the earliest traditions of learning in the English-speaking race.[29] Certainly Princetonians, because they have lived in the shadow of Pyne Hall, Little Hall or Joline, Holder or Madison take with them through life a better appreciation of the beautiful, are better men, with higher ideals. Yet there are some who regret that the Georgian of the Middle Colonies as represented in Nassau Hall was not adopted instead of the Gothic, as more typically American and more in keeping with Princeton history. But there can be only gratitude to Dean West and those who supported him for putting an end to architectural chaos on the campus and giving to the college a style which is as practical as it is beautiful.

Stafford Little Hall, a new dormitory south of Witherspoon, overlooking the old railway station, was designed by Cope and Stewardson in architectural harmony with Blair Hall. The first section of the building was completed in 1899 and the lower section in 1902. "There are to be baths in the new Little Hall!" announced the *Alumni Weekly*. "This will be astonishing news to many old graduates, alarming news to certain older graduates, who shook their heads once upon a time when bath-rooms were put in . . . Reunion Hall and who said, 'I told you so,' when an epidemic of typhoid broke out. . . . Some of the Trustees, it is said, have never believed in baths since. In dormitories, that is."[30] The long sweep of the west front, the graceful bays of the second story, the Flemish gables, the Tudor chimney stacks, the pedimented doors, the four-story tower added a new element of beauty and charm to the campus.

In the meanwhile a movement had been set on foot to replace the old Whig and Clio Halls, which had graced the back quadrangle for more than half a century, with larger and more handsome buildings. There had been increasing alarm among the alumni over the gradual decline of the

[29] *Ibid.*, Dec. 13, 1902.     [30] *Ibid.*, Nov. 9, 1901.

societies. Formerly, to be left out of Whig and Clio was considered a kind of ostracism; now there were hundreds who did not care to join. Though the work which went on behind the classic porticoes of the Halls was still invaluable to those who participated in it, something of the old zest, the old glamour had gone.

Some put the blame upon the many other interests, formerly almost unknown, which now demanded a share of the student's time. Athletics, especially, had become a serious rival of the societies, and it was the latest victory over Yale or Harvard which was the general topic of conversation in the dormitories or around the dining table, rather than the debates in the Halls or even the selection of the commencement orators. The *Bulletin* pointed out that "the enormous increase in the number of undergraduates has made it more difficult for every one to get the share which he desires of Hall work, and with diminished opportunity has frequently come diminished zeal." To make matters worse, the growing influence of the eating clubs was robbing the literary societies of their fraternal character, formerly so important. Perhaps the erection of two large, handsome buildings might put an end to decline and restore to the two venerable Halls something of the glory of past days.[31]

In 1889 the work of demolition was begun and at the commencement of 1890 the cornerstones of the new Halls were laid with impressive ceremonies.[32] In response to the plea of the alumni, the classic style was adhered to, but the stucco of the old buildings gave way to two-inch slabs of marble, and the old wooden pillars to solid marble columns, twenty feet high and three in diameter. Within were libraries, reading rooms, club rooms, and on the third floors spacious senate chambers. To the very old alumnus, who remembered the meetings in the little rooms over the library in Stanhope Hall, the new Halls seemed luxurious in the extreme. But had he lingered to hear the orations and de-

[31] *Princeton College Bulletin*, v, p. 2, Jan., 1892.
[32] *Moses Taylor Pyne Scrap Book*, IX, p. 25.

bates, he would no doubt have found them less inspiring, less convincing than those of 1833 or 1834. In fact, it was apparent that "marble halls" were a poor substitute for enthusiasm, and with the passage of a few more decades the societies suffered a decline so pronounced that in the end they retained but a shadow of their former ascendancy in undergraduate life.

Athletics, on the other hand, especially football, absorbed more and more of undergraduate interest. Crowds flocked to the field to watch the practice, an injury to this player or that spread dismay through the campus, the prospects of winning from Harvard and Yale were debated at every club and in every dormitory. The members of the team were looked up to as heroes whom it was a privilege to honor. The freshman who received a friendly nod or a kind word from "Tilly" Lamar, or Hector Cowan, or Arthur Poe, was as thrilled as though he had been invited to dine with President Patton or even Grover Cleveland. If this kind of adulation did not turn the heads of the players, they still had to stand the strain of "write-ups" in the New York and Philadelphia papers. Those were the days when Princeton, Yale, Harvard, Pennsylvania, Cornell, and a few others had almost a monopoly of the game of football, so that the spotlight was focused upon their players.

On the day of a major game the center of Princeton life was transferred from Nassau Hall to the Murray Hill Hotel, New York. In the lobby a throng, gay with their orange and black pennants, sang and cheered, while alumni greeted each other and introduced their families to classmates. As the hour for the game approached tallyhos drew up before the hotel door and, after thirty or forty youths had got aboard, some actually standing on the top seats, jolted off over the rough cobblestones to the Polo Grounds or Berkeley Oval. At the gates they might encounter a crowd jostling each other in an attempt to get through, while within the throng waited impatiently for the game to begin. "Even the clergy cut short their Thanksgiving Day service of song and praise, and dismissing their congregations, gather their families about them and hasten with all speed from the pulpit to the ball-field. And old men, learned and dignified judges, men of letters, actors and physicians . . . can be seen among the thousands of college lads shouting with the best of them."[33]

There were many members of the faculty, old fogies the boys called them, who were seriously alarmed at the unexpected growth of interest in football. Was it wholesome, these men asked, for college boys to stage great spectacles which drew thousands of spectators, involved the handling of large sums of money, and elicited column after column of comment in the daily papers? Would it not lead to the temptation to bring in young men because of their promise as athletes rather than as students? Would the teams not become semiprofessional and no longer be representative of the undergraduate body? Would there not be attempts to conceal irregularities by misrepresentation, if not by actual dishonesty? Wholesome exercise was an excellent thing and intercollegiate games of themselves proper, but the emphasis upon the physical side of student life had gone too far, so that the hearts of the boys were in the Yale or the Harvard game rather than in their class work. It was charged, also, that the undergraduates had become "athletes by proxy." "Forty years ago," wrote an old graduate, "no self-respecting young man or boy would have been content to be always a mere onlooker at any athletic sport; he was not happy until he held the bat or the ball, however clumsily, in his own hand. . . . The invertebrate fashion of today is to gape and shout at a game."[34] This brought an indignant denial from the *Alumni Weekly*. If the old graduate would take the time to come to Princeton and stroll over the campus, he would find that the football team had no monopoly on athletics. He would see the track team trot out of the field-house, the class baseball nines at practice, the freshman foot-

[33] *Illustrated American*, Dec. 16, 1893.
[34] *Princeton Alumni Weekly*, Feb. 22, 1902.

ball squad at work over by the Osborn clubhouse, the tennis players wielding their rackets on Brokaw terrace, youngsters informally booting footballs for points in front of Reunion, back of the chapel, over the cannon, north of Blair or between Dod and Brown. Athletic participation was far from universal, the *Weekly* concluded, but "the habit of regular bodily exercise is more general to-day than it was ten years ago."[35]

The wider interest in athletics, together with the increase in the number of students, made the old gymnasium quite inadequate as early as 1888. "It is too small and crowded," the president reported, "large numbers of students being constantly turned away. . . . The apparatus is scanty, old-fashioned and worn out."[36] In 1896 the trustees made an appeal for funds for a new building, and this brought a prompt and enthusiastic response. There were some whose contributions ran into thousands of dollars, some who gave only ten or five, but the gift of one dollar from Jimmy Johnson, the old Negro fruit and candy vendor who had fled from slavery before the war and had been purchased from his master by the Princeton students, was appreciated most of all. In February 1902 ground was broken and soon the stone walls of the huge building began to rise just north of Brokaw athletic field. With its fine trophy hall, its running track, its many lockers, its hot and cold baths, its handball courts, its fine apparatus, its offices, it was pronounced the finest gymnasium in the country.

The increase in interest in athletics was paralleled by the growth of the club system. Ivy was followed by Cottage, Cottage by Tiger Inn, Cap and Gown, Colonial, Elm, and others. On Prospect Avenue arose one handsome building after another, with dining rooms, reception rooms, libraries, billiard rooms, sleeping quarters for alumni, kitchens, etc. "Visit one of these clubs after supper to get an idea of the life," wrote one correspondent. "Some try a game of bil-

[35] *Ibid.*
[36] *Trustees Minutes*, Nov. 8, 1888.

liards, others go to the reading room and surround themselves with a large armchair or sprawl out on a window seat,
behind the folds of a comic weekly or magazine, others
gather round the large fireplace with their feet distributed
everywhere from the floor to the mantelpiece." Here they
discuss any or all phases of college life, the dryness of one
professor, the "squareness" of another, why Princeton lost
the Yale game, the prospects for the baseball team. But soon
one student, remembering that he has an examination to
prepare, "whacks out" his pipe against the fireplace and
makes his departure. One by one the others follow and the
club is deserted for the night.[37]

All this seemed harmless enough. Princeton men boasted
that their club life lacked many of the evils so apparent in
the Greek letter fraternities of other colleges. The clubs
were not secret, there were no dangerous and degrading
initiations, they entered less into undergraduate politics, the
men did not room in the houses so that in the dormitories
they were thrown into contact with members of other clubs
or with non-club men and often made close friendships with
them. "Our good old democratic traditions live on as before
the advent of the clubs and the members of clubs are just
as likely as their less fortunate (?) classmates to wear 'slick-
ers' to the football games where they may see their best
girls. . . . Princeton is itself the grandest fraternity, and
the most closely knit, in the country," declared the *Alumni
Weekly*.[38]

But before the end of Patton's administration the clubs
came under fire. The elections, which were held in April,
were for weeks the burning topic of discussion among the
students, and seriously disrupted their studies. Membership
in a club took on an exaggerated importance chiefly because
of the dread of the stigma of being left out.[39] "The business
of making friends had been organized even in my time, with
the 'right' freshmen and sophomore groups . . . leading you

[37] *Moses Taylor Pyne Scrap Book*, XIII, p. 30.
[38] *Princeton Alumni Weekly*, Dec. 8, 1900.     [39] *Ibid.*

into one of the upper-class clubs," wrote Ernest Poole '02. "I was headed for one of the four at the top. . . . But when elections came I learned that one junior blackball had kept me out! The news came like a thunderbolt. With a cold sick feeling, the bottom dropped out of my college life." But when his roommate refused to join without him, the hard-hearted junior relented, young Poole "was in," and life once more seemed worth living.[40]

Gradually there arose a demand from faculty members and alumni that the establishment of additional clubs be prohibited. Why should half the undergraduate body be stigmatized as undesirable, perhaps as "queer, unlikable, non-clubbable?" The more clubs you establish, they pointed out, the more attention you call to those who are left out. Others sought the remedy in expanding the system until it included all, or nearly all, the students. "It is a perplexing question, and some day it is going to give us trouble," said the *Alumni Weekly* prophetically.[41]

The young Princetonians of the last decade of the century were a virile group. They were on the average older and more mature than the boys of 1840 or 1850—whose chief joy was to bedevil their teachers—more self-reliant; they were less studious, less interested in intellectual things than the students of 1940. They were "a generation infused with terrific vitality and love of life, sweeping through the calm places of the little country village, vibrant with faith in each other, with the fierce joy of loyalty . . . laughing and exuberant and with no doubt as to the stability and abiding purpose of the universe."[42] As Booth Tarkington put it, the student of today has criticism, whereas the student of the 'nineties had faith.

It was this overflowing vitality which caused the famous battle with Pawnee Bill's wild west circus in May 1899. When the parade started down Nassau Street, with the

<hr>

[40] Ernest Poole, *The Bridge*, p. 61.
[41] *Princeton Alumni Weekly*, April 19, 1902.
[42] M'Cready Sykes '94, in *Princeton Alumni Weekly*, Feb. 13, 1931.

Indians and cowboys lined up on either side of the wagons, the sidewalks for two blocks were crowded with students. Suddenly a rock came out of the throng, striking a cowboy named Big Mouth on the wrist. When Big Mouth retaliated by lashing several students with a whip, the mob began bombarding the wagons with cannon crackers and old eggs. This caused a stampede down the street until Pawnee Bill rallied his forces and charged the students. Numbers were against him, however, and in the end Indians, cowboys, and wagons were in full flight for the circus grounds. President Patton called a meeting of the student body at five o'clock that afternoon and after gazing at them through his glasses rebuked them for their unprovoked attack on the circus and forbade them to attend the performance in the evening.[43]

It was hazing, however, which gave the faculty and trustees most anxiety. The general college sentiment condemned the more violent forms of hazing, and the *Princetonian* was strong in its denunciation, but the custom was difficult to eradicate. Sophomores who had been the victims the year before insisted upon getting their revenge upon the incoming freshmen. Dean Murray and the proctor did their best to detect the offenders, but they had to admit that the task was beyond them. "Even when hazing is carried on in rooms it almost defies detection," Murray told the trustees, "and outside it would take a corps of college police to ferret it out."[44]

Following a widely publicized incident in which a victim of hazing disappeared temporarily and was at first believed to have been drowned in the Canal, sentiment turned strongly against hazing. Final action was taken at a mass meeting in 1894. When all had crowded into Alexander Hall H. C. Brown '95 rose, saying: "I move that we, the undergraduates of Princeton College, agree to abolish hazing." This was seconded and ably supported in brief addresses by T. G. Trenchard '95, Gordon Johnston '96, and

[43] *New York Sun*, May 16, 1899.
[44] *Trustees Minutes*, Nov. 14, 1889.

W. A. Reynolds '97. When the question was put the motion was carried by acclamation. Thereupon President Patton and Dean Murray were called in, informed of the action, and asked to address the assemblage. They were highly gratified, they said, for it meant that one of the greatest blots on Princeton's name would be removed. After all, only the students themselves could put an end to the brutal practice of hazing, as discipline had proved to be ineffective. The incongruity between the splendid buildings and the intellectual life of the college and student rowdyism would now be a thing of the past.[45]

Though this did not put a complete end to hazing, the practice gradually died out, although "horsing," or what Dean Murray called "mild hazing," continued for years. *The Nassau Literary Magazine* gave its support to "raillery and things of that sort," on the grounds that they were deeply rooted in tradition and were wholesome for the freshman.[46] But Dean Murray did not agree. "The whole theory of mild hazing is wrong in principle and rests on wrong tradition," he said. "A campaign of education is needed to convince the students that hazing in no form should be tolerated."[47] Nonetheless, the freshman still was treated as an inferior being, was still the victim of merciless "guying," was still restricted by annoying, if humorous, rules. He must not wear golf trousers, fedoras, "horse hats" or monogram caps; he must not smoke a pipe; he must not enter the grandstand at University Field unless accompanied by visitors; he must not be seen on the streets after nine o'clock in the evening before Washington's Birthday, he must not play ball or loaf on the campus save in the company of a sophomore, junior or senior.[48]

Whatever criticisms there may have been of undergraduate life in the 'nineties, there was something about it which

[45] *Daily Princetonian*, Oct. 1, 1894.
[46] *Nassau Literary Magazine*, XLIX, pp. 219, 220.
[47] *Trustees Minutes*, Nov. 9, 1893.
[48] *Princeton Alumni Weekly*, Sept. 28, 1901.

gave the students an intense loyalty. The compact class system, the life in a country village, the growing voice of the students themselves in matters of discipline and even educational policies, and success in intercollegiate athletics all tended in the same direction. "In an intensely democratic, comradely community the college spirit burned in passionate loyalty to Princeton," said Alfred Pearce Dennis '91.[49] How great an asset this was for the college was fully appreciated by the faculty and the trustees. Patton declared that there was everything to hope from the enthusiasm of the undergraduates for their Alma Mater and their belief that her future was very largely in their hands.[50]

To the students themselves must go most of the credit for the adoption of the honor system, for it was in response to their outspoken wishes that the faculty agreed to put an end to espionage in the examination room. The honor system was practiced first by William and Mary in the eighteenth century and later spread to other southern colleges and preparatory schools. At Princeton there had been a growing resentment against the old system, for many undergraduates considered it a reflection upon their honor. It is to the lasting credit of the faculty that a majority at least understood this sentiment and knew how to use it for Princeton's good. "I can't imagine Dr. Patton's keeping watch over a student taking an examination," wrote M'Cready Sykes '94. "In fact, he would sometimes announce that he had an engagement . . . and ask that the man finishing last be kind enough to leave the papers at the president's house."[51]

The matter came to a head in January 1893 with an editorial in the *Princetonian* deploring the presence in many examinations of professors and proctors, and pleading for the honor system. The demand for fair play on examinations was not less strong than for fair play in athletics, it declared, and predicted that the adoption of the new system would create a sentiment against cheating so strong and universal

[49] *Princeton Alumni Weekly*, April 25, 1930.
[50] *Trustees Minutes*, June 8, 1891.    [51] *Alumni Weekly*, Feb. 13, 1931.

as to make violations exceedingly rare.[52] This was the faculty's opportunity, and a few days later it resolved "that until due notice is given to the contrary, there shall be no supervision of examinations, each student, simply, at the end of his paper, subscribing the following declaration: "I pledge my honor as a gentleman that, during this examination, I have neither given nor received assistance."[53]

The new system was a success from the first. During the mid-term examinations of 1893 four underclassmen were brought before a committee of investigation appointed at a public meeting. All four were found guilty, but as it was deemed wise to treat the first offenders with leniency they were pardoned on condition that they confess their guilt to their professors and take zero for their grades. Three of the four did so. But the fourth, according to Dean Murray, "set himself deliberately at work to break down the new honor method." Thereupon proof of his guilt was submitted to the faculty, who immediately asked his father to withdraw him from college.[54]

Princeton was proud of its new system and greatly heartened by the approval voiced in the press. "Praise for such honor and manliness can hardly find words strong enough to express itself," said the *Cleveland Leader*.[55] "No Faculty could have dealt more judiciously with such a case than these students have done," declared the *New York World*.[56] And though in the years that followed there were isolated cases of cheating at Princeton, they were always dealt with promptly and effectively. "Only once did I see a man break that pledge," wrote Ernest Poole. "Sitting just in front of me, furtively he kept looking at notes. Beside me the president of the class leaned forward and touched his arm and said: 'Tear up your paper and flunk this.' He did."[57]

President Patton, seconded by Dean Murray, made a very

[52] *Daily Princetonian*, Jan. 13, 1893.   [53] *Faculty Minutes*, Jan. 18, 1893.
[54] *Trustees Minutes*, June 12, 1893.
[55] *Daily Princetonian*, Feb. 22, 1893.
[56] Feb. 19, 1893.
[57] Ernest Poole, *The Bridge*, pp. 63, 64.

real contribution to Princeton in relying more and more upon student opinion and student self-government for the suppression of hazing and other disorders. But what in matters of discipline may be termed his *laissez-faire* policy, in the classroom became plain laxity. Patton knew that a large proportion of the students were not taking advantage of their opportunities and several times sought to make a distinction between honor men and ordinary men. He was conscious, also, of the existence of snap courses, which were habitually elected by loafers. But he opposed any stringent stiffening of standards, believing that young men gained much by merely being at college and perhaps having leisure to read the books which interested them. Whether or not he uttered the famous aphorism,

> "Tis better to have gone and loafed
> Than never to have gone at all"

it fairly represented his views.

Although the president had no intention of inviting idleness, many undergraduates took advantage of his laxness. "To use the vernacular of the street, we got away with murder," says M'Cready Sykes. "We resisted culture with a vigor, a resourcefulness, an invincible clan spirit that must have been the despair of the devoted and frequently scholarly men whose task it was to train our adolescent minds." A large part of each class went through college and received their diplomas with a minimum of effort and a minimum of real scholarship. "A student would really have had to try pretty hard to flunk on examinations."[58] As the courses were often too large for effective quizzing, it was the examination which determined the student's grade, so that habitual neglect of class work was followed by hasty cramming for the final test. Then it was that the boys really burned the midnight oil, interrupting the unaccustomed work at nine o'clock with the din of horns and the report of pistols in celebration

[58] *Princeton Alumni Weekly*, Feb. 6, 1931.

of "poler's recess."[59] Disorders in class were frequent and there was much outright disrespect for the professors. On the other hand, there were courses requiring hard work into which the students crowded because they were interested in the subject or because the teacher stirred their intellectual curiosity. "Twinkle" Young's astronomy, Sloane's history, Hunt's English, Hibben's logic, Daniel's public finance, were more extensively elected than the easiest course in college.[60] "Jerry Ormond, carrying something of the spacious tradition of Spinoza and Kant, radiated a serenity of scholarship that fortified one against the chaos of a meaningless universe. . . . To Harry Fine many of us became bound by lasting ties of friendship. Sloane was a thorough cosmopolitan, at his best in small classes, forcing men to think for themselves." Andy West, "urbane, witty, versed in the ways and speech of the race which traces its line to Olympus," aroused new interest in the classical age.[61]

Certainly the intellectual fires lighted by McCosh were not extinguished under his successor, and the instruction of learned and inspiring teachers was by no means ignored. Professor Hunt declared that despite far too many idle and irresponsible students, three-fourths of them were in college with a definite intellectual purpose and were doing creditable work.[62] There were no disorders in Woodrow Wilson's lectures, because the students were eager to hear. "To listen to Wilson was a delight, and his lectures were crowded," M'Cready Sykes tells us. "More important, Wilson was penetrating our defenses. He was leading us in the way of some real intellectual interest. He started us reading, and showed glimpses of a world so attractive and worth while that we went in a little way in spite of ourselves."[63]

Nevertheless, it must be said that although President Patton's regime produced excellent results in student conduct, it

[59] The "poler" was the very diligent student, the "grind."
[60] *Trustees Minutes*, Feb. 8, 1894.
[61] *Alumni Weekly*, Feb. 13, 1931.
[62] *Moses Taylor Pyne Scrap Book*, XV, p. 91.
[63] *Princeton Alumni Weekly*, Feb. 13, 1931.

was far from being successful in educational and administrative matters. Before the first session had passed the faculty were complaining of a general relaxation, and the comment that "Patton is letting things slide," was heard on all sides.[64] The brilliant promise of the inaugural address, with its grasp of educational policies, its vision of future progress, was not being fulfilled. Had Patton carried through his own ideas, he might have ranked with the great educators of the day, but he lacked the persistence to put his own theories into practice. "Dr. Patton would sit for hours in his study grasping a cologne-scented handkerchief in his thin hands," said Alfred Pearce Dennis '91. "Occasionally he would lay down the handkerchief, take up a pen, and make a few calligraphic scratches on a sheet of paper. He hated the manual labor of writing and would often add the completing touches to a sermon during the singing of the second hymn." Such a man was out of place as the administrative officer of a modern and growing college.

Moreover, the 'nineties was no time for inactivity. Great changes were under way in the nation. The United States was taking its place as a world power, the ever greater use of machinery was pouring out wealth in undreamed of quantities, new and broadening currents of thought were changing the outlook on life. The colleges had to meet changed conditions, for they could not go on preparing young men for an age which had passed. The very undergraduates were changing, while the old-fashioned professor, with his wide general scholarship and his paternal attitude toward the student, was being replaced by the highly trained specialist, a master in some one branch of knowledge. The introduction of elective courses had produced momentous problems, the correct solution of which was of vital importance to the future of education; the alumni and others were pouring in funds which could be used wisely for the upbuilding of the colleges, or could be frittered away upon unessential proj-

---

[64] W. B. Scott, *Materials for an Autobiography*, III, p. 712.

ects; the rapid increase in the number of undergraduates demanded radical changes in the methods of teaching.

In the absence of vigorous leadership by the president, it was inevitable that the initiative should fall to the faculty, perhaps to some one member of the faculty. In Patton's administration it was Andrew Fleming West who seized the reins. West it was who, as we have seen, fixed the architectural style of the Princeton buildings; he it was who planned and managed the Sesquicentennial celebration in 1896; who built up the graduate department and originated the idea of a Graduate College; who became secretary of the Committee on the Schedule and so was influential in shaping the curriculum and advancing undergraduate standards; who was entrusted with the vital work of building up the endowment.

It was in November 1892 that a special committee of the faculty reported to the trustees in favor of October 22, 1896, as the proper date for the Sesquicentennial celebration. Not only had the first charter of the college been granted on October 22, 1746, but the date commended "itself by reason of the beauty of the season, the convenience of foreign visitors and the fact that the college at that time is living its characteristic life and so is more interesting to strangers."[65] As the months passed plans for the celebration began to take shape under the able guidance of West. It was decided to invite "a highly representative academic body" from both American and foreign universities, to confer a large number of honorary degrees, to secure some distinguished poet to prepare an ode on Princeton, to announce an enlargement of the endowment, to have addresses to the delegates and responses by them. As the climax of the celebration the president was to declare that the title of the institution had been changed from the College of New Jersey to Princeton University.[66]

The last proposal was not received with universal ap-

[65] *Trustees Minutes*, Nov. 10, 1892.
[66] *Ibid.*, Nov. 8, 1894.

proval by the trustees. Eight years previously, when Mc-
Cosh had urged the change of title, they had voted against
it on the grounds that the funds and equipment necessary for the work of a university were not available. Was
Princeton better prepared for the step now than then? Might
it not be a change from "the best college to the worst university?" But the committee urged it strongly. "If we are
ever to become in name a university the committee can conceive of no better opportunity for doing so. . . . We suffer in
prestige for lack of this name, and it is feared that some day
we shall suffer in pocket. . . . We believe that this step in
itself will greatly encourage the alumni, . . . that it will be
regarded generally as notice that we intend to keep in the
front rank in educational progress."[67] In the end the trustees
were convinced, admitting that the college was already
doing "real university work of a high order" which should
not only be continued but expanded.

To West, also, fell the chief responsibility of securing a
large increase in the endowment, "through the united efforts
of alumni and other friends of the college," as one of the
most important features of the Sesquicentennial. This, in
turn, gave him a large, if not determining, voice in the dis-
posal of the money. "Our great need is the strengthening
and extension of the various departments of instruction, his
committee reported. It would require a million dollars, laid
out for the teaching staff and equipment, to place the undergraduate work on a proper basis. For the graduate work,
which "so urgently called for development" another million was needed immediately and more in the near future
if Princeton was to rank as a great university.[68] In the original report there was no mention of West's plan for a Graduate College, but President Patton specifically endorsed it in
his Sesquicentennial address.[69]

The most interesting but the least noticed feature of the
celebration was the series of lectures by distinguished foreign

[67] *Ibid.*                                    [68] *Ibid.*, Feb. 14, 1895.
[69] *New York Evening Post*, Oct. 23, 1896.

scholars, a feature which "did more to make the occasion memorable than the burning of any amount of colored fire or the delivery of any number of after-dinner speeches."[70] Among those who spoke were Edward Dowden of Trinity College, Dublin; Felix Klein of Göttingen; J. J. Thomson of the University of Cambridge; Karl Brugmann of the University of Leipzig; A. A. W. Hubrecht of the University of Utrecht; and Andrew Seth of the University of Edinburgh. Arriving in Princeton the week before the celebration proper, these scholars were entertained in the hospitable homes of the college and village. Their lectures, delivered in Alexander Hall, attracted scholars from all parts of the country, who listened with rapt attention to expositions on the Mathematical Theory of the Top, the French Revolution and English Literature, The Discharge of Electricity in Gases, Theism, the Descent of the Primates, etc. "I am not aware that the authorities of Princeton have stated formally what they understand by the transformation of a college into a university," wrote one visiting scholar, "but may we not infer" that these distinguished lectures "betoken a true university spirit?"[71]

With dawn on the morning of October 20, 1896, the college and town became alive with excitement. Every store on Nassau Street was decorated; on all sides the national flag waved side by side with pennants of orange and black; spanning the street at one end was an arch with the inscription "From the Town to the University"; opposite Nassau Hall was another decorated with flags and bearing the inscription "Ave Vale Collegium Neo Caesariensis." On the campus, nature took a hand in the decorations, for the autumn yellow of the maples mingled harmoniously with the green shadows of the grass. Here one saw gray-haired delegates from foreign universities, brilliant in their varicolored hoods; here a group of undergraduates in slouch hats, or golf-suits or orange and black sweaters; here alumni greeting each other happily and noisily.

[70] A. G. Webster in the *Nation*, Nov. 12, 1896.     [71] *Ibid.*

At 10:30 the academic procession left the Marquand Chapel and began the march across the campus to Alexander Hall. Leading were President Patton and Charles E. Green of the board of trustees, while delegates, trustees, and faculty followed, the crimson, orange, green, white, purple glistening in the sunlight. When all had been seated Patton arose to deliver a sermon, in which he pledged anew the adherence of the college to the religious ideals of the past. "The spirit of the founders has been kept alive in their successors. The interest of the college has always been in the hands of religious men and of men, I may say, belonging as a rule to a particular branch of Protestant Christendom, but it has never been under ecclesiastical control."[72]

In the afternoon Dr. Howard Duffield delivered the address of welcome to the visiting delegates. President Eliot of Harvard responded for the American universities and learned societies and Professor J. J. Thomson of Cambridge for the European universities and learned societies. In the evening under the direction of Walter Damrosch an orchestra played Schubert's *Unfinished Symphony*, Brahms' *Academic Festival Overture*, and other compositions.

The next morning Henry van Dyke delivered his anniversary ode, *The Builders*:

> "Fair Harvard's earliest beacon tower had shone;
> Then Yale was lighted, and an answering ray
> Flashed from the meadows by New Haven Bay.
> But deeper spread the forest, and more dark,
> Where first Neshaminy received the spark
> Of sacred learning to its frail abode,
> And nursed the holy fire until it glowed.
> Thine was the courage, thine the larger look
> That raised yon taper from its humble nook.
> Thine was the hope and thine the stronger will
> That built the beacon here on Princeton hill."

The reading of the ode was followed by an oration by Woodrow Wilson, who gave, in his usual eloquent way, his interpretation of Princeton's history, "It moves her sons very

[72] *Philadelphia Press*, Oct. 21, 1896.

deeply to find Princeton to have been from the first what they know her to have been in their own day—a school of duty. . . . It has been Princeton's work, in all ordinary seasons, not to change, but to strengthen society."[73]

At 8:40 in the evening, the torchlight procession started from the cannon. In the van was the 71st Regiment Band of New York, followed by Head Marshal Libbey, the Mercer Blues, a delegation of Yale seniors, the undergraduates, and the alumni headed by two representatives of the class of 1839.[74] Many of the classes held aloft transparencies proclaiming their achievements in Princeton history. "We first adopted the Orange and Black," proclaimed the class of 1873; "We were the sponsors of the Honor System," boasted the boys of 1894. The class of 1881, attired in colonial costume and headed by "George Washington" in a coach drawn by four horses, drew vigorous applause along the route. The procession advanced to University Place and, after winding through the western part of the village, returned to the campus in front of Nassau Hall. There, in the presence of President and Mrs. Cleveland, the crowd sent up repeated cheers and sang Princeton songs, while fireworks burst overhead. Nassau Hall itself, outlined by hundreds of electric lights, stood out clearly in the night, while the campus was gay with orange-colored Chinese lanterns.[75]

On the third day of the celebration, the 150th birthday of the college, Alexander Hall was again crowded with an excited, expectant throng, while on the platform sat the President of the United States, surrounded by a group of distinguished men. There was deep silence as President Patton rose, and a "common tide of emotion swelled and rose in the hearts of the alumni" as his words, full and clear, penetrated every part of the hall. The efforts for an endowment had been successful, he said, and had given Princeton several fellow-

[73] *Princeton Sesquicentennial Celebration* (Charles Scribner's Sons, for Trustees of Princeton University, 1897).

[74] *Torchlight Procession*, pamphlet issued by William Libbey.

[75] *Daily Princetonian*, Oct. 22, 1896; *Philadelphia Press*, Oct. 22, 1896.

ships, a professorship, Blair Hall, the library quadrangle, and other needed improvements. He then proclaimed the change in title. "It is my pleasure, for expression of which I have no equivalent in words, to say that the wishes of the alumni in this respect have at last been fully realized; to say that the faculty, trustees and alumni stand together, and, as with the voice of one man, give their hearty approval. . . . It is my great pleasure to say that from this moment what heretofore for one hundred and fifty years has been known as the College of New Jersey shall in all future time be known as Princeton University." This announcement was received with uproarious applause, interspersed with cheers for "Princeton University."[76]

When quiet was restored honorary degrees were conferred upon a distinguished group including Lord Kelvin, Otto von Struve, James B. Angell, Karl Brugmann, Ira Remsen, and Andrew Seth. Patton then introduced President Cleveland and the assemblage, rising to their feet, greeted him with enthusiastic and prolonged applause. Making an earnest plea for a greater participation in governmental activities by university graduates, the President declared that he would like to have graduates of such institutions as Princeton not only as the counselors of their fellow countrymen, but the tribunes of the people. The exercises closed with the singing of the national anthem.[77]

During the Sesquicentennial celebration there was abundant evidence that the era which was dawning for Princeton was to be marked by the declining influence of the Presbyterian church and an ever-increasing interest of the alumni in educational problems. President Patton, in his opening sermon, stated: "I hope that Princeton will always stand for belief in the living God, the immortal self, an imperative morality and the Divine Christ. On this broad platform all the true friends of Princeton can meet."[78] Broad this, indeed —so broad that it must have shocked some of the older

[76] *Ibid.*, pp. 153, 154.    [77] *Ibid.*, p. 45.
[78] *Trustees Minutes*, Oct. 19, 1900.

trustees who could not forget that Presbyterians had founded the college and for a century and a half had been dominant in its counsels. They could console themselves, however, with the thought that Patton himself was a Presbyterian minister, and that when he took his seat at the trustee meetings he had at his elbow such pillars of the church as Samuel B. Dod, J. Addison Henry, Elijah R. Craven, William M. Paxton, John Hall, W. H. Green, Francis B. Hodge, and Melancthon W. Jacobus. In the faculty some of the ablest scholars—John Grier Hibben, Theodore W. Hunt, Henry van Dyke, C. W. Shields and others—were of the same calling, while as late as 1900 almost half of the freshman class were Presbyterians.[79]

But within a year after the Sesquicentennial there occurred an incident which not only revealed the secularizing tendencies at work at Princeton but actually brought on a serious breach with a large faction of the Presbyterian church. "Princeton University or the College of New Jersey, born of high Presbyterian parentage, and for a century and a half diligently nursed by the Church, has taken to the bottle in its old age," proclaimed the *New York Voice*, of July 29, 1897. "The talk of the town at this time is regarding the recent action of several professors, doctors of divinity and LL.D.'s . . . in signing the petition for a saloon licence for the duly authorized university rumshop." This sensational story grew out of the serving of beer and wine at meals and in the grill room of the Princeton Inn,[80] which faculty members described as an honest experiment in temperance, since it lessened the temptation of students to patronize the real saloons and kept drinking within moderate bounds.

Within a few weeks the matter became the subject of a violent controversy within the Presbyterian church. At the session of the synod of New York on October 21, the Reform Committee reported "with humiliation and astonishment" that a drinking-bar, legalized through the signing of a peti-

---

[79] *Trustees Minutes*, Oct. 19, 1900.
[80] Now Miss Fine's School.

tion by professors, had been established at Princeton. In view of these facts, "how long may we hope to keep the pulpit, and even the ministry from the calamity of the cup?" On the same day, in the synodical convention at Plainfield, the presbytery of New Brunswick was urged to discipline such of its members as had signed the petition for the license.

In the face of these attacks the Princeton trustees and faculty stood their ground. "I am going to fight this question out, if I have to fight the whole Presbyterian Church," declared President Patton.[81] Some members of the faculty were so outraged at the storm of abuse that they advocated the withdrawal of the privilege of free tuition to ministers' sons. Grover Cleveland declared emphatically: "I am glad I signed the petition and I would do it again. All the presbyteries and synods in the United States wouldn't change my view of that question."[82] When Professor Shields, another signer, in the face of impending charges, resigned from the Presbyterian church, he had the complete sympathy of his colleagues.

A few weeks later, President Patton, addressing the New York alumni at Delmonico's, declared: "I am loyal to my Church. I know the law and the constitution of my Church and I know that much of what has lately been quoted as the law of that Church is not law and has no binding authority. But whether it has or not, I cannot consent to have the law of that Church, as such, imposed on Princeton University. . . . While I hold my place as the head of your alma mater I will do what in me lies to keep the hand of ecclesiasticism from resting on Princeton University."[83] These words, which were greeted with cheers, marked the end of one epoch in Princeton history and the beginning of another, by announcing to the world that the college of Dickinson and Edwards and Witherspoon had yielded to the secularizing influences of the day.

[81] *New York Sun*, Oct. 31, 1897.
[82] *Illustrated American*, Nov. 27, 1897.
[83] *New York Herald*, Jan. 21, 1898.

As the influence of the Presbyterian church declined, that of the alumni increased. Even though there was no official alumni representation on the board of trustees, the loyal support of the graduates, a support which often expressed itself in dollars and cents, made that body pay respectful attention to their wishes. This it was which had rendered it so difficult to root out the Greek-letter fraternities, even though but a fraction of the alumni had supported them. And it would have been a bold president indeed who would have dared commit himself to the suppression or even serious restriction of intercollegiate athletics.

But with this "virtual representation" the alumni were not contented, and in April, 1900, the *Alumni Weekly* asked pointedly why it was that Princeton men, whose loyalty to their university was so ardent, had no official voice in the conduct of its affairs. "The great body of the alumni have always considered this . . . to be as unjust as it was unwise, and as unwise as it was unnecessary."[84] Moreover, as "taxation without representation," it defied one of America's oldest traditions. The Princeton Club of New York, under the leadership of John L. Cadwalader, set things in motion by drawing up a plan of alumni representation and submitting it to the trustees, and other regional clubs followed suit. But it was the plan of the Western Association of Princeton Clubs, presented by James Laughlin, Jr., '68, John D. Davis '72 and Harlan Cleveland '85, which, with slight modifications, was adopted by the board.[85]

It called for the addition to the trustees of five members who were to hold office for five years, one being elected each year by alumni of ten years' standing. The new trustees were to choose a secretary and treasurer to take charge of the enrollment of the graduates.[86] On June 11, 1901, when the first election was held, the dining room of University Hall was crowded with alumni seated at the tables or standing up or perched in the windows. The announcement that

[84] April 7, 1900.
[85] *Princeton Alumni Weekly*, Sept. 29, 1900.
[86] *Trustees Minutes*, Oct. 19, 1900.

no fewer than 1,200 alumni had enrolled as voters was received with general satisfaction, while the results of the balloting which resulted in election of John D. Davis '72 of St. Louis; John L. Cadwalader '56 of New York; James Laughlin, Jr., '68 of Pittsburgh; David B. Jones '76 of Chicago, and Alexander van Rensselaer '71 of Philadelphia, were greeted with prolonged applause. "Alumni representation is now an established fact; the experiment has worked," declared the *Alumni Weekly*.[87]

With the alumni behind him, President Patton turned his thoughts to the revision of educational policies. Despite the School of Science, he thought that not enough emphasis was placed on vocational training. The average age of the undergraduates had advanced greatly in recent years so that they were still devoting themselves to mathematics or Latin or philosophy at an age when former groups had started business careers or had entered law or medical schools. "I feel confident that some decided modification of our existing curriculum must be made in the near future, unless we are to face the probability of a decided falling off in the number of our students," Patton told the trustees. To meet this threat he favored the introduction of courses in anatomy and physiology and also in common law, "so that those who desire may have . . . in senior year the full equivalent of one year of professional study in Medicine or Law. He also suggested that ambitious students might be permitted to take twenty hours of work a week instead of fifteen, so that they could win the bachelor's degree in three years.[88]

It was also Patton's ambition to establish a law school. "We have Princeton philosophy, Princeton theology, but we have to go to Harvard and Columbia for our law," he said in a commencement address to the alumni in 1890. "Gentlemen, that is a shame. Just as soon as I find a man with a half a million, I am going to found a law school."[89]

[87] June 15, 1901.      [88] *Trustees Minutes*, March 14, 1901.
[89] *Philadelphia Press*, June 11, 1890.

The next year when the retirement of Theodore W. Dwight from the Columbia Law School caused serious dissatisfaction among the students there, it seemed that Patton's opportunity was at hand. Why not found a new law school in New York, it was urged, financed by the friends and alumni of Princeton, to form an integral part of Princeton University? If Dwight could be induced to become dean, bringing with him many of his former students, the success of the project would be assured. But Patton failed to press the matter, funds were not forthcoming, and the opportunity passed.[90]

More successful were Patton's efforts for the social sciences. The Spanish-American War, the acquisition of possessions in the Far East and the increased interest in world affairs, the enormous expansion of American industry with its greater use of machinery and its mass production, the pleas of Grover Cleveland and others for better leadership in politics were demanding a shift of emphasis by the colleges from the study of man the individual to man as a unit of society. That the undergraduates sensed the spirit of the times was shown by the unprecedented elections to the courses in history, jurisprudence, or economics as soon as they were established. The alumni, not wishing Princeton to fall behind its rivals in the new field, gave important financial support with the endowment of the Edwards professorship of American history, the McCormick professorship of jurisprudence[91] and a gift of $100,000 from John W. Garrett and Robert Garrett for an endowment for the teaching of politics.[92] In 1892 Wilson and Sloane had the field of social sciences to themselves; ten years later Wilson, John H. Finley, Winthrop More Daniels, Walter A. Wyckoff, Paul van Dyke, John H. Coney and Robert McN. McElroy constituted the nucleus of a strong department of history, politics and economics.

The development of graduate teaching met with more

[90] *Moses Taylor Pyne Scrap Book*, XVI, p. 78.
[91] *Trustees Minutes*, Jan. 23, 1897.    [92] *Ibid.*, Dec. 14, 1899.

opposition and so was far slower in its advance. The trustees were lukewarm, the alumni were lukewarm, Patton himself was lukewarm. Graduate teaching was well enough in itself, but it would require hundreds of thousands of dollars to erect the buildings, secure the proper equipment and bring in research professors. Would this not divert funds from the proposed law school? Would it not "cripple the undergraduate department?" The faculty, alone, ably led by Dean West, stood stanchly by this stepchild of the university, insisting that it was of vital importance to the intellectual life of the campus and that, far from being a drag on undergraduate teaching, it was essential to it, because it tended to renew the enthusiasm and scholarly interest of the professors in their subjects. But all they could secure from Patton was a promise that he would not stand in the way of advanced study.

A measure of order had been brought out of the former confusion in graduate work as early as 1887 by the adoption of a plan for conferring advanced degrees, patterned after the German university system. The candidate for the doctor's degree had to select a major subject, with two cognate subjects, and might proceed to his final examination after two years of study and the completion of a satisfactory thesis. To be admitted as a candidate it was necessary to have a bachelor's degree and to pass an entrance examination. This, it was thought, would "elevate the scholarly tone of graduate life at Princeton," and "recruit a respectable though moderate number of special scholars."[93] Later the plan was so modified as to have the bachelor of arts degree lead to the master of arts, and this in turn to the degree of doctor of philosophy.[94]

But the growth of the graduate department continued to be slow. In 1895 the number of students was 116, of whom sixty were candidates for the master's degree and only ten for the doctor's degree. Six years later the enrollment was 109, of whom 68 were students of the Princeton Theological Seminary who were supplementing their work there with a few

[93] *Princeton College Bulletin*, II, pp. 52, 53, June, 1890.
[94] *Ibid.*, IV, pp. 48, 49, June, 1892.

graduate courses.[95] In fact, the facilities for graduate work were quite inadequate, for the faculty had to devote so much time to undergraduate teaching that little was left for graduate courses; laboratories and libraries were limited; there was no graduate building or endowment.

Fortunately, a number of seminar rooms had been included in the new library, and this proved invaluable in the development of graduate work. For this the chief credit is due Professor John Howell Westcott. In a report to the president, in 1894, just prior to the drawing of the library plans, he pointed out the inadequacy of the facilities for study by advanced students in the classics. "We need a 'laboratory' where our apparatus can be gathered together," he said. "Where our students can be shown their tools and taught how to use them, where they can work under the eye of their instructor and be in communication with him every day. A place where they can go at any hour of the day or night to carry on their work. The Latin seminary . . . should be provided with a library suited to the needs of students working in small classes. . . . We need a full line of lexicons, works of reference in history, archaeology, etc. We should have on file some of the classical periodical literature to enable us to form a club to keep up with the contemporary progress of the world in classical studies."[96]

At first the new seminars with their paneled walls, leaded panes, and stiff Gothic chairs, seemed more artistic than useful, for the shelves were empty and the chairs almost unoccupied. Gradually, however, they were transformed. By 1898 four seminars—ancient history and archeology, English, classics, and philosophy—were fairly well equipped.[97] In the summer of 1901 the history seminar was handsomely refurnished and supplied with books by an anonymous donor.[98] To secure properly prepared graduate students was not so easy, and some of the handsome rooms either remained idle or were

[95] *Trustees Minutes*, Oct. 15, 1901.
[96] *Trustees Minutes*, June 11, 1894.
[97] *Ibid.*, Oct. 21, 1898, Dec. 8, 1898.
[98] *Princeton Alumni Weekly*, Oct. 5, 1901.

used by members of the faculty for purposes of research or for their undergraduate pro-seminars.[99]

As time passed the difference of opinion between the trustees and the faculty as to the emphasis to be placed upon the development of graduate work became more pronounced. When the board gave it as their opinion that an appeal for funds for "distinctly University work" would not receive the cordial approval of many of the best friends of Princeton, especially those able to make large gifts,[100] the professors were aroused to earnest protest. Princeton had committed itself to graduate work by assuming the title of university, they urged, and moreover was especially fitted for it because of its academic seclusion, its fine undergraduate department and its religious, patriotic, and intellectual traditions. To use the Sesquicentennial endowment exclusively for undergraduate purposes would create the impression that the institution was not interested in a genuine university development. "We therefore beg earnestly to suggest that, even at the cost of postponing for a time such a symmetrical strengthening of the undergraduate work as we all desire, some substantial portion of the new income be pledged toward the endowment of instruction in a graduate college."[101]

The conception of a graduate college, a household of knowledge, where graduate students would have their rooms and studies and take their meals, was originated by Professor West.[102] In his visits to Oxford and Cambridge he had been impressed with the life in the colleges. As he looked in at the beautiful dining halls where students in academic gowns were spicing their meals with discussions of cultural things, as he wandered through grassy courts, and charming chapels and ancient libraries and study halls, as he viewed time-worn walls and towers and Gothic windows, the thought came to him that education in America might take on new meaning could it be carried on in surroundings such as these. So when he was

[99] *Trustees Minutes*, Dec. 8, 1898.
[100] *Trustees Minutes*, March 14, 1895.
[101] *Ibid.*, Dec. 10, 1896.      [102] *Ibid.*, Oct. 21, 1902.

entrusted with raising the Sesquicentennial endowment, he suggested as one of the chief purposes the erection of a residential graduate college, and he secured the endorsement of both the faculty and board of trustees.[103]

So Cope and Stewardson were called upon to make the plans, which were published in 1897 in the Princeton book of *Plans and Sketches of New Buildings*. It was to be in the form of an irregular quadrangle, with one side on Washington Road, another occupying the site of the present chapel, another back of Marquand Chapel, and another on McCosh walk where the main entrance was to be through an archway in a tower similar to Blair Tower. The architecture was Tudor Gothic. There were to be suites of rooms for the students, a master's house with garden, a library, a large dining hall, a breakfast room, a drawing room, kitchen, etc. To West, as he thumbed over the architect's plans and visualized the beautiful group of buildings arising in the old Academy Lot, the realization of his dream seemed near.

But buildings on paper are not buildings in stone and mortar, and the raising of the necessary funds proved a discouraging task. In 1897 West reported to the trustees that for months he had been trying to get a million dollars, and although he had left no stone unturned, had had no success. West thought the blame could be placed at the door of William Jennings Bryan, whose campaign for the presidency on the free silver platform had frightened businessmen and made them keep their hands in their pockets.[104] In 1898 the committee on the graduate college reported that if it were not for the active interest of the faculty in this project and the discouragement which failure would produce, they would ask to be discharged.[105]

West, however, was not easily discouraged. In October 1900, following organization of a Graduate School, he was appointed dean and entrusted with the responsibility for graduate students, courses, degrees, fellowships. That he

[103] *Ibid.*, Dec. 10, 1896.      [104] *Trustees Minutes*, June 14, 1897.
[105] *Ibid.*, Dec., 1898.

might have a free hand in building up the new school, the trustees gave him the unusual privilege of picking the members for the faculty graduate committee.[106] This seems to have been a mistake, for it was a slight to Patton's authority, so that the assurance of an enthusiastic and able committee was won at the price of the president's resentment.[107]

Perhaps Patton would not have taken this matter so to heart had he not again been under fire from the faculty. There were complaints of his failure to enforce discipline, of the need for higher entrance requirements and higher standards in the classrooms, of the chaotic condition of the curriculum, of the inefficiency of administration. Whenever individual trustees visited Princeton they were cornered by faculty members and made to understand that the university was drifting aimlessly. By 1897 the discontent was so general that the board appointed a Committee on University Affairs to make an investigation. As one professor after another came before this body—West, Wilson, Brackett, Scott and others—the need for more vigorous leadership became clear, even though there was no manifestation of an "unkind spirit" in the charges of inefficiency.

Patton, in his turn, had no trouble in convincing the committee of his full and comprehensive grasp of the local situation and his "broad and intelligent" views on education in general. But these had never been in question. It was his failure to put his policies into operation which had brought him into conflict with the faculty, and which now resulted in a mild rebuke from the trustees. "It would be well that discipline be administered with a firmer hand, that studies should be better coordinated, and methods of administration be somewhat changed in order to [attain] greater efficiency," they thought. Perhaps it would be wise to appoint a secretary for the university and inaugurate the offices of Dean of the Academic Faculty and Dean of the Scientific Faculty.[108]

[106] *Ibid.*, Dec. 13, 1898.
[107] W. B. Scott, *Materials for an Autobiography*, III, p. 913, MSS.
[108] *Trustees Minutes*, June 14, 1897.

Unfortunately these suggestions were not acted on, the investigation failed to infuse new energy into the president, and Princeton continued to drift. Within three years another committee of the trustees reported that the university was suffering from a "lack of cooperation between the various departments and from the want of some one person whose duty it should be to follow up details. . . . This results in friction, delay, neglect and omissions. Friends and patrons are alienated by failure to procure exact information when needed. Letters remain unanswered for an unnecessary length of time. Committees and resolutions are overlooked. Inquiries are handed from one officer to another, and the general impression is given that the university is suffering from a lack of system and business methods."[109]

There was complaint, also, that Princeton was not taking advantage of the opportunity to advance its standards of undergraduate work presented by the growth and development of the preparatory schools. Despite the increasing age of the entering classes, many courses continued on the level of thirty or fifty years before. The excuse for this, if there could be an excuse, was the laxness shown in enforcing entrance requirements. M'Cready.Sykes has stated that "any boy of fair intellectual endowment and reasonable powers of application could be admitted."[110] The College Entrance Examination Board was still in the experimental stage, and in 1901 only thirty-three boys entered Princeton through this channel.[111]

When ill-prepared young men entered, they were faced with a group of required courses, some of which were fairly difficult, and a few who could not surmount this hazard were dropped. But once safely in the junior class it was a dull youth indeed who could not select enough easy courses to complete his work in comparative idleness. When certain professors tried to stiffen their courses they found themselves confronted with empty benches. Winthrop More Daniels

---

[109] *Ibid.*, Oct. 19, 1900.     [110] *Princeton Alumni Weekly*, Feb. 6, 1931.
[111] *Ibid.*, Oct. 5, 1901.

"caused a panic" by announcing that economics "would no longer be a snap," and it was only his able teaching and the growing interest in the subject which permitted him to survive the "consternation caused by this bold break with tradition."[112]

The problem was complicated by the rapid increase in undergraduate numbers. For the session of 1889-1890 the total enrollment had been 653; in 1901-1902 it was 1,237. Yet the heavy burden of teaching which this entailed could have been met by the equally large increase in the faculty, had it not been accompanied by a wide expansion of courses. As it was, popular courses such as Wilson's jurisprudence or Young's astronomy or Sloane's history were woefully undermanned and had to depend chiefly upon lectures, while in others the professors devoted their time to two or three students. In 1893-1894 there were no fewer than fifty courses in which the elections were ten or less, and of these, twenty-seven had five students or less and five had only one.[113] These tiny classes were stimulating to the men who gave them, but they produced a maladjustment of teaching power and lowered the level of efficiency. For the mass of the students the old intimate touch with the teachers was missing, and the only real test of their grasp of the matter presented to them was the examination.

In the meanwhile new problems concerning the curriculum were pressing for solution. Princeton was steeped in the classical tradition. To Jonathan Edwards, or Witherspoon, or Maclean it would have been unthinkable to confer a degree upon a young man who had not read his Homer, his Xenophon, his Cicero, his Ovid—all of which was thought not only essential to mental discipline but the key to theology, philosophy, ancient literature, and other basic studies. In Patton's day Dean West was the sturdy defender of the classics, and any suggestion in faculty meetings that their place in the curriculum should be weakened brought him instantly to his feet. But the dean was powerless to stem a tide which was nationwide in its sweep, for how could the conservative colleges hold

---

[112] *Ibid.*, Feb. 13, 1931.  [113] *Trustees Minutes*, Feb. 8, 1894.

firm, when the schools were beginning to yield, especially in the teaching of Greek? In 1897-1898 nearly fifty per cent of the students in the high schools and preparatory schools were studying Latin, but only four and a half per cent were taking Greek.[114] So Princeton, with its rigid requirement that every candidate for the bachelor's degree must take courses in Greek in both the freshman and sophomore years, was closing the door on hundreds of bright, ambitious youths.

The bachelor of science degree, with its comparatively mild requirement of three hours of Latin in freshman year, offered a partial solution, and the School of Science became a haven for youthful "barbarians" fleeing the phalanx of Greek case relations and irregular verbs. In 1889-1890 there had been but 111 undergraduates in the School of Science, two years later the number had doubled; in 1901-1902 it had quadrupled. At the beginning of Patton's administration the School of Science men constituted exactly one-sixth of the undergraduate body; at its end they were 37 per cent. This threat to the bachelor of arts degree alarmed and divided the faculty. Some thought that Princeton should yield to the inevitable and drop Greek as a requirement for this degree; others stood firm; still others suggested the offering of the bachelor of letters degree as a compromise.

Not less important were the efforts to bring order out of confusion in the curriculum. In former days when very few electives were open to the students and these chiefly in long established subjects such as philosophy, Greek, Latin and chemistry, spiced with one or two in modern languages or history, no serious problem had presented itself. But with the adding of scores of new subjects it was possible for the students to make schedules leading only to mental indigestion. The conferences of the faculty committee on the schedule of studies became long and earnest. Some thought it unwise to limit the choice of electives because freedom developed a sense of responsibility; others argued that American undergraduates were too immature to choose for themselves.

[114] Dean A. F. West in the *Educational Review*, Oct. 1899, p. 261.

The latter group urged that electives be so coordinated as to make them preparatory to the study of law, medicine, or theology; or to insure a broad cultural training; or to require concentration in the pure sciences, the humanities, or the social sciences. This would leave to the students the freedom to elect a prescribed field, while putting an end to the existing chaos. Leaders of undergraduate thought leaned to this solution. "We are firmly convinced that the ill-judged courses and the aimless, superficial and disintegrated education made possible by the unguided and unrestricted choice of Senior year especially, could be largely avoided if the elections had to be made of groups of homogeneous studies," declared Andrew C. Imbrie, in the *Nassau Literary Magazine* of November 1894.

But the opposing group in the faculty argued that this plan would break up the college into a number of little graduate schools, turning out narrow specialists. Were undergraduates in their junior and senior years ready for this? Was it wise to put the roof on a house before the foundation had been laid? It was well enough for the German universities to specialize, for their students had had eight or nine years of secondary work in the gymnasiums, but for the American youth who seldom remained more than four or five years at the preparatory school, the case was different.[115]

President Patton, while admitting that much was to be gained by restricting elections to a "congruous course of study," was opposed to radical changes. "It is probable that this evil is to a very considerable extent incurable and it is the inevitable result of the elective system which is in vogue in all the leading universities," he told the trustees.[116] Possibly much could be gained by making course elections a privilege granted only to high-standing students rather than a right enjoyed by all. But he could not convince his colleagues and the conflict of opinion became heated. Whenever it was known

[115] *Princeton Alumni Weekly*, April 28, 1900; *Trustees Minutes*, Dec. 13, 1900.
[116] *Ibid.*

that the committee on the schedule of courses was going to report to the faculty and that Patton, Dean West, Woodrow Wilson, and others were to argue the question, the meetings, overflowing the narrow limits of Stanhope Hall, had to be adjourned to the School of Science building.

It may have been Patton's resentment at the refusal of the faculty to follow his leadership in this matter, it may have been the accumulated force of the criticism of his administration, it may have been the pressure brought to bear by certain members of the board of trustees which convinced him that it would be wise to tender his resignation. In 1902 David Jones, in behalf of himself and other trustees, approached him and in a frank but kindly manner suggested that he ought to relinquish the presidency in order to make way for "urgent needs in the matter of university reform." Patton hesitated. It was not pleasant to retire under fire. Perhaps it was not too late to make himself master in his own household, to define his own policies for the university, and push them through to a successful completion. On the other hand, he did not relish the conflict and the exertion which this would entail. Far more pleasant it would be to retire to the peace and seclusion of his study, and there, surrounded by his volumes on ethics, philosophy and theology, devote his remaining years to research. In the end he yielded. On May 31, 1902, he wrote Jones stating that he could well believe that it would be better for the university for him to retire, and concurring in Jones's belief that by freeing himself of "the burdens of administration" he could render notable service in his "literary and philosophical work."[117]

So, on June 9, when Patton submitted his formal resignation the trustees accepted and proceeded at once to ballot for his successor. Many persons had thought that Dean West would be the next president because of his great services to the university and his activity in shaping its educational policies. But when Patton advised strongly against West he was passed over in favor of Woodrow Wilson.

[117] *Patton Letter Book*, Princeton Library, XVI, pp. 487-495.

The news that Patton had resigned and that Wilson had been elected in his place created a sensation among the alumni assembled for commencement. Why had Patton not given some intimation of his intention? it was asked. Why such haste to elect Wilson? In the past the trustees had often deliberated months or even years before selecting a president; was there any reason for breaking this precedent? The press took up the matter, publishing unconfirmed rumors of a series of plots and counter-plots.[118] And though the *Alumni Weekly* took pains to deny these sensational stories, pointing out that it was quite understandable that Patton should have wished to give up his administrative duties for the scholarly work for which he was so well suited, months passed before the life of the university resumed its even way.

Despite the failure of President Patton to capitalize to the full upon the many opportunities which presented themselves for advancing the educational interests of Princeton, the fourteen years of his administration are among the most important in the history of the institution. It was a time of rapid physical development, with new buildings arising to the south, west, and east of Nassau Hall—the huge gymnasium, Alexander Hall, the new library, Blair Hall, and many others. It witnessed a marked increase in student enrollment and an equally remarkable expansion of the faculty. In under-graduate life there had grown up a tremendous interest in athletics, with football games becoming great public spectacles bringing in large sums of money and entailing troublesome problems of eligibility. Even more important was the de-velopment of student self-government, which found its finest expression in the honor system. The multiplication of clubs and the erection of handsome houses were already producing problems which were to vex the university for decades to come.

The Patton era also witnessed the passing away of the "old guard" in the faculty, many of whom had come to Princeton in Maclean's day and represented a past age—Kargé, the

[118] *New York Sun*, June 12, 13, 14, 1902.

sturdy old soldier; Shields, the religious philosopher; Murray, the kindly dean; Duffield, the mathematician; Schanck, Packard, Cameron. And as they went a new type of professor took their places, men who were perhaps less concerned with religion and with discipline and more with scholarship and with the educational trends of the day. It was West, Fine, Scott and others like them who carried on and expanded the intellectual revival initiated by McCosh. This it was, typified by the Graduate School and by the scholarly work of faculty members, rather than the change of corporate title, which made Princeton a real university.

Patton's failures were chiefly failures of omission. Had proper steps been taken to stiffen easy courses, to maintain rigid entrance requirements, to drop incorrigibly idle students, and to inaugurate a logical scheme of coordinated electives, Princeton could not, even in jest, have been dubbed a delightful country club. At the same time it must be emphasized that throughout the 'nineties there was much excellent teaching, much scholarly attainment, much earnest work on the part of undergraduates. The era of Andrew Fleming West, of Woodrow Wilson, of William B. Scott, of Charles A. Young, of Henry B. Fine, of Winthrop M. Daniels, and others of like stamp cannot be stigmatized as an era of sterility.

# CONCLUSION

O F first importance in the history of Princeton is leadership. The college was fortunate in having a long line of presidents farseeing enough to map the road of progress and strong enough to conduct her along it. Without Witherspoon, Smith, Maclean, McCosh the institution might have remained a small college with limited influence in American education and scholarship.

But leadership would have been ineffectual without the support of the alumni. From the days when the first tiny group of students gathered around Jonathan Dickinson in his residence in Elizabeth, the sons of the college have taken with them into life an abiding love for Alma Mater, and this love has expressed itself not only in gifts for professorships, scholarships, buildings, and equipment, but in constructive advice.

The institution owes much also to its teachers and scholars. The two have gone hand in hand, for the college has always believed in inspiring, rather than drilling, its undergraduates. It was the distinguished physicist, Samuel Stanhope Smith, to whom the students listened with rapt attention a century and a half ago; it was the rush for seats at the lectures of Joseph Henry that created a near riot fifty years later; it was the astronomer Stephen Alexander, the geologist Arnold Guyot, and others like them who aroused the enthusiasm of the students and opened to them new intellectual vistas.

This alliance of teaching and scholarship presaged the metamorphosis from college to university. The scholar demands relief from work in the classroom so that he may devote part of his time to investigation, he demands an adequate library equipped with the important books in his field, he demands laboratories and scientific equipment, he demands graduate courses so that he can have the stimulus of contact with advanced students, he demands the privilege of exchanging views with other scholars whose interests parallel his own. When Witherspoon purchased the Rittenhouse orrery and installed it in Nassau Hall, when John Maclean, Senior, performed an experiment in chemistry, when Stephen Alexander installed a tiny telescope in his residence with which to carry on his investigations, they were unwittingly laying the foundations of Princeton University.

On the other hand, when these men took their enthusiasms into the classroom, when Samuel Stanhope Smith declared that every experiment in physics was an act of devotion to God, when Joseph Henry made his huge magnet lift a group of students, these men were preparing the way for the preceptorial system and the four-course plan. Princeton's emphasis upon teaching, which dates back to the days of President Burr, was thus implemented by productive scholarship, and in turn implemented scholarship by demanding for the classrooms the stimulus of creative minds.

As we look back over the history of Princeton during the eighteenth and nineteenth centuries, it divides itself into several fairly well-defined periods. The first of these, the period of the founders, of Jonathan Dickinson, Aaron Burr, Jonathan Belcher, Samuel Davies and Samuel Finley, extends from 1746 to 1768. During these years the college devoted its best energies to buttressing the reformed wing of the Calvinistic congregations, by educating young men for its ministry and by providing it with intellectual leadership. It was this which extended the influence of the institution far beyond the confines of New Jersey, for it drew students not only from those parts of the middle colonies and the south where the Presbyterian church had established itself, but from the New Lights congregations of New England.

In the second period, ushered in with the appointment of John Witherspoon and continuing until the close of his presidency, the emphasis shifted from preparation for the ministry to preparation for civic leadership. Witherspoon himself was a statesman as well as a theologian, so that fathers who envisioned careers for their sons in political life were eager to entrust them to his guidance. It was not by accident that

Princeton had such a large contingent in the Constitutional Convention at Philadelphia.

At the same time the gradual dying out of the controversy within the Calvinistic denominations, the reuniting of congregations and the reconciling of conflicting views cut from under the foundations of the college the ground upon which it had originally stood. It was this which drew off the New England contingent, for with the old hostility of Harvard and Yale to the reform movement no longer a matter of moment, there was no reason why they should be by-passed for the college in New Jersey. On the other hand, in the middle colonies and the south the college profited from the spirit of reconciliation, since it gave it undisputed religious leadership over the reunited Presbyterian church which was so strong in those sections.

This position it lost in the third period of its history, which extended approximately from 1794 to 1828, with the reflection in the student body and to some extent among the alumni of the growing liberalism of the age, a liberalism which was impatient of disciplinary restraint and in some cases of religion itself. The determination of the trustees and the faculty to crush what they termed Jacobinism resulted in a conflict with the undergraduates which brought great misfortunes to the college. The riots in Nassau Hall, the explosions of giant crackers, the wholesale suspensions and expulsions were but incidents in the clash between the spirit of the old age and the new, between the eighteenth century and the nineteenth. But before they died out, before the government of the college became more tolerant and the undergraduates less rebellious, the diminishing student body, the loss of prestige, the sterility in scholarship, and the dullness of teaching gave striking evidence of Princeton's decline.

From its nadir the college emerged slowly through the efforts of the alumni and the leadership of John Maclean. Funds came in, the faculty was enlarged, the number of undergraduates increased rapidly, new buildings were erected, scientific equipment was acquired. With alumni support came increased alumni influence and a corresponding weakening of Presbyterian influence. Throughout the fourth period of Princeton history, the period from 1828 to 1868, this development continued and, although it was not completed until the end of the century, its effects upon educational policies became more and more apparent. Had it not been for the strength acquired during the third, fourth, and fifth decades, the college might not have survived the shock of the Civil War. As it was, the great intersectional struggle greatly diminished Princeton's following in the south and made the institution, for the time being, less national.

With the election of James McCosh as president, Princeton entered the fifth period, the period from 1868 to the beginning of the twentieth century, which was marked by the transition from the college to the university. Taking a leading part in the great liberalizing movement in education, loyally and generously supported by the alumni, led by the far-sighted McCosh, the institution entered upon an era of expanding influence. The curriculum was broadened, the faculty enlarged, graduate courses were added, scholarship encouraged, new buildings erected, new schools added. The College of New Jersey became officially Princeton University in 1896, but the transition began many years before that date and was completed only many years later.

As we review the history of Princeton our thoughts revert to the men who dedicated their lives to her service—those who laid the foundations two centuries ago, those who guided her through the storms of the Revolution and the War between the States, the men who poured out their largesses into her lap, those who brought her distinction by the excellence of their teaching or by their scholarly contributions. The thousands of youths who enter Princeton, to study and live in the shadow of Nassau Hall, owe a debt of gratitude to these men and we could wish that they knew them better.

Perhaps the time will come when there will be in some appropriate building on the campus a mural in the style of Raphael's School of Athens, showing in one group the men who have contributed most to Princeton's upbuilding. Then all who pass in and out will see the seven founders—Jonathan Dickinson, Aaron Burr, Ebenezer Pemberton, John Pierson, William Smith, Peter Van Brugh Livingston, and William Peartree Smith—gathered for the conference which "concocted the plan of the college"; nearby, the sturdy Gilbert Tennent, the pious Jonathan Belcher, the gentle Samuel Davies, and the ruddy-faced Samuel Finley. They will see the heavy-set John Witherspoon, the scholarly Samuel Stanhope Smith, John Maclean, Senior, at work with his chemical retorts, and Joseph Henry bending over his epoch-making electromagnetic telegraph, John Maclean, Junior, his famous cape thrown over his shoulders, the diminutive Stephen Alexander peering through his telescope. Then Princeton's great will become something more than names to Princeton's sons, and every undergraduate will become acquainted, if not with the careers, at least with the faces, of the men who won a place in The School of Princeton.

# APPENDIX

## Charters of the College of New Jersey, October 22, 1746 and September 14, 1748*

GEORGE THE SECOND, BY THE GRACE OF GOD, OF GREAT BRITAIN, FRANCE AND IRELAND, KING, DEFENDER OF THE FAITH &c. TO ALL TO WHOM THESE PRESENTS SHALL COME, GREETING.

Whereas sundry *of our loving subjects*, well disposed & publick spirited Persons, have lately by their humble Petition presented to our Trusty and well beloved [JOHN HAMILTON ESQ^r. the President of OUR COUNCIL,] *Jonathan Belcher, Esq., governor* and Commander in Chief of our Province of New Jersey in America, represented the great Necessity of coming into some Method for encouraging and promoting a learned Education of Our Youth in New Jersey, and have expres'd their earnest Desire that a College may be erected in our Said Province of New Jersey *in America* for the Benefit of the *inhabitants of the* Said Province *and other*, wherein Youth may be instructed in the learned Languages, and in the Liberal Arts and Sciences. . . . And whereas by the fundamental Concessions made at the first Settlement of New Jersey by the Lord Berkley and Sir George Carteret, then Proprietors thereof, and granted under their Hands, and the Seal of the said Province, and bearing Date the Tenth Day of February [1664], *in the year of our Lord one thousand six hundred and sixty-four*, it was, among[st] other Things, conceded and [granted] *agreed*, "that no Freeman within the said Provence of New Jersey, should at any Time be molested, punished, disquieted, or Called in Question for any difference in opinion or practice in matters of Religious Concernment, who do not actually disturb the civil Peace of the Said Province, but that all and every such Person [and] *or* Persons might from Time to Time & at all Times *thereafter* freely & truly have and enjoy his and their Judgments and Consciences in Matters of Religion throughout the said Province,

*The parts of the Charter of 1746 which were omitted in the Charter of 1748 have been placed in brackets; the parts of the Charter of 1748 not included in the Charter of 1746 appear in italics. The capitalization of the first charter has been followed, but not the punctuation. It is obvious that a few of the omissions in the first charter were made by the transcriber and did not occur in the original.

they behaving themselves Peaceably and quietly and not using this Liberty to Licentiousness nor to the Civil Injury or outward Disturbance of others." As by the Said Concessions on Record in the Secretary's Office of New Jersey, at Perth Amboy, in Lib. 3 fol*io* 66 &c may appear. Wherefore *and for that* the said Petitioners have also expressed their earnest Desire that those of every Religious Denomination may have free and Equal Liberty and Advantage of Education in the Said College [notwithstanding] any different Sentiments in Religion *notwithstanding*. We being willing to grant the reasonable Request*s* & Prayer*s* of all our loving Subjects, and to promote a liberal and Learned Education among them—KNOW YE, therefore that we considering the Premises, and being willing for the future that the best Means of Education be established in our Province of New Jersey, for the Benefit and Advantage *of the inhabitants* of that our said Province *and others*, Do of Our special Grace, certain Knowledge and mere Motion, by these Presents, will, ordain, grant, and constitute that there be a College erected in Our Said Province of New Jersey for the Education of Youth in the Learned Languages and in the Liberal Arts and Sciences. And that the Trustees of the said College and their Successors *for* ever May, and shall be one Body Corporate & Politick, in Deed, action & Name, and shall be called, *and* named and distinguis*h*ed, by the Name of the Trustees of the College of New Jersey.—And further we have willed, given, granted, Constituted and [Ordained] *appointed*, and by this our present Charter of Our especial Grace, certain Knowledge & meer Motion. We do for Us, our Heirs and Successors [For ever] will, give, grant, constitute & ordain that there shall in the Said College from henceforth, and for ever be a Body politick Consisting of Trustees of the said College of New Jersey, and for the more full & perfect Erection of the said Corporation and Body Politick consisting of Trustees of the College of New Jersey, we of our Especial Grace, Certain Knowledge and meer Motion, do by these Presents for Us, our Heirs & Successors, create, make, ordain, constitute, Nominate and appoint [our Trusty & well beloved WILLIAM SMITH, PETER VAN BRUGH LIVINGSTON & WILLIAM PEARTREE SMITH, of the City of New York, Gentlemen, and our trusty & well beloved JONATHAN DICKINSON, JOHN PIERSON, EBENEZER PEMBERTON & AARON BURR, Ministers of the Gospel with such others as they shall think proper to Associate until them not Exceeding the Number of twelve to be the Trustees of the Said College of New

Jersey with full power and Authority to them, or any four, or greater Number of them, to nominate & appoint & associate unto them any Number of Persons, as Trustees, so that the whole Number of Trustees exceed not Twelve.] *the Governor and Commander in Chief of our said province of New Jersey, for the time being, and also our trusty and well beloved John Reading, James Hude, Andrew Johnston, Thomas Leonard, John Kinsey, Edward Shippen and William Smith, Esquires, Peter Van-Brugh Livingston, William Peartree Smith and Samuel Hazard, gentlemen, John Pierson, Ebenezer Pemberton, Joseph Lamb, Gilbert Tennent, William Tennent, Richard Treat, Samuel Blair, David Cowell, Aaron Burr, Timothy Jones, Thomas Arthur and Jacob Green, ministers of the gospel, to be Trustees of the said College of New Jersey.*

*That the said Trustees do, at their first meeting, after the receipt of these presents, and before they proceed to any business take the oath appointed to be taken by an act, passed in the first year of the reign of the late King George the First, entitled, "An act for the further security of his Majesty's person and government, and the succession of the crown in the heirs of the late princess Sophia, being protestants, and for extinguishing the hopes of the pretended prince of Wales, and his open and secret abettors"; as also that they make and subscribe the declarations mentioned in an act of parliament made in the twenty-fifth year of the reign of King Charles the Second, entitled, "An act for preventing dangers which may happen from popish recusants"; and likewise take an oath for faithfully executing the office or trust reposed in them, the said oaths to be administered to them by three of his Majesty's justices of the peace, quorum unus; and when any new member or officer of this corporation is chosen, they are to take and subscribe the aforementioned oaths and declarations before their admission into their trusts or offices, the same to be administered to them in the presence of the Trustees, by such persons as they shall appoint for that service.*

*That no meeting of the Trustees shall be valid or legal for doing any business whatsoever, unless the clerk has duly and legally notified each and every member of the corporation of such meeting; and that before the entering on any business, the clerk shall certify such notification under his hand to the Board of Trustees.*

*That the said Trustees have full power and authority or any thirteen or greater number of them, to elect, nominate and appoint and associate unto them, any number of persons as Trustees upon any vacancy, so the whole number of Trustees exceed not twenty-three whereof the President of the said college for the time being, to be chosen as hereafter mentioned, to be one, and twelve of the said Trustees to be always such persons as are inhabitants of our said province of New Jersey.*

AND We do further of our special Grace, certain Knowledge & meer Motion, for us, Our Heirs & Successors, will, give, grant and appoint That the said Trustees and their Successors shall forever hereafter be in Deed, Fact & Name a Body corporate, & politick, and that they the Said Body Corporate & Politick shall be known & distinguished in all Deeds, Grants, Bargains, Sales, Writings, Evidences, [Monuments] *muniments* or otherwise howsoever, and in all Courts for ever hereafter Plead and be impleaded by the Name of the Trustees of the College of New Jersey. And that *they* the Said Corporation, by the Name aforesaid shall be able, and in Law capable for the use of the said College to have, get, acquire, purchase, receive and possess Lands, Tenements, Hereditaments, Jurisdictions & Franchises for themselves and their Successors, in Fee Simple or otherwise howsoever, and to purchase, receive, or build any House or Houses, or any other Buildings, as they shall think needful [and] *or* Convenient for the Use of the said College of New Jersey, and in such Place or Places in New Jersey as they the said Trustees shall agree upon. And also to receive, and dispose of any Goods, Chattels and other things of what Nature soever for the Use aforesaid. And also to have, accept & receive any Rents, profits, Annuities, Gifts, Legacies, Donations and Bequests of any kind whatsoever for the Use aforesaid, so nevertheless that the Yearly *clear* Value of the premi[s]ses do not exceed the Sum of two thousand Pounds Sterling. And therewith or otherwise to support and pay as the Said Trustees & their Successors, or the Major Part of such of them as according to the Provision herein after*wards* [made] are regularly convened for that Purpose shall agree and see Cause, the President, [&] Tutors and [their] *other* Officers [and] *or* Ministers of the Said College, their respective annual Salaries, or Allowances, and all such other necessary & contingent Charges as from time to time shall arise and accrue relating to the said College.—And also to grant, Bargain, sell, let, set or Assign Lands, Tenements or Hereditaments, Goods or Chattels, contract or do all other things whatsoever, by the Name Aforesaid, and for the Use aforesaid, in as full and ample Manner, to all intents & Purposes, as any Natural Person or other Body politick or corporate is able to do by the Laws of our Realm of Great Britain, or of our said province of New Jersey. And of our further Grace, certain Knowledge, meer Motion, to the Intent that our said Corporation & Body politick may answer the End of their Erection & Constitution, and may have perpetual Succession, and continue for ever, We do for Us, our Heirs and Successors, Hereby will, give and grant unto the said Trustees of the College of New Jersey, and to their Successors for ever, that when any [seven] *thirteen* of the *said* Trustees, or of their Successors, are convened & met together *as aforesaid* for the Service of the said College *The Governor and Commander in Chief of our said province of New Jersey, and in his absence, the President of the said college, and in the absence of the said Governor and President, the eldest Trustee present at such meeting, from time to time, shall be President of the said Trustees in all their meetings, and* at any Time or Times such [seven] *thirteen* Trustees *convened and met as aforesaid*, shall be capable to act as fully and amply to all Intents and Purposes as if all the Trustees of the said College were personally present, *provided always, that a majority of the said Thirteen Trustees be of the said province of New Jersey, except after regular notice they fail of coming in which case those that are present are hereby empowered to act, the different place of their abode notwithstanding*, And all Affairs and Actions whatsoever under the Care of the said Trustees shall be Determined by the Majority or greater Number of Those [seven] *thirteen* [Trustees] so convened & met together, *the President whereof shall have no more than a single vote.* And we do for us, our Heirs and Successors hereby will, give & grant full Power & Authority to any [Three] *six* or more of the said Trustees, to [appoint] *call* Meetings *of the said Trustees* from time to time [of the said seven Trustees] and to order Notice to the said [seven] Trustees [or any greater Number of them] of the Times & Places of Meeting for the Service aforesaid. . . . And also we do hereby for us, Our Heirs and Successors will, give & grant to the Said Trustees of the College of New Jersey, and to their Successors for ever, that the Said Trustees do elect, nominate and appoint such qualified persons as they or the Major Part of any [Seven] *thirteen* of them convened for that purpose, as above directed, shall think fitt to be the President of the Said College and to have the immediate Care of the Education & Government of such Students as shall be sent to & admitted in to the Said College for instruction and Education. . . . And also that the said Trustees do Elect, nominate

[ 400 ]

and appoint so many Tutors and Professors to assist the President of the Said College in the Education & Government of the Students belonging to it, as they the said Trustees or their Successors, or the Major Part of any [Seven] *thirteen* of them, which shall convene for that Purpose as above directed, shall from time to time, and at any time hereafter think needful and serviceable to the Interests of the Said College. . . . And also that the Said Trustees and their Successors, or the Major Part of any [Seven] *thirteen* of them which shall convene for that Purpose as above directed, shall at any time Displace and discharge from the Service of the said College such President, Tutors or Professors and to elect others in their Room and Stead. . . . And also that the said Trustees or their Successors or the Major Part of any [seven] *thirteen* of them, which shall convene for that purpose, as above directed, do from time to time, as Occasion shall require elect, constitute and appoint a Treasurer, a Clerk, an Usher and a Steward for the Said College, and appoint to them, and each of them, their respective Business & Trust, & Displace & Discharge from the Service of the said College such Treasurer, Clerk, Usher or Steward, and to elect others in their Room & Stead, which President, Tutors, Professors, Treasurer*s*, Clerks, Ushers & Steward, so elected and appointed, We do for us, our Heirs & Successors by their Presents Constitute and Establish in their several Offices, and do give them, and Every of them, full Power and Authority to Exercise the same in the said College of New Jersey according to the Direction[s] and during the pleasure of the Said Trustees, as fully and freely as any other the like officers in our Universities or any of our Colleges in our Realm of great Britain Lawfully may or ought to do. . . . And also that the said Trustees and their Successors or the Major Part of any [seven] *thirteen* of them, which shall convene for that Purpose as above directed, as often as one, or more of the said Trustees shall happen to die, or by Removal or Otherwise shall [according to their Judgment] become unfitt, or uncapable *according to their judgment* to serve the Interest[s] of the said College, do as soon as conveniently may be after the Death, Removal or such Unfittness and Incapacity of such Trustee or Trustees *to serve the interest of the said college elect and appoint such other Trustee or Trustees,* as shall supply the place of him or them so dying or otherwise becoming unfitt or Uncapable to serve the Interest[s] of the said College, and every Trustee so Elected or appointed shall by virtue of these Presents and *of* such Election and Appointment be vested with all the powers and Privile[d]ges which any of the Other Trustees of the said College are hereby vested with. . . . And we do further of our especial Grace, certain Knowledge and meer Motion will, give, and grant and by these Presents do for us, our Heirs and Successors will, give, and grant unto the said Trustees of the College of New Jersey, that they and their Successors or the major part of any [seven] *thirteen* of them which shall convene for that Purpose, as is above directed, may make, and they are hereby fully [i]empowered, from Time to Time freely and lawfully to make & Establish such Ordinances, Orders and Laws as may tend to the good and whole-some Government of the said College, & all the students & the several[1] Officers & Ministers thereof, and to the publick Benefit of the same not repugnant to the Laws and Statutes of our Realm of great Britain, or of this our Province of New Jersey, and not ex-cluding any Person of any religious Denomination whatsoever from free and Equal Liberty and Advantage of Education, or from any of the Liberties, Privile[d]ges or immunities of the Said College on account of his or their [speculative Sentiments in Religion and of his, or their] being of a Religious profession Different from the said Trustees of the College[.] and such ordinances, Orders & Laws which shall [as aforesaid be made] *be so as aforesaid made,* . . . We do by these Presents for us, our Heirs and Successors, ratify, allow of and Confirm, as good and Effectual to oblige and bind all the *said* students, and the several Officers & Ministers of the said College, and we do hereby authorize & [impower] *empower* the said Trustees of the College, and the President, Tutors and Pro-fessors by them elected and appointed to put such Ordinances, [Orders] and Laws in Execution, to all proper Intents and pur-poses. And we do further of our especial Grace, certain Knowledge and meer Motion, will, give and grant unto the said Trustees of the College of New Jersey, that for the Encouragement of Learn-ing and Animating of the Students of *the* Said College to Diligence, Industry and a Laudable Progress in Literature that they and their Successors, [and] *or* the Major Part of any [seven] *thirteen* of them convened for that Purpose, as above directed, Do by the President of the said College for the time being, or by any other Deputed by them Give and Grant any such Degree or Degrees to any of the Students of the said College, or to any others by them thought worthy thereof as are usually granted in either of our Universities, or any

other College in our Realm of great Britain, and that they do sign
& seal Di[a]plomas or Certificates of such Graduations to be kept
by the Graduates as perpetual Memorials and Testimonials thereof. . . .

And further of our especial Grace, certain Knowledge & meer
Motion we do by these Presents for us, our Heirs and Successors,
give and grant unto the said Trustees of the College of New Jersey
and to their Successors that they and their Successors shall have a
Common Seal under which they may pass all Di[a]plomas, or
Certificates of Degrees, and all Other the Affairs & Business of and
Concerning the said Corporation, or of and Concerning the Said
College of New Jersey which shall be [i]engraven in such form,
and with such Inscriptions as shall be devised by the said Trustees
of the said College [for the Time being,] or [by] the Major Part
of any [seven] *thirteen* of them convened for the Service of the
Said College as above directed. . . .

And we do further for us, Our Heirs and Successors, give &
Grant unto the said Trustees of the [Said] College of New Jersey
and their Successors, or the Major Part *of any thirteen* of them
convened for the Service of the said College, as [is] above directed,
full Power and Authority from time to time to Nominate and
Appoint all other Inferio[u]r Officers & Ministers which they shall
think to be convenient & necessary for the Use of the [said]
College, not herein particularly named or mentioned, and which
are accustomary in our Universities or any of our Colleges in our
Realm of great Britain, which Officers or Ministers we do hereby
[i]empower to execute their Offices or Trusts as fully & freely
as any other the like Officers [&] *or* Ministers in *and of* our Universities or any *other* College[s] in our Realm of great Britain,
Lawfully may or ought to do.—

And Lastly our express Will and Pleasure is, and we do by these
presents for us, our Heirs and Successors, give and grant *un*to the
said Trustees of the College of New Jersey and to their Successors
forever, that these our Letters patent, or the Enrol[l]ment thereof
[in our Secretarys Office of our Province aforesaid] shall be good
& effectual in the Law, to all intents & Purposes against us, our
Heirs & Successors without any Other Licence, Grant or Confirmation
from us, our Heirs & Successors hereafter by the said Trustees, to be
had & attained, notwithstanding the not [writing] *reciting* or
Misrecital, [of] *or* not naming or misnaming of The Aforesaid
Offices, Franchises, Privileges, Immunities or Other the Premis[s]es,

or any of them, and notwithstanding a Writ of ad quod Damnum hath not issued forth to [e]inquire of the Premis[s]es or any of them before the ensealing hereof, any Statute, Act, Ordinance or Provision, or any other' Matter or thing to the Contrary notwithstanding.

To have [&] to hold *and enjoy* all & Singular the Privileges, Advantages, Liberties, Immunities and all other the Premis[s]es herein & hereby granted & given, or which are meant, mentioned or intended to be herein and hereby given and granted Unto them the Said Trustees of the Said College of New Jersey and to their Successors forever.

In Testimony whereof we have caused these our Letters to be made patent, and the great seal of our Said Province of New Jersey to be hereunto Affixed. Witness our Trusty and well Beloved [John Hamilton Esqr. the President of our Council] *Jonathan Belcher, Esquire, Governor* and Commander in Chief of our said Province [&c] *of New Jersey.* This [Twenty second] *fourteenth* Day of [October] *September, and* in the [twentieth] *twenty second* Year of our Reign [Annoq: Domini 1746] *year of our Lord,* one thousand seven hundred and forty eight.

L.S.　*I have perused and considered the written Charter of incorporation, and find nothing contained therein inconsistent with his Majesty's interest or the honor of the Crown.*
*(Signed)*　　　J. WARRELL, *Att. Gen'l*

*September the 13th, 1748.—This Charter, having been read in Council was consented to and approved of.*
CHA. READ, *Cl. Con.*

*Let the Great Seal of the Province of New Jersey be affixed to this Charter.*
*(Signed)*　　　J. BELCHER
*To the Secretary of the Province of New Jersey.*

# INDEX

Academies, American, in Middle Colonies, 10-13; on frontier, 114-115

Adams, John, student letter to, 1798, 209

Admission to college, under Witherspoon, 73-74; early requirements, 89-90; to upper classes, 89-90; Greek and Latin required, 91-92; English emphasized, 90-92; 1790-1830, 184; lax under Patton, 384

Aiken, Charles A., elected professor, 284; joins seminary faculty, 284

Aiken, John, teaching of, 83-84

Alexander, Archibald, describes S. S. Smith, 118; proposes theological seminary, 147; trustee, 1824, 239

Alexander, Henry M., suggests D. A. Gregory as trustee, 239

Alexander, James, contributes to college, 21, 31; advises granting charter, 21-22

Alexander, James W., criticizes drinking water, 200; professor, 1833, 221; on library deficiencies, 228; speaks at centennial, 231; resigns, 1844, 254; favors Maclean for presidency, 257

Alexander, Stephen, adjunct professor, 222; professor, 1840, 225; description of, 225-226; teaching of, 226; a distinguished scientist, 226; private telescope, 228, 282; teaches mathematics, 253; teaching of, deteriorates, 259; lectures of, 277; address of, 1867, 283; makes Princeton collection, 311

Alexander, William C., launches endowment campaign, 1863, 274-275

Alexander Hall, building of, 348-349; anti-hazing meeting in, 361-362; sesquicentennial celebration in, 371-373

Alford, John, gift to college, 31

Alison, Francis, attacks Log College, 13; Old Sides' candidate for presidency, 48-49; welcomes Witherspoon, 52; criticizes college finances, 52

Alumni, potential source of income, 180-181; Alumni Association of

Nassau Hall, 1826, 181-182; affection for Princeton, 181; share control of college, 182; denounce suppression of fraternities, 323; representation on trustees, 322, 376-377; Alumni Council proposed, 332-333; associations established, 333; support change to university, 340; Patton wins, 344-345; Patton favors participation, 347; Patton renounces church control before, 375; influence of increases under Patton, 376-377; save Princeton, 1828-1868, 393-394

Alumni Weekly, on dormitory baths, 354; defends athletics, 357-358; defends clubs, 359; demands alumni representation, 376

American Philosophical Society, address before, of S. S. Smith, 96; Princeton members of, 227

American Whig Society, see Whig Society

Anglican Church, 6; opposes college charter, 21, 23

Architecture, of Nassau Hall, 37-38; changes in Nassau Hall, 1802, 130-131; literary halls neo-classic, 252; of rebuilt Nassau Hall, 1855, 263-264; era of bad taste, 297; of Dod Hall, 347-348; of Brown Hall, 348; of Alexander Hall, 348-349; hodge-podge of, 352-353; Tudor Gothic introduced, 353; influence of, 353-354; of Blair Hall, 353; of proposed graduate college, 382

Art, School of, founded, 309; museum for erected, 309; dedication of Museum, 336

Ashworth, Caleb, academy of, 82

Athletics, early need for, 138; advocated by Lindsley, 162-163; unorganized in early days, 193-194; skating and sleigh-riding, 194; under Carnahan, 245; first gymnasium, 1859, 277-278; games under Maclean, 278-279; baseball introduced, 279; gymnastics, 324-325; baseball under McCosh, 325; first football match, 325-326; develop-

lege planned, 381-382; Graduate
School organized, 382-383
Graham, William, academy of, 114-
115
Great Awakening, Princeton results
from, 3-9; Old Side oppose, 9; education of ministers, 10-13; excesses
of, 17; Princeton founded, 22;
Presbyterians reunite, 52
Green, Ashbel, on lost charter, 22; on
Princeton during Congress session,
65; valedictorian, 1783, 65; professor of mathematics, 70; resigns, 70-
71; deplores "vice" of students, 77;
investigates S. S. Smith, 121-122;
acting president, 1802-1803, 128;
plans theological seminary, 147-148;
elected president, 1812, 153; plans
his administration, 154-155; hopes
for religious revival, 154-155; the
"big cracker," 156-157; discipline
under, 1814, 157-158; ignores
Lindsley's theories, 164; organizes
religious societies, 164; religious revival cheers, 165-166; riot of 1817,
167-169; expels fourteen students,
167-168; ice thrown at, 168; parent reproves, 169-170; on causes of
student riots, 169; raises funds for
seminary, 170; asks aid from Legislature, 170; trustees offend, 171;
resigns, 171-172; administration a
failure, 172; Samuel Miller reproves, 172; Maclean's opinion of,
172; distinguished graduates under,
182-183; as undergraduate actor,
197; preaching of, 199; aids in epidemics, 200
Green, Chancellor Henry W., speaks
at centennial, 230-231; a trustee,
239; library named for, 296; asked
to prosecute hazers, 315-316
Green, Jacob, acting president, 44
Green, Jacob, professor, 1817, 171;
forced out, 171
Green, James S., professor of law, 230
Green, John C., benefactions of, 294;
gives Dickinson Hall, 295-296;
gives library, 296-297; endows
School of Science, 308; endows department of engineering, 308-309;
endows Lawrenceville, 314-315

Green, William Henry, declines presidency, 1868, 290
Gregory, Dudley A., suggested for
trustee, 239
Gummere, William S., football captain,
1869, 325
Guyot, Arnold, professor, 1854, 254,
274; a distinguished scholar, 260;
his Chair endowed, 275; lectures of,
277, 304
Gymnasium, first erected, 1859, 278;
burned, 278; second erected, 1869,
295; funds raised for third, 358;
erection of, 358
Gymnastics, under McCosh, 324-325;
at Commencement of 1883, 330

Halsey, Jeremiah, proposed as profes-
sor, 49; tutor, 99
Halsey, Joseph J., describes Dod, 224
Halsey, Luther, professor, 176; resigns,
1829, 179
Halsted, N. H., gives observatory, 282-
283
Hamilton, John, grants college charter,
21-22; Anglicans assail, 23
Hamilton, William, Whig disciplines,
204-205
Hampden-Sydney, 3; Princeton men
found, 114; S. S. Smith at, 118-119
Hancock, John, gift to college, 53
Hargous, Lewis, teacher of modern
languages, 179; professor, 1830,
221
Harris, John, patriot preacher, 112
Hart, John S., values research, 221;
adjunct professor, 221; suggested
for professorship, 283
Harvard, 3; New Jersey ministers
from, 6; opposes New Lights, 14;
Princeton trustees from, 27; government control, 86-87; New Lights
reconciled to, 113; gifts from, for
Nassau Hall, 129; riots at, 142;
disorders of 1823, 158; faculty no
longer Puritan, 159-160; influence
of Everett and Ticknor, 160; curriculum of, criticized, 305-307;
early football games with, 327;
celebrations, 1886, 333-335
Hazard, Samuel, trustee, 1748, 27
Hazing, under McCosh, 315-317; exaggerated reports, 317; McCosh